D0849658

Also by Heather Dubrow

Captive Victors: Shakespeare's Narrative Poems and Sonnets

Genre

A Happier Eden:
The Politics of Marriage in the Stuart Epithalamium

The Historical Renaissance:
New Essays on Tudor and Stuart
Literature and Culture (coeditor)

ECHOES OF DESIRE

ENGLISH PETRARCHISM AND ITS COUNTERDISCOURSES

Heather Dubrow

CORNELL UNIVERSITY PRESS

Ithaca and London

First published 1995 by Cornell University Press.

Library of Congress Cataloging-in-Publication Data

Dubrow, Heather
  Echoes of desire : English Petrarchism and its counterdiscourses / Heather Dubrow.
    p. cm.
  Includes bibliographical references and index.
  ISBN 0-8014-2966-8
  1. English poetry—Early modern, 1500–1700—History and criticism. 2. Love poetry, English—History and criticism. 3. Petrarca, Francesco, 1304–1374—Influence. 4. Sonnets, English—History and criticism. 5. English literature—Italian influences. 6. Power (Social sciences) in literature. 7. Man-woman relations in literature. 8. Sex role in literature. 9. Desire in literature. 10. Petrarchism. I. Title.
  PR535.L7D83   1995
  821'.0409—dc20   95-8916

Printed in the United States of America

CONTENTS

ACKNOWLEDGMENTS

I thank the Graduate School Research Committee of the University of Wisconsin–Madison for supporting my research on this book; I am also grateful for both the released time and the collegiality I enjoyed during my semester at the University of Wisconsin Institute for Research in the Humanities. Librarians at the University of Wisconsin Library and the Harvard College Library were patient and helpful throughout the project. David Rowe, computer whiz, repeatedly rescued a scholar in distress by fighting off software and hardware gremlins. It has been a pleasure to work yet again with the staff of Cornell University Press, especially Bernhard Kendler, my editor. Susannah Brietz, Stacey Knowlton, Amy McConnell, and Amelia Nearing provided valuable assistance with research on this book, and I look forward to reading their own books in due course. I am happy to record long-standing debts to two of my undergraduate teachers: honors tutorials with the late David Kalstone and with Neil Rudenstine sparked my fascination with the sonnet tradition over twenty-five years ago. Much more recently, the University of Wisconsin English Department Draft Group provided fruitful suggestions about sections of this book, as did audiences at Bryn Mawr College, the University of California at Los Angeles and at Riverside, Claremont McKenna College, Dickinson College, the University of Southern California, and here at the University of Wisconsin. I am indebted to more individuals than I can enumerate for help with the manuscript; in particular, I thank Ilona Bell, Barbara Bono, Douglas Bruster, Nona Fienberg, Susan Stanford Friedman, Jane Hedley, Constance Jordan, William Kennedy, Mary Ellen Lamb, Barbara Kiefer Lewalski, David Loewenstein, Naomi Miller, Sherry Reames, Johann Sommerville, Michael Stapleton, Marguerite Waller, Susanne Lindgren Wofford, and Cathy Yandell. For years I have been fortunate enough to enjoy the friendship and collegial generosity of Gwynne Blakemore Evans and Anne Lake Prescott; their extensive work on the manuscript of this book deepened my gratitude to them. I hope to repay these two unpayable debts, at least in part, by heeding the suggestion of Sandy Mack, another colleague and friend, when I tried to thank him for professional help: "Thank me by doing it for someone else."

I have retained Renaissance spelling but modernized i/j and u/v; capitalization in the titles of sixteenth- and seventeenth-century texts has been regularized.

Quotations from scholarly editions have been reprinted by permission of the publishers as follows: Basil Blackwell *(The Works of Michael Drayton*, ed. J. William Hebel, 1931–1941); Harvard University Press *(Petrarch's Lyric Poems*, ed. Robert M. Durling; copyright © 1976 by Robert M. Durling); Houghton Mifflin *(The Riverside Shakespeare*, ed. Gwynne Blakemore Evans, 1974); Johns Hopkins University Press (The Variorum Spenser, ed. Edwin Greenlaw et al., 1943–1957); Macmillan *(John Milton: Complete Poems and Major Prose*, ed. Merritt Y. Hughes; copyright 1957; copyright © 1985 by Macmillan Publishing Company); Oxford University Press *(The Poems of Thomas Carew*, ed. Rhodes Dunlap, 1957; *The Poems English and Latin of Edward Lord Herbert of Cherbury*, ed. G. C. Moore Smith, 1923; *The Poems of Sir Philip Sidney*, ed. W. A. Ringler, 1965; *The Divine Poems of John Donne*, ed. Helen Gardner, 1952; *John Donne: The Elegies and the Songs and Sonnets*, ed. Helen Gardner, 1965; *John Donne: The Satires, Epigrams, and Verse Letters*, ed. W. Milgate, 1967; *John Donne: The Epithalamions, Anniversaries, and Epicedes*, ed. Wesley Milgate, 1978); Yale University Press *(Shakespeare's Sonnets*, ed. Stephen Booth, 1977; © 1977 by Yale University); University of Wisconsin Press *(The Poems of John Collop*, ed. Conrad Hilberry, 1962).

H. D.

ABBREVIATIONS

CL   *Comparative Literature*
EIC   *Essays in Criticism*
ELH   *English Literary History*
ELR   *English Literary Renaissance*
HLQ   *Huntington Library Quarterly*
JEGP   *Journal of English and Germanic Philology*
MLN   *Modern Language Notes*
MLQ   *Modern Language Quarterly*
MLR   *Modern Language Review*
MP   *Modern Philology*
NLH   *New Literary History*
NQ   *Notes and Queries*
PMLA   *Publications of the Modern Language Association*
PQ   *Philological Quarterly*
RES   *Review of English Studies*
RQ   *Renaissance Quarterly*
SEL   *Studies in English Literature, 1500–1900*
SP   *Studies in Philology*
SQ   *Shakespeare Quarterly*
TSLL   *Texas Studies in Language and Literature*

Echoes of Desire

CHAPTER ONE

INTRODUCTION: LOVE IN THE TIME OF CHOLER

I

Author. In all this world I thinke none lov's but I.
Echo. None lov's but I. *Auth.* Thou foolish tattling ghest,
    In this thou telst a lie. *Echo.* thou telst a lie.
Author. Why? *Love* him selfe he lodgeth in my brest.
Echo. He lodgeth in my brest. *Auth.* I pine for griefe;
    And yet I want reliefe. *Echo.* I want reliefe.
Author. No starre more faire then she whom I adore.
Echo. Then he, whom I adore. *Auth.* Herehence I burne
    Stil more and more. *Echo.* I burne stil more and more.
Author. Love, let my heart returne. *Echo.* my heart, returne.
Auth. Is then the *Saint*, for whom thou makest mone,
    And whom I love, but one? *Echo.* I love but one.
Author. O heav'ns, is ther in love no ende of ills?
Echo. In love no ende of ills. *Auth.* Thou pratling voyce,
    Dwelst thou in th'ayre, or but in hollow hills.
Echo. In hollow hills. *Auth.* Cease of to vaunt thy choyse.
Echo. Cease of to vaunt thy choyse. *Auth.* I would replie,
    But here for love I die. *Echo.* for love I die.
                                        (Watson, *Hecatompathia*, 25)[1]

Thomas Watson's dialogue between a lover and Echo might well tempt literary critics themselves merely to echo the conventional wisdom about Petrarchan poetry. Though published in 1582, the poem is in many ways representative both of earlier Tudor sonnets and of

---

[1] I cite Thomas Watson, *The Hecatompathia or Passionate Centurie of Love* (London, 1582).

those that appeared in the 1590s. It invokes the diction of Petrarchism when its author describes the mistress as a saint and compares her to a star. It confirms the ideology of Petrarchism when Echo assents, "In love no ende of ills" (14). And it not only exemplifies but also enacts the repetitiveness that is the fundamental praxis of Petrarchism, typically realized on levels ranging from diction to stanzaic structure to plot: if the speaker named Author is trapped in repeating sentiments from which he cannot escape, that process itself is replicated when Echo mimes his words. All these mirrorings are ironically played against the dialogue form, which normally implies their opposite, a give-and-take conversation.

Yet by turning the dyad of Petrarchan lover and mistress into a triad whose third member, Echo, in some sense rivals the lover ("he lodgeth in my brest. / Echo. He lodgeth in my brest" [4–5]), Watson directs our attention to an often neglected aspect of Petrarchism: the significance of competition, whether with other poets or other lovers. As we will see, not only texts participating in that movement but also ones reacting against it are triangulated in this and many other ways. More to our purposes now, if in some respects Watson's dialogue substantiates the conventional wisdom about Petrarchism, in others it challenges both that discourse and our critical perspectives on it. Certain passages in the lyric render this apparently straightforward Petrarchan poem anti-Petrarchan in at least the broadest senses of that contested and complex term. And the text calls into question as well many of the academic discourses that examine Petrarchism.

These interrogations of Petrarchism begin when the poem itself does: lines one and two, as well as lines seven and eight, draw our attention to the deceptions inherent in Petrarchan rhetoric. If both Author and Echo can claim that no one is fairer than their beloved, that commonplace assertion is revealed as at the very least hyperbolic, and thus the absolutes favored in Petrarchan diction and exemplified by the opening of this poem are challenged. Echo not only repeats the words of Author but mimes and even mocks his literary enterprise in that he too is echoing the conventional language associated with his genre. Like her prototypes in classical mythology, Watson's Echo is variously pathetic shadow and powerful satirist.[2]

Lines seven and eight also embody a more unsettling subversion. Despite the explanatory note in the text, "S. Liquescens immutat sensum" ("the elision of S. changes the sense"),[3] more than the sense is being changed: a

---

[2]On the varied mythological versions of this figure, see John Hollander, *The Figure of Echo: A Mode of Allusion in Milton and After* (Berkeley: University of California Press, 1981), chap. 1; and Joseph Loewenstein, *Responsive Readings: Versions of Echo in Pastoral, Epic, and the Jonsonian Masque* (New Haven: Yale University Press, 1984), chap. 1.

[3]I am grateful to my colleague Denis Feeney for assistance with this translation.

female voice is praising Narcissus in terms usually reserved for a female Petrarchan mistress. The transgression here is recognized and intensified when the author asks if they love the same person, a decidedly unconventional question that Echo finesses with a return to the most conventional of sentiments, "I love but one" (12). While one should avoid the temptation to make too much of this confusion of gender boundaries (its subversion is, after all, contained by the obvious explanation for Echo's words, the myth starring herself and Narcissus), its unresolved undertones remain and again call into question the workings of Petrarchism.

Moreover, the poem complicates and even compromises some common critical assumptions about the connections between gender and power in Petrarchism. If this lyric is read as an instance of the dependency that the Petrarchan lover shares with the client in a patronage system, an interpretation many new historicists would favor,[4] the ways the name "Author" draws attention to the lover's power of speech are neglected. Alternatively, one might cite the poem in support of the feminist argument that Petrarchism is both source and sign of male potency: after all, not only does Watson literally give his fictive Echo her words, but that authorial power is replicated when his alter ego in the poem does so as well.[5] Yet in merely repeating what has been said, Echo occasionally challenges it as well. Thus an ostensibly powerless female voice achieves some types of agency. Moreover, the speaker, like Echo, claims to die at the end; his power of speech culminates in a statement about the ultimate loss of power, the loss of life itself. If storytelling is an assertion of male power,[6] what happens when a man tells stories about his own defeat?

Seemingly conventional enough to exemplify Petrarchism, seemingly unremarkable enough to invite the briefest summary of how it does so, the lyric thus twists and turns in a way that the third line implicitly glosses: "In this thou telst a lie. *Echo.* thou telst a lie." Although that assertion initially refers to Echo's claim that no one else loves, the doubled lines of the poem hint that line three could apply to other types of duplicity as well. Is Author's claim that Echo lies itself a lie? And, in a broader sense, might the author's claims throughout the poem be lies, as Echo's response

[4]For the most influential presentation of this case, see Arthur F. Marotti, " 'Love is not love': Elizabethan Sonnet Sequences and the Social Order," *ELH*, 49 (1982), 396–428.

[5]Compare Maureen Quilligan's different but related suggestion that the mythological figure of Echo represents the situation of the Jacobean woman author ("The Constant Subject: Instability and Authority in Wroth's *Urania* Poems," in *Soliciting Interpretation: Literary Theory and Seventeenth-Century English Poetry*, ed. Elizabeth D. Harvey and Katharine Eisaman Maus [Chicago: University of Chicago Press, 1990], pp. 310–312).

[6]Many critics have argued this position. See, e.g., Peter Brooks, *Reading for the Plot: Design and Intention in Narrative* (New York: Random House, 1985), esp. chap. 4.

to his first assertion would suggest? In recognizing that Echo challenges the veracity of Author, we should recognize as well that her voice interrogates the author and the authority of Petrarchan love poetry.

Watson's poem, then, exemplifies and examines the subject of this book: how Petrarchism is variously criticized, contradicted, and countermanded in Tudor and Stuart culture. In so doing, it introduces a range of related issues, such as the linkage between formal decisions and cultural conditions, the role of rivalry in love poetry, the workings of repetition, the paradoxes of recounting one's own failures, and, above all, gender, that nexus of questions about sameness and difference. The relationship between Echo and Author also alerts us to another manifestation of sameness and difference: the difficulty of distinguishing the discourses and counterdiscourses of Petrarchism. Many attacks on Petrarchism can be traced to members of its own battalions. The problem of differentiating friend and foe, Petrarchan and anti-Petrarchan text, is echoed and in part generated by the difficulty of clearly distinguishing masculine and feminine in Petrarchism and in Tudor and Stuart culture.

II

Protean and pervasive in sixteenth- and seventeenth-century England, both Petrarchism and the reactions against it prove notoriously hard to define. The *Rime sparse*, a collection as variable as Laura herself, includes many characteristics that might otherwise be labeled anti-Petrarchan, such as a renunciation of love in favor of spiritual values. Moreover, the *Rime sparse* was read in editions festooned with lengthy and often contradictory commentaries, editions that, like some Bibles, frequently sported a relatively brief passage from Petrarch surrounded by far bulkier glosses.[7] The very presence of these lengthy explications attests to both the cultural significance and the intellectual complexity of Petrarch's sequence. Far from re-

---

[7]On the commentators, see esp. two studies by William J. Kennedy, "Petrarchan Textuality: Commentaries and Gender Revisions," in *Discourses of Authority in Medieval and Renaissance Literature*, ed. Kevin Brownlee and Walter Stephens (Hanover, N.H.: University Press of New England, 1989), and *Authorizing Petrarch* (Ithaca: Cornell University Press, 1995). I am indebted to the author for making his book available to me before publication and for a number of useful suggestions about my work. The commentators' influence on Wyatt in particular is analyzed in Maxwell S. Luria, "Wyatt's 'The Lover Compareth His State' and the Petrarchan Commentators," *TSLL*, 12 (1971), 531–535; and Patricia Thomson, *Sir Thomas Wyatt and His Background* (Stanford: Stanford University Press, 1964), pp. 190–200, and her earlier version of the argument, "Wyatt and the Petrarchan Commentators," *RES*, 10 (1959), 225–233.

solving the interpretive problems posed by the *Rime sparse*, however, Petrarch's early commentators often confound them. William J. Kennedy has persuasively demonstrated the variety in Renaissance interpretations of the author of the *Rime sparse*: he is read as devout Christian, civic humanist, monarchist, and so on.[8] "The history of Petrarchism," as Kennedy aptly observes, "is a narrative of multiple Petrarchs."[9]

When one turns from Petrarch to his Continental heirs and assigns, the challenges of describing and defining Petrarchism are further confounded. Categorizing the poems in this tradition is itself problematical. Donald Stone Jr., for example, observes that the twenty-third sonnet of Ronsard's *Continuation* ("Mignongne, levés-vous") "abandons Petrarchism indirectly by creating an intimacy between poet and lady unparalleled in the Italian tradition";[10] others, however, might expand their definitions of Petrarchism to include frankly erotic lyrics like this one. Even authors who are clearly writing Petrarchan poetry respond very differently to the *Rime sparse* and in so doing create alternative Petrarchan traditions; witness the contrast between respectful imitators like Bembo and more radical reinterpreters like Serafino.[11]

By the time the sonnet was in vogue in England, then, poets who wished to write within or react against that tradition confronted not one but several traditions—and not one but several Petrarchs. Hence scholars debate whether the reinterpretation of Petrarch's Poem 190 that shapes Wyatt's "Whoso List to Hunt" should be traced to Giovanni Antonio Romanello (the Italian poet who recast the poem) or to commentaries on Petrarch himself.[12] Moreover, all these problems are further complicated in light of the historical perspective of sixteenth-century sonneteers. The tradition must have seemed even more flexible, inchoate, or both to poets composing sonnets in 1592—or even 1594 or 1595—than it does to us today. Its sixteenth-century practitioners could not turn to their Norton Anthologies for a convenient summary of its characteristics and development, and they may well not have defined Petrarchism in all the ways a twentieth-century scholar would. At what point, for instance, was the fourteen-line

[8]See Kennedy, "Petrarchan Textuality," and his *Authorizing Petrarch*, esp. chap. 2.

[9]William J. Kennedy, "Colonizing Petrarch," paper presented at 1990 meeting of the Modern Language Association, Chicago.

[10]Donald Stone Jr., *Ronsard's Sonnet Cycles: A Study in Tone and Vision* (New Haven: Yale University Press, 1966), p. 64.

[11]Compare F. T. Prince, "The Sonnet from Wyatt to Shakespeare," in *Elizabethan Poetry*, Stratford-upon-Avon Studies, 2 (London: Edward Arnold, 1960), pp. 11-12.

[12]See Alastair Fowler, *Conceitful Thought: The Interpretation of English Renaissance Poems* (Edinburgh: University of Edinburgh Press, 1975), pp. 3-4; Kenneth Muir and Patricia Thomson, eds., *Collected Poems of Sir Thomas Wyatt* (Liverpool: Liverpool University Press, 1969), pp. 266-267; and Thomson, *Sir Thomas Wyatt*, pp. 190-200.

poem established as one of its principal norms? To be sure, most sonneteers do adopt it. Yet in 1582 Watson himself publishes eighteen-line poems that, despite their prosody, are insistently Petrarchan in other ways. Fifteen years later another minor sonneteer, Richard Tofte, calls his heroine "Laura" and puns on "laurel." He does not, however, feel constrained to write fourteen-line poems, and, given how derivative his poems are in other respects, the absence of that norm suggests not excitement with prosodic experimentation and variation (a desire, so to speak, to wear his laurel with a difference) but a lack of concern for the verse form now considered one of the central markers of Petrarchism. Indeed, in asking how Petrarchism was interpreted by those writing within it and hence in some sense re-creating it, one needs to entertain the possibility that in some instances Petrarch himself might not have been seen as the central source for the love lyrics critics now associate primarily with him. Certainly many sonneteers are keenly conscious of their classical antecedents and insistently draw attention to them, in part, perhaps, to lend respectability to the dubious enterprise of writing love poetry; the title page of Giles Fletcher's *Licia* reads "to the imitation of the best Latin Poets, and others,"[13] while the prose passages attached to each sonnet in Watson's *Hecatompathia* explicate his sources, including many classical ones.[14]

Defining anti-Petrarchism is no less complicated.[15] In some instances, of course, the label fits neatly. One has no more trouble designating the satiric poem about Mopsa in Sidney's *Arcadia* anti-Petrarchan than we do categorizing its sources and analogues, notably so-called ugly beauty poems by Berni and Ronsard, as such. Often, however, the process of classification is less clear-cut. To begin with, a definition of anti-Petrarchism necessarily draws on that perilous enterprise of defining Petrarchism. Because many poems, including Watson's, oppose Petrarchism at certain points and embrace it at others or oppose it with the ambivalence that characterizes Petrarchism itself, the very category anti-Petrarchan is itself often problematical. Petrarchism regularly incorporates attacks on its own vision, so distinguishing lyrics that participate in that movement from ones that rebut it is by no means easy—should we, for example, label poems that

---

[13]Fletcher is cited from *Licia, or Poemes of Love* (Cambridge, Eng., 1593?).

[14]Two studies, though dated, provide detailed background on the range of sources behind the English sonnets. See Lisle Cecil John, *The Elizabethan Sonnet Sequences: Studies in Conventional Conceits* (1938; rpt., New York: Russell and Russell, 1964); and Janet G. Scott, *Les Sonnets Elisabéthains: Les sources et l'apport personnel* (Paris: Librairie Ancienne Honoré Champion, 1929).

[15]In chap. 2 of her unpublished book, "Passion Lends Them Power: The Poetry and Practice of Elizabethan Courtship," Ilona Bell attempts to negotiate this problem by distinguishing what she terms *anti-Petrarchism* from *pseudo-Petrarchism*, which refashions a tradition.

reject *cupiditas* for *caritas* anti-Petrarchan or simply acknowledge that they are replicating a move made by Petrarch himself? One critic, in fact, mis-leadingly claims that until the eighteenth century, so-called anti-Petrarchism is merely a convention of Petrarchism which never seriously challenges it, a common interpretation that neglects the intensity and even choler with which certain poets attack Petrarchism.[16] In fact, the dialogue between the two movements is as complex and variable as the interchange between Watson's Echo and Author; in both cases the voices are sometimes antagonistic opponents, sometimes virtually indistinguishable alter egos.

Neither is it easy to delimit the scope of the movement generally called anti-Petrarchism. Given the prevalence and significance of Petrarchism in sixteenth- and even seventeenth-century England, texts that never explic-itly allude to it may well respond to it implicitly. Petrarchism is a basso continuo against which arias in different styles and genres are sung. Thus in the 1590s, as I will suggest later, the decision to write an epyllion is in important ways a decision not to write a Petrarchan love poem. Similarly, many seventeenth-century texts are grounded in an unspoken commentary on Petrarchism; as Gordon Braden and William Kerrigan persuasively dem-onstrate, the development of lyric poetry during that era may virtually be plotted as a series of different reactions to Petrarchism.[17] "Renaissance love poetry," Ilona Bell observes, "cannot be a-Petrarchan."[18]

The present book responds to the methodological challenges inherent in its vast subject by defining its topic narrowly in some ways and broadly in others. I direct my attention to the sixteenth and earlier seventeenth cen-turies, though both Petrarchism and its counterdiscourses are exemplified by such contemporary poets as John Berryman and Marilyn Hacker,[19] and I focus mainly on texts whose relationship to Petrarchism is overt. I refer

[16]See Leonard Forster, *The Icy Fire: Five Studies in European Petrarchism* (Cambridge: Cam-bridge University Press, 1969), pp. 56–58.

[17]In emphasizing the continuing influence of that movement, Gordon Braden maintains, however, that seventeenth-century poetry typically refracts Petrarchism rather than rejecting it; the validity of this thought-provoking but ultimately unpersuasive assertion once again depends on how one defines Petrarchism and anti-Petrarchism ("Beyond Frustration: Pe-trarchan Laurels in the Seventeenth Century," *SEL*, 26 [1986], 5–23). For a related inter-pretation of seventeenth-century responses to Petrarchism, see also an essay he coauthored with William Kerrigan, "Milton's Coy Eve: *Paradise Lost* and Renaissance Love Poetry," *ELH*, 53 (1986), 28–38.

[18]Ilona Bell, "Milton's Dialogue with Petrarch," in *Milton Studies*, 28 (1992), 109.

[19]See esp. Lynn Keller's essay on Hacker, "Measured Feet 'in Gender-Bender Shoes': Marilyn Hacker's *Love, Death, and the Changing of the Seasons*," in *Feminist Measures: Soundings in Poetry and Theory*, ed. Lynn Keller and Cristianne Miller (Ann Arbor: University of Mich-igan Press, 1994). I am grateful to the author for making this text available to me in man-uscript.

briefly to Continental poems when they are especially germane, but this is a study of English Petrarchism, not a comparatist analysis. Indeed, I am particularly interested in certain characteristics of Petrarchism and anti-Petrarchism which specifically interact with Tudor and Stuart culture: advantages as well as limitations accrue from the decision to read the movement in part as a response to local conditions.[20] Tip O'Neill repeatedly observed that all politics is local; in some senses the politics of even as international a movement as Petrarchism is so too. I further delimit my topic by concentrating mainly on lyric poetry, though my conclusion considers reactions against Petrarchism in other genres and modes; there, as elsewhere, I respond to the breadth of my subject by trying to allude suggestively to issues I could not hope to analyze definitively.

This book also counters the problems inherent in the term *anti-Petrarchism* by attempting to avoid it. Because, as I have noted, that label is at best imperfect and at worst misleading, when possible I substitute the concept of the counterdiscourse, itself in turn redefined. As deployed by Richard Terdiman in *Discourse/Counter-Discourse: The Theory and Practice of Symbolic Resistance in Nineteenth-Century France*[21] and by other critics as well, that term is meant to apply to a range of reactions against a dominant discourse. Because it can readily be declined in the plural, "counterdiscourse" aptly suggests the variety of ways Petrarchism was resisted and rejected. Moreover, this label is more appropriate than "anti-Petrarchism" for describing the many instances in which a text both espouses and rejects Petrarchism or the cases in which its relationship to that discourse is, in more senses than one, too close to call. Like Terdiman, in using the term in question I want to suggest a continuing process of struggle and one that often ends in the containment of the transgressive assertions in the texts that criticize Petrarchism. The containment of the reactions against Petrarchism is not, however, inevitable or even normative, as the paradigm deployed in *Discourse/Counter-Discourse* is prone to suggest. Nor is Petrarchism itself a stable or monolithic discourse with the hegemonic ability to repel all challenges. The relationship between discourse and counterdiscourse is a closely matched and often indeterminate power struggle, once again as volatile and variable as the relationship between Watson's Author and Echo.

---

[20]Roland Greene also alludes to local conditions influencing Petrarchism, though his approach to that issue is very different from mine (*Post-Petrarchism: Origins and Innovations of the Western Lyric Sequence* [Princeton: Princeton University Press, 1991], p. 3).

[21]Richard Terdiman, *Discourse/Counter-Discourse: The Theory and Practice of Symbolic Resistance in Nineteenth-Century France* (Ithaca: Cornell University Press, 1985).

III

However we define and label them, the reactions against Petrarchism deserve more attention than they have hitherto received. To understand Petrarchism, certainly one of the most significant discourses in Tudor and even Stuart England, we must understand its counterdiscourses; this book is itself in some important ways a study of Petrarchan poetry, as any study of anti-Petrarchism is virtually bound to be. Analyzing the reactions against Petrarchism also allows us to address many questions currently at the center of early modern studies, notably problems about gender, the female body, male subjectivity, and nationalism. At the same time, studying the counterdiscourses of Petrarchism invites us to reexamine the kind of issues that are variously dismissed and celebrated as the staples of traditional criticism. Thus the problems of repetitiveness and of modes of difference and sameness in Watson parallel prosodic questions: the sonnet may play the sameness of its quatrains against the difference of the couplet, or, similarly, it may play the recurrence of the sonnet form from one poem to the next against variations within their sestets, and so on. Generic questions also explicate the relationship of Petrarchism and its assailants, for rejections of that discourse are often expressed by invoking a range of alternative genres.

Because of what they do and what they fail to do, previous studies of early modern English literature further encourage us to examine both Petrarchism and the reactions against it. The contemporary predilection for analyzing Tudor and Stuart drama at the expense of the poetry and prose of the period guarantees that the sonnet tradition has received less attention than it deserves during the past two decades. In this book I attempt to redress that imbalance and to encourage further work on lyric poetry in general.

Although neither the Petrarchan discourse nor its counterdiscourses have received the attention they deserve and demand, the former, at least, has not been completely disregarded. Contemporary studies of Petrarchism, notably important books and articles by Ilona Bell, Gordon Braden, and Roland Greene, among other scholars, have demonstrated its continuing significance and have generated an exciting climate in which to address the subject.[22] At the same time, however, the lacunae and limitations in many current analyses invite reinterpretation. In particular, critics often claim that

[22]Bell, "Passion Lends Them Power"; Gordon Braden, "Love and Fame: The Petrarchan Career," in *Pragmatism's Freud: The Moral Disposition of Psychoanalysis*, ed. Joseph H. Smith, M.D., and William Kerrigan (Baltimore: Johns Hopkins University Press, 1986); Greene, *Post-Petrarchism*.

Petrarchism is really about politics, not love.[23] Like most correctives, these statements demonstrate both the polemical benefits and the intellectual limitations of hyperbole. The tendency to read love as a decoy for another subject may well remind us of the type of allegorical temper that sees allusions to religious ideas virtually everywhere; in the case at hand, the equivalent of the original, transcendental signified is politics. As the title of this chapter insists, both Petrarchism and anti-Petrarchism are indeed often about subjects like politics, history, or the relationships among men, but they are always—and often primarily—about love, desire, and gender as well.

A second interpretive problem, which we have already encountered in passing, arises in some, though by no means all, new historicist and feminist commentaries on love poetry. Engaged in demonstrating parallels between courtship and courtiership, a number of new historicists have identified the Petrarchan lover with the subservient and often unsuccessful candidate for patronage.[24] Thus this tradition becomes a narrative of failure and the loss of agency. Alternatively, some feminist scholars encapsulate Petrarchism as a successful assertion of male power and the concomitant erasure of the female. As one typical presentation of that position puts it, "The Petrarchan love poem is a theater of desire—one in which men have the active roles and the women are assigned silent, iconic functions, and are notable primarily for their absence in the script."[25]

In this book I adopt a complex and often contestatory stance towards such arguments about power and silence. One can make a case for either the passive subservience or the aggressive if often masked dominance of the Petrarchan lover precisely because Petrarchism typically enacts a dynamic, unending slippage between power and powerlessness and between one of their principal sources, success and failure.[26] Hence readings that

[23]See Marotti," " 'Love is not love' "; for a related argument that connects love and politics without suggesting that the first is primarily a screen for the second, cf. Ann Rosalind Jones and Peter Stallybrass, "The Politics of *Astrophil and Stella*," *SEL*, 24 (1984), 53–68.

[24]See esp. Marotti, " 'Love is not love' "; and Jones and Stallybrass, "Politics of *Astrophil and Stella*." The argument has, however, been widely disseminated.

[25]Gary F. Waller, "Struggling into Discourse: The Emergence of Renaissance Women's Writing," in *Silent but for the Word: Tudor Women as Patrons, Translators, and Writers of Religious Works*, ed. Margaret Patterson Hannay (Kent, Ohio: Kent State University Press, 1985), p. 242. Also cf. the version of this argument in an essay by Margaret Homans, " 'Syllables of Velvet': Dickinson, Rossetti, and the Rhetorics of Sexuality," *Feminist Studies*, 11 (1985), 569–593, a study that connects Petrarchism with developments in poetry of later centuries.

[26]Though critics have slighted this aspect of English Petrarchism, Thomas M. Greene trenchantly traces the uneasy relationship between success and failure in Petrarch's own poetry (*The Light in Troy: Imitation and Discovery in Renaissance Poetry* [New Haven: Yale University Press, 1982], chaps. 6 and 7).

emphasize the potency and agency that Petrarchism bestows on its poets tell a partial story at best.[27] As we will see, the lurch between success and failure which characterizes that movement corresponds to recurrent problems in other arenas of Tudor and Stuart England, notably the conflicts among several different systems for assessing social status, and hence accounts in no small measure for the attraction of this mode of love poetry. Similarly, I maintain that reexamining female speech as constructed both in Petrarchan texts and elsewhere in the culture complicates frequently asserted connections among gender, speechlessness, and passivity. Although the Petrarchan mistress is sometimes silenced, in many instances she is not. Her voice, like that of Watson's Echo, is threatening not least because it comprises such varied and even contradictory registers.

The paradigm of the dominant and manipulative poet and silenced mistress is deceptive not merely because it neglects that variety but also because it typically presupposes the stability of gender categories. Writing poetry, according to this model, is gendered masculine, and it is associated with many forms of power and agency, not least the power to silence the female voice. But other studies have drawn our attention to the problematics of gender categories in sixteenth- and seventeenth-century England,[28] and queer theory in particular has encouraged us to see both gender and sexuality in terms of overlapping and unstable subject positions rather than clear-cut binaries.[29] Petrarchism, I will argue, repeatedly challenges the boundaries between characteristics that might be gendered masculine and feminine; whereas its counterdiscourses react to those challenges in many different ways, one of the most common and most revealing is their attempt to reestablish gendered distinctions.

Despite, and because of, the confusions of gender which are so characteristic of Petrarchism, this book focuses on what I term *diacritical desire*, a phrase intended to refer to the desire to make distinctions, its relationship to desire in the erotic sense, and the markers that attempt to establish such boundaries. Petrarchism, however imitative its style may be, is grounded in attempts at differentiation. Its poets distinguish themselves from their

---

[27]For an example of those readings, see Braden, "Love and Fame."

[28]See, e.g., Phyllis Rackin, "Androgyny, Mimesis, and the Marriage of the Boy Heroine on the English Renaissance Stage," *PMLA*, 102 (1987), 29–41; and Linda Woodbridge, *Women and the English Renaissance: Literature and the Nature of Womankind, 1540–1620* (Urbana: University of Illinois Press, 1984), esp. pt. 2. My argument about the eroded boundaries in Petrarchism between male and female is also related to the observations by Jonathan Dollimore about the threat of sameness (*Sexual Dissidence: Augustine to Wilde, Freud to Foucault* [Oxford: Clarendon, 1991], chap. 17).

[29]See, e.g., Jonathan Goldberg, *Sodometries: Renaissance Texts, Modern Sexualities* (Stanford: Stanford University Press, 1992), esp. the Introduction.

predecessors and from contemporary love poets as sedulously as Petrarch marks the divide between himself and Dante and between the youthful and mature Petrarchs. And Petrarchan poets emphasize the divide between the poet and the mistress—even as they erase it. For Petrarchism also stages the breakdown of distinctions; witness the relationship between Author and Echo, analogous confusions about gender in other poems, and the oxymoron itself. More to our purposes, diacritical desire is both the impulse behind and the defining characteristic of anti-Petrarchism. I am concerned throughout to stress the contiguities—chronological, ideological, and stylistic—between Petrarchism and its counterdiscourses, one of which is the replication of diacritical desire in those counterdiscourses. They are, of course, based almost by definition on distinguishing one's own poem and sometimes, too, one's own lady from their counterparts in conventional Petrarchism. We will see that the diacritical agendas of anti-Petrarchism are realized as well in nuances of diction, patterns of syntax, and choices of genre. Cultural conditions, notably the often neglected consequences of early parental death, help to explain the attraction to these manifestations of diacritical desire.

The adjective *diacritical* typically refers not only to the impulse to make distinctions but also to the markers that do so. Focusing on them, I ask, What strategies, whether formal, ideological, or otherwise, serve to establish distinctions between one poet and another or between the poet and his lady? Why are both those markers and the desire to deploy them so attractive to the culture and the specific poets who do so? And why, given the prevalence and efficacy of these diacritical markers, are the texts in question characterized not by clear-cut separations between male and female, powerful and powerless, successful and unsuccessful, Petrarchan and anti-Petrarchan, but by slippages within and between those sets of categories?

In stressing the instability of both power and gender, however, I do not simply posit a kinder, gentler patriarchy. To be sure, I argue that to read Petrarchism primarily as an exercise in domination and silencing is to misread it, and I maintain as well that responses to some of the cultural tensions I explore are more complex than critics often acknowledge. But this book also uncovers anxieties about gender in some arenas that have been neglected by many students of literary and cultural history, notably demographics and the history of medicine. And, as the title of this introduction would suggest, I argue that the misogynistic hostility and anger that often impel both Petrarchism and the reactions against it can be even more pervasive and virulent than we sometimes acknowledge. In lyrics in these traditions, choler is variously directed towards the Petrarchan mistress and deflected onto women from whom she is seemingly different or onto other poets. Patriarchy may be most threatening when it is most threatened, most offensive (in both senses) when it is most defensive.

I approach broad questions like these by focusing closely on particular authors and movements and above all on particular texts within the counterdiscourses of Petrarchism. One aim of this book is to direct attention to some neglected poets and poems, notably the writing of that obscure but intriguing seventeenth-century figure John Collop. My close scrutiny of specific texts is, however, also polemical. We too often conflate the ideological agendas that were frequently though not always characteristic of New Criticism with its methodological protocols and therefore dismiss the latter out of hand; by precept and example, *Echoes of Desire* attempts to demonstrate how close readings can illuminate the questions that interest even—or especially—new historicists and feminists. If all politics is local, so too are many avenues for understanding politics.

In these and other respects, the methodology of this book is eclectic. It dovetails some of the concerns of more traditional critical modes, notably genre studies and formalism, with the agendas of newer ones. In particular, though I take issue with the ways certain new historicists and feminists have interpreted the sonnet tradition, I am profoundly indebted to those two approaches. Indeed, one of my principal goals is to bridge new historicism and feminism, a project more often advocated than attempted by students of Renaissance literature.

In Chapter 2 I examine the poetry of Petrarch and its relationship to the dynamics of English culture, asking why both that discourse and its counterdiscourses were so popular and so influential in England. My third chapter provides an overview of the counterdiscourses within the sonnet tradition as a whole, whereas the fourth concentrates more intensely on the work of three of the most important participants in that tradition: Sidney, Shakespeare, and Wroth. Chapter 5 studies a particularly significant manifestation of the counterdiscourses of Petrarchism, the so-called ugly beauty tradition, aiming as well to direct attention towards Collop. John Donne, often considered monarch of anti-Petrarchism as well as of the adjoining kingdom of wit, is the subject of Chapter 6, and I engage there not only with the love lyrics that are generally studied when critics evaluate his relationship to Petrarchism but also with his work in other genres. My conclusion, Chapter 7, extends the scope of the book by surveying some specimen instances of the counterdiscourses in genres other than lyric poetry. In addition, I extend the discussions of our profession and our discipline which appear from time to time in previous chapters. Commentaries on issues like professional rivalries and tenure policies are typically confined to the pages of journals such as *Profession* or the *ADE Bulletin* rather than being integrated into a scholarly study. I mention such problems in passing within early chapters and at greater length in the conclusion partly because Petrarchism, like other literary topics, provides an apt analogue to many of them. And I do so as well because I believe that in our own time of opposing and often choleric critical movements, these professional issues are at once so pressing and so intriguing that we should expand the forums in which we address them.

CHAPTER TWO

PETRARCHAN PROBLEMATICS:
TRADITION AND
THE INDIVIDUAL CULTURE

I

Petrarchism, itself a discourse of extremes, demands from its critics a rhetoric of qualifications and modulations. For lyrics in this tradition resist easy generalizations as determinedly as Laura flees her Apollo: their meaning is as tantalizingly veiled as her face, as evanescent as the snow that so often figures her. The tradition not only stages but also represents a series of paradoxes; its poems are, for example, more likely than texts in many other genres to be either singularly conventional or strikingly transgressive or both, and they may variously celebrate and subvert ideologies of gender. More to our purposes here, the reception of these lyrics was no less paradoxical than their own agendas: they enjoyed an extraordinary vogue throughout much of Europe yet endured repeated attacks from the very cultures and poets who seemed most enamored of them.

Petrarch's love poems are particularly liable to problems in interpretation. Critics part company on the most basic issues: Is their fundamental aim the praise of the lady, as some scholars of an earlier generation assumed, or the establishment of the poet's own subjectivity, as many of their contemporary counterparts would assert?[1] Is the final poem the culmination of a movement towards spiritual resolution or an instance of the ways that movement has been compromised throughout the sequence?[2] The rhetoric of the

---

[1]For instances of these positions, see, respectively, Leonard Forster, *The Icy Fire: Five Studies in European Petrarchism* (Cambridge: Cambridge University Press, 1969), esp. p. 9; and Gordon Braden, "Love and Fame: The Petrarchan Career," in *Pragmatism's Freud: The Moral Disposition of Psychoanalysis*, ed. Joseph H. Smith, M.D., and William Kerrigan (Baltimore: Johns Hopkins University Press, 1986).

[2]Many critics have espoused each of these positions; for example, see, respectively, Mar-

lyrics thwarts efforts to resolve these and other debates. From the very opening of the *Rime sparse*, Petrarch qualifies and undermines his statements: "quand' era *in parte* altr' uom da quel ch'i'sono" (1.4, emphasis added; "when I was *in part* another man from what I am now").[3] As the sequence progresses, terms like *forse* (perhaps) and forms of the verb *parere* (to seem) repeatedly destabilize declarative statements. It is no accident that these poems have attracted and rewarded deconstructive analyses.[4]

Far from resolving such paradoxes, Petrarch's early commentators have confounded them, as we have already observed.[5] Similarly, Petrarch's imitators repeatedly construct different versions of both the type of Petrarchism they are writing and the type they are eschewing. As Roland Greene acutely demonstrates, all sonnets after the *Rime sparse* are "post-Petrarchan" in that they reinterpret their heritage.[6] Nor have contemporary critics achieved a consensus. Witness, for example, the gap between Marjorie O'Rourke Boyle's claim that the *Canzoniere* exemplify the theological and spiritual values expressed elsewhere in the canon,[7] Aldo S. Bernardo's assertion that the *Triumphs* achieve the fusion of the classical and heavenly for which Petrarch has striven with varied success in the *Rime sparse*,[8] and John Freccero's contrast between Augustine's spirituality and Petrarch's fallen vision.[9]

Generalizing about Petrarchan love is, then, almost as perilous as prac-

---

jorie O'Rourke Boyle, *Petrarch's Genius: Pentimento and Prophecy* (Berkeley: University of California Press, 1991), esp. p. 149; and Robert M. Durling, *The Figure of the Poet in Renaissance Epic* (Cambridge: Harvard University Press, 1965), pp. 83–84.

[3]All citations and translations from Petrarch's *Rime sparse* are to *Petrarch's Lyric Poems: The Rime sparse and Other Lyrics*, ed. and trans. Robert M. Durling (Cambridge: Harvard University Press, 1976). The play on "in parte" is also noted by Sara Sturm-Maddox in *Petrarch's Laurels* (University Park: Pennsylvania State University Press, 1992), p. 232. For a different but compatible reading of the instability of Petrarch's language, see William J. Kennedy, *Authorizing Petrarch* (Ithaca: Cornell University Press, 1995), esp. pp. 5–24.

[4]See esp. Marguerite Waller, *Petrarch's Poetics and Literary History* (Amherst: University of Massachusetts Press, 1980).

[5]See esp. two studies by William J. Kennedy: *Authorizing Petrarch*, and "Petrarchan Textuality: Commentaries and Gender Revisions," in *Discourses of Authority in Medieval and Renaissance Literature*, ed. Kevin Brownlee and Walter Stephens (Hanover, N.H.: University Press of New England, 1989).

[6]Roland Greene, *Post-Petrarchism: Origins and Innovations of the Western Lyric Sequence* (Princeton: Princeton University Press, 1991).

[7]Boyle, *Petrarch's Genius*.

[8]Aldo S. Bernardo, *Petrarch, Laura, and the Triumphs* (Albany: State University of New York Press, 1974).

[9]John Freccero, "The Fig Tree and the Laurel: Petrarch's Poetics," in *Literary Theory/ Renaissance Texts*, ed. Patricia Parker and David Quint (Baltimore: Johns Hopkins University Press, 1986).

ticing it. In this chapter I counter such risks partly by delimiting my own agenda: I aim not to survey the entire tradition but to anatomize the particular characteristics that help to explain why Petrarch inspired both so many imitations and so many correctives in sixteenth- and seventeenth-century England. And I concentrate mainly on Petrarch himself, though at several junctures I develop or qualify generalizations about him by alluding to other Continental writers. The influence of French poets on the English sonnet tradition was profound, pervasive, and protean, as Anne Lake Prescott has shown: Gorges translates texts by Du Bellay, Ronsard, and Desportes, four poems in Daniel's *Delia* are based on sonnets to Du Bellay's *Olive*; Lodge borrows entire lyrics from Ronsard; and so on.[10] In 1594, when decrying slavish imitation in the dedicatory poem of *Ideas Mirrour*, Drayton mentions Desportes as well as Petrarch. Yet the author of the *Rime sparse* is, after all, still the main influence on English Petrarchism, and discussions of English Petrarchism can profitably ground generalizations in a detailed analysis of his work.

In the end, all the cautions and caveats demanded by a study of Petrarchism enrich, not endanger, that enterprise. For the problems of interpretation and representation exemplified by that tradition are central to its attractiveness and its agendas in the English Renaissance.[11] Those challenges help us to address the central question about Tudor and Stuart culture on which this chapter pivots: Why does Petrarchism attract both so many adherents and so many detractors, inspire slavish imitations and embittered rejections? While some answers to those questions are predictable and familiar (Petrarchism clearly did offer intriguing technical challenges and an arena for nationalistic pride and competitiveness), other answers will involve a radical reinterpretation of both Petrarchism itself and the culture, or rather cultures, of Tudor and Stuart England. In particular, analyzing responses to English Petrarchism reveals the conjunctions between that international literary discourse and more local problems. These patterns emerge most clearly when we approach the movement from five interrelated perspectives: the movement between success and failure, the nature of narrative and lyric, the dangers of repetition, the problems of gender, and the drive to differentiate.

---

[10]Anne Lake Prescott, *French Poets and the English Renaissance: Studies in Fame and Transformation* (New Haven: Yale University Press, 1978).

[11]Other critics have noted that the problems of interpretation are central to the meaning of these poems. See, e.g., Guiseppe Mazzotta's analyses of the instability of both language and desire ("The *Canzoniere* and the Language of the Self," *SP*, 75 [1978], 271–296; reprinted in *The Worlds of Petrarch* [Durham, N.C.: Duke University Press, 1993]).

II

Sonnet 118 is neither one of the best known lyrics in the *Canzoniere* nor one of the best, but it is typical of the collection in ways germane to those five perspectives and hence to the reception and reinterpretation of Petrarchism in England.

> Rimansi a dietro il sestodecimo anno
> de' miei sospiri, et io trapasso inanzi
> verso l'estremo; et parmi che pur dianzi
> fosse 'l principio di cotanto affanno.
>
> L'amar m'è dolce, et util il mio danno,
> e 'l viver grave; et prego che gli avanzi
> l'empia fortuna; et temo no chiuda anzi
> Morte i begli occhi che parlar mi fanno.
>
> Or qui son, lasso, et voglio esser altrove,
> et vorrei più volere, et più non voglio,
> et per più non poter fo quant' io posso;
>
> et d'antichi desir lagrime nove
> provan com' io son pur quel ch' i' mi soglio,
> né per mille rivolte ancor son mosso.

(Now remains behind the sixteenth year of my sighs, and I move forward toward the last; yet it seems to me that all this suffering began only recently. The bitter is sweet to me, and my losses useful, and living heavy; and I pray that my life may outlast my cruel fortune; and I fear that before then Death may close the lovely eyes that make me speak. Now here I am, alas, and wish I were elsewhere, and wish I wished more, but wish no more, and, by being unable to do more, do all I can; and new tears for old desires show me to be still what I used to be, nor for a thousand turnings about have I yet moved.)

Characteristically preoccupied with time, Petrarch here plays several conflicting interpretations of it against one another. The opening line introduces an objective chronological sequence by alluding to years that can be measured—yet "parmi" (3; "it seems to me") signals a subjective time sequence at variance with the first one. Moreover, lines seven to eight introduce a mode of time which was to prove particularly significant in the work of Petrarch's English imitators: allusions to the future, a realm that may be variously associated with uncontrolled fears or soaring hopes, with the authority of the successful prophet or, as in this case, the helplessness of the fearful prognosticator.

In any event, all these time schemes are contrasted with the psychological stasis that is the most significant temporal mode of these texts. Thus "d'antichi desir lagrime nove / provan com' io son pur quel ch' i' mi soglio" (12–13; "and new tears for old desires show me to be still what I used to be") starts on an antithesis that seems firmly to establish the *then/now* pattern that Roland Greene rightly claims is central to the sequence—but that pattern is blurred by the admission that in the psyche of the speaker, *then* and *now* collide and elide.[12] As the conclusion of the poem indicates, for all the volatility of his emotions, he moves without moving. But this paradox was in fact anticipated in lines nine through eleven, where the traductio associated with *volere* (to wish) and *potere* (to be able) rhetorically stages the conjunction of change and its lack to which the concluding lines refer more overtly. Those reduplicated verb forms demonstrate how rhetorical repetition can figure the many types of entrapment that Petrarchism involves, the "thousand turnings" that fail to produce movement. Stasis is the physical state that represents an emotional state of depression and compulsive repetition, of wishing that one was not unable even to wish.

That paradox prepares us for the approach to agency in this lyric and elsewhere in the sequence as well. On the one hand, for all his frustration, on some level Petrarch is in charge of his medium. Even though Laura speaks often, in several ways he has the last word. And he also has a kind of autonomy that Laura, who is present in the poem only in terms of her effects on him, lacks. On the other hand, line eight reminds us that his speech is generated elsewhere, in her eyes. Such lines should not be dismissed with the claim that the woman is merely assuming gendered roles that in fact figure her subordination, such as the Muse. Indeed, to redeploy Margaret Homans's phrase, it is the male poet who bears the word of another.[13] Hence one cannot preserve the critical commonplace of the masterful Petrarchan poet by arguing that, despite the unruliness of his emotions, his power and agency reside in his skillful deployment of language: his poetic gifts are as much a source and symptom of his problems as a solution to them.

Yet neither is Laura's agency uncompromised; if she can make the poet

[12]Greene, *Post-Petrarchism*, esp. pp. 33–34.

[13]Margaret Homans, *Bearing the Word: Language and Female Experience in Nineteenth-Century Women's Writing* (Chicago: University of Chicago Press, 1986).

speak, Death, he fears, will close her eyes and hence stifle one source of her potency. Indeed, the grammatical structures of "et temo no chiuda anzi / Morte i begli occhi che parlar mi fanno" (7–8; "and I fear that before then Death may close the lovely eyes that make me speak") body forth this paradoxical power structure: Laura's eyes are poised on the hinge of a phrase, variously object and subject, a double role that mimes the ambiguities of the speaker's own agency.[14] In this as in so many other ways they are twinned: if Laura is both subject and object in the sentence, thus eliding the two roles, so too do Petrarch and Laura, the figures who are normally interpreted as the antithetical subject and object of love poetry, themselves elide.[15]

In this lyric, then, we repeatedly encounter the poet's slide between mastery and loss, the temporal patterns that often figure it, and a related slippage, the instability of gender. Thus Poem 118 introduces some of the five conflicts in Petrarchism on which this chapter focuses—success versus failure, narrative versus lyric, repetition versus closure or stasis, masculine versus feminine, and differentiation versus sameness—as well as the elisions that typically recur in those areas. Or, to put it another way, this and many other texts in the *Rime sparse* enact and interpret dramas about male subjectivity and its relationship to gender like those that were to be played in many of the theaters, literal and metaphoric, of sixteenth-century England.

III

Although many readers have noted that the *Rime sparse* repeatedly resorts to the trope of the pilot, Petrarch's deployment of that metaphor deserves more scrutiny, not least because it represents the careening relationship between success and failure in the sequence. Sometimes the speaker himself is the pilot; sometimes, as in Sonnet 189 ("Passa la nave"), which inspired several English imitations, Petrarch is merely a passenger in a ship steered by his enemy. And even in the lyrics where he takes over the rudder, he is by no means assured of retaining his control of it: this is a pilot who, overwhelmed by storms or by the lady, repeatedly loses the ability to steer.

---

[14]Compare Ilona Bell's observations about a male pronoun Milton uses when recounting Eve's creation ("Milton's Dialogue with Petrarch," *Milton Studies*, 28 [1991], 100).

[15]Many critics have noted these elisions. For a particularly thought-provoking reading of them, different from but compatible with my own, see Marguerite Waller, "Historicism Historicized: Translating Petrarch and Derrida," in *Historical Criticism and the Challenge of Theory*, ed. Janet Levarie Smarr (Urbana: University of Illinois Press, 1993), pp. 192–204. I thank the author for making this text available to me before publication.

Sonnet 235 juxtaposes statements that themselves seem paradoxical, driven off course: first the speaker admits that he is carried off against his will by love, then celebrates his ability to protect his ship from the lady, and then admits that the weather has buffeted that vessel to the point where it lacks sails and tiller. Similarly, as we saw, Sonnet 151 opens by comparing the lover to a pilot fleeing a wave, a comparison subverted by the "Non" on which the lyric begins. (As that negative reminds us, Petrarch resembles Herrick, a fellow student and victim of desire, loss, and their connections, in that in the text of both poets, presence is repeatedly promised, then denied.) Thus the pilot who ostensibly controls his ship yet is often driven astray draws our attention to storm systems in the epistemological and psychological climate of this sequence. Like the speaker in the poem by Watson on which this book opened, its lover is tossed back and forth between success and failure, as both a poet and a lover, as well as between more specific manifestations of those states: agency and its absence, mastery and loss of control.

Our current professional preoccupations may at times tempt us to neglect one source of the Petrarchan poet's success and mastery: solving formal problems. I am not denying that the construction of and participation in an aesthetic realm are necessarily implicated in cultural agendas. But that recognition need not preclude tracing the workings of technical virtuosity. In the case at hand, when the Petrarchan pilot does manage to steer his nautological craft, he does so in no small part by displaying and practicing his aesthetic craft: the skill involved in mastering a sestina or playing on a small number of rhymes or weaving into one's own text lines written by one's predecessors is a source and symbol of achievement. If the rhetorical agenda of Petrarchism often is announcing one's failure as a lover or that of the alter ego one invokes, the aesthetic agenda frequently includes manifesting and celebrating one's success as a poet. Yet that agenda may be undermined in many ways in the course of the poem. English Petrarchism and its counterdiscourses recur repeatedly to these paradoxes.

Most obviously, writing poetry, pursuing the laurel, represents both success and failure. In the *Rime sparse*, as in the Coronation Ode, the achievements of the poet are often celebrated; but Petrarch never allows us to forget the Augustinian distrust of the imagination, and he repeatedly suggests that his own verse may misrepresent what it claims to describe and that his readers may in turn misunderstand what they claim to interpret or even refuse to believe what they read. While the inexpressibility conceit is a literary commonplace, all these other references to the limitations of the poet's power ensure that it is resonant on the many occasions when Petrarch himself invokes it. As Guiseppe Mazzotta, one of the most acute students of Petrarch, points out, achieving a vision of the beloved is, paradoxically, associated with losing one's voice.[16] Nor is regaining that voice an unmixed blessing, for speech in general and poetic speech in particular are fraught with danger as presented by Petrarch. In Poem 23, one of his most revealing texts, he is identified with Battus, whose transgression is speaking;[17] as Francesco learns in the *Secretum*, one of the chains that binds him is the love of glory, including the glory achieved by the poet. Poem 239 is a sestina that rings the changes on *versi* (verses) and *note* (notes) and in so doing reminds us how those manifestations of the poetic impulse can lend themselves to both positive and negative valuations. Given these contradictory judgments on poetry, it is no wonder that Petrarch so often invokes Orpheus, another multivalent poet, who in medieval and Renaissance commentaries variously represented everything from Christ to the eloquent lover to the dangers of base passions.[18]

The frustrated wandering to which Petrarch refers so often in his love lyrics, as well as his epistle about the ascent of Mount Ventoux, aptly figures the paradoxical presentation of agency in this sequence: wanderers have some control over their movements, but they experience difficulty when they attempt, as it were, to climb the mountain as they had hoped. Similarly, witness the paradoxical treatment of agency in the well known lines of Sonnet 5:

> vostro stato RE-al che 'ncontro poi
> raddoppia a l'alta impresa il mio valore;
> ma "TA-ci," grida il fin, "ché farle onore
> è d'altri omeri soma che da' tuoi."

> Così LAU-dare et RE-verire insegna
> la voce stessa,

(5.5–10; Your RE-gal state, which I meet next, redoubles my strength for the high enterprise; but "TA-lk no more!" cries the ending, "for to do her honor is a burden for other shoulders than yours." Thus the word itself teaches LAU-d and RE-verence.)

[16]Mazzotta, "The *Canzoniere* and the Language of the Self," p. 278.

[17]Compare Leonard Barkan, *The Gods Made Flesh: Metamorphosis and the Pursuit of Paganism* (New Haven: Yale University Press, 1986), p. 211.

[18]On the varied interpretations of Orpheus, see John Block Friedman, *Orpheus in the Middle Ages* (Cambridge: Harvard University Press, 1970).

While this text ostensibly celebrates the poet's skill in crafting anagrams with Laura's name, in much of the poem his agency is denied or deflected. As I have emphasized, English poets often approached Petrarch's lyrics through the filters of both commentators and Continental poets. The latter group was to reinterpret his slippages between agency and its absence and between triumph and its opposite in varied and often contradictory ways. Although Petrarch's *Rime sparse* embodies a struggle between assertions of success and admissions of failure, the balance tilts towards the latter; that is not invariably the case in the work of later Petrarchan poets. The emphasis on fame in the texts of many French sonneteers is one source of this difference; on occasion they celebrate their achievements in a tone foreign to Petrarch himself. Ronsard, for example, sometimes exhibits a confidence that borders on arrogance, a note seldom present in Petrarch. Witness, for example, the declaration in the poem that opens the first book of *Sonnets pour Hélène*: "Je suis de ma fortune auteur" (1.12; "I am author of my destiny").[19] Similarly, his "Elégie a son livre" defies not only women but also the poet's audience, which he often engaged in conflict. Yet, for all his defiance, even Ronsard admits to despair and powerlessness on occasion; in the poem immediately following that boast about his sovereignty over fortune, for example, he acknowledges that Hélène's cruelty induces such fear that he dare not speak, a confusion that anticipates the loss of agency in the work of many English poets.

This tempestuous tossing back and forth between representations of success and failure, agency and impotence, and control and helplessness is, then, at the core of Petrarch's poetry and that of many of his followers as well. And it should be at the core of our interpretations. Such upheavals have been acknowledged in some quarters, particularly by comparatists and Italianists: Thomas M. Greene has offered an especially incisive survey of the tensions within the Petrarchan speaker, noting as I do struggles between mastery and helplessness.[20] And a few important studies have described similar patterns within certain English sequences.[21] Yet critics from a range

[19]The citation is to Pierre de Ronsard, *Les Amours*, ed. Albert-Marie Schmidt and Françoise Joukovsky (Paris: Gallimard, 1974).

[20]In *The Light in Troy: Imitation and Discovery in Renaissance Poetry* (New Haven: Yale University Press, 1982), esp. chaps. 6 and 7, Thomas M. Greene acutely describes Petrarch's slippage between success and failure, though many of his conclusions differ from mine. I am indebted to his work throughout this chapter.

[21]See, e.g., Clark Hulse, "Stella's Wit: Penelope Rich as Reader of Sidney's Sonnets," in *Rewriting the Renaissance: The Discourses of Sexual Difference in Early Modern Europe*, ed. Margaret W. Ferguson, Maureen Quilligan, and Nancy J. Vickers (Chicago: University of Chicago Press, 1986); and Michael McCanles, "Love and Power in the Poetry of Sir Thomas Wyatt," *MLQ*, 29 (1968), 145–160.

of different methodologies continue to emphasize the potency of the Petrarchan poet, downplaying how his power is subverted, his vessel taken
over and driven off course by someone or something stronger than its pilot.
Thus, for example, while acutely acknowledging the threats to the sovereignty of the Petrarchan poet, Gordon Braden nonetheless argues that the
tradition focuses instead on his achievements.[22] Similarly, though feminism
has been varied in this and other regards, many studies of the sonnet do
emphasize the unassailable hegemony of patriarchy. The image—or mirage—of the omnipotent male poet satisfies many agendas of feminism, at
once demonstrating the force of patriarchy in early modern England and
exemplifying patterns of domination that indubitably occur in other cultures as well, not least our own.[23]

What case might be made, then, for interpretations like these that deny
or downplay any challenges to the poet's power? In analyzing Petrarch and
his followers, as in the more specific instance of Poem 118, some critics
are tempted to protect the conventional wisdom about the power of the
poet by discounting Petrarch's lurches between success and failure. One
might argue that he succeeds as a poet even if he fails as a lover, a net gain
because his main concern is not Laura but the laurel.[24] But the pun that
unites those two goals reminds us that they cannot in fact be divided so
easily; Petrarch's problems in achieving speech parallel his difficulties in
winning Laura. As Lynn Enterline has demonstrated, he, like Ovid, connects male subjectivity with linguistic problems.[25] Nor can one dismiss his
problems with language as a mere convention, a type of hyperbolic modesty topos: certainly an element of self-consciousness and role-playing informs the poetic speaker's allusions to difficulty in writing, like virtually
everything else he says, but Petrarch clearly realizes how soon the mask
adheres to the face. In this instance and many others, to dismiss convention
as "mere convention" is to misunderstand its workings. Moreover, calling
Petrarch's allusions to failure into question in these ways forces us to ask

[22]Gordon Braden, "Love and Fame," and "Beyond Frustration: Petrarchan Laurels in the
Seventeenth Century," SEL, 26 (1986), 5–23. Also cf. Lauro Martines, who, writing primarily about Italian Petrarchism, finds in that movement an alternative to the frustrated
powerlessness its poets experienced in a culture of religious corruption and political and
social upheaval (Power and Imagination: City-States in Renaissance Italy [New York: Knopf,
1979], chap. 15).

[23]See, e.g., Margaret Homans, " 'Syllables of Velvet': Dickinson, Rossetti, and the Rhetorics of Sexuality," Feminist Studies, 11 (1985), 569–593.

[24]Many critics have made this case; see, e.g., Braden, "Beyond Frustration."

[25]Lynn Enterline, "Embodied Voices: Petrarch Reading (Himself Reading) Ovid," in
Desire in the Renaissance: Literature and Psychoanalysis, ed. Valeria Finucci and Regina M.
Schwartz (Princeton: Princeton University Press, 1994).

to what extent his celebrations of his own poetic success may also be rhetorical ploys that are not completely persuasive. Alternatively, reverting to conceptions of the persona, one might attempt to distinguish the success of the historical personage Petrarch from the failure of the speaker within the sequence—but again the two figures are twins, fraternal though not Siamese or even identical. Above all, they are both subject to the same theological accusations: their indubitable poetic triumphs are always shadowed by the Augustinian condemnation of the imagination. Similar difficulties arise if one tries to dismiss the problems connected with agency: without in any way denying the poetic achievement and historical impact of the *Rime sparse*, it remains true that those successes are built on a bedrock of writing about failure, a paradox to which we will return several times.

The figure of the pilot who is, paradoxically, victor and victim, captain and captor, is, then, central to Petrarchism—and central as well to why it flourished in England and why it also invited repeated attacks. The seesaw between power and powerlessness which defines the Petrarchan voice was especially attractive to sixteenth-century English poets. Like Laura herself, it was a kind of living magnet that drew them to the perilous islands, shoals, and storms of Petrarchism.

Needless to say, a preoccupation with the elision between power and powerlessness reappears in many cultures: this and the other characteristics that I am identifying as distinctive of the English Renaissance are not unique to it. Yet seldom if ever has that preoccupation been more central than it was in sixteenth-century England. It takes very different forms there, of course, than it does in the *Rime sparse*; nonetheless, similar issues and tensions arise. It is no accident that *The Shepheardes Calendar*, the text that inspired so many later Elizabethan poets, balances precariously on that very seesaw between potency and impotence: Spenser celebrates his own debut as a poet and the potentialities of a national literature in a sequence of texts which begins with a broken pipe and ends on a discarded one. Nor is it an accident that *The Faerie Queene*, as influential in and characteristic of its period as Spenser's pastoral sequence, repeatedly qualifies even the most triumphant moments of its knights with intimations, or worse, of failure: the Red Crosse Knight cannot remain with his beloved, Scudamour does not stay around long enough to enjoy the consummate moment granted him at the end of the 1590 version, and the Blatant Beast survives, sharpening its teeth for the scholarly conferences and conventions that it eagerly foresaw.

The uneasy relationship between success and failure assumes several different but related forms in the texts, in the many senses of that noun, of sixteenth-century England, forms that correspond to the movements of

Petrarchism itself. At times a triumphant assertion of mastery is followed in rapid succession by its opposite, an acknowledgment of failure; at times success from one vantage point is failure from another; at times one cannot clearly distinguish the two. These patterns stem above all from the coexistence of conflicting status systems, competing values, contesting ideologies, and contrasting communities within the larger culture, a coexistence that by its very nature did not always yield a clearly dominant victor.[26]

These unresolved conflicts are manifest in the conditions of authorship in the period. Defenses of poesy, as Margaret W. Ferguson among many others has demonstrated, are indeed defensive in that culture and its Continental counterparts;[27] writing love lyrics was particularly suspect in some circles because of the taint of immorality. (Indeed, the fraught status of creative writers in certain of our own English departments, an issue that in itself deserves more attention, might alert us to the dangers of equating poetic achievement and power in the different but not wholly unrelated milieu of sixteenth-century England, as some analyses of Petrarchism do.)[28] Petrarch's anxieties on the subject had been reinterpreted and reduced in the two centuries that intervened between the *Rime sparse* and the flowering of the sonnet vogue in England—reinterpreted, reduced, but not erased. Witness, most obviously, Sidney's defensive posture when protecting his Second Maker from accusations of immorality and impiety; consider his admission that despite the virtues of art it may be abused to "infect the fancy with unworthy objects."[29] By referring to his treatise as an "ink-wasting toy" (p. 141) at a crucial moment, his peroration, he is indulging in a common rhetorical ploy, a modesty topos—but surely he is using that topos so that he can at once express his own doubts and distance himself from them by constructing them as a conventional strategy. And, of course, such doubts were intensified in the instance of the author of love lyrics, who is especially liable to the danger of infecting the fancy. Nor were the standards for evaluating secular poetry consistent. Pleasing one's cohorts at the Inns did not ensure a following at court; writing sonnets did not guarantee admission to the coterie that was circulating Donne's lyrics in manuscript.

[26]On the presence of multiple communities in the Renaissance, compare Jane Tylus, *Writing and Vulnerability in the Late Renaissance* (Stanford: Stanford University Press, 1993), esp. chap. 1. I thank the author for sharing her work with me before publication.

[27]Margaret W. Ferguson, *Trials of Desire: Renaissance Defenses of Poetry* (New Haven: Yale University Press, 1983).

[28]See, e.g., Braden, "Beyond Frustration."

[29]The citation is to Sir Philip Sidney, *An Apology for Poetry or The Defence of Poesy*, ed. Geoffrey Shepherd (London: Nelson, 1965), p. 125. Future citations from this edition will appear in my text.

Success and failure were also strange bedfellows in the patronage system in which writers and many others participated, though in this case they were likely to follow each other in rapid succession rather than to coexist. As we have seen, many readers posit a metaphoric link between patronage and the sonnet tradition: sonnets flourished when they did, as Arthur F. Marotti and others have maintained, because their discussions of service to a lady figured the patterns of service at court.[30] But patronage is most relevant to love poetry because it provides an experience of uncertainty analogous to the Petrarchan seesaw between success and failure. The lament for the "variable, and therefore miserable condition of man" on which Donne opens his *Devotions upon Emergent Occasions* could aptly gloss not merely the medical and spiritual transformations that he is primarily addressing but also the patronage system that he knew all too well.[31] A patron could prove unable to exercise the influence at court that he and his dependents had anticipated, as did Donne's own unreliable mentor Sir Robert Drury.[32] Or the royal personage whom the patron was influencing could die; Leonard Tennenhouse has documented the seismic shifts caused by the death of Prince Henry and the consequent unmooring of the many courtiers who had turned to him for patronage.[33]

Both the frequency with which sumptuary laws were promulgated and the frequency with which they were flouted remind us that in sixteenth-century England, social position and one of its principal components, financial status, were as frangible and variable as was literary success. Their volatility during this period is, of course, a commonplace; witness Spenser's metamorphosis from scholarship boy at his school to landowner in Ireland. But social ranking was further complicated by the coexistence of different systems for assessing it, a cultural pattern that literary critics sometimes overlook. The complex social position enjoyed by widows like Bess of Hardwick reminds us that gender, inherited wealth, recently acquired wealth, and birth all provided different and often conflicting markers of social status. Nor was that status necessarily consistent throughout the country; as I argue in Chapter 4, in assessing systems of ranking, one should not focus only on the court, thus making one little world an everywhere.

---

[30]Arthur F. Marotti, " 'Love is not love': Elizabethan Sonnet Sequences and the Social Order," *ELH*, 49 (1982), 396–428.

[31]I cite John Donne, *Devotions upon Emergent Occasions* (Ann Arbor: University of Michigan Press, 1959), p. 7.

[32]On Drury's fortunes, see R. C. Bald, *John Donne: A Life* (Oxford: Oxford University Press, 1970), esp. p. 238.

[33]Leonard Tennenhouse, "Sir Walter Ralegh and the Literature of Clientage," in *Patronage in the Renaissance*, ed. Guy Fitch Lytle and Stephen Orgel (Princeton: Princeton University Press, 1981).

Success and failure enjoyed an intimate relationship, then, not only because achievements were fragile but also because perceptions of them could differ so much, with what would be seen as success in one social circle or region coded as failure in another. For this and many other reasons, the Petrarchan pilot who slides back and forth between commanding his ship and being buffeted by unfavorable winds could be an emblem for the position of many writers—and many readers—in Tudor England.

IV

If its uneasy juxtapositions of mastery and impotence help to explain the attraction of Petrarchism in England, two of its central formal patterns, which are often connected to those juxtapositions, do so as well. Both the relationship between the narrative and lyric potentialites of Petrarchism and its predilection for repetition preoccupy, even obsess, its adherents, its detractors, and the many writers who cannot be fairly classified through either label. And both of these formal dynamics correspond to cultural dynamics, thus further explaining the position of Petrarchism in English culture.

The poems of both Petrarch and his followers compromise the connections between narrative and masculinity, as well as narrative and masculine power. The relationship between narrative and lyric in Petrarch's *Rime sparse* is significant in part, then, because this arena is one of many in which that slippage between mastery and impotence is staged. But his poems can also help to illuminate broader theoretical questions about those two modes. What happens when theories of narrativity, which have most frequently been developed through and applied to nineteenth- and twentieth-century novels, are played against medieval or Renaissance lyrics? What happens to conventional critical assumptions about the gendering of narrative when they are played against the storytelling propensities of that master and slave of gender, Petrarch?

Lyric has traditionally been seen as an unmediated expression of the subjective and of subjectivity itself. It is frequently associated, too, with the absence of a specific time and place, characteristics that help to explain its use of what George T. Wright describes as the "lyric present."[34] Many critics would agree that narrative, in contrast, is generally rooted in a specific time and place. Narrative theorists ranging from Peter Brooks to Te-

---

[34]George T. Wright, "The Lyric Present: Simple Present Verbs in English Poems," *PMLA*, 89 (1974), 563–579.

resa de Lauretis have connected narrativity with male desire;[35] for this and other reasons, it is often seen as gendered masculine, whereas lyric is feminine, even though male poets predominate among its writers.[36] Such distinctions have, however, been challenged in many quarters and from many perspectives. For example, several students of lyric remind us that the apparent lack of mediation may itself be a rhetorical ploy.[37] Sharon Cameron's important study of that mode, incisive despite the problems created by treating Dickinson as its normative case, suggests that the concern with death that so often characterizes lyric directs attention towards temporality.[38] Notwithstanding such disputes, the familiar descriptions of lyric as ahistorical and subjective remain influential. To carve a working definition from among these controversial interpretations of that mode, I will focus on two frequently accepted characteristics of lyric, atemporality and subjectivity, though I attempt as well to problematize those and other categorizations.

Not the least of the many ways Petrarch distinguishes himself from Dante is his approach to the relationship between narrative and lyric (indeed, as Roland Greene rightly notes, Petrarch's principal transformation of his models centers on a question connected to that relationship, temporality).[39] Whereas the *Vita Nuova* links its poems with narrative commentary, the *Rime sparse* establishes a more covert and conflicted relationship between the two modes. This much is clear, but critics part company on how to describe Petrarch's approach to narrative and lyric. For example, in one of the most powerful treatments of the subject, Teodolinda Barolini argues that Petrarch manipulates the narrative elements in the sequence to defuse and conquer time.[40] Aldo Scaglione emphasizes open notions of form and

---

[35]See Peter Brooks, *Reading for the Plot: Design and Intention in Narrative* (New York: Vintage Books, 1985), esp. chaps. 2, 4; and Teresa de Lauretis, *Alice Doesn't: Feminism, Semiotics, Cinema* (Bloomington: Indiana University Press, 1984), chaps. 1, 5.

[36]For a refutation of that conventional wisdom from a perspective different from my own, see Susan Stanford Friedman, "Lyric Subversion of Narrative in Women's Writing: Virginia Woolf and the Tyranny of Plot," in *Reading Narrative: Form, Ethics, Ideology*, ed. James Phelan (Columbus: Ohio State University Press, 1989).

[37]On revisionist readings of lyric, see Sharon Cameron, *Lyric Time: Dickinson and the Limits of Genre* (Baltimore: Johns Hopkins University Press, 1979); Jonathan Culler, "Changes in the Study of the Lyric," in *Lyric Poetry: Beyond New Criticism*, ed. Chaviva Hošek and Patricia Parker (Ithaca: Cornell University Press, 1985); and Patricia Parker, introduction to *Lyric Poetry*.

[38]Cameron, *Lyric Time*, esp. chap. 3.

[39]Roland Greene, *Post-Petrarchism*, p. 22.

[40]Teodolinda Barolini, "The Making of a Lyric Sequence: Time and Narrative in Petrarch's *Rerum vulgarium fragmenta*," *MLN*, 104 (1989), 1–38.

the presence of an order that is not based on logic.[41] In an influential essay, Thomas P. Roche Jr. identifies calendrical patterns in the sequence, adducing them to demonstrate that secular desires are played against spiritual verities;[42] such patterns, like the many other types of shape critics have (with widely varying degrees of persuasiveness) located in the sonnet tradition, complicate analyses of temporality and narrativity.

Poem 142 exemplifies the complex relationship between narrative and lyric in Petrarch's sequence:

> A la dolce ombra de le belle frondi
> corsi fuggendo un dispietato lume
> . . . .
> Però più fermo ogni or di tempo in tempo,
> seguendo ove chiamar m'udia dal cielo
> . . . .
> Tanto mi piacque prima il dolce lume
> ch' i' passai con diletto assai gran poggi
> per poter appressar gli amati rami;
> ora la vita breve e 'l loco e 'l tempo
> mostranmi altro sentier di gire al cielo
> et di far frutto, non pur fior et frondi.
>
> Altr'amor, altre frondi, et altro lume,
> altro salir al ciel per altri poggi
> cerco (che n'è ben tempo), et altri rami.

(142.1–2, 19–20, 31–39; To the sweet shade of those beautiful leaves I ran, fleeing a pitiless light. . . . Therefore, more and more firm from season to season, following where I heard myself called from Heaven. . . . So pleasing to me at first was that sweet light that joyfully I traversed great hills in order to approach the beloved branches. Now the shortness of life and the place and the season show me another pathway to go to Heaven and bear fruit, not merely flowers and leaves. Another love, other leaves, and another light, another climbing to Heaven by other hills I seek [for it is indeed time] and other branches.)

---

[41]Aldo Scaglione, "La struttura del *Canzoniere* e il metodo di composizione del Petrarca," *Lettere Italiane*, 27 (1975), 129–139.

[42]Thomas P. Roche Jr., "The Calendrical Structure of Petrarch's *Canzoniere*," *SP*, 71 (1974), 152–172.

In one sense the whole poem pivots on the concept of temporal change so central to lyric: then the speaker sought Laura, now he seeks heaven. This emphasis on diachronic shifts is underscored as well by descriptions of changes in the material world (now, lines twenty-five and twenty-six declare, woods, rocks, and so on are conquered by time) and by the repetition of *altre* (other) no fewer than three times in line thirty-seven. As these instances would suggest, narrativity both describes and enables the movement from earthly to heavenly love. It is precisely the ability to contrast *then* and *now* that permits him to contrast *here*, the world of secular love that at its best encourages him to seek the divine, and *there*, the world of heavenly love. And it is the ability to tell a story that synecdochically represents the possibility of spiritual change and growth.

And yet not so. Or at least, as is so often the case with Petrarch, and yet not quite so. The poem seems to contradict itself at several points, as when Petrarch follows the observation that the laurel is the tree most favored in heaven with the statement that it defended him against the heavens (12–13). The repeated rhymes of the sestina figure the underlying question that destabilizes the patterns I have been describing: Is change really possible? Perhaps, as the identity of "l'aura" and "Laura" would suggest, the speaker cannot truly distinguish the light that comes from heaven and that which comes from Laura. Perhaps, as his sometimes contradictory commentary would suggest, the poem attempts to establish and inhabit a world of linearity and narrativity but instead is pulled back into the lyric stasis suggested by its repetitive rhymes. In a sense the slippage into lyric here culminates in other texts whose repeated reliance on apostrophe is the syntactical analogue to the breakdown of narrative: "O passi sparsi, o pensier vaghi et pronti, / o tenace memoria, o fero ardore" (161.1–2; "O scattered steps, O yearning, ready thoughts, O tenacious memory, O savage ardor").

Similarly, many poems in Petrarch's sequence could be classified as a vision or that sibling of the vision, the dream, and both of those modes inherently challenge distinctions between narrative and lyric.[43] Thus the vision often involves narrating a story ("One day as I walked by the river I saw") and an insistently teleological story culminating in some apocalyptic change at that ("and at the end he arose from the dead" or "and it was just a dream"). But visions, like lyric, are by definition also intensely subjective, and they are often though not inevitably located in an indetermi-

---

[43]One of the best studies of narrative and lyric, Jay Clayton's *Romantic Vision and the Novel* (Cambridge: Cambridge University Press, 1987), emphasizes the complex overlappings of the modes but primarily links the visionary to lyric.

nate landscape rather than a specific time and place. Moreover, visions often involve repetition, which itself frequently blurs the line between narrative and lyric.

Petrarch's anniversary poems demonstrate how the visionary mode encourages complex combinations of narrative and lyric. In one sense these lyrics are typically narrative, involving as they do not one but two stories: the original tale of seeing Laura and the tale of recalling that moment. In addition, they firmly foreground time and place by emphasizing the number of years since the first sight of Laura and referring specifically to the locales in which she has been sighted. If, as Tzvetan Todorov has claimed, narrative is based on the tension between difference and resemblance,[44] these poems certainly focus on that tension by reminding us that the passage of time, the graying of the narrator's hair, separates this vision from the original one—and yet that original one is relived in the course of the poem. Petrarch's anniversary poems are, however, also intensely lyric in their emphasis on the static and subjective experience they evoke.

Bearing in mind, then, the complexity of labeling the modes of the *Canzoniere,* how does that sequence engage with the gendering of narrative and lyric, one of the Petrarchan legacies that was to prove of especial significance to English poets, and with related issues of empowerment? Here narrative is male, both in the obvious sense that Petrarch himself shapes stories about his experience and in so doing shapes that experience and in the less obvious but no less significant sense that he tells stories about the future as well. If he is the victim Actaeon, he is also Apollo, god of prophecy. Indeed, the Coronation Ode emphasizes the poet's role as seer.[45] Such narratives about the future were to figure prominently in the work of many of his successors, notably Shakespeare. Narrative, too, is associated very specifically with what is potentially the principal triumph of the sequence: the movement towards God. For that movement depends on distinguishing a past of loving only Laura, a present of moving towards God, and a future of achieving spiritual peace. Witness the emphasis on temporality in Sonnet 1. And yet, as that poem and many others remind us, the movement towards God—and the narrativity that expresses it—are at the very least destabilized by the pull back towards Laura.

Indeed, Petrarchan narrative is often connected not with the empow-

[44]Tzvetan Todorov, *The Poetics of Prose,* trans. Richard Howard (Ithaca: Cornell University Press, 1977), p. 233.

[45]Compare Aldo S. Bernardo, "Petrarch and the Art of Literature," in *Petrarch to Pirandello: Studies in Italian Literature in Honour of Beatrice Corrigan,* ed. Julius A. Molinaro (Toronto: University of Toronto Press, 1973), 27-30.

erment of the male speaker and of the masculine in general but with their loss of power. Though in one respect Petrarch shapes narratives, in another respect narrative is associated with what happens to him against his will: the discontinuous storytelling in Canzone 23, among others, figures the sense in which his metamorphoses, like the changes that constitute narrative, are outside his control. With due respect to Barolini, although Petrarch the poet obviously crafts skilled narratives, the poetic speaker with whom he is so intimately associated is more often a victim of narrativity than its manipulator.[46] One of the many senses in which Laura is linked to the lyric world of stasis and Petrarch to the narrative world of linear change is that, despite her death, she is frequently described as evergreen while, as he repeatedly reminds us, he ages and grows gray. Sometimes the ultimate loss of power and control, the disappearance of the vision of Laura, is presented as a fall from lyric contemplation to narrative movement. Witness the sonnet in which that loss involves a literal fall: "quand' io caddi ne l'acqua et ella sparve" (190.14; "when I fell into the water, and she disappeared").

If narrative is sometimes gendered male, then, it is not necessarily or invariably associated with male power. The customary association between storytelling and the quest of male desire is compromised as well. Inasmuch as that desire takes the form of a movement towards God, it is certainly expressed through narrative; indeed, in the *Rime sparse* the movement from lyric to narrative is often a shift from entrapment in earthly love to a progress, however impeded, however distrusted, towards the spiritual. But loving Laura is a very different matter, one expressed not as a narrative quest but as the inability to pursue that or any other quest. Loving Laura is the state that, as we observed, is memorably encapsulated at the end of Poem 118: "né per mille rivolte ancor son mosso" ("nor for a thousand turnings about have I yet moved"). Loving Laura is a sestina of apparent shifts that are really just repetitions.

This compromising of the connection between narrative and male sexual desire is not, however, sui generis. Conventional definitions of narrative suffer from the literary equivalent of that bête noire of contemporary criticism, essentialism: they do not allow sufficiently for the variations engendered by different cultures and different historical periods. In the Middle Ages, I would suggest, writers besides Petrarch were more likely to associate desire with lyric than with narrative. As analyzed by Aristotle and Aquinas, concupiscence, in contrast to irascibility, may be seen as passive and fem-

---

[46]Barolini, "The Making of a Lyric Sequence."

inine; it is no accident that it is often connected with Venus.[47] Moreover, affective piety, the highly influential religious movement that emphasizes emotional rather than speculative approaches to religion, frequently stresses a passive receptivity rather than an active search for God.[48] To be sure, the commonplace metaphor of spirituality as a journey survives in these writers, but often they describe the quest for union with God in more passive terms. Thus Bernard of Clairvaux stresses both the difficulty and the importance of surrendering one's will to God; in his commentary on the Song of Songs, the Bride, having strewn the chamber of her heart with flowers, waits there for God, and elsewhere he describes her as being led into the chamber.[49] Similarly, St. Bonaventure stresses that we must be "led in the path of God."[50] As Caroline Walker Bynum points out, such passages demonstrate that medieval writers often see spiritual experience as an acceptance of a position otherwise gendered female.[51] Paradoxically, much as Pandarus's condemnations of Troilus's effeminate behavior establish and buttress a conventionally masculine norm in Chaucer's text,[52] so this medieval construction of desire as passive and effeminizing might perhaps be seen as preserving and even strengthening an alternative model of male desire. By loving in a feminine way, this argument would run, Troilus draws attention to the masculine alternative, the connection of narrative and male action. But, as many studies of androgyny have indicated, when men are repeatedly portrayed in relation to a state normally gendered female or vice versa, binary gender categories may be challenged as well as, or rather than, asserted.[53] In short, many medieval texts serve to confound, not confirm or contradict, the connections between narrative and male desire.

Hence Petrarch's approach to narrative and lyric invites us to pose

[47]On Christian theories of love and desire, see esp. Anders Nygren, *Agape and Eros*, trans. Philip S. Watson, rev. ed. (Philadelphia: Westminster, 1953).

[48]For a useful summary of affective devotion, see Douglas Gray, *Themes and Images in the Medieval English Religious Lyric* (London: Routledge and Kegan Paul, 1972), chap. 1.

[49]Bernard of Clairvaux, *Selected Works*, trans. G. R. Evans (New York: Paulist, 1987), esp. pp. 179–181.

[50]Bonaventure, *The Soul's Journey into God, The Tree of Life, The Life of St. Francis*, trans. and ed. Ewert Cousins (New York: Paulist, 1978), p. 60.

[51]Caroline Walker Bynum, " ' . . . And Woman His Humanity': Female Imagery in the Religious Writing of the Later Middle Ages," in *Gender and Religion: On the Complexity of Symbols*, ed. Caroline Walker Bynum, Stevan Harrell, and Paula Richman (Boston: Beacon, 1986), esp. p. 258.

[52]I am grateful to Donald W. Rowe for suggesting the Chaucerian parallel to me.

[53]Androgyny has been widely discussed by feminists and other students of gender during the 1980s and 1990s. For a particularly influential treatment, see Phyllis Rackin, "Androgyny, Mimesis, and the Marriage of the Boy Heroine on the English Renaissance Stage," *PMLA*, 102 (1987), 29–41.

broader revisionist questions about those modes and their role in English Petrarchism and anti-Petrarchism. To what extent can critics accept the conventional wisdom on masculine empowerment via narrative? Is the relationship between the two modes often, as in the instance of Petrarch himself, an unresolved struggle? And does that conflict between narrative and lyric stage a struggle to define male subjectivity and assert male power, a process that is complicated both because gender categories erode and overlap and because narrative does not in fact necessarily establish the power of its narrator? In refining and redefining the connections between narrative and lyric which they encountered in Petrarch and his continental imitators, English poets map subjectivity and its discontents.

V

Repetition, we have just observed, may erode the line between narrative and lyric in much the same way and for many of the same reasons that the refrain erodes the line between the closural and the anticlosural; one of the most deconstructive of tropes, it both announces and erases temporality.[54] But repetition is also central in many other ways in Petrarch's sequence, and its role has hardly gone unnoticed. Thomas M. Greene, for example, writes about Petrarch's "iterative present"[55] Guiseppe Mazzotta trenchantly observes that the *Rime sparse* appears to represent "a coherent unity and totality, but the unity always appears to be made of contiguous, adjacent parts that steadily repeat themselves, even while they aspire to mark new imaginative departures."[56]

As these commentaries would suggest, repetition assumes many forms within the *Rime sparse*. Most obviously, it is apparent in the stanzaic patterns of the Petrarchan sonnet, like those of its Shakespearean counterpart. The poet may return to and re-create an action or an incident or an image, as he does in the anniversary poems. Or he may repeat an action continuously, as he does in many of the poems that describe his wandering movements. Frequently that form of repetition generates the paradox of movement without change—"l'aura mi volve et son pur quel ch' i' m'era" (112.4; "the breeze turns me about, and I am still just what I was"). And while I have argued that repetition often threatens narrative, some of the passages

---

[54]For a related but different argument, see Clayton, *Romantic Vision*, esp. pp. 108–115; he argues that repetition is central to both narrative and lyric.

[55]Thomas M. Greene, *The Light in Troy*, esp. pp. 118–120.

[56]Guiseppe Mazzotta, "Petrarch's Song 126," in *Textual Analysis: Some Readers Reading*, ed. Mary Ann Caws (New York: Modern Language Association, 1986), p. 129.

in question could be explained by Brooks's emphasis on the centrality of repetition to narrative.[57]

But perhaps the most revealing instance is a section of Canzone 23, the altered rendition of the Actaeon myth. Although Nancy J. Vickers's influential study of the passage adduces it subtly to analyze Petrarch's fear of dismemberment, especially castration, that argument neglects the fact that dismemberment is precisely what does not occur in these lines.[58] To be sure, when Actaeon is evoked elsewhere in the sequence, he is, like his stepbrother Orpheus, torn apart. But the passage at hand, the locus classicus for Petrarch's rendition of the myth, in fact culminates not in decisive destruction but in the repetition of an action:

> ch' i' senti' trarmi de la propria imago
> et in un cervo solitario et vago
> di selva in selva ratto mi trasformo,
> et ancor de' miei can fuggo lo stormo.

(23.157–160; for I felt myself drawn from my own image and into a solitary wandering stag from wood to wood quickly I am transformed and still I flee the belling of my hounds.)

The poet's experience repeats that of Actaeon and of the lady; and that experience is presented as one form of repetition, the inability to escape from a continuing action.

Such passages help us to understand why repetition is so important within the *Rime sparse* and why it proved so significant a legacy to Petrarch's followers and detractors. Recurrence is associated with sin in several ways. Petrarch repeats the Fall of Adam, as Sara Sturm-Maddox has shown us,[59] and what is more, he repeats his repetition of it in each anniversary poem. Similarly, when Petrarch's alter ego Orpheus looks back, he represents man's tendency to return to sin, according to some medieval and Renaissance commentators.[60] But Petrarchan repetition is also the trope that writes and is written by erotic desire. For repetition represents the way that impulse is never finally satisfied and hence never finally controlled—

[57]Brooks, *Reading for the Plot*, esp. chap. 4.

[58]Nancy J. Vickers, "Diana Described: Scattered Woman and Scattered Rhyme," *Critical Inquiry*, 8 (1981), 265–279.

[59]Sara Sturm-Maddox, "Petrarch's Serpent in the Grass: The Fall as Subtext in the *Rime sparse*," *Journal of Medieval and Renaissance Studies*, 13 (1983), 213–226.

[60]See, e.g., the commentary on Boethius's version of the myth in John Block Friedman, *Orpheus in the Middle Ages*, pp. 89–96.

"Had, having, and in quest to have, extreme" (Shakespeare, Sonnet 129, 10).[61] Its obsessive, uncontrolled reversions exemplify the loss of agency that we have traced from other perspectives. And its erosion of the boundaries between narrative and lyric, between past and present, recalls yet again the erosion of gender distinctions which characterizes Petrarchism.

Petrarchan repetition also often represents a drive that is exemplified by but not confined to desire: the urge towards reenactment in the psychoanalytic sense, that is, repeating an action to assert mastery. In Freudian terms, reenactment is the attempt to turn failure and powerlessness into success and power[62]—in other words, it is the attempt to arrest the seesaw between failure and success which is at the heart of Petrarchism, which helps to explain why repetition is itself at the heart of the sequence. Lacan, however, glosses this form of reenactment more accurately than Freud, for Petrarch's is a reenactment that, like so much in the sequence, is doomed to failure. Thus although repetition that attempts to assert mastery, to win the game of *fort-da* once and for all, seems the opposite of repetition that relives the Fall and returns to sin, in reality the two are closely allied, for Petrarch's version of reenactment merely repeats the problems it attempts to resolve. Indeed, throughout the sequence, repetition is associated with entrapment. Therefore, as we have already seen, the repetitions of lyric may represent Petrarch's inability to escape from Laura—or rather from the images of her, images that Augustine would consider the dangerous detritus of the imagination.

An attraction to repetitive literary structures and the formal and other cultural agendas they embody is not, of course, unique to early modern England; indeed, many literary theorists have even seen repetition as a central structuring force in virtually all literature.[63] The English Renaissance, however, manifests a particularly intense attraction to this mode. Three of its most popular literary types—the sonnet, romance, and pastoral—involve multiple forms of it. *The Faerie Queene* may at first seem an

---

[61]Stephen Booth, ed., *Shakespeare's Sonnets* (New Haven: Yale University Press, 1977).

[62]On reenactment and *fort-da*, see esp. chap. 2 of Sigmund Freud, *Beyond the Pleasure Principle, The Standard Edition of the Complete Psychological Works of Sigmund Freud*, trans. James Strachey et al., vol. 18 (London: Hogarth Press and Institute of Psycho-analysis, 1955). For Lacan's more pessimistic reinterpretation, see esp. "The Function and Field of Speech and Language in Psychoanalysis," in *Ecrits: A Selection*, trans. Alan Sheridan (New York: Norton, 1977), pp. 102–104. After completing this book, I found that Gary Waller also notes connections between Petrarchism and fort-da, though he applies the analogy differently from the way I do (*The Sidney Family Romance: Mary Wroth, William Herbert, and the Early Modern Construction of Gender* [Detroit: Wayne State University Press, 1993], p. 149); I regret that his volume appeared after my own book was virtually finished.

[63]See, e.g., Todorov, *The Poetics of Prose*, esp. pp. 116–117.

exception to this fascination: epic, after all, distinguishes itself from romance through its linear thrust and intense closural drive. But this is an exception that proves the rule, for Spenser's poem characteristically eschews closure in favor of repetition. His Blatant Beast, the poem implies, will be repeatedly chased and will repeatedly escape.

One of the deepest fantasies in Tudor and Stuart England, I suggest, is uncontrolled repetition emanating from a single case, a single error—a metaphoric rendition of contagion. Revenge plays are so popular in both Tudor and Stuart England in part because they anatomize precisely this pattern. Compare too *Arden of Faversham*, which presents the repetitiveness associated with an attempted murder, or Spenser's reduplicated evil triplets, Sansloy, Sansjoy, and Sansfoy. Indeed, it is no accident that two of the telling passages in the literature of that culture—Spenser's description of Error's brood and Milton's case study of Sin's obstetrical records—involve a similar version of the fear that a single transgression will repeat and multiply, in these instances multiply in the most literal sense.[64] As these texts remind us, the fear that one error will breed another recalls original sin,[65] and it is telling that Thomas M. Greene's reading of repetition in the *Rime sparse* alludes to a "fall into iteration."[66]

Texts of the English Renaissance respond to these anxieties about uncontrollable and unstoppable reduplication in three principal ways. First, the culture devises myths for and about itself which incorporate potentially threatening repetition into overarching patterns of linearity and teleology. Witness above all the notion of Trojan descent, which includes but subsumes repetition. Witness too the central model for a poetic mission, the Virgilian wheel, which acknowledges repetition in the emphasis on replicating Virgil's career and in the image of circularity itself, yet plots that repetition in terms of a progressive, linear growth from pastoral to georgic to epic. Second, many apparently disparate practices in both Tudor and Stuart England may in fact be seen as attempts to redefine repetition as control and order. The refrain uses repetition to suggest a reassuring aesthetic order; typology, like liturgy, uses repetition to suggest a reassuring spiritual order. As those instances indicate, one way of redefining recur-

---

[64] I am indebted to Linda Gregerson for fruitful discussions of these episodes.

[65] Compare Thomas P. Roche Jr.'s observation that in Barnes's poetry, like that of Spenser, verbal repetition is connected with sin (*Petrarch and the English Sonnet Sequences* [New York: AMS Press, 1989], p. 173). For a different but not incompatible argument about religion and repetition, see Kristen Poole, "Saints Alive! Falstaff, Martin Marprelate, and the Staging of Puritanism," *SQ*, 46 (1995), 47–75. She demonstrates that Puritans were seen in terms of grotesque proliferation.

[66] Thomas M. Greene, *The Light in Troy*, p. 126.

rence is to recast it as repetition-with-a-difference[67]—which is, of course, the dynamic behind the psychoanalytic process of reenactment—as writers in the African-American tradition were to assert when they developed their practices of signifying.[68]

Finally, Petrarchism itself serves to negotiate cultural attitudes towards repetition. Both Petrarchism and its counterdiscourses attract writers and readers in Renaissance England in no small measure because they are, above virtually all other traditions, the discourses of repetition. The subjectivity of the Petrarchan lover in England, like that of his Continental counterparts, is mapped by means of several coordinates of repetition: he repeats a conventional literary language that is itself loaded with tropes of repetition, he perpetually reenacts previous attempts to win the lady's favor in the hope that this time the game of fort-da can cease, and he sometimes constructs his relationship to his counterparts in the tradition as a version of repetition-with-a-difference. The counterdiscourses of Petrarchism, as we will observe throughout this study, attempt both to escape and to exemplify Petrarchan repetition; often they provide a release from Petrarchan problematics which is at best partial, on the one hand asserting types of agency denied the Petrarchan poet while on the other rehearsing some patterns from that discourse.

VI

Petrarch's own poetry, then, helps us to understand how and why repetition attracted his followers. Petrarch himself does not, however, provide a clear blueprint for later writers' approach to the Petrarchan mistress and many of the questions about both male and female gender categories that she poses: constructions of both gender and the Petrarchan lady vary significantly from culture to culture, sequence to sequence, and even of course from poem to poem within a given cycle. But reading the *Rime sparse* does serve to indicate some of the problems in these areas which were to shape English Petrarchism and its counterdiscourses.

Even more to the point, reading Petrarch's text warns us against underestimating the significance of gender in explaining the popularity of those

[67]Sandra L. Bermann also alludes to repetition-with-a-difference in her analyses of Petrarchism, but she focuses on asymmetical repetitions and the tensions they create (*The Sonnet over Time: A Study in the Sonnets of Petrarch, Shakespeare, and Baudelaire* [Chapel Hill: University of North Carolina Press, 1988], pp. 2–5).

[68]On this influential concept, see Henry Louis Gates Jr., *The Signifying Monkey: A Theory of African-American Literary Criticism* (New York: Oxford University Press, 1988).

traditions. Sparked by Marotti's influential observation that "love is not love" and by related articles by Ann Rosalind Jones and Peter Stallybrass among others,[69] many critics have found the ostensible subject of these poems a guise for their true concerns, arguing in effect that the erasure of the female is reduplicated in that not only is the mistress silenced within the poems but their putative romantic plot is essentially silenced as well by their actual agenda. This corrective, though initially valuable, has been taken too far. Although these poems address a range of cultural issues, including ambition, Laura is far more than a decoy and gender far more than the vehicle of a political metaphor. Indeed, Laura's role involves confusions of gender and reinterpretations of speech and silence which are central to the popularity of Petrarchism and its counterdiscourses in Elizabethan—and Elizabeth's—England.

Once again Petrarch's poetry resists generalizations, for Laura is portrayed in varied and contradictory ways. Gentle and stonelike, loving and cruel, she both generates and exemplifies the oxymoron. Yet despite, or sometimes because of, these contradictions, some general patterns emerge. In particular, the poetry seesaws between the denials of her subjectivity which one might anticipate and assertions that she possesses not only subjectivity but considerable agency too.

To begin with, Laura is repeatedly aestheticized. Her tears are described as "belle" (158.13; "lovely") and her braids compared not just to gold but also to polished gold (196.8). In such passages, Petrarch certainly objectifies her much as Gilbert Osmond tries to objectify the wife he adds to his collections; but, as we will see, aestheticization serves different functions elsewhere in the sequence.

Petrarch, that Pygmalion who celebrates her, variously erases and redesigns her body as well, describing her gold braids and eyes with particular intensity. But he, unlike many of his French followers, refers only rarely to other, more erotic body parts; though critics talk about Petrarch's blazons, what he in fact generally provides are truncated blazons that dwell on just a few areas of her body. As Peter Hainsworth reminds us, on one of the unusual occasions when he does refer to her breast, he chooses a Latinate term.[70] And even the bodily parts to which Petrarch does allude are as disembodied as the smile of the Cheshire cat, for descriptions of Laura repeatedly slide away from materiality. This is to some extent true of other descriptions in the sequence as well—Hainsworth notes the telling

---

[69]Ann Rosalind Jones and Peter Stallybrass, "The Politics of *Astrophil and Stella*," *SEL*, 24 (1984), 53–68.
[70]Peter Hainsworth, *Petrarch the Poet*, p. 121.

lack of shapes and of precise shades of color throughout the *Rime sparse*[71] —but it is especially marked in the case of Laura herself. Her very body is evoked through absence and emptiness, through a footprint rather than a foot.

What prevents us, then, from simply endorsing the many readings that emphasize the erasure of Laura herself and the construction of the female as lack in more than one sense of that word? In many of the texts of Petrarch, she is erased to the extent and in the ways the male poet is himself: the construction of gendered categories is rooted in their deconstruction. For, as we have already observed, Petrarch and Laura, like Watson and his Echo, are repeatedly elided in a text that blurs boundaries in so many other ways as well. The fusion of subject and object, Joel Fineman reminds us throughout *Shakespeare's Perjured Eye*, is common in love poetry;[72] but in few sequences is it effected as frequently as in this one. Most obviously, of course, Petrarch's emblem, the laurel, is hers as well. If the text alludes to her veil, he at times sports one too (see, for example, Poem 119, in which a reference to her veil is succeeded fifteen lines later by a reference to his). If she is a stone, so too is he, and if she sings, he does so as well. This confounding of subject and object, male and female, complicates gender categories in ways that English poets were to pursue.

It is above all in the treatment of Laura's voice that the complex process through which she is variously denied and granted subjectivity and agency is effected. Two revealing passages demonstrate, however, the problems of analyzing her speech. In one, words are dismissingly labeled "queste dolci tue fallaci ciance" (359.41; "these sweet deceptive chatterings of yours"); in the other, the failure to obey the injunction " 'Di ciò non far parola' " (23.74; " 'Make no word of this' ") leads to punishment. Textbook examples, then, of the cultural imperative to silence woman metaphorically by devaluing her speech or to silence her literally by forbidding it—except that these instances refer to Petrarch's speech. Male speech is as multivalent in this sequence as the biographies of two of its prime representatives, Battus and Orpheus, would suggest. My main point, however, is not that the ambiguity of gender categories which marks this sequence creates an elision between male and female speech together with so many other elisions; that happens occasionally, but by and large the two forms of language are more clearly distinguished in the sequence than are other characteristics

[71]Hainsworth, *Petrarch the Poet*, p. 194.
[72]Joel Fineman, *Shakespeare's Perjured Eye: The Invention of Poetic Subjectivity in the Sonnets* (Berkeley: University of California Press, 1986). Many other critics have commented on that fusion in Petrarchism and elsewhere; see, e.g., Braden, "Beyond Frustration," p. 9.

of Petrarch and Laura. More to our purposes now, because Petrarch constructs his own speech in very much the terms his readers might anticipate for Laura's, it is not surprising to find that the sequence as a whole challenges many assumptions about the relationship among speech, power, and gender.

Another medieval text (if indeed Petrarch should be classified among medieval writers) may also prepare us for those challenges by complicating the resonances of silence. In the Corpus Christi play the raucous noise of Christ's tormentors contrasts with his silence, which seems, like the final silence of Shakespeare's Iago and Melville's Babo, to represent a form of power.[73] Indeed, far older precedents testify to the value of silence: Egyptian discussions of rhetoric stress its efficacy.[74] And if Christ's refusal of speech can be decoded positively, under many circumstances the possession of language was coded negatively as well. To Petrarch and his contemporaries, language in its current form was a sign of the Fall as well as a tribute to the reason that separates man from beast, and, as several commentators have pointed out, Saussure could have taught them little they did not already know about the separation between signifier and signified.[75] Analogues like these warn us again against merely reading speech positively and silence negatively or associating the first with agency and the second with its absence.

Allusions to Laura's speech are as frequent as they are paradoxical. Dante had celebrated the "salute" or greeting of Beatrice, comparing her speech to that of God. But Laura's speech is even more central to the sequence. First, as I already suggested, it is one of the characteristics in the litany by which she is praised: in the Rime sparse and in the Secretum as well, Petrarch evokes Laura by referring to her eyes, her voice, and her movements, a list ritualized enough to recall descriptions of a locus amoenus. Moreover,

---

[73]Compare V. A. Kolve, The Play Called Corpus Christi (Stanford: Stanford University Press, 1966), pp. 182–186. The power of silence is also discussed in Mimi Still Dixon's unpublished paper, "Seeing and Saying in The Winter's Tale," which relates Hermione's silence to her martyrdom, and in Christina Luckyj, " 'A Moving Rhetorike': Women's Silence and Renaissance Texts," Renaissance Drama, 24 (1993), 33–56. I thank these authors for making their work available to me.

[74]Michael V. Fox, "Ancient Egyptian Rhetoric," Rhetorica, 1 (1983), 12–14.

[75]Medieval attitudes towards language have, of course, been widely discussed. For instances of several different approaches, see, e.g., R. Howard Bloch, Etymologies and Genealogies: A Literary Anthropology of the French Middle Ages (Chicago: University of Chicago Press, 1983); G. L. Bursill-Hall, Speculative Grammars of the Middle Ages: The Doctrine of "Partes Orationis" of the Modistae (The Hague: Mouton, 1971); Marcia L. Colish, The Mirror of Language: A Study in the Medieval Theory of Knowledge, rev. ed. (Lincoln: University of Nebraska Press, 1983); and R. H. Robins, Ancient and Medieval Grammatical Theory in Europe with Particular Reference to Modern Linguistic Doctrine (London: Bell and Sons, 1951).

he repeatedly emphasizes how deeply her words have affected him. Yet Laura is granted direct discourse relatively infrequently, and almost all the instances occur in the "in morte" sonnets.

Several of the paradoxes associated with Laura's speech and with speech in general in the *Rime sparse* are resolved if one distinguishes patterns in the "in vita" sonnets from those in their "in morte" counterparts. Although the precise point of delineation between those two groups is the product of scholarly convention more than authorial intention, the fact remains that the second group of poems does differ from the first in a range of ways; for example, as Oscar Büdel demonstrates, Laura is, paradoxically, further removed from Petrarch when she is presented as alive than she is after her death.[76]

The nexus of gender, silence, and impotence is variable and unstable in the "in vita" lyrics. In some sonnets Laura is surely silenced in every sense of that complex term. In others, as we have seen, lacking her own voice, she merely repeats the words Love has taught her. So too, however, does Petrarch on other occasions, and Dante before him as well, for in the twenty-fourth chapter of the *Vita Nuova*, its author describes himself as learning what Love dictated to him. Indeed, might not the fear that male speech is itself ventriloquized, whether by a patron, a previous author, or a force like Cupid, attract certain Tudor and Stuart writers to the myth of Echo on which this book opened? That story, like so many other narratives in the mythologies of gender, deflects behavior men fear within themselves onto a woman.

Moreover, in other instances Petrarch's "in vita" poems more overtly challenge the linkage of literal silence (or its analogue, dictated speech), powerlessness, and gender. For Laura does speak frequently, and although her speech is not equivalent to male speech, neither is it denigrated as clearly inferior. The repeated association between her words, her eyes, and her movements gestures towards some of the characteristics of her speech in the "in vita" sonnets. It is connected not with the intellectual or rational but with the emotive. And it is constructed as a precious aesthetic object. In Poem 200, for example, her mouth is described as "di perle / piena et di rose, et di dolci parole" (200.10–11; "full of pearls and roses and sweet words"). While the pearls and roses gracefully signal anatomical features, they also serve to categorize the words less as intellectual counters than as beautiful natural objects. They are yet another ornament for a body con-

---

[76]Oscar Büdel, "Illusion Disabused: A Novel Mode in Petrarch's *Canzoniere*," in *Francis Petrarch, Six Centuries Later: A Symposium*, ed. Aldo Scaglione, North Carolina Studies in the Romance Languages and Literatures: Symposia, 3 (Chapel Hill and Chicago: University of North Carolina Press and Newberry Library, 1975), p. 135.

structed in terms of adornments of all sorts. (Petrarch's heir Bembo was to describe a woman's speech, like the teeth through which it issues, in terms of pearls, and Petrarchan poems as well as their counterdiscourses recur to the figure too.) But whereas the aestheticization we examined earlier served to objectify and hence diminish the woman, here its valuation is more complicated. One cannot simply maintain that the aestheticization is a ploy for silencing Laura under the guise of praising her, for her speech is repeatedly described in terms of its overwhelming effect on its primary listener. Similarly, the inhabitants of sixteenth- and seventeenth-century England, schooled as they were in the precepts of classical rhetoric, were far less likely than contemporary critics to associate the aestheticization of speech merely with objectification and diminution. Laura's pearls, like those of some of her English counterparts, are as powerful as bullets, invisible or otherwise.

Or, to put it another way, in certain respects Laura's speech in the "in vita" sonnets is located in the semiotic, not the symbolic, though it also gestures towards the complexities of those categories and the problems of applying them to premodern texts. Repeatedly associated with the breeze, it is a natural force. Frequently linked to her songs and sighs, in a sense it is described in terms of prelinguistic impulses. (Indeed, while Sturm-Maddox, one of the relatively few critics who discusses Laura's speech in any detail, draws attention to distinctions between Laura's speech and her songs, the text itself tends to merge, not distinguish, the two modes of communication.)[77] But Julia Kristeva's warnings against neat separations and facile genderings of the symbolic and semiotic and against assuming the privileging of the one over the other are nowhere more germane than here.[78] Male speech, even when it has the qualities usually attributed the symbolic, is by no means always a marker or source of power in this sequence. Nor is it always associated with positive qualities. Conversely, in the "in vita" sonnets Laura's semiotic speech has both the power and the agency that many paradigms, feminist and otherwise, would associate only with the symbolic.

These patterns are further confounded by the "in morte" sonnets. Laura's speech changes in several ways. Whereas it is sometimes, as before, described in aesthetic terms and constructed as gestural, by and large it is now represented through direct discourse, with its ethical content emphasized.

[77]Sara Sturm-Maddox, "Petrarch's Siren: 'Dolce Parler' and 'Dolce Canto' in the *Rime sparse*," *Italian Quarterly*, 103 (1986), 5–19; see also the later version of this argument in Sturm-Maddox, *Petrarch's Laurels*, pp. 46–62.

[78]Julia Kristeva, *Revolution in Poetic Language*, trans. Margaret Waller (New York: Columbia University Press, 1984), pp. 23–24.

Like Beatrice, whom she increasingly resembles as the sequence progresses, in this group of poems Laura takes responsibility for the spiritual salvation of her lover. Here she instructs, warns, threatens. In particular, she repeatedly admonishes Petrarch about the dangers of Petrarchism itself; hence, like Watson's Echo and many other women in the sonnet tradition, she herself represents a type of counterdiscourse.[79] In so doing, Laura, again like Beatrice, may recall the Greek and Hebraic traditions of the figure of Wisdom, who was often, though not invariably, gendered female.[80] And yet at the very point where she seems to have the most agency, Laura's power is the most delimited, for there is no question but that she is a mediator expressing the wisdom of God and of a patriarchal order. She is at most a law clerk recording and repeating the Law of the Father.

In short, Laura's speech, like Petrarch's, is constructed in contradictory ways; her voice is associated with power and powerlessness, with cruelty and kindness, with divine wisdom and all too human temptation. If Petrarch wants to suppress and distance her speech, he wants to celebrate it as well. Sometimes the contradictions stemming from these divided visions generate contradictions within a single poem, as when Laura's speech is labeled with the diminutive "parolette" (253.1; "little words") yet also described as "accorte" (1; "eloquent") and associated with "chiuso inganno" (7; "loving deceptions").[81] But most of the time Petrarch attempts to resolve his conflicting responses to woman's speech through a strategy we will encounter repeatedly in the discourses and counterdiscourses of English Petrarchism. That is, by distinguishing Laura's voice in the "in vita" and "in morte" poems, he recasts synchronic complexity as diachronic diversity: rather than acknowledging that female speech, like woman herself, can be both semiotic and symbolic, he creates a narrative in which it switches chronologically from one to the other. Thus he unties the oxymoron. This strategy for attempting to control conflict, which might be termed *narrative displacement*, is common in both the discourses and the counterdiscourses of English Petrarchism.

Hence reading the *Rime sparse* impels us to ask certain questions of English Petrarchan texts and also of the theoretical models to which they bear

---

[79]Ilona Bell also suggests that the female critique of love language represents an alternative to traditional Petrarchism which she terms *Elizabethism* ("Passion Lends Them Power: The Poetry and Practice of Elizabethan Courtship," esp. chap. 2, forthcoming); her interpretations of Laura's speech, however, differ significantly from mine.

[80]On Wisdom, see John Donne, *The Anniversaries*, ed. Frank Manley (Baltimore: Johns Hopkins University Press, 1963), pp. 20–40.

[81]I am indebted to Robert Rodini and Marguerite Waller for useful discussions of this passage and to Christopher Kleinhenz for additional assistance with Italian translation.

such an uneasy relationship. Should one assume that speech and power, or, more specifically, speech and agency, are necessarily linked? Under what circumstances and to what extent can silence itself be a form of power?[82] What are the connections between the poet's valuations of his own speech and that of the woman? And how do these problems contribute to the popularity of Petrarchism and its counterdiscourses? As these queries would suggest, the assumption that Petrarchism exemplifies masculine expressivity and female silence is very problematical;[83] for example, male subjectivity in these sequences is often rooted as much in the difficulty of speaking or writing as in the act of doing so, while to describe the female voice as silenced is to impose a teleological model on a process of incessant struggle.

At their best, feminist discussions of speech and silence have been exemplary in their subtlety: witness Margaret Homans's anatomy of the process she terms "bearing the word" or Margaret Higonnet's discussion of suicide as a type of speech, among other examples.[84] A few more recent analyses of female agency in early modern texts have questioned the assumption that women's voices are erased,[85] and other feminist books, notably the work of Patricia Yaeger, have refuted some common assumptions about the silencing of women in nineteenth- and twentieth-century texts.[86] Such studies could serve as models for the much needed reinterpretation of both female and male speech in Petrarchism. Trenchant discussions like these have, however, coexisted with a curiously uncritical return to a type of positivistic social history. In particular, many otherwise acute scholars continue to repeat the bald assertion that women were silenced in early modern England, neglecting the complexities that we have been tracing. Studying English Petrarchism impels us variously to nuance and to negate that assertion.

But however one adjudicates these issues about gendered speech, ex-

[82]This and other questions about speech and silence are discussed, though from perspectives different from mine, in the incisive essay by Jonathan Goldberg, "Shakespearean Inscriptions: The Voicing of Power," in *Shakespeare and the Question of Theory,* ed. Patricia Parker and Geoffrey Hartman (London: Methuen, 1985); and Mary Ann Radzinowicz, "The Politics of Donne's Silences," *John Donne Journal,* 7 (1988), 1–19.

[83]A different challenge to that position appears in Bell, "Passion Lends Them Power."

[84]Homans, *Bearing the Word*; and Margaret Higonnet, "Speaking Silences: Women's Suicide," in *The Female Body in Western Culture: Contemporary Perspectives,* ed. Susan Rubin Suleiman (Cambridge: Harvard University Press, 1986).

[85]See, e.g., Mary Beth Rose's observations about heroic drama in " 'The Observed of All Observers': Gender and the Performance of Heroic Identity in Marlowe and Jonson," paper delivered at the 1994 Shakespeare Association of America meeting, Albuquerque, New Mexico.

[86]Patricia Yaeger, *Honey-Mad Women: Emancipatory Strategies in Women's Writing* (New York: Columbia University Press, 1988).

amining the ways Petrarchism constructs the female in general and the Petrarchan mistress in particular guides us towards further explanations for its appeal in England. Although some critics have argued that patriarchy either changed little in the course of that century or veered towards more intense repression,[87] in fact it was struggling with only partial success to contain rival social practices about marriage and the family and alternative ideologies about gender.[88] (Some have even argued for the appearance of a protofeminism both in England and on the Continent.)[89] Gynecological treatises, for example, were far less uniform than Thomas Laqueur has encouraged us to believe;[90] on the issue of heredity, say, they variously attribute all power to the male seed, declare that the mother's seed is more likely to determine characteristics of a female child than a male, explain that the mother may influence the traits of a child of either sex only if the sperm is weak, and so on. Similarly, marriage manuals and sermons disagree among and even within themselves on questions ranging from what constitutes a valid marriage to how much power the wife should have in running the family.[91] There is some evidence that tensions about gender, particularly the problems of androgyny, intensified towards the end of the sixteenth and beginning of the seventeenth centuries.[92] During the English Renaissance, then, the discourse of patriarchy was in fact multivocal and cacophonous, including as it did a series of conflicting discourses that compromise the very use of that noun.

Recognizing those conflicts helps us to understand the dual attraction of Petrarchism in England. First, in some respects it offered a monolithic image—the Petrarchan mistress is unfailingly beautiful—whose simplicity appealed at a time when many issues about gender were problematical. If, as Mario Praz observes, the discourse was almost as conventional as Byzantine painting,[93] in a sense that intensified its attraction: the assurance that in

[87]See, e.g., Lisa Jardine, *Still Harping on Daughters: Women and Drama in the Age of Shakespeare* (Sussex, Eng.: Harvester Press, 1983).

[88]For a lengthier exposition of this argument, see Heather Dubrow, *A Happier Eden: The Politics of Marriage in the Stuart Epithalamium* (Ithaca: Cornell University Press, 1990), esp. chap. 1.

[89]See esp. Constance Jordan, *Renaissance Feminism: Literary Texts and Political Models* (Ithaca: Cornell University Press, 1990).

[90]See Thomas Laqueur, *Making Sex: Body and Gender from the Greeks to Freud* (Cambridge: Harvard University Press, 1990); and Laqueur, "Orgasm, Generation, and the Politics of Reproductive Biology," *Representations*, no. 14 (1986), 1–41.

[91]Compare Dubrow, *A Happier Eden*, esp. pp. 5–27; and Mary Beth Rose, *The Expense of Spirit: Love and Sexuality in English Renaissance Drama* (Ithaca: Cornell University Press, 1988), esp. chap. 1. Rose's treatment of the question, unlike mine, posits a clear movement towards an idealized Protestant model of marriage despite this variety.

[92]Rackin, "English Renaissance Stage."

[93]Mario Praz, *The Flaming Heart: Essays on Crashaw, Machiavelli, and Other Studies in the*

England in, say, 1594 women could be praised in the same terms Petrarch had deployed in a different century and Ronsard had used in a different country offered a comforting alternative to changing and conflicting social norms connected with gender. On another level, however, Petrarchism flourished in that milieu less because it offered a model for a normative woman than because, like the rest of the culture, it staged a struggle to establish norms in the face of contradictions. And if English Petrarchism at once replicates and rejects cultural contradictions about gender, its counterdiscourses often do so as well.

VII

Studies have asserted that in many respects gender is constructed between and among men,[94] a claim I will variously develop and challenge. But for now we can observe that Petrarch's poetry provided English poets not only with a model, however difficult to interpret, for male-female interactions but also with a paradigm of one important manifestation of diacritical desire, the relationship between men, especially male rivals. For desire in Petrarch is, as I have stated, linked to and even enabled by a diacritical response to other men and even to earlier versions of oneself. While the *Rime sparse* incorporates a number of texts inspired by male friendship and political allegiance, such as the poems concerning Giovanni Colonna, its subtext is a relationship between men based on repudiation rather than affinity. Similarly, for all their imitativeness, Petrarch's followers often emphasize their rejections of other Petrarchan poets; witness the edginess in the preface to the second edition of *Olive* when Du Bellay answers imputations of slavish imitation. (Twentieth-century critics are not necessarily immune to the attractions of a similar ideal. Notice how J. W. Lever, whose own work on the sonnet is pioneering in many positive ways, links English rejections of earlier Petrarchan models with male potency and then proceeds to make them seem both natural and inevitable, as descriptions of male potency are wont to do: "The Tudor poets were indeed true pioneers both in form and content, breaking a virgin soil on which, in the

Relations between Italian and English Literature from Chaucer to T.S. Eliot (Garden City, N.Y.: Doubleday, 1958), pp. 264–265.

[94]Two of the most influential statements of this position are Gayle Rubin, "The Traffic in Women: Notes on the 'Political Economy' of Sex," in *Toward an Anthropology of Women*, ed. Rayna R. Reiter (New York: Monthly Review, 1975); and Eve Kosofsky Sedgwick, *Between Men: English Literature and Male Homosocial Desire* (New York: Columbia University Press, 1985).

fullness of days, the great Elizabethans were to raise their golden harvest." Throughout his study he also interprets the development of the sonnet as a nationalistic triumph curiously reminiscent of the Whig view of history.)[95]

That subtext of repudiating other writers structures the *Rime sparse* as a whole: as many critics have pointed out, Petrarch repeatedly defines himself in contrast to Dante.[96] This agenda mirrors his diacritical construction of his own subjectivity: from the first poem onwards, the deictic contrasts between *here* and *there* and between *then* and *now* which are so characteristic of this text often take the form of contrasts between two stages in his own development. Later poets were to adduce this emphasis on repudiation and distinction to define their own relationship to Petrarch and to other Petrarchan writers. Reactions against Petrarch are not an occasional anomaly in French Petrarchism, critics of that tradition have demonstrated, but a central characteristic.[97] "There is nothing more quintessentially Petrarchan," Reed Way Dasenbrock observes, "than an attempt to go beyond Petrarchism."[98] While that attempt is by definition the drive behind anti-Petrarchism, it is also, I maintain, not the least impetus behind apparently "straight" Petrarchism as well: this is one of many ways in which the two are allied and aligned and one of many reasons it can be harder to distinguish them than the label "anti-Petrarchism" might seem to suggest.

These contrasts between the then and there of earlier poets and the now and here of one's own verse have not gone unremarked or unexplained by previous critics. Petrarch's reactions to Dante, like the interplay in many other instances of literary imitation, can be fruitfully explicated in terms of the anxiety of influence; if Laura, who is sometimes presented in maternal terms, is threatening, so too are two fathers who oversee the sequence, the heavenly one whom Petrarch attempts to approach and the author of the *Divine Comedy*. Similarly, unease about the extent of their imitations sparks later Petrarchan poets to repudiate other practitioners of Petrarchism and thus stress their own originality. Any reader of epic knows that relationships with fathers and father surrogates are no less significant in the birth of a nation than in the development of its members, and diacritical desire can also be explained, of course, in familiar though still important nationalistic

---

[95]J. W. Lever, *The Elizabethan Love Sonnet*, 2d ed. (London: Methuen, 1966), p. 13.

[96]For discussions of this pattern, see two books by Sara Sturm-Maddox, *Petrarch's Metamorphoses: Text and Subtext in the Rime sparse* (Columbia: University of Missouri Press, 1985), esp. chaps. 3, 4, and *Petrarch's Laurels*; and Waller, *Petrarch's Poetics and Literary History*.

[97]Robert J. Clements, "Anti-Petrarchism of the Pléiade," *MP*, 39 (1941–1942), 15–21; and Yvonne Hoggan, "Anti-Petrarchism in Joachim du Bellay's *Divers Jeux Rustiques*," *MLR*, 74 (1979), 806–819.

[98]Reed Way Dasenbrock, *Imitating the Italians: Wyatt, Spenser, Synge, Pound, Joyce* (Baltimore: Johns Hopkins University Press, 1991), p. 17.

terms: distinguishing oneself from Petrarch and his Continental imitators is one way of both celebrating and stimulating national pride.[99] Psychoanalytic criticism offers a different though not incompatible etiology for the distinctions so central to Petrarchism. Male development, according to a number of otherwise divergent models, is rooted in an act of separation from the mother. The cartographers of post-Freudian psychology provide a number of alternative mappings for that act: Lacan relates it to the passage between the Imaginary and the Symbolic, certain object relations psychologists focus on its different implications for male and female development,[100] and Jessica Benjamin asserts that failure in differentiation generates a need to dominate.[101] Hence, if one agrees that the drive towards differentiation from the mother is the cornerstone of male development, one might merely interpret the relationship between Petrarch and Dante, Sidney and Petrarch, or John Collop and Sidney as a redirection and reenactment of that drive.

But such an explanation, while true in part, begs several questions that deserve more scrutiny. Automatically attributing the relationship among Petrarchan and anti-Petrarchan poets to that drive assumes without debate the transcultural and transhistorical centrality of differentiation. There is in fact a persuasive case for positing its significance in the Tudor period in particular, though not necessarily in other eras and countries. This pattern is more likely to occur in a culture in which the divisions between male and female are at once sharply defined and seriously challenged, as was certainly the case in a nation ruled for some years by a queen and engaged with many forms of cross-dressing, and the influential work of object relations critics such as Coppélia Kahn and Carol Thomas Neely further substantiates the significance of differentiation in sixteenth- and seventeenth-century England.[102] But even if one does accept that differentiation was significant in some form in that milieu, distinctions between what it

---

[99]Compare Christopher Kleinhenz's analysis of the urge to develop the sonnet as a uniquely Italian form ("Petrarch and the Art of the Sonnet," in *Francis Petrarch*, ed. Scaglione, esp. p. 179).

[100]The most seminal statement of this position is Nancy Chodorow, *The Reproduction of Mothering: Psychoanalysis and the Sociology of Gender* (Berkeley: University of California Press, 1978). Many psychoanalytic critics have developed the principles of object relations psychology; see, e.g., Coppélia Kahn, "Excavating 'Those Dim Minoan Regions': Maternal Subtexts in Patriarchal Literature," *Diacritics*, 12 (1982), 32–41.

[101]Jessica Benjamin, "Master and Slave: The Fantasy of Erotic Domination," in *Powers of Desire: The Politics of Sexuality*, ed. Ann Snitow, Christine Stansell, and Sharon Thompson (New York: Monthly Review, 1983).

[102]See, e.g., Coppélia Kahn, *Man's Estate: Masculine Identity in Shakespeare* (Berkeley: University of California Press, 1981).

might mean in twentieth-century America as opposed to sixteenth-century England must be addressed. And why is diacritical desire more intense in the sonnet form than, say, in pastoral? What are the connections between the drive to distinguish oneself from other men and the drive to pursue a woman?

Reinterpreting the psychoanalytic models of differentiation addresses all these questions. Although many critics have persuasively suggested that psychoanalysis should be historicized rather than rejected out of hand, that project is still in its early days. The suggestive but brief commentaries on the influence of wet-nursing on developmental psychology demonstrate one direction in which it might move.[103] The uprooted and rerouted family structures of Tudor and Stuart England, however, offer an even more fruitful arena for pursuing such historicizing and thus rethinking the workings of differentiation both in the culture at large and in Petrarchism in particular. Donne, Herrick, and Jonson all lost their fathers early in childhood, a pattern that directs our attention to the frequency of parental loss and remarriage.[104] It was especially significant in the lives of the writers and readers of English sonnets, for England endured a major mortality crisis in 1557–1559.[105] Although the death rate varied from one area of the country to the next, as was the case in mortality crises throughout the century, in many regions the toll was heavy, with, for example, about 10 percent of the population of Stratford dying.[106] Remarriage rates differ according to variables of gender and class, but remarriage within a few years was not uncommon, especially for widowers.[107] Hence many members of the gen-

---

[103]See Janet Adelman, *Suffocating Mothers: Fantasies of Maternal Origin in Shakespeare's Plays, "Hamlet" to "The Tempest"* (New York: Routledge, 1992), pp. 4–5, 7.

[104]For a more detailed discussion of parental loss and its effects on family structure, see Heather Dubrow, "The Message from Marcade: Parental Death in Tudor and Stuart England," in *Attending to Women in Early Modern England*, ed. Betty S. Travitsky and Adele S. Seeff (Newark and London: University of Delaware Press and Associated University Presses, 1994).

[105]See E. A. Wrigley and R. S. Schofield, *The Population History of England, 1541–1871: A Reconstruction* (1981; rpt., Cambridge: Cambridge University Press, 1989); and Paul Slack, "Mortality Crises and Epidemic Disease in England, 1485–1610," in *Health, Medicine, and Mortality in the Sixteenth Century*, ed. Charles Webster (Cambridge: Cambridge University Press, 1979).

[106]See two articles by J. M. Martin, "A Warwickshire Market Town in Adversity: Stratford-upon-Avon in the Sixteenth and Seventeenth Centuries," *Midland History*, 7 (1982), 26–41, and "The Parish Register and History," *Warwickshire History*, 2 (1973–1974), 3–15. I am most grateful to the author for also making available to me his unpublished research on the parish registers.

[107]Remarriage rates have been extensively discussed by social historians. See, e.g., Vivien Brodsky, "Widows in Late Elizabethan London: Remarriage, Economic Opportunity, and Family Orientation," in *The World We Have Gained: Histories of Population and Social Structure,*

eration born during the 1550s and 1560s grew up in what today would be called a blended family, with a stepparent and quite possibly step- and half-siblings.

Analyses of these complex subjects need to be inflected to allow for differences in cultural attitudes to both death and family structure, and even then they should be parsed in conditionals, subjunctives, and interrogatives. But the significance of these family patterns, however provisionally it is analyzed, is documented by the many tracts, such as Gouge's marriage manual, *Of Domesticall Duties*, that warn in great detail about the problems involved in introducing a stepparent into a family. (Or, as Petrarch himself puts it in Twyne's sixteenth-century translation of his *Phisicke against Fortune*, "Who so having children by his first marriage, bringeth a Stepmother among them, he setteth his house afire with is [sic] owne handes.")[108]

More to our purposes here, however, the prevalence of the early modern version of blended families invites us to challenge models of differentiation. Varied though they are in other ways, these discussions of male development reveal their own paternity, traditional Freudianism, in their emphasis on infancy and childhood. But might not that initial process of differentiation from the mother have been complicated and perhaps compromised if one was distinguishing oneself from a stepparent, as could readily happen if the birthmother died in childbirth or shortly afterwards? And, more to the point, might not an alternative form of differentiation, defining subjectivity in contrast to a stepparent or stepsibling, have been quite as formative an experience, in part, perhaps, because it echoed and intensified incomplete versions of the differentiation of early childhood?

These processes of differentiation must also have complicated and often intensified the rivalries customarily present in the family romance. Recognizing this possibility again warns us against a mechanical and ahistorical application of psychoanalytic models and in so doing provides a further etiology for the competitiveness in the sonnets read and written by members of the generation who endured the mortality crisis of 1557–1559. Literary critics are sometimes too ready to assume that intragenerational tensions merely displace intergenerational ones; in this instance, it is more than possible that rivalries with a half- or stepsibling are echoed in the

---

ed. Lloyd Bonfield, Richard M. Smith, and Keith Wrightson (Oxford: Basil Blackwell, 1986); B. A. Holderness, "Widows in Pre-industrial Society: An Essay upon Their Economic Functions," in *Land, Kinship, and the Life-Cycle*, ed. Richard M. Smith (Cambridge: Cambridge University Press, 1984); and Barbara J. Todd, "The Remarrying Widow: A Stereotype Reconsidered," in *Women in English Society, 1500–1800*, ed. Mary Prior (London: Methuen, 1985).

[108]Petrarch, *Phisicke against Fortune*, trans. Thomas Twyne (London, 1579), sig. Nviiiᵛ.

diacritical rivalry between poets of the same generation which is so characteristic of English Petrarchism.[109]

Familial patterns of differentiation also resemble the distinctions between
self and Other which make up the foundations of nationalism, thus suggesting connections between the birth of a nation and the multiple rebirths
of Petrarchism. In particular, the stepparent or stepsibling metaphorically
echoes those who both were and were not part of the English family at
the moment of rising nationalistic consciousness: the Scots, Irish, Welsh.
Richard Helgerson opens his recent examination of English nationalism on
the observation that a group of writers who were particularly engaged in
nationalistic self-fashioning were all born between 1551–1564.[110] It may be
no accident that this generation witnessed the mortality crisis of 1557–1559
and its aftershocks at close quarters: whether or not their own families
suffered losses, they are likely to have been surrounded early in their lives
by an unusually high percentage of blended families. For this generation of
the 1550s and 1560s, the process of distinguishing self and Other was enacted in two arenas: the nation and its microcosm, the family. Might the
nationalistic construction of the Other have been sparked and shaped by
its domestic equivalent and vice versa? Might the need to distinguish the
self and the Other, especially the Other gendered female, have been especially intense in the type of uprooted families I am postulating? There is
no clearer instance of the need to historicize psychological patterns—or of
a more neglected imperative, the need to render historical patterns psychological as well, particularly by orchestrating family and cultural history.

In short, differentiation played a significant role in both familial and
national dynamics of Tudor England, though not necessarily the role suggested by the paradigms of Freudian and object relations theory. Petrarchism was simultaneously attractive and threatening in sixteenth-century
England, I maintain, because it offered both a reenactment of failed differentiation and a solution to it. We have repeatedly traced the elision between male and female, subject and object, in Petrarchan poetry.
Paradoxically, the very discourse that aims to define male subjectivity does
so in terms that subvert that aim: the activities constructed as prototypically
male, notably the quest for Laura and the laurel, are precisely those pursuits
that blur the line between male and female. For the devotee of erotic love

---

[109]Though the research of modern psychoanalysts cannot be uncritically adduced in studying the families of Tudor England, cf. Theodore Lidz's observation that interactions among
siblings may be almost as important as Oedipal tensions (*The Person: His Development throughout the Life Cycle* [New York: Basic Books, 1968], pp. 218–219).

[110]Richard Helgerson, *Forms of Nationhood: The Elizabethan Writing of England* (Chicago:
University of Chicago Press, 1992), p. 1.

as for the devotee of affective piety, gender lines break down, imprisoning the lover in a labyrinth of conflicting definitions of male and female. Petrarch, like his followers, is a prisoner of gender no less than a prisoner of sex.

Through its emphasis on differentiation as the defining characteristic of many male relationships, however, Petrarchism also offers a key to and an escape from that prison. The lover who is unable to ground his subjectivity in the differences between himself and Laura can ground it instead in those that separate him from Dante. He can, in other words, transpose into another arena his battle with his lady, his fair warrior, a battle whose outcome is as indeterminate as almost everything else in the sequence. His relationship with women is not the excuse for homosocial desire but rather the conundrum that necessitates and shapes his relationship with men; the male-female interaction is not erased. At the same time that he achieves differentiation in one arena, however, he keeps losing it in another: success and failure once again collide and elide. The counterdiscourses of Petrarchism in turn allow an even deeper and clearer version of this reactive differentiation. The availability of such opportunities for distinguishing self and Other, however compromised they might on occasion prove, is yet another reason both Petrarchism and those counterdiscourses enjoyed the extraordinary vogue they did.

VIII

We are now in a position, as it were, to merge some files and to prepare to load others—in a position, that is, to summarize observations about the appeal of Petrarchism and to begin to interpret the workings of its counterdiscourses. The popularity of both straightforward Petrarchism and its counterdiscourses, like so many other phenomena in literary and cultural history, is overdetermined, and the scholar who privileges a single explanation shows more about her or his own ideology than that of the culture. The broader etiologies that explain the vogue Petrarchism enjoyed on the Continent as well as in England, and in both the medieval period and later, certainly should not be rejected; as I suggested earlier, Leonard Forster is correct in connecting the tradition to the rise of the vernacular, Marotti is persuasive in linking it to the struggles of courtiership, and a culture that delighted in literary craft surely enjoyed the technical challenges of the sonnet. Similarly, anti-Petrarchism is clearly rooted partly in an international recoil from the affectations of Petrarchism; witness among a host of other examples Du Bellay's attacks in the poem whose two versions are entitled, respectively, "A une dame" and "Contre les Petrarquistes." But in explicating the appeal of both Petrarchism and its counterdiscourses, we also need to explore explanations that are related to—though not necessarily unique to—a particular country, a particular class, even a particular decade or generation. If the texts by Du Bellay to which I just referred level accusations that recur in counterdiscourses from different periods and countries, they are also connected to a local controversy, the so-called *querelle des Amyes*.[111] Similarly, in some important respects both English Petrarchism and its challengers can best be understood when viewed in their native habitat, the culture of Tudor and Stuart England.

Pace Marotti, love is indeed love, and I have been demonstrating that Petrarchism was attractive in that culture partly because its ambivalences about gender, desire, and their embodiment in the Petrarchan mistress enact cultural anxieties about those subjects. But the tradition drew on and contributed to conflicting constructions of male subjectivity as well. It typically emphasizes the struggles involved in establishing that subjectivity; in more senses than one, Petrarchism bodies forth the *sujet en procès*. In particular, medieval descriptions of desire interpellated the lover into the prototypically female position of the bride awaiting the arrival of the bridegroom, and as we will see, secular ideologies also established Petrarch's Renaissance counterparts in a role generally gendered female. Yet because in another sense the Petrarchan lover was a prototypically male role, those gender categories were confounded. Furthermore, the elision between the roles of lover and beloved which is so characteristic of Petrarchism blurred what was left of the boundaries between male and female. Displaying its own version of cross-dressing, Petrarchism both explicated and intensified the concerns about gender categories that characterized the end of the sixteenth century in England. The appeal of anti-Petrarchism stems in part from its attempts to reestablish firm definitions of gender.

At the same time, as we have observed, Petrarchism replicates and redefines many cultural problems unconnected or only partly connected to gender, such as the dangers of repetition and the slippery paths between success and failure and between agency and passivity, the latter pairing being often but not invariably one manifestation of the former. Once again the discourse involves continuing struggles and a sujet en procès. Petrarchism shapes and is shaped by cultural tensions in these arenas. Its counterdiscourses often attempt to resolve those tensions more definitively, only

---

[111]For a useful summary of that literary controversy, see *A New History of French Literature*, ed. Denis Hollier et al. (Cambridge: Harvard University Press, 1989), pp. 188–189.

to end up replicating them. Their authors play fort-da without ever winning.

These replications of cultural tensions suggest further parallels with film theory, a field that has already interacted with feminist criticism in so many ways. To understand Petrarchism more fully, literary critics should foster in their own discipline a shift comparable to one in film studies. The highly influential model that Laura Mulvey established in "Visual Pleasure and Narrative Cinema," with its emphasis on monolithic male power and the erasure of female subjectivity,[112] was soon nuanced by some critics, including Mulvey herself, and challenged by others.[113] Just as certain film critics have come to argue that male subjectivity is neither assured nor monolithic, so critics of Petrarchism need to emphasize the ways both Petrarchism and its counterdiscourses pivot on unresolved struggles about both male and female gendering. To be sure, in Petrarchism as in Hollywood films, male power is preserved in many important ways. It is still the male poet who creates the sequence and literally and metaphorically utters its last word, and still the discourses of patriarchy that he often speaks, much as both the diegetic authoritative voices and the voice-over in Hollywood films are male.[114] Yet Petrarchism, like many of the films in question, more frequently reenacts the struggles that compromise male power, whether represented by a single lover or by patriarchy itself, than it protects that power from threats. Those and many other struggles, as we will now see, sparked the growth of the counterdiscourses of English Petrarchism and, paradoxically, were replicated within them.

[112]Laura Mulvey, "Visual Pleasure and Narrative Cinema," *Screen*, 16 (1975), 6-18; reprinted in *Women and the Cinema*, ed. Karyn Kay and Gerald Peary (New York: E. P. Dutton, 1977).

[113]See, e.g., Laura Mulvey, "Afterthoughts on 'Visual Pleasure and Narrative Cinema' Inspired by *Duel in the Sun*," *Framework*, 6 (1981), 69–79; Tania Modleski, *The Women Who Knew Too Much: Hitchcock and Feminist Theory* (New York: Methuen, 1988); and Linda Williams, "When the Woman Looks," in *Re-Vision: Essays, in Feminist Film Criticism*, ed. Mary Ann Doane, Patricia Mellencamp, and Linda Williams (Frederick, Md.: University Publications of America, 1984).

[114]See two studies by Kaja Silverman, "Dis-Embodying the Female Voice," in *Re-Vision*, ed. Doane, Mellencamp, and Williams, and *The Acoustic Mirror: The Female Voice in Psychoanalysis and Cinema* (Bloomington: Indiana University Press, 1988).

CHAPTER THREE

FRIENDLY FIRE: CONFLICT AND
CONTRAVENTION
WITHIN THE SONNET TRADITION

I

Committed to focusing on drama at the expense of lyric, many
critics today are prone to read only the best known poems by
major sonneteers and none at all by subsidiary figures such as Barnabe Barnes and Bartholomew Griffin. Describing his generation's reactions
to the sonnet tradition, C. S. Lewis observes: "Critics reading them, as they
were never meant to be read, hastily and in bulk, are gorged and satiated
with beauty, as a fish can be choked by holding its head upstream. The
water is good water but there is too much of it for the fish."[1] Now, in
contrast, Lewis's successors are swimming in very different streams, and
rather than choking on the sonnet tradition, they are likely to enjoy only
the slightest taste of its major texts and none at all of the minor ones.

But another of Lewis's remarks, his assertion that this genre cannot be
dismissed as a mere repository of trite conceits, remains apt.[2] One result of
both the long-standing tendency to neglect the minor sequences and the
contemporary desire to focus on drama at the expense of the major ones
is missing the aesthetic pleasures of Petrarchism—a regrettable loss despite
the contemporary suspicion of aesthetic values. Admittedly, those pleasures
are not uniformly present. Griffin's sonnets are indeed thought-provoking,
but even his mother would be hard pressed to argue that most of these
lyrics are skillfully written; few hearts would leap up with joy at the discovery of a previously lost manuscript of sonnets by, say, Henry Constable.

---

[1]C. S. Lewis, *English Literature in the Sixteenth Century excluding Drama* (New York: Oxford
University Press, 1954), p. 498.
[2]Lewis, p. 498.

But many sequences, including minor and otherwise unsuccessful ones, exhibit impressive technical virtuosity. Witness, for example, Henry Lok's acrostic or the tour de force that Griffin executes when he ends every line of a sonnet on the same word. And Barnabe Barnes's extensive prosodic experiments encompass examples of that notoriously difficult form the sestina, including a triple sestina and one with an unorthodox rhyme scheme.[3]

Notice, too, the often clever use of concatentio, the device of ending one poem in a group with the same line that begins the next text, in sequences by writers as varied as Samuel Daniel, William Percy, and William Smith. Because the major sonnet writers do not generally deploy this device (Daniel represents a significant exception), its appearance in the sonnet tradition has seldom been scrutinized at length. Yet, like its sibling, anadiplosis, it often adds attractive complexity to the structure of the sequence. Gascoigne, for instance, uses concatentio not simply to repeat the same point but also to connect two assertions, as Jane Hedley has demonstrated.[4] And, like its cousin, the prosodic structure of the sonnet, it draws attention to both sameness and difference. In these and other ways concatentio may serve to represent the complex relationship between movement and stasis and hence between narrative and lyric which, as I have demonstrated, is central to the workings of the sonnet and the subjectivity of its speaker. Similarly, the juxtaposition of likeness and unlikeness recalls the erosions of gender boundaries in Petrarchism. Just as marking essays without knowing the student's name can make one more receptive to the achievements of even the students who are less talented—or whom we have classified as such—so reading through Elizabethan sonnets without identifying the author and hence anticipating only banality can lead to uncovering some impressive technical skill.

Neglecting the minor sonnet sequences and granting the major ones only a passing glance also encourages us to neglect the variety of the tradition. Poets eager to define themselves diacritically have played their own apparent innovations against the putative sameness of Petrarchism, and critics have often taken them at their word. Admittedly, descriptions of netlike golden hair, tropes of icy fire, and allusions to legal cases do recur with depressing predictability. Yet, pace all our generalizations about chaste Petrarchan ladies and respectful if embittered Petrarchan speakers, the English tradition also encompasses Barnabe Barnes's extraordinary fantasy of a rit-

[3]Barnes's technical virtuosity is the subject of Philip E. Blank Jr., *Lyric Forms in the Sonnet Sequences of Barnabe Barnes* (The Hague: Mouton, 1974); on his sestinas in particular, see pp. 46–48.

[4]Jane Hedley, *Power in Verse: Metaphor and Metonymy in the Renaissance Lyric* (University Park: Pennsylvania State University Press, 1988), p. 83.

ualized rape and Richard Barnfield's homoerotic sonnets.[5] Some of Alexander Craig's fickle ladies are émigrées from the households—and, more to the point, the bedrooms—of Latin elegies, not the woods or the courts of Petrarchan tradition as critics generally conceive it. As the instance of Craig suggests, Scottish Petrarchism differs from its English counterparts in several ways,[6] but for all the current attacks on cultural imperialism, that tradition is seldom acknowledged by critics in England and the United States. "Who reads an American novel?"—and who in those countries reads a Scottish sonnet?

The third sonnet in Griffin's *Fidessa*, a collection published in 1596, demonstrates further reasons for examining the less well known sonnets—reasons especially germane to the issue of gender.

> *Venus,* and yong *Adonis* sitting by her,
>   Under a Myrtle shade began to woe him:
> She told the yong-ling how god *Mars* did trie her,
>   And as he fell to her, so fell she to him.
> Even thus (quoth she) the wanton god embrac'd me,
>   (And then she clasp'd *Adonis* in her armes)
> Even thus (quoth she) the warlike god unlac'd me,
>   As if the boy should use like loving charmes.
> But he a wayward boy refusde her offer,
>   And ran away, the beautious Queene neglecting:
> Shewing both folly to abuse her proffer,
>   And all his sex of cowardise detecting.
> Oh that I had my mistris at that bay,
> To kisse and clippe me till I ranne away![7]

Apparently trite in its sentiments, undoubtedly unaccomplished in its style, this lyric would at first seem to merit no more than a passing glance. Yet closer attention uncovers intriguing oddities. In recounting Venus's failure to woo Adonis through her parallel with Mars, the text stages the limitations of the very strategies it deploys: narrative and one of its minions, analogy. Venus tells the tale of her relationship with Mars in a vain attempt

[5]The neglect of Barnfield may, of course, be in part homophobic. On the homoerotic elements in his sonnets and the critical response to that issue, see George Klawitter, ed., *Richard Barnfield: The Complete Poems* (Selinsgrove and London: Susquehanna University Press and Associated University Presses, 1990), pp. 45–51.

[6]See R. D. S. Jack, "Petrarch in English and Scottish Renaissance Literature," *MLR*, 71 (1976), 801–811.

[7]All citations from Bartholomew Griffin are to *Fidessa, More Chaste Then Kinde* (London, 1596).

to seduce Adonis, while Griffin presumably repeats the story of that storytelling to advance the aim of sonneteers: winning the lady. Similarly, Venus fails to persuade her beloved when she adduces and imitates her ostensibly analogous relationship, whereas Griffin calls on the analogy of Venus and Adonis to express his fondest hopes for his own relationship. Structured around syntactical as well as rhetorical similitude (anaphora links lines, parallel constructions connect phrases), the poem nonetheless stages the breakdown of the process of comparison.

The paradoxical workings of these literary strategies may draw our attention to the peculiar blurring of boundaries throughout this sonnet. Here, as so often in both Petrarch's *Rime sparse* and the texts of his English followers, the relationship between success and failure is disrupted, and narrativity impels not the success of the male lover but rather that disruption itself. Thus the story pivots on the failures in love of both Venus and Adonis, and yet Griffin recounts it when he wishes for his own success in that arena. The ostensible resolution of these paradoxes lies, of course, in the diacritical implication that the speaker, unlike Adonis, would not truly run away—but the fact remains that Griffin figures his potential triumphs through the parallel with the pathetically reluctant Adonis, a fantasy that involves identifying with an unsuccessful lover who assumes the passive role normally gendered female while casting the chaste Fidessa in the dominant role. Line twelve glosses these implications, suggesting that Adonis's behavior implicates "all his sex" in cowardice. On another level, however, the sonneteer engages in the type of cross-dressing that recurs in his genre: while he apparently identifies with Adonis, as a sonneteer he is attempting to woo his lady and hence is assuming the aggressive role assigned in this poem to Venus. These contradictions and paradoxes are never resolved. And thus this seemingly transparent sonnet raises in thought-provoking form the issues we explored in Petrarch's poetry: the complex relationship between mastery and impotence, the ways narrativity negotiates that relationship rather than resolving it, the permeability of roles critics sometimes assume to be unambiguously gendered, and, in particular, the ambivalences, deflections, and denials that many sonneteers bring to their own position as sexual aggressor.

Griffin's lyric, then, gestures towards important continuities with the poems studied in Chapter 2. In so doing it defines the aims of this chapter as well: charting the manifestations of diacritical desire in the English sonnet tradition as a whole and exploring the problematics of the speaker's subjectivity and of gender in relationship to reactions against the Petrarchan tradition. English Petrarchism, we will discover, deserves far more attention from new historicists than it has received—if only because its construction of its speaker repeatedly circles back to questions about autonomy and power.[8] And it deserves far more attention from feminists as well, if only because its explication of gender variously emphasizes and obscures the speaker's hostility towards his lady. Many problems in Petrarchism are addressed by its counterdiscourses, but their attempts to renegotiate that autonomy and that hostility are at the top of their agendas.

II

The counterdiscourses of English Petrarchism assume a wide range of forms, echoing the range of Petrarchism itself. Occasionally, as in Sir John Davies' *Gulling Sonnets,* an entire group of poems is indubitably parodic. One can only hope that *Zepheria,* a group of singularly infelicitous sonnets published anonymously in 1594, is parodic as well, but critics have parted company on that issue.[9] In any event, more often poems criticize Petrarchan norms in the company of other texts that apparently espouse them unabashedly; witness *Astrophil and Stella* and a host of minor sequences. The counterdiscourses also vary in both the consistency and the grounds of their attacks. These poems typically focus on one of three principal targets, variously substituting (or allegedly substituting) their spirituality for the amorality of Petrarchism, their frank eroticism for its frustrated desires, or their more direct styles of writing and loving for its banalities and excesses. The "ugly beauty" tradition, as we will see later, enacts a fourth type of diacritical desire.

First, then, either by appending a few religious poems to an otherwise secular sequence or by composing an entire cycle of religious lyrics, poets may announce their rejection of love in favor of spiritual values. Thomas Watson's *Hecatompathia* culminates on a group of sonnets with the repeated title "My Love Is Past." Fulke Greville punctuates *Caelica,* his sequence of straightforwardly Petrarchan sonnets, not only with a fabliau-like poem that anticipates Restoration lyrics but also with several religious texts; the se-

[8]Stephen Greenblatt does address those issues in relation to Wyatt's will to power (*Renaissance Self-Fashioning from More to Shakespeare* [Chicago: University of Chicago Press, 1980], chap. 3), but his analysis did not inspire many other new historicists to examine the sonnet. I contend that the issues of dominance and submission that Greenblatt finds in Wyatt and traces to the Henrican court are characteristic of other sonneteers and other decades as well; I also, unlike many early new historicists, emphasize the instability of power.

[9]See, e.g., Janet G. Scott's contention that the sequence is weak but not parodic (*Les Sonnets Elisabéthains: Les sources et l'apport personnel* [Paris: Librairie Ancienne Honoré Champion, 1929], pp. 181–184), and Lu Emily Pearson's suggestion that it may be intended as parody (*Elizabethan Love Conventions* [Berkeley: University of California Press, 1933]), p. 138.

quence then concludes on a spiritual poem that rejects love, much as Sidney's *Certaine Sonnets* ends on two such lyrics.

The sixteenth century also witnessed several collections devoted entirely to religious poems, documented in detail in Thomas P. Roche Jr.'s *Petrarch and the English Sonnet Sequences.*[10] Among the texts in this category are sonnets attributed to Anne Lok, a little known woman writer;[11] these lyrics, based on the fifty-first psalm, were published in 1560 with her translation of a series of Calvin's sermons, which perhaps suggests yet again that even in a period where women did compose religious verse, doing so was facilitated if one assumed the roles of appendage and translator.[12] Translation was not, however, gendered exclusively female: in 1593, Anne Lok's son Henry Lok published his own rendition of the psalms together with a much longer collection of religious sonnets, *Sundry Christian Passions.* This cycle also focuses entirely on godly pieties rather than Petrarchan goddesses. In his prefatory "To the Christian Reader," Lok attributes his choice of the sonnet to readers' impatience with longer texts; the absence of any reference—defiant, apologetic, or otherwise—to its customary role in love poetry could be explained in many ways, but one strong implication is that even in 1593 the attributes of that stanzaic form were not firmly fixed. Barnabe Barnes, having published the highly controversial love sonnets *Parthenophil and Parthenophe* in 1593, gets religion in *A Divine Centurie of Spirituall Sonnets,* which appeared in 1595; this collection reacts explicitly against Barnes's own youthful error in writing love sonnets and implicitly against the popularity such sonnets were enjoying in the 1590s.

The relationship of these and other pious texts to Petrarchism, however, is by no means clear. They exemplify the familiar but important point that Petrarch himself was anti-Petrarchan in that his sequence pivots on a renunciation of the love of Laura in favor of the love of God. This paradox is manifest in the difficulty of even deciding what poems should be classified within this counterdiscourse—poems that renounce love without referring directly to spiritual alternatives, such as Wyatt's "Farewell, Love, and All Thy Laws Forever," and texts that echo Petrarch in alluding to desire as a youthful error may read very like ones that more overtly embrace a spiritual alternative to human love. Yet other texts ironize the choice of

---

[10]Thomas P. Roche Jr., *Petrarch and the English Sonnet Sequences* (New York: AMS Press, 1989), esp. chap. 3.

[11]On the background and attribution of these poems, see Susanne Woods, "The Body Penitent: A 1560 Calvinist Sonnet Sequence," *ANQ* (formerly *American Notes and Queries*), 5 (1992), 137–140.

[12]Compare Mary Ellen Lamb's observations about the permissibility of translating in *Gender and Authorship in the Sidney Circle* (Madison: University of Wisconsin Press, 1990), p. 10.

cupiditas over caritas by reminding us of the world elsewhere that the love poet is abandoning. Thus, for example, the disjunctive version of polyptoton in a peculiar sonnet in Constable's *Diana*, "My God, how I love my goddesse" (5.10), draws attention to the dangers of worshipping false, golden-haired idols, but there is no sign that the poem consistently or even consciously wishes to pursue that issue.

Roche, fashioning a version of Renaissance Robertsonianism, has argued that English sonneteers routinely criticize the privileging of secular love;[13] in such a reading, poets like Henry Lok are not sports but rather more overt versions of the norms that emerge in the line I quoted from *Diana*. This argument usefully redirects our attention to the spiritual dimensions of both Tudor culture at large and the literary tradition at hand, and Roche uncovers important subtexts in certain lyrics. But on the whole his arguments are not convincing: in particular, his study too often relies on strained numerological interpretations to prove the presence of religious implications. Rather, those implications constitute a sustained counterdiscourse in sonnets by a small group of writers, notably Spenser; an intermittent one in sequences like Fulke Greville's *Caelica* or Sidney's *Certaine Sonnets;* and an occasional and perhaps even unwitting strain in texts such as *Diana.*

If it is hard to classify spiritual sonnets in relation to Petrarchism, it is no less difficult to evaluate the actual or imputed piety of writers in this counterdiscourse. The fact that assertions of religious feeling were themselves a convention of Petrarchism does not necessarily establish such claims as counterfeit. As I argue throughout this book, anti-Petrarchism as a whole was certainly conventional, but that need not mean its sentiments were superficially experienced and mechanically expressed. The types of anti-Petrarchism in question are, however, liable to the charge of another type of bad faith. Discordant, disjunctive, and dissonant on so many levels, Petrarchan poetry regularly undermines its own statements; unstable and inconsistent in so many ways, Petrarchan poets regularly reverse the courses of action on which they confidently embark. One has no reason to doubt the protestations of faith in a group of sonnets devoted entirely to the spiritual, such as Henry Lok's *Sundry Christian Passions,* but in many other cases one wonders, as Anne Ferry rightly points out, whether this renunciation is any more final and definitive than that of Petrarch himself.[14] Indeed, the act of giving up the goddess for the godly may be yet another instance of the cyclical patterns of reenactment which characterize Pe-

---

[13]Roche, in *Petrarch and the English Sonnet Sequences,* chap. 1, provides a useful overview of his argument.

[14]Anne Ferry, *The "Inward" Language: Sonnets of Wyatt, Sidney, Shakespeare, Donne* (Chicago: University of Chicago Press, 1983), pp. 122–123.

trarchism. Barnes might conceivably follow the spiritual sonnets that repudiate their secular counterparts with yet another series of love poems
and yet another renunciation. Give me chastity, O Lord, but not yet.

A second type of counterdiscourse inverts the pieties of the first: if writers
such as Anne Lok react against the amorality associated with Petrarchism
by espousing a spiritual alternative, poets like Barnes and Alexander Craig
react against the morality associated with it by embracing an erotic alternative. They variously celebrate consummated, not frustrated, desire, or
they evoke libidinous, not virtuous, ladies. Craig's *Amorose Songes, Sonets,
and Elegies*, published in 1606, builds the concept of this and other counterdiscourses into its very structure: rather than addressing one woman, he
directs sonnets to a group of different mistresses, some of whom would
certainly bring a blush to Laura's cheek. Note the ironic juxtaposition of
Petrarchan vocabulary with more bawdy language and the equally bawdy
behavior it describes in one of his poems to Lais: "So that my Sainct for
falshood I am sure, / May match the *Grecian* or the *Troian* whore" ("To
Lais" ["When *Cressid* went"], 13–14).[15] It is sometimes difficult to determine to what extent and in what ways such lyrics do constitute a counterdiscourse: consummation is present in Petrarch himself, though distanced
by the dream format, and a number of his Continental followers, such as
Ronsard, overtly condemn chastity. In many instances, however, the defiant tone of such poems does clearly indicate their transgressively diacritical
agenda.

One of the most intriguing—and most disturbing—examples of that and
many other forms of transgression is the final poem in Barnes's *Parthenophil
and Parthenophe*, a fantasy of a consummation engendered through classical
magical rituals. When Barnes ends his sonnet sequence not with a lament
on the absence of the lady, not with yet another expression of frustrated
desire, but with a sestina recounting sexual consummation, he is surely
signaling his violation of not only his lady but also his Petrarchan tradition.[16]
He intensifies that signal by preceding this lyric, Sestine 5, with Sonnet
105. Since the final section of *Parthenophil and Parthenophe* had included
odes and sestinas but no sonnets, he is, I suggest, reintroducing that form
to establish a contrast with what follows. To escape the fruitless laments of
the Petrarchan sonneteer, Barnes implies, one must change genres, escaping
from the sonnet to some other form of writing and form of loving. Al-

---

[15]Alexander Craig, *The Amorose Songes, Sonets, and Elegies* (London, 1606).

[16]In so doing, however, Barnes draws heavily on the classical tradition; on his debt to
Latin writers in this poem, see Victor A. Doyno, ed., *Parthenophil and Parthenophe: A Critical
Edition* (Carbondale and London: Southern Illinois University Press and Feffer & Simons,
1971), "Introduction," pp. xxxix–xlii.

though the final lines of Sonnet 105 anticipate the poem that will follow, much of it reads very like the despairing poems that end other sequences— "At thy long absence like an errant page / With sighes and teares long journeyes did I make" (5–6). Thus Barnes juxtaposes two alternatives for ending a collection of love poems: frustrated desire, represented by and expressed through the sonnet, versus consummated love, signaled and chronicled in a different genre. This instance is, then, one of many in the Petrarchan tradition where literary types serve as metaphors for perspectives and attitudes—and one of many reminders that critics neglect formal issues at their peril. And while numerological readings of the sonnet tradition are not uniformly persuasive, it is worth noting that Sestine 5, the lyric in which the relationship is consummated, is 111 lines long, a number reso-nant to the many readers who would have known that Augustine and others associate the number eleven, which goes beyond the decalogue, with transgression.[17]

The sestina form also serves to draw attention to the literary power of its creator while describing the sexual potency of his persona, thus provid-ing us with one of many instances of the connection between the two in Petrarchism. Sometimes its repetitions demonstrate the speaker's obsession with his emotions, especially anger. Thus the repetition of "furies" in sev-eral senses reminds us, if readers needed any reminding, that he is over-whelmed with fury in the sense of rage:

> At length yet, wilt thou take away my furies?
> Ay me, embrace me, see those ouglye furies.
> Come to my bed.
>
> (78–80)

Elsewhere the recurring words imitate how sexual fantasies dwell on the same image: "Hence goate and bring her from her bedding bare" (36), and "Ah me! *Parthenophe* naked and bare" (72).

The poem is deeply, disturbingly violent: Webster could have taught Barnes nothing he did not already know about the workings of revenge. Barnes repeatedly dwells on his rage and his desire for retribution: "You goddes of vengance, and avenge-full furies / Revenge" (22–23). Whether

---

[17]The connection between the number eleven and sin is explicated in Augustine, *The City of God against the Pagans*, trans. George E. McCracken et al., 7 vols. (Cambridge and London: Harvard University Press and Heinemann, 1957–1972), 4:535. Vincent Foster Hop-per traces the development of the connection in medieval mystical philosophers (*Medieval Number Symbolism: Its Sources, Meaning, and Influence on Thought and Expression* [New York: Columbia University Press, 1938], p. 101).

or not a seduction effected through magic can strictly speaking be prose-
cuted as rape, it remains worth noting that many theorists of rape cite anger,
not desire, as one of the primary motivations of its perpetrators.[18] That
violence and the guilt associated with it are briefly directed towards Parthenophil himself when he describes intercourse as being "buried" (111)
in Parthenophe, but most of the time, of course, she is the victim of his
violent rage. Though women within the sonnet tradition are generally not
silenced in the way or to the extent some studies would lead us to believe,
here Barnes's destruction of Parthenophe's virginity is foreshadowed by his
destruction of her words, including, apparently, her claim to be a rival
poet: "These letter's, and these verses to the furies / (Which she did write)
all in this flame be kindled" (50–51). And if he deprives her of her language
in these lines, he deprives her of her very name through the sexual act on
which the poem culminates, for *parthenophe* is based on a Greek word for
virgin.[19] The envoi to the poem again casts that act in terms of a revenge
ostensibly rendered respectable by a legal term: "Tis now acquitted" (109).
Because legal tropes recur so frequently in the sonnet tradition, this phrase,
like Barnes's use of the sestina, draws attention to the complex relationship
between this poem and Petrarchism.

Barnes's vengeful violence is all the more disturbing because the poem
excuses it. By dwelling on the accusation that Parthenophe, like other
Petrarchan mistresses, is unconscionably hard-hearted and omitting signals
to criticize her lover, the poem implies that the violence against her is
justified, even mandated, by her own behavior. She was, as the saying goes,
asking for it, though through behavior opposite to that which the phrase
usually implies. Also all too familiar is the implication that Parthenophe
was asking for it in the more customary sense. The poet's ritual invocations
repeatedly raise the possibility—and the hope—that she may feels desire
(*"Hecate* reveale if she like passion bare" [37]). The text remains ambiguous
on this issue, with some lines implying that the magic may inspire passion
even in a Parthenophe; thus, for example, "See whence she comes with
loves enrag'd and kindled" (61) apparently suggests that she shares the poet's
desire and that the resulting events should not be seen as a rape, but references to her tears cast doubt on her consent. In any event, the poem also
deploys the trappings of mythology to put its own fantasy in quotation
marks. On some level, the references to Hecate, the Furies, and magical

[18]See two studies by A. Nicholas Groth and H. Jean Birnbaum, "The Rapist: Motivations
for Sexual Violence," in *The Rape Crisis Intervention Handbook: A Guide for Victim Care*, ed.
Sharon L. McCombie (New York: Plenum, 1980), and *Men Who Rape: The Psychology of the
Offender* (New York: Plenum, 1979), esp. pp. 12–17.

[19]On this etymology, see Doyno, *Parthenophil and Parthenophe*, p. xxix.

rituals imply that the rape is not really happening, and thus the poem allies itself to the Petrarchan lyrics in which consummation is possible because it was all only a dream.

More to the point, the speaker in this poem denies his responsibility for the very acts he engineers. He seems possessed both by desire and by the gods.[20] His sleepiness even before sex—"Now I waxe drousie, now cease all my teares" (70)—implies that he, like her, is under the spell of magic and not fully responsible for his actions. It is no accident that Spenser's "Epithalamion," though it describes a very different sort of consummation, screens the groom's passion by associating the sexual act itself, not just its aftermath, with sleep.[21] Similarly, the final declaration that Parthenophil is "buried" (111) in Parthenophe's body not only chronicles the physiology of sex but also reduces the speaker to the ultimate state of powerlessness. In short, whereas their loss of agency haunts other Petrarchan poets, Barnes deploys that loss implicitly to excuse Parthenophil's treatment of Parthenophe.

Though in one sense Barnes, by writing this extraordinary lyric, is reacting against the Petrarchan tradition, in another sense he is exemplifying and illuminating it. By both dwelling on and denying the violence of male desire, Barnes creates a poem that clarifies the workings not only of Petrarchism and its counterdiscourses but also of broader issues about gender in Tudor and Stuart England. The counterdiscourses of Petrarchism help us to understand its more straightforward discourses, and thus Barnes's transgressive eroticism can illuminate the very different eroticism of more typical English Petrarchan poetry, much as his apparent pathologies can clarify the less disturbed behavior of other poets. In particular, this sestina forces us to acknowledge how much potential violence and rage may be latent in Petrarchan demands for revenge. The conventional vocabulary of war, like Spenser's controversial allusions to his lady as a bloody beast, acknowledges the fevered hostility and yet at the same time offers avenues for delimiting or excusing it. Much as fantasies of consummation are excused with the tag "it was only a dream," so fantasies of destruction could be explained away as only tropes—and commonplace ones at that. At times Petrarchism relies on its own conventionality to say the unsayable, to make the unacceptable tolerable. Barnes's sestina reminds us, too, that the drive to blame the victim that has interested contemporary feminists so much has some thought-provoking counterparts in the Petrarchan tradition.

[20]Compare Scott's suggestion that Barnes seeks to imply that he is demonically possessed (*Sonnets Elisabéthains*, p. 81).

[21]Heather Dubrow, *A Happier Eden: The Politics of Marriage in the Stuart Epithalamium* (Ithaca: Cornell University Press, 1990), pp. 37–38.

Though religious and erotic poems challenge Petrarchism, a third type of counterdiscourse is more prevalent: its authors explicitly criticize Petrarchism, often by differentiating their verse from that of other writers in the tradition. This third version of diacritical desire, which is the brand of anti-Petrarchism recognized by most critics and practiced by poets ranging from Shakespeare to Sir John Davies, assumes many distinct forms. They encompass everything from playful inversions of Petrarchan conventions to radical challenges to them; they include both attacks on the social behavior of other Petrarchists and critiques of their literary style.

Davies's *Gulling Sonnets* are among the best known instances. Consisting of nine poems plus a dedicatory sonnet, the collection parodies stylistic excesses common in Petrarchism. One lyric, for example, is a frenzy of anadiplosis, thus also mocking concatentio, which, we observed earlier, simply transposes anadiplosis from the syntax of a single poem to the structure of the whole sequence. Another of Davies's sonnets exaggerates the Petrarchan predilection for correlative verse, so that literally every line consists of a list of five terms that correspond to a list in another line. (Notice too that here the enumeration of the lady's charms includes her speech.) The Petrarchan delight in elaborately articulated conceits is taken to task in a poem that describes Cupid's apparel, not failing to include his codpiece, garters, and so on. Nor is the legal language in which sonneteers indulge immune from attack, with one poem declaring that Cupid has been admitted into the Middle Temple of the speaker's heart and others breaking out in a veritable rash of legalisms. Thus Davies' collection demonstrates that contemporaries were very aware of many of the faults that modern critics associate with Petrarchism.

It is not surprising that Sir John Davies, the author of a series of epigrams, composes this collection. If, as we recalled earlier, Rosalie L. Colie acutely traces the connections between epigram and sonnet, here Davies in effect splits the two, turning the epigrammatic wit of the sonnet on itself or, to adapt Colie's terms, sprinkling epigrammatic salt on amatory honey.[22] (Alexander Craig concocts a similar recipe.) Thus Davies draws attention to the characteristics of each genre and to their symbiosis, reminding us in particular that without an admixture of epigrammatic wryness, the sonnet can readily descend into vacuous excesses. And by grounding so much of his parody in the unchecked recurrence of rhetorical devices, he demonstrates yet again that Petrarchism is the discourse that rehearses, returns, relives—in short, repeats.

---

[22]Rosalie L. Colie, *Shakespeare's Living Art* (Princeton: Princeton University Press, 1974), chap. 2.

Though it is not surprising that Davies wrote these satirical poems, it is at first surprising that more poets did not follow his lead in composing a set of consistently parodic or satiric sonnets. With the possible exception of *Zepheria,* which may or may not be parodic, his *Gulling Sonnets* is the only such collection in the language. Other practitioners of this counter-discourse choose instead to insert poems critical of Petrarchism within a sequence of lyrics that practice it; witness, for example, the twentieth lyric in Lodge's *Phillis,* as well as a host of the better known instances like Shakespeare's Sonnet 130. Such juxtapositions of Petrarchism and its counterdiscourses testify yet again that their relationship is no less volatile and variable than Petrarchan love itself.

The best example of the type of diacritical desire which differentiates the sonnet at hand from other love poetry is a set of lyrics by Michael Drayton, poems important enough to be discussed at length. The dedicatory sonnet in the first version of *Ideas Mirrour,* which was published in 1594, reads:

> To the Deere Chyld of the Muses, and his Ever Kind Mecænas,
> Ma. Anthony Cooke, Esquire

> Vouchsafe to grace these rude unpolish'd rymes,
>   Which long (deer friend) have slept in sable night,
> And come abroad now in these glorious tymes,
>   Can hardly brooke the purenes of the light.

> But sith you see their desteny is such,
>   That in the world theyr fortune they must try,
> Perhaps they better shall abide the tuch,
>   Wearing your name theyr gracious livery.

> Yet these mine owne, I wrong not other men,
>   Nor trafique further then thys happy Clyme,
> Nor filch from *Portes* nor from *Petrarchs* pen,
>   A fault too common in thys latter tyme.
> Divine Syr *Phillip,* I avouch thy writ,
> I am no Pickpurse of anothers wit.[23]

Doubly diacritical, this poem is engaged in distinguishing Drayton both from Desportes and Petrarch and also from the poets who are more reliant

[23]I quote Drayton from J. William Hebel, Bernard H. Newdigate, Kathleen Tillotson, eds., *The Works of Michael Drayton,* 5 vols. (Oxford: Basil Blackwell, 1931–1941).

on their Continental predecessors. He may, as J. William Hebel suggests, be resting his claim to independence on the absence of direct translation,[24] but one should acknowledge as well that his assertion of autonomy has broader implications. It is clearly, proudly nationalistic, which may explain why he is willing to permit the paradox of declaring his independence by quoting a line from the seventy-fourth sonnet in *Astrophil and Stella.* (All Cretans are liars, indeed.)

Drayton defines his nationalistic independence through his legal trope. The word "avouch" (13), commonplace though legal language may be in sonnets, serves to set up a contrast between the lower beings who "filch" (11) and their respectable opposite numbers, who are on the right side of the law and the literary scene. Yet in the late sixteenth century, "avouch" could mean "to appeal or refer for confirmation to some warrant or authority," "to give one's own warrant or assurance; to guarantee, confirm," or "to acknowledge (or claim) solemnly as one's own."[25] The three meanings constitute a spectrum stretching from respectful dependence to proud independence: in the first instance, Drayton is relying on Sidney for authority; in the second, he himself lends that authority to the author of *Astrophil and Stella;* and in the third, he appropriates the work of Sidney. The sonnet ostensibly emphasizes independence from foreign models and enthusiastic acceptance of native antecedents, but Drayton's own ambivalences about even his English predecessors are staged in the multiple meanings of the word.

Recognizing the hidden meanings of "avouch" triggers queries about the hidden motives of the whole poem and of diacritical desire. Is it any accident that Drayton asserts his independence from other poets in the very lyric that acknowledges his dependence on a patron? His discomfort about patronage emerges in his attempt to lend respectability to the relationship by alluding to Virgil's participation in it and in the effort to decrease Cooke's potency by implying that he himself is dependent on the Muses. In any event, it seems likely that the necessity of relying on patronage intensified Drayton's desire to be—and to be seen to be—independent from other putative authorities. Potential, inexpressible resentment of Cooke is deflected onto realized and expressed resentment of other poets. Similarly, misogyny, a strong undercurrent in later editions of the sonnets, is barely present in the 1594 edition, in part because Drayton is espousing a model of sonnet style that does not encourage the type of intense bitterness that appears in the 1619 version of his sonnets. So might not such

---

[24]Hebel, 5:13.
[25]*OED*, s.v. "avouch."

gendered resentment, suppressed elsewhere in the volume, also be deflected onto the "Pickpurse[s]" (14) that Drayton here condemns?

One of the sonnets appended in 1599 to *Englands Heroicall Epistles*, the poem beginning "Many there be excelling in this kind," can be paired with the dedicatory sonnet of the 1594 *Ideas Mirrour:* in attempting to distinguish himself from imitative poets, Drayton again expresses the divided feelings about his distinguished English predecessors which were latent in the 1594 poem.[26] But in "To the Reader of these Sonnets," the prefatory poem in the 1619 edition of his sonnets, Drayton resolves the struggle between independence and dependence enacted in its two earlier counterparts by unequivocally opting for the former:

> Into these Loves, who but for Passion lookes,
> At this first sight, here let him lay them by,
> And seeke else-where, in turning other Bookes,
> Which better may his labour satisfie.
> No farre-fetch'd Sigh shall ever wound my Brest,
> Love from mine Eye a Teare shall never wring,
> Nor in *Ah-mees* my whyning Sonnets drest,
> (A Libertine) fantastickly I sing:
> My Verse is the true image of my Mind,
> Ever in motion, still desiring change;
> And as thus to Varietie inclin'd,
> So in all Humors sportively I range:
> My Muse is rightly of the *English* straine,
> That cannot long one Fashion intertaine.

Here, as in 1594, Drayton connects independence and nationalism, forging that link all the more strongly by positioning it in the couplet. "Farrefetch'd" (5) couples onto its more obvious meaning a reference to fetching from distant places, perhaps foreign climes, which is exactly how Sidney uses the term in the fifteenth sonnet of *Astrophil and Stella,* one of his own sorties in anti-Petrarchism. But Drayton's targets are broader than in his previously examined poems. Rather than simply focus on the imitation of foreign models, the octet attacks the most common clichés of all Petrarchism (and hence implicitly attacks as well the imitative style that encourages those clichés). Rather than merely condemn inferior poets, Drayton also warns off the readers who appreciate them. Given how ruthlessly Drayton

---

[26]A lengthy discussion of this poem is outside my scope here, but see the useful observations in Hebel, *Works of Michael Drayton,* 5:138.

pruned sonnets from earlier versions of his sequence, one suspects another target: his earlier verses, which had their share of tears and sighs.

Against that and other targets, Drayton opposes the positive aesthetic values defined in his sestet. In light of the context, *Libertine* may well take as its primary meaning simply "one who follows his own inclinations," but the implication of amorality, also documented in the *Oxford English Dictionary*, is surely present as well, if only as an undertone.[27] The counterdiscourses of Petrarchism typically costume questions about gender as questions about style, or vice versa, and here too the suggestion about literary variety may hint at a taste for sexual variety and inconstancy. If so, Drayton is distinguishing himself from typical Petrarchan poetry—or what he constructs for his own ends as typical Petrarchan poetry—in yet another way. Rejecting faithfulness and constancy, he turns instead to the delight in a range of women which is so often expressed in Cavalier poetry.

Firm though the anti-Petrarchism of this sonnet may be, it is not consistently realized throughout the sequence. To be sure, Drayton purges many of the *"Ah-mees"* (7) from his earlier collections; and in much of the 1619 edition, he refuses to accept Petrarch as teacher, let alone as *il miglior fabbro,* and matriculates instead at the School of Donne. Yet the collection does retain certain passages liable to the very criticisms so effectively detailed in "To the Reader of these Sonnets." Consider, for example, "I ever love, where never Hope appeares, / Yet Hope drawes on my never-hoping Care" (26.1–2), or "My Sighes be spent in utt'ring of my Woe." (41.7) Drayton's rejection of Petrarchism, however wittily expressed in the 1619 edition of his sonnets, is clouded with the inconsistencies we have already found in other counterdiscourses and will most memorably encounter in Sidney.

As these examples from Drayton suggest, the type of differentiation which is at the core of anti-Petrarchism—contrasting one's own texts with those of other love poets—can be traced to a number of tangled roots, thus providing some new explanations for diacritical desire. To begin with, one should not neglect the obvious: some poems are inspired by exactly what they claim: dismay at the excesses of second-rate Petrarchism. But Drayton's anti-Petrarchan poems invite us to consider additional etiologies. Just as the gendered tensions in the sonnet tradition repeatedly demonstrate how often reactions against the Other repress and represent reactions against the self, might not poets' commentaries on bad sequences often also deflect anxiety about the sort of poetry they themselves once wrote or, they fear, might still write? As is so often the case, the Other is the dark double of

---

[27] *OED,* s.v. "libertine."

the self. In some sense Sidney challenges his *Certaine Sonnets* both in the poems that conclude that sequence and in the lyrics in *Astrophil and Stella* which mock other sonneteers. Similarly, scripting a different type of diacritical desire, Barnes attacks poets who celebrate "foule affections" *(A Divine Centurie of Spirituall Sonnets*, 42.11) and thus implicitly continues the apologia for his own love poetry initiated in the opening sonnet of the sequence.[28] Much as some of the critics who today condemn traditional scholars do so all the more ferociously because of an uneasy consciousness that some of their own early publications might fly under that flag, so, too, a kind of nervous deflection is the undertow in many instances of the kind of diacritical desire that attacks other sonneteers.

The Renaissance fascination with genre is another, more straightforward motivation.[29] Discussions of literary form in sixteenth-century England manifest a curious paradox: writers of the period are keenly conscious of generic issues, as Sidney's *Defense of Poesy*, together with many more minor texts, demonstrates, and yet by and large they do not participate in the type of lengthy, systematic debates about it that were provoked in Italy by, for example, the publication of Guarini's *Pastor Fido*. English writers do not neglect genre criticism, but they often incorporate it not in tracts devoted to that purpose but in texts in a rival genre; thus one reason for the appeal of formal verse satire is that it was a medium for critiquing texts in other literary forms. Diacritical desire is, besides so much else, an opportunity to write genre criticism, to define the sonnet by precept in the very course of defining it by example.

Nationalism, as Drayton's poems clearly demonstrate, is in some cases both yet another source and an important consequence of the type of diacritical desire which attacks other versions of Petrarchism.[30] As so often happens in nationalistic assertions, the self is defined in contrast to the alien, here represented by poems by Continental poets. In one sense, then, the convention of declaring one's independence from convention permits the poet to turn a potential weakness to a strength: in the very course of writing within a form borrowed from Petrarch, Drayton declares the superiority of English poetry. From another perspective, however, that process rep-

---

[28]Citations from Barnes's religious poetry are to *A Divine Centurie of Spirituall Sonnets* (London, 1595).

[29]On Renaissance genre theory, see esp. Rosalie L. Colie, *The Resources of Kind: Genre-Theory in the Renaissance* (Berkeley: University of California Press, 1973).

[30]On the growth of English nationalism, see Richard Helgerson, *Forms of Nationhood: The Elizabethan Writing of England* (Chicago: University of Chicago Press, 1992); Helgerson stresses throughout that nationalism developed diacritically, through a series of contrasts with the Other.

resents an unresolved paradox: for all their declarations of independence, English sonneteers define and advertise their nationalism in the course of writing in a Continental genre, much as they define their masculine subjectivity by participating in Petrarchism, a mode of writing which repeatedly confounds the boundaries between male and female.

But do the attacks on Petrarchism in poems within this counterdiscourse represent a considered evaluation or an offhand nod to the Petrarchan convention of attacking itself? Admittedly, sometimes the counterdiscourses of Petrarchism appear to be only a casual sentiment, a passing aside as it were, but by and large they are seriously engaged in the issues they raise. When they do sound half-hearted or ambivalent, it is not because the poet is unconcerned with the issues but because his concern creates, or aggravates, yet another form of obsessive vacillation. Examples include Drayton's attacks on Petrarchism and, as we will see, the relationship between Spenser's *Amoretti* and the other poems with which it was published.[31]

Yet for all their sustained criticisms of Petrarchism, its counterdiscourses resemble it in many ways and not least in its predilection for reenactment. Their repeated attempts to give up Petrarchism replicate the Petrarchan attempt to eschew love; their criticism of styles in which they indulge themselves replicates the Petrarchan criticism of forms of behavior exemplified by the *Rime sparse*. Thus the layering of anti-Petrarchan and Petrarchan sentiments within the same sequence again demonstrates the inappropriateness of a linear approach to their relationship. In any event, the patterns of rejection in the counterdiscourses are driven by the same motives that impel reenactment in other arenas, including that of Petrarchism itself. The desire for revenge emerges both in overt attacks on women in poems like Barnes's final sestina and Drayton's description of his aging mistress; the desire to achieve mastery, whether over a literary discourse or a psychological state, is manifest in Drayton's introductory poems, as well as in many other instances. Indeed, that striving for mastery involves the attempt to transform the role of passive sufferer into active agent, the very process Freud identifies in his main discussion of reenactment, a section of *Beyond the Pleasure Principle*:[32] rather than merely parroting the clichés of Petrarchism, the poets in question assert their free will. Yet that assertion is at times compromised and confounded. Thus the counterdiscourses of

[31]On the serious issues raised by anti-Petrarchism, compare Thomas M. Greene's explication in *The Light in Troy: Imitation and Discovery in Renaissance Poetry* (New Haven: Yale University Press, 1982), esp. the discussion of Wyatt in chap. 12.

[32]See Sigmund Freud, *Beyond the Pleasure Principle*, in *The Standard Edition of the Complete Psychological Works of Sigmund Freud*, trans. James Strachey et al., vol. 18 (London: Hogarth Press and Institute of Psycho-analysis, 1955).

Petrarchism, no less than that discourse itself, engage in a game of fort-da whose rules question the possibility of ever winning the game—or even ever halting it. Petrarchism and its counterdiscourses are about a drive to escape which is always present and often frustrated, and in no arena is this more true than the urge to escape Petrarchism itself.

III

Petrarchan poets frequently practice both diacritical desire and genre criticism by playing different literary types against one another. Although many of the best known English cycles, such as the *Amoretti,* include only sonnets, a number of English poets, like Petrarch himself, incorporate lyrics in other stanzaic forms and genres within what would be termed a sonnet sequence, thus building a series of comparisons between the visions and values realized in the different poems. Hence Barnes presents the rape in a sestina rather than a sonnet. William Smith's *Chloris,* which appeared in 1596, includes among its sonnets a twenty-six line poem, its different stanzaic status perhaps signaling its different phenomenological status as a dream. Similarly, Alexander Craig's *Amorose Songes, Sonets, and Elegies* (1606) encompasses poems to a range of women and in a range of genres; the epigrammatic qualities of some of his poems to Laia, for example, represent generically the other ways she is unlike the typical sonnet mistress.

The most thought-provoking instances of generic differentiation, however, occur when a poem in a different genre is appended to or appears after the conclusion of the sequence.[33] This juxtaposition of different literary types—and hence, frequently, different takes on love, narrativity, gender, and so on—corresponds to the juxtaposition of different calendrical structures and thus different perspectives. Witness in particular the complex relationship between Daniel's *Delia* and the poem that appears in the same volume, his "Complaint of Rosamond."[34] These texts are overtly linked by Rosamond's appeals for Delia's sympathy and by Daniel's reference in the complaint to the errors of his youth (740), which echoes Petrarch and hence focuses specifically on the moral failings connected with his Petrarchism, and such connections signal the ways that the poems covertly

[33]For a brief but fruitful discussion of this issue, see Carol Thomas Neely, "The Structure of English Renaissance Sonnet Sequences," *ELH,* 45 (1978), 379–380; she observes that these poems sometimes offer alternative ways of fulfilling desire, an argument related to my own.

[34]Some of the sonnets in *Delia,* however, were originally published as an appendage to the 1591 edition of *Astrophil and Stella* (see Arthur Colby Sprague, ed., *Samuel Daniel: Poems and "A Defence of Ryme"* [Chicago: University of Chicago Press, 1930], p. xiii).

comment on each other. Delia's chastity and modesty appear all the more precious when contrasted with the alternative that Rosamond represents: the contrast between chaste love and lust within so many sonnet sequences here is worked out through two different stories in two different genres. Another hint that emerges from the juxtaposition of the two texts is more disturbing and more transgressive: different though they are in other ways, Delia and Rosamond are alike in the power they exercise over men, and so whatever subtext of gendered resentment or anxiety is latent in the mild-mannered sonnets of Delia becomes activated when that text is played against its companion.

Profoundly dialogic, the relationship between the two poems in Daniel's collection demonstrates how seriously M. M. Bakhtin erred in associating that mode primarily with the novel.[35] The relationship between Daniel's texts can also be understood in terms of those visually dialogic forms the diptych and triptych.[36] The "Complaint of Rosamond" is in no sense a simple continuation or culmination of *Delia,* but neither is it a completely separate work. Compare Hubert van Eyck and Jan van Eyck's Ghent Altarpiece (*The Mystic Adoration of the Lamb*): its panels are distinguished iconographically and pictorially, but the figures of Adam and Eve remind us of Christ's mission, and the more restrained coloration of those figures makes the rich greens and reds of the extraordinary Flemish palette all the more striking. Similarly, both the parallels and the differences that connect the texts clarify Daniel's agendas, and each of the texts draws attention to elements in the other that might otherwise be readily overlooked.

The most complex instance of interrelated texts is surely the volume Spenser published in 1595, which includes his *Amoretti,* the Anacreontic poems, and the "Epithalamion." As contested and vexed a question as the connections among the various avatars of Elizabeth in *The Faerie Queene,* the relationship among the lyrics in this book has generated considerable scholarly debate. These disagreements are germane as well to interpretive problems raised by particular texts within the book, notably the question of why the *Amoretti* apparently ends on loss.

Varied though the scholarship on these issues is, three principal approaches recur, sometimes in opposition to one another but sometimes interconnected by particular scholars. Certain critics emphasize a literal,

---

[35]See M. M. Bakhtin, *The Dialogic Imagination: Four Essays,* ed. Michael Holquist, trans. Caryl Emerson and Michael Holquist (Austin: University of Texas Press, 1981), esp. chap. I.

[36]Compare O. B. Hardison Jr.'s suggestion that we read the *Amoretti* itself as a triptych, with each panel representing a different perspective on the lady ("*Amoretti* and the *Dolce Stil Novo,*" *ELR,* 2 [1972], 209–214).

biographical relationship among the poems, with the *Amoretti* tracing the events of Spenser's courtship and the "Epithalamion" those of his wedding;[37] thus the inconclusive conclusion of the *Amoretti* would commemorate a period of literal separation. Though this approach is dated, a version of it paradoxically returns when numerological studies relate their symbolic patternings to biographical events. Other students of Spenser have uncovered both within the *Amoretti* and in its relationship to the other poems in the volume patterns of ethical and spiritual growth. Lisa Klein, for example, finds in the sonnets a radical new version of Petrarchism which accords to a Protestant ideal of mutual love.[38] Similarly, Reed Way Dasenbrock argues that the sequence is more Petrarchan than most of its English counterparts precisely because its author, like the author of the *Rime sparse*, rejects Petrarchism.[39] Carol V. Kaske, emphasizing Spenser's allegiance to the principles of Christian humanism, maintains that each of the genres in the volume moves from sexual conflict to resolution, miming as they do three stages of courtship; the otherwise troubling conclusion of the *Amoretti*, as well as the presence of the Anacreontics, represent the anticlimactic period of betrothal.[40] Finally, many studies have traced patterns of numerological symbolism, positing correspondences to Christian liturgy both within the *Amoretti* and in the volume as a whole.[41] Such readings invite us, for example, to relate the sense of loss at the end of the sequence to how the church calendar terminates.[42]

Even skeptics about numerology—a subject whose slipperiness is man-

[37]See, e.g., Yvette Marchand, "Hypothesis for an Interpretation of the Later Poems of Edmund Spenser," *English Miscellany*, 28–29 (1979–1980), 7–18.

[38]Lisa Klein, " 'Let us love, dear love, lyk as we ought': Protestant Marriage and the Revision of Petrarchan Loving in Spenser's *Amoretti*," *Spenser Studies*, 10 (1992), 109–137.

[39]Reed Way Dasenbrock, *Imitating the Italians: Wyatt, Spenser, Synge, Pound, Joyce* (Baltimore: Johns Hopkins University Press, 1991), esp. p. 48. I part company with Dasenbrock when he claims that Spenser's reactions against Petrarchism are atypical of the English tradition (see esp. pp. 32–33, 39).

[40]Carol V. Kaske, "Spenser's *Amoretti* and *Epithalamion* of 1595: Structure, Genre, and Numerology," *ELR*, 8 (1978), 271–295. For similar arguments about the relationship among the poems in the volume, also see Peter M. Cummings, "Spenser's *Amoretti* as an Allegory of Love," *TSLL*, 12 (1970), 163–179; Donna Gibbs, *Spenser's "Amoretti": A Critical Study* (Aldershot, Eng.: Scolar Press, 1990), esp. pp. 13–14; and William J. Kennedy, *Authorizing Petrarch* (Ithaca: Cornell University Press, 1995), chap. 5.

[41]See, e.g., two essays by Alexander Dunlop, "The Unity of Spenser's *Amoretti*," in *Silent Poetry: Essays in Numerological Analysis*, ed. Alastair Fowler (New York: Barnes and Noble, 1970), and "The Drama of *Amoretti*," *Spenser Studies*, 1 (1980), 107–120; and William C. Johnson, *Spenser's "Amoretti": Analogies of Love* (Lewisburg, Penn. and London: Bucknell University Press and Associated University Presses, 1990).

[42]See Anne Lake Prescott, "The Thirsty Deer and the Lord of Life: Some Contexts for *Amoretti* 67–70," *Spenser Studies*, 6 (1986), 58.

ifest in the conflicting and even contradictory patterns sometimes uncovered by its proponents—should find certain of the calendrical and liturgical allusions attributed to the *Amoretti* totally persuasive. It is quite clear, for example, that Sonnet 68 links Easter and the spiritual development of its speaker, ending as it does on the affirmation that the Lord taught him and his lady how to love. Here, as in other versions of Petrarchan counterdiscourses, Christianity at once exposes the limitations of Petrarchism and provides an alternative version of it. Figured as a stone in Sonnet 54, the lady elsewhere resembles Beatrice.[43]

Yet critics need to resist the corollaries that some, though by no means all, adherents have associated with symbolic patternings, Christian and otherwise, in the sequence. A steady and consistent trajectory of maturation does not in fact occur either within sections of the 1595 volume or in the relationship among its parts.[44] Much of the sequence moves back and forth between intensely negative presentations of the lady and more positive, even adulatory ones, as does the *Rime sparse*; Spenser juxtaposes tropes ranging from the bestial ("cruell and vnkind, / As is a Tygre" [56.1–2]) to the divine ("resembling heauens glory in her light" [72.6]).[45] The recurrence of those negative constructions of Spenser's lady demonstrates not that the speaker wants to rehearse the presentation and rejection of old views, as some critics have claimed,[46] but that he is repeatedly pulled between Petrarchism and its counterdiscourses or, to put it another way, between various versions of Petrarchism. Like Redcrosse, he encounters Error after apparently destroying it: anti-Petrarchan pride, like so many other versions of that deadliest of sins, cometh before a fall.

From another perspective, the juxtaposition of these negative images of the lady with more positive ones demonstrates the persistence of misogyny in and because of Petrarchism. *The Faerie Queene* allows Spenser to explicate and negotiate the tension between misogyny and more positive responses to women by attaching those reactions to evil and good characters respectively. This process of dramatic displacement by Spenser himself is not

[43]Compare Robert G. Benson, "Elizabeth as Beatrice: A Reading of Spenser's *Amoretti*," *South Central Bulletin*, 32 (1972), 184–188.

[44]Compare the rejection of that trajectory, though from a perspective different from my own, in Prescott, "The Thirsty Deer and the Lord of Life," esp. pp. 61–62; unlike many practitioners of numerological criticism, she too finds loss and suffering at the end of the *Amoretti*.

[45]All citations from Spenser are to The Variorum Spenser, ed. Edwin Greenlaw et al., 11 vols. (Baltimore: Johns Hopkins University Press, 1943–1957). Because of the special problems associated with Spenser's spelling, in this instance, unlike other citations in this book, I have not regularized u/v.

[46]For this argument, see, e.g., Klein, " 'Let us love, dear love,' " esp. pp. 117–118.

unlike the narrative displacement that leads some readers variously to assert that the darker views of the mistress in the *Amoretti* are the product either of sonnets written at an earlier stage or of a form of Petrarchism which the sequence firmly eschews as it progresses.[47] In the 1595 volume, however, Spenser challenges such strategies of reassurance.

Similarly, to read the movement towards the "Epithalamion" as merely the triumph of mature Protestant love is to subscribe to a partial truth. While critics should beware of the revisionist corrective that emphasizes the tensions in the "Epithalamion" at the expense of adequately acknowledging the joy that earlier critics highlighted, some passages of this poem, such as the descriptions of threats in the nineteenth and twentieth stanzas, do translate the laments about loss and sexual threat in the *Amoretti* into a different key by suggesting that they could imperil marriage itself.[48]

> And in thy sable mantle vs enwrap,
> From feare of perrill and foule horror free.
> . . . .
> Ne let false whispers breeding hidden feares,
> Breake gentle sleepe with misconceiued doubt.
>
> (321–322, 336–337)

Monitory and apotropaic, such passages at once introduce and contain the possibility of danger, ensuring that the contrast between Spenser's epithalamium and his sonnets, though real, is by no means complete or unchallenged.

Above all, the relationship among the poems in the volume is complicated by Spenser's playing his liturgical resonances against other and sometimes conflicting perspectives. In particular, the Christian calendar does suggest that the sense of loss on which the sequence ends is temporary; influenced by that perspective, many readers interpret the conclusion of the sequence as the speaker eagerly awaiting the return of his beloved. Yet the Petrarchan habit of ending sequences on a note of despair invites a less optimistic reading, which is supported by the dark language in these final sonnets: "And dead my life that wants such liuely blis" (89.14), the final line of the *Amoretti*, exemplifies a tone that is somber enough to undermine the argument that the sequence merely ends on waiting and expectation. The first interpretation suggests a successful escape from the dangers of

---

[47]See, e.g., J. W. Lever, *The Elizabethan Love Sonnet* (London: Methuen, 1956), pp. 99–100.

[48]One of the most acute examples of that revisionist reading is Joseph Loewenstein, "Echo's Ring: Orpheus and Spenser's Career," *ELR*, 16 (1986), 287–302.

profane love, a liberation that might be described as either the rejection of Petrarchism or the espousal of a better version; the second assaults the hope of escaping. Characteristically, Spenser does not merely contrast the gloomy endings of other writers' sequences with the hopefulness of a cycle infused with Christianity; rather, his zoo, like Shakespeare's, is populated by a Wittgensteinian menagerie of incompatible ducks and rabbits.[49] Conflicting structural patterns stage conflicting interpretive possibilities, much as *The Faerie Queene* repeatedly juxtaposes the teleology of epic against the cyclical movements of romance.

Spenser, like other practitioners of Petrarchan discourses and counter-discourses, is a practitioner of genre criticism as well: he is not merely deploying genres to chart spiritual development but also adducing forms of spirituality to reexamine forms of literature.[50] In particular, he is concerned to demonstrate how courtship and marriage in general appear from the perspectives symbolized by three genres. Radically different though the poets and their texts may be in other ways, Spenser's changing of genres to signal shifting viewpoints on love is not unlike the generic pattern we traced at the end of Barnes's collection. Recognizing that such patterns appear in Spenser as well helps to explain the Anacreontics, which are slighted in some though not all liturgical interpretations of the sequence.

Thus the *Amoretti* practices genre criticism by juxtaposing different versions of Petrarchism. According to one interpretation, its concluding sonnets, even the apparently somber final ones, celebrate the achievement of a mature love, with the liturgical calendar explaining what would otherwise seem a curiously unoptimistic ending for that love. Yet that trajectory is undermined by the alternative reading of Spenser's ending: his *Amoretti* terminates darkly because loss is the predictable outcome of a relationship grounded in adulation, unconsummated desire, and bitterness, the kind of relationship which the Petrarchan sonnet so often represents. Such relationships are by their very nature anticlosural and uncertain. Whether the arena is the sequence itself or the culture, Spenser suggests, attempts to reform Petrarchism—in the several senses of that verb—are likely to be at best partly successful. The Anacreontics then pose the question of how the texts of frustrated desire differ when they appear in, as it were, the Greek

---

[49]Ludwig Wittgenstein, *Philosophical Investigations*, trans. G. E. M. Anscombe, 3d ed. (Oxford: Basil Blackwell, 1968), pp. 194–196, 199, 205–206. Norman Rabkin cleverly deploys the metaphor of ducks and rabbits in relation to *Henry V* in *Shakespeare and the Problem of Meaning* (Chicago: University of Chicago Press, 1981), chap. 2.

[50]For a different view of Spenser's genres, see Patrick Cheney, *Spenser's Famous Flight: A Renaissance Idea of a Literary Career* (Toronto: University of Toronto Press, 1993), chap. 4.

Anthology rather than *The Passionate Pilgrim*. In this way Spenser plays both the secular and the spiritual elements of his *Amoretti* against the urbane and amoral vision of his Anacreontics. Since, as Janet Levarie points out, two of those poems are renditions of the same story,[51] he characteristically is also playing two versions of this type of verse against each other, much as he juxtaposes different responses to Petrarchism in the *Amoretti*. And finally, in the "Epithalamion" he suggests that marriage and its genre offer a partial resolution of the problems of the *Amoretti* and the short lyrics that follow it. Yet in resolving it also replicates, in so doing providing two different perspectives on its own genre: Spenser, like other practitioners of the discourses and counterdiscourses of Petrarchism, is engaged in attacking the very contrasts he establishes.

Hence, as I have already suggested, simply describing the relationship among the poems in the volume as a narrative movement from the pains of courtship to the pleasures of marriage is a partial truth at best. An alternative model, the painting with multiple panels, each of which lends itself to multiple interpretations, is yet again germane. Though critics have suggested that the *Amoretti* be read as a triptych,[52] that mode of composition provides a more apt analogy for the relationship among that sequence and its neighboring poems. Another analogy is the patterning of Book 3 of *The Faerie Queene*: in both, Spenser shows "How diuersly loue doth his pageants play" (*Faerie Queene*, III.v.1). The concept of diacritical desire is, however, the best way of explicating and summarizing these and other complex patterns in the 1595 volume. Spenser, like so many other poets in his culture, is engaged in strategies of differentiation: he is contrasting different modes and valuations of Petrarchism with one another and contrasting the principal genre of Petrarchism with other genres. Yet the distinctions he attempts to establish are repeatedly inscribed and repeatedly washed away, like the name of the beloved in Sonnet 75. As in the oxymoron and the rhyme scheme of the Spenserian sonnet, difference and sameness collide and elide. Spenser, born into the generation that witnessed the mortality crisis of 1557–1559, creates in his 1595 volume a family of poems which resembles some of the families that resulted from that event: its texts are variously stepsons, prodigal sons, half- and stepsiblings, and so on of Petrarch and of his imitators.

[51]Janet Levarie, "Renaissance Anacreontics," *CL*, 25 (1973), 234.
[52]See, e.g., Dunlop, "The Unity of Spenser's *Amoretti*," p. 155, which posits a central group of forty-seven Lenten sonnets, preceded and followed by sets of twenty-one poems; Hardison, "*Amoretti* and the *Dolce Stil Novo*," pp. 209–214, argues that they are a triptych in their treatment of opposing images of the lady.

IV

The subjectivity of the male speaker, I have suggested, impels the attraction of both Petrarchism and its counterdiscourses in Tudor and Stuart
England. In particular, a nexus of different but overlapping issues related
to power—success and failure, agency and impotence, speech and its discontents—proved especially resonant in the late sixteenth century, and both
Petrarchism and anti-Petrarchism strive to mediate the relationships between these positions. Indeed, the shifts between Petrarchism and anti-
Petrarchism represent a movement between alternative models of
masculinity.

An attempt to map those patterns, however, immediately thrusts us to
the center of a conundrum, the relationship of speaker and poet.[53] The
New Critical separation of the two has been challenged in many quarters.
Impelled by different perspectives and different motivations, practitioners
of both new historicism and feminism often do so; poststructuralism, too,
discourages us from assuming the kind of aesthetic control presumed by
earlier conceptualizations of a persona—or even, according to Foucault and
Barthes, from positing an author at all.[54] We will return to these problems
when examining *Astrophil and Stella*, which raises them in thought-
provoking form, in the next chapter. But other sequences clearly manifest
a real but imperfect and volatile separation between fictive lover and fic-
tionalizing poet. Renaissance sonneteers draw attention to that separation
in many ways. They may relegate the speaker to a category by affixing
titles such as "The lover compareth his state . . ." to their poems, as Anne
Ferry points out;[55] they may allude to and even quote from other sequences, thus reminding us that they are participating in a literary discourse;
they may also draw attention to their own role-playing, as Spenser does in
the theatrical metaphor that structures *Amoretti* 54. These poets try, in short,
to achieve some detachment from desire and its most favored genre, a
version of the process of distancing which is enacted on so many levels in
the sonnet tradition. Indeed, the relationship between writer and fictive
speaker is yet another example of the diacritical drive of Petrarchism.[56]

[53]For a particularly useful overview of this problem, see Ferry, *"Inward" Language*, esp.
pp. 16–30.
[54]The alleged death of the author has been widely discussed in contemporary criticism;
for one of the most influential statements of that position, see Roland Barthes, "The Death
of the Author," in *Image, Music, Text*, trans. and ed. Stephen Heath (London: Fontana,
1977).
[55]Ferry, *"Inward" Language*, p. 18.
[56]I am grateful to William Kennedy for this insight.

Nonetheless, as the instances of Sidney and Shakespeare will demonstrate shortly, that attempt at detachment, like so much else in the sonnet tradition, repeatedly breaks down, and the similarities between poet and persona are intensified.

The tensions associated with male subjectivity in the *Rime sparse* recur in the English discourse of Petrarchism, generating counterdiscourses that variously resolve, reinterpret, and, most frequently and most disturbingly, replicate them. In particular, the authors of the straightforward Petrarchan sonnets against which the counterdiscourses rebel, like Petrarch himself, typically and repeatedly slide between announcements of triumph and admissions of defeat. Writing love poetry, as we have already seen, is not an unambiguously positive achievement; a distrust of that activity runs very deep in the English tradition, as J. W. Lever demonstrates,[57] and it is not surprising that Barnes attempts to disown his poems by labeling them "barstard Orphan[s]" ("Go barstard Orphan," 1). They have been out nine years, and away they shall again. Nor is male speech inevitably either source or sign of male power. Petrarchan mistresses regularly deprive their poets of a voice, a situation confounded but certainly not resolved by the paradox that they manage to write about their inability to write. In *Amoretti* 43 the poet laments that his speech will only renew the lady's anger, while his silence will only break his own heart. His solution—"I my hart with silence secretly / Will teach to speak" (9–10)—reminds us how complex the relationships among speech, silence, success, and failure may be and warns us once more against merely equating speech with power and silence with powerlessness. Neither is male agency firmly established. By variously blaming Cupid, Venus, and the lady for their own behavior, sonneteers avert some guilt, but they sacrifice even an illusion of autonomy. Often, too, the poet stresses his own passivity when confronted with love; thus Barnes reduces himself to object in both grammatical and other senses through his trope of fishing: "Loves golden hooke on me tooke soddeine holde" (43.9). "In one sense," Arthur F. Marotti rightly observes, "sonneteering was perceived as an activity for losers,"[58] and his observation is apt not only for the socioeconomic pressures on which he focuses but also for the many other types of loss in the tradition.

Narrativity in the English sequences, as in Petrarch's, further complicates all these issues and hence further helps us to understand the pressures against

---

[57]See Lever, *Elizabethan Love Sonnet*, esp. pp. 8–12.

[58]Arthur F. Marotti, " 'Love is not love': Elizabethan Sonnet Sequences and the Social Order," *ELH*, 49 (1982), 408.

which the counterdiscourses struggle. Multiple narrative patterns often structure English sonnet cycles, with the calendrical structures that have received so much attention functioning somewhat like the political events in drama which Harry Levin termed the *overplot*;[59] witness above all the *Amoretti*. More to our purposes, however, English sequences, like Petrarch's, typically include a range of types of narrative, each of which bestows on the speaker a different admixture of power and powerlessness. Thus Drayton opens his 1619 *Idea* by comparing himself to an "adventurous Sea-farer" (1) who "call'd to tell of his Discoverie" (3), the journey miming the more overt reference to narrative in line three. An implicit allusion to other Petrarchan poems intensifies the heroism evoked by "adventurous," for whereas those other sonneteers typically construct themselves as passengers on a tossing, listing, careening boat, a vessel as out of control as love itself, Drayton's seafarer is a confident traveler. But power again proves as unstable as language itself in Petrarchism and its counterdiscourses; in the case at hand, the speaker's confidence is significantly qualified when the couplet refers to his "tedious Travels" (14).

In many, indeed most, instances, however, narrative is associated either with the failure or with the fusing and confusing of failure and success which sparks Petrarchan counterdiscourses. The dream vision, borrowed most immediately from Petrarch's own reveries of consummation, transforms that confusion into narrative: having triumphed in sleep, the poet wakes up to discover that his victory was only a dream. Or, to adapt Hedley's framework, the moment of awakening jolts the poem from metaphorical inner realms to the metonymic social world.[60] This form of storytelling attracts Petrarchan poets not simply because it permits the fulfillment of desire but also because it mimes how English Petrarchism itself works both in its slippage from success to failure and in its construction of that slippage in terms of a struggle between narrative and lyric. For such poems are doubly narrative: they tell the story of the dream and the story of dreaming, and yet the moment of awakening redefines that first narrative as lyric in the senses of internal and subjective. (Thus here, as in Petrarch, fulfilled desire is positioned in the realm of lyric.)

Once again a poem in a minor sequence, the thirteenth lyric in William Smith's *Chloris,* offers an instructive example of major patterns in its tradition. Smith dreams that he rescues his lady from a "lust-led Satyre" (11) and that she rewards him by promising never again to react with "rigor"

---

[59]On the concept of the overplot, see Harry Levin, *The Overreacher: A Study of Christopher Marlowe* (Cambridge: Harvard University Press, 1952), p. 67.

[60]See Hedley, *Power in Verse*, esp. p. 67, on the relationship of narrative to the metonymic.

(19)—but then he awakes. On one level the poem allegorizes a commonly expressed but seldom achieved agenda of sonnet sequences: the satyr externalizes his own uncontrolled sexuality, which he kills off and replaces with a more acceptable version of masculinity (his weapon against his adversary being "a sturdy bat" [14], just in case anyone might have missed the point). From another perspective, a narrative of success, the dream itself, is encased within a narrative of failure, the story of waking to discover that the triumphs within the dream did not really occur. And so the dream vision of the sonnet sequence actually dramatizes the movements between success and failure at the core of the entire tradition.

These examples demonstrate, then, that a series of issues centering on power and its loss, success and its opposite, and agency and its absence are as central to English Petrarchism as to its principal Continental forebear. The counterdiscourses respond by offering a rival vision of male subjectivity, variously reinterpreting and rejecting the issues in question. In particular, they often posit a more confident poet, triumphant in the arena of love or literature or, frequently, both. Deflection, as common a strategy in the counterdiscourses as in Petrarchism itself, permits and sustains such triumphs, for the counterdiscourses typically transfer characteristics of both the poet and his lady to other beings.[61] Once again, however, apparent reinterpretation often collapses into mere reenactment, and triumph segues into defeat.

Thus spiritual sonnets like Henry Lok's eschew the failure implicit in writing love poems by not writing them and even, as in Barnes's opening poem, by openly rejecting such poems and renouncing one's own earlier involvement with them. Yet, as we observed earlier, the reader sometimes questions whether the spiritual vision in such poems represents a final, secure position or merely a moment on a giddy merry-go-round, one more continuing struggle between desire and its renunciation. The erotic counterdiscourse of English Petrarchism reinterprets the subjectivity of the speaker in a different way: the unsuccessful lover, unappreciated in his devotion and unfulfilled in his desire, is replaced with one who actually wins the lady. Yet the consummation itself may be problematical; Barnes is "buried" (111) in his lady's body, and the sexual availability of Shakespeare's Dark Lady enables only the darkest and briefest of triumphs. Similarly, the anti-Petrarchan poems that criticize the styles of writing and loving which characterize other Petrarchan poets allow their authors to lay

---

[61]Compare Gibbs's argument that although in other sequences the poet normally blames something or someone other than the mistress for his entrapment in her hair, Spenser holds the lady herself responsible (*Spenser's "Amoretti,"* pp. 76–79).

claim to many types of success, centering especially on agency and autonomy. They are, as Drayton among others declares, more discriminating,
more independent, even more English than poets turning out boilerplate
imitations of Petrarch. Yet these poets frequently replicate the very faults
they lampoon. Despite all Drayton's delight in ranging "sportively" ("To
the Reader of these Sonnets," 12), his attacks on the sonnet tradition could
be turned against some of his own poems.

V

The English sonnet may participate in patronage, react to Elizabeth, and
allude to connections between and among men—but, pace the worst excesses of first-generation new historicism, it is still mainly concerned with
gender, still mainly addressed to sexual rather than courtly politics. To
begin with, then, English poets, like Petrarch, typically stage the relationship between male and female in terms of elisions, reversals, displacements,
and confusions of gender. The mistress's hair is conventionally figured as
a net, but in the fifteenth sonnet of *Ideas Mirrour*, Drayton declares that he
will bind the lady in his own hair. In *Fidessa* 31, Griffin rhetorically dis-
members his own body. Tofte, performing a common reversal of the metaphor of hunting, describes himself as the hart and his beloved as the huntress
(Laura, III.15).

In certain respects especially germane to its counterdiscourses, however,
the English tradition approaches gender very differently from the way Petrarch does. In particular, while hostility is hardly absent from the *Rime
sparse,* in English sonnets it is prone to be more overt, more virulent, and
more aggressive.[62] To deny the presence of more beneficent responses
would be merely fashionable, but to deny the intensity of this antagonism,
merely foolish. If English Petrarchism thrives partly because it allows such
hostility to be expressed in an apparently acceptable form, critics themselves
are sometimes guilty of accepting, not exposing, this pattern, that is, of
assuming that the hostility of the Petrarchan poet is an understandable
response to the disdain of the lady rather than realizing that the disdain
may be constructed precisely to excuse hostility. In any event, while English sonnets do differ in their degree of anger, the tradition includes poems
like the eighth text in Drayton's 1619 *Idea,* the description of his aging
mistress which is significantly harsher than comparable poems on aging by

[62]See, e.g., Michael McCanles's thoughtful analysis of the workings of hostility in Wyatt's
poetry ("Love and Power in the Poetry of Sir Thomas Wyatt," *MLQ,* 29 [1968], 145–160).

Petrarch and Ronsard. Spenser's evocations of his mistress as a violent beast are so antithetical to the tone of his other sonnets that one otherwise acute critic even hypothesizes that they are imported from a different, earlier collection, thus demonstrating that literary critics, like poets, may themselves practice narrative displacement to keep disturbing realities at bay.[63] Rather, just as the creator of Busirane was not totally free of the gendered hostility he deflects onto the villains of The Faerie Queene, so the English sonnet tradition as a whole is marked by such hostility, however deflected, however denied it may sometimes be.

The treatment of female speech varies significantly within English Petrarchism; but it cannot be summarized as silencing.[64] To begin with, certain assumptions behind common generalizations about silencing are based on faulty logic and skewed readings. Thus to substantiate the assertion of silencing on the grounds that female speech is always reported by the male speaker and created by the male poet is to obscure the fact that the same must be said of, say, the powerful courtiers who rebuke Sidney or even of God's voice in religious sonnets and other lyrics. Moreover, female silence is only rarely mentioned directly, and the explanation that it is instead simply effected is not borne out by the poems: in some sonnets the female voice is certainly smothered, but in many others women are neither literally silenced, in that they do speak, nor metaphorically silenced, in that the import of their words often remains even when partly challenged.

In particular, one cannot persuasively maintain that metaphoric silencing occurs in that the female voice is denigrated as a merely aesthetic characteristic, preferably devoid of intellectual content. In English sonnets, as in the Rime sparse, it is certainly aestheticized, but, as I have argued, the sonneteer's own identification with Orpheus and the delight in aesthetic achievement manifest in texts such as Sidney's Apology for Poetry warn us against interpreting this process as only objectification and diminution. Moreover, the woman's words themselves are also often praised; witness, for example, Amoretti 81. Therefore a more precise and nuanced description of the workings and failings of female voices is needed to clarify both the discourses and counterdiscourses of Petrarchism.

One respect in which its women do resemble Laura is that their voices are among their most attractive attributes. Sonnet 22 of Richard Linche's

[63]Lever, Elizabethan Love Sonnet, esp. pp. 99–103, 136–137.
[64]On the silencing of women in the culture as a whole, see Lynda Boose, "Scolding Brides and Bridling Scolds: Taming the Woman's Unruly Member," SQ, 42 (1991), 179–213. Although this article is important and persuasive in many ways, certain of its conclusions are based on thin evidence (e.g., some arguments about the bridles are speculative, though intriguing) and others are complicated by my revisionist reading of silencing.

Diella, one of the minor sequences that appeared in 1596, praises his lady's cheeks, breasts, and voice, giving one line to each of the first two attributes but two lines to her voice; the twenty-fifth poem in Daniel's *Delia* celebrates the lady's "faire hand, sweete eye, rare voyce" (1) as "my harts triumvirat" (2); the eighty-first text in Spenser's *Amoretti* goes so far as to describe the woman's mouth as her fairest feature. And Watson's *Hecatompathia* devotes not one but a whole series of poems to the lady's voice.

Indeed, so common is praise of the woman's voice that it impels us to consider whether the voice, the mouth, or more likely both may have been viewed as principal sites of eroticism in Tudor England. Despite all the contemporary emphasis on gender as a constructed, not inherent, category, we have as yet devoted inadequate attention to the problem of exactly what was considered attractive in that culture—and why. The emphasis on the voice itself in so many sonnets thus encourages us to wonder to what extent sounds in general and the female voice in particular were more eroticized in early modern England than students of that culture acknowledge. And how about the mouth—was it perhaps even a fetishized representative of another, unquestionably sexual female orifice? Though, as we noted earlier, adducing theories of the grotesque body is a risky enterprise,[65] such hypotheses often comment acutely on orifices and the connections among them. Although Lynda Boose has argued that female speech, as an assertion of female power, may be seen as an appropriation and relocation of the male sexual organ,[66] women's voices are more closely associated with the female genitals. (Debating the sexuality of both the voice and the mouth provokes further speculations about texts and even periods outside our scope here. Are the allusions to gaping mouths in Marston's satires, among their other resonances, another sign of his hostility to women? Might the gaping hell-mouth in medieval literature and iconography be related to the experience, frightening though common, of catching a glimpse of a woman giving birth? If so, it would represent an unusually explicit version of the *vagina dentata*.) But more to the point now, recognizing the eroticism of the voice explicates the divided ways English Petrarchism responds to it, which range from its suppression to its celebration.

Yet that celebration, of course, is only part of the story. If the female voice may well be eroticized, it is subject to the same anxieties attending

---

[65]The most influential application of the Bakhtinian model to Renaissance literature is Peter Stallybrass, "Patriarchal Territories: The Body Enclosed," in *Rewriting the Renaissance: The Discourses of Sexual Difference in Early Modern Europe*, ed. Margaret W. Ferguson, Maureen Quilligan, and Nancy J. Vickers (Chicago: University of Chicago Press, 1986).

[66]Boose, "Scolding Brides," 203–204.

on other erotic bodily parts. Hence the ambivalences critics have long noted in treatments of female speech are in part, though only in part, sexual in the most narrow and specific sense; and hence anxieties about the voice and the organ from which it emanates are directly related not solely to woman's potential social power but also to her sexual power. Observe, for example, that the voice is clearly associated with sexual seduction in Watson's *Hecatompathia* 12. Watson describes his lady's speech as angelic but proceeds to lament its effect on him ("My hart is hurt with overmuch delight" [14]) and to portray the speaker as a latter-day Ulysses, tied to the mast.[67]

These complexities prepare us for the contradictions and variations in Petrarchan and anti-Petrarchan treatments of female speech. In some sonnets the woman, like Laura in the "in morte" poems, delivers a definitive pronouncement. In the fourth and seventeenth lyrics in Percy's *Cælia*, one of the several sequences that appeared in 1594, the poet and his mistress argue, but she literally and metaphorically has the last word. Elsewhere, as in the twenty-second poem in Fletcher's *Licia*, she plays straight man, delivering a line from which the poet can conveniently launch his sonnet. And often poems permit female speech only to counter it: the woman makes a point, variously expressed in direct or indirect discourse, and the poet then devotes the sonnet to rebutting her argument. Thus in *Diana* V.1, the mistress scornfully dismisses the poet's love as lust in line two, and in the succeeding twelve lines he disagrees; in the seventy-fifth poem of the *Amoretti*, lines five through eight are given over to the lady's warning against inscribing her name on the seashore, but in the next six lines Spenser defends his action.

Whereas many English sonnets simply do not silence the Petrarchan mistress, others, like the two just mentioned, invite us at once to adduce and to modify the concept of silencing. Devoting most or all of a sonnet to rebutting the lady's sentiments surely mutes her in several ways, yet even in these instances it is not unimportant that she is, as it were, given significant air time. When studying the poems where the female voice yields to male domination, the model of control is often more apt than that of silence in either its literal or its metaphoric senses, partly because it opens the door to the presence of some measure of agency, even in poems where the speaker dominates the beloved in many respects. Control is a more precise model in other instances as well. Thus, for example, the authors of English sequences frequently attempt to control female speech in the sense

---

[67]All citations from Watson are to *The Hecatompathia or Passionate Centurie of Love* (London, 1582).

of preserving its attractiveness while ensuring that it is unthreatening; more disturbingly, other sonnets manipulate the lady's language to express and justify the poet's own darker purposes. The Echo poems that we will examine shortly exemplify both these modified versions of silencing. Alternatively, rather than denying the power of female speech, sonneteers may render that power ambiguous and qualified; hence, as we will see, the repetitiveness of Stella's "No, no, no, my dear, let be" in Sidney's Fourth Song indicates a resolve whose potency should not be underestimated in the way some readers have done, but, like the repetitions typically associated with the Petrarchan poet himself, it also suggests a loss of power.[68]

Acknowledging such complexities prepares us to examine two entwined roles that female speech plays in the English sonnet tradition. First, it is surely significant that the woman often expresses doubts about Petrarchism, including the very doubts the poet himself may utter elsewhere. When the woman in *Amoretti* 75 dismisses as folly "a mortall thing so to immortalize" (6), she is evaluating Petrarchism from an implicitly but firmly Christian perspective, much as its religious counterdiscourse does; she is, as it were, imposing a spiritual calendar on secular temporality. And when Percy's Cœlia attacks his sighs in Sonnet 4, she is targeting the very Petrarchan mannerism that is so often condemned by anti-Petrarchan poets. Hence the female voice becomes in effect the voice of a counterdiscourse: as Ilona Bell demonstrates, it attacks not only the importunities of a specific Petrarchan lover but also the predilections of Petrarchism itself.[69] And, like the other counterdiscourses we have explored, it often engages in a continuing and unresolved battle rather than being taken prisoner, bound and gagged.

In a broader sense, the female voice in Petrarchism can stand for any unruly subordinate discourse. Involved in the often transgressive activity of writing love poetry, Petrarchan sonneteers often deploy within their verse a transgressive voice, thus again eliding the separation between subject and object. While resisting the temptation to turn these writers into proto–new historicists, one may speculate that this voice interests them not least because through it they can explore the potentialities and the limitations of

---

[68]I cite *The Poems of Sir Philip Sidney*, ed. William A. Ringler Jr. (Oxford: Clarendon, 1962).

[69]This is one of the central contentions in Ilona Bell, "Passion Lends Them Power: The Poetry and Practice of Elizabethan Courtship" (forthcoming); although our interpretations of female voices differ in a number of significant respects, I am indebted throughout to her work on female speech as an alternative to Petrarchism. Also cf. Gibbs's commentary on female speech in the *Amoretti* and other sequences (*Spenser's "Amoretti,"* pp. 44–56); the latter argues that whereas the sonnet mistress is sometimes mute, in a number of important passages her speech is quoted or reported.

many different kinds of rebellion, including their own—as long as one acknowledges that in the sonnet as in other arenas, the politics of subversion is explored through, not instead of, gender.

Insistently and even obsessively deployed in Renaissance sonnet sequences, the myth of Echo attracts Petrarchan poets for many reasons, as the poem on which this study opened would suggest.[70] It is the corollary to those writers' narcissistic posturing; its emphasis on imprisonment and repetition speaks to some of their deepest preoccupations. The sixteenth-century delight in mythology, the type of traditional etiology that is too often overlooked today, should be acknowledged. And when Echo speaks words that poets themselves might hesitate to utter, the myth allows them again to practice strategies of deflection: they devise yet another plot for excusing their own hostility, attributing it to a voice that is explicitly or, given the myth, at least implicitly female. Above all, however, Renaissance sequences so often embody the bodiless Echo because her story calls into play specific problems of female speech as a type of counterdiscourse[71] and larger issues of subversion in general.

The treatment of the myth varies greatly from poem to poem, which again warns us to avoid easy generalizations about the female voice in Petrarchism. Sometimes, as in the fifteenth sonnet in Percy's *Cælia*, the woman's words contradict and undermine the male discourse to which she is responding and in so doing undermine central assumptions of Petrarchism, recalling its counterdiscourses. Her words are particularly powerful because they turn the lover's own language against him:

> Then unto Saints in mind, She'is not unlike? *Unlike.*
> ....
> Fie, no, it is impossible. *Possible.*
>
> (3, 7)

[70]For discussions of the myth from perspectives very different from my own here, see Leonard Barkan, *The Gods Made Flesh: Metamorphosis and the Pursuit of Paganism* (New Haven: Yale University Press, 1986), esp. pp. 48–52; John Hollander, *The Figure of Echo: A Mode of Allusion in Milton and After* (Berkeley: University of California Press, 1981); and Joseph Loewenstein, *Responsive Readings: Versions of Echo in Pastoral, Epic, and the Jonsonian Masque* (New Haven: Yale University Press, 1984). Daniel's use of the myth is discussed in Bell, "Passion Lends Them Power," chap. 4.

[71]Compare Maureen Quilligan's related though different observation that Echo represents the situation of the Jacobean woman author in general and Lady Mary Wroth in particular ("The Constant Subject: Instability and Female Authority in Wroth's *Urania* Poems," in *Soliciting Interpretation: Literary Theory and Seventeenth-Century English Poetry*, ed. Elizabeth D. Harvey and Katharine Eisaman Maus [Chicago: University of Chicago Press, 1990], pp. 310–312).

Similarly, in the poem by Watson on which this book began, Echo's words challenge those of Author. Even in these instances, however, transgressive lines are juxtaposed with ones that support the aspirations of the poet and the assumptions of his discourse; thus Percy writes, "What is her face, so angel-like? *Angel-like*" (2). Echo apparently undermines not only the poet but also herself. (These contradictions suggest yet another reason the myth is appealing: Echo stages the problems with representation that are often though not invariably gendered female, because she herself is bodiless and formless and her words may likewise be paradoxical.) More often, as in Smith's *Chloris* 22, the echo conveniently backs up what the poet is saying or, as in Barnfield's thirteenth sonnet, offers new but uncontroversial answers to a query ("Speake Eccho, tell: how may I call my love? *Love*" [1]).[72] And in Percy's *Cælia* 16 as well as Barnes's Sestine 4, the echo advises aggression against an obdurate woman. Women beware women—or, rather, beware the men who speak through them.

As these instances suggest, the Echo myth allows poets to engage with the gendering of power and agency, approaching from a different vantage point many of the issues explored throughout this chapter. In a number of sonnets, Echo's voice is dependent on and secondary to the words of a man. At the same time, however, the lyrics in which the echo surprises, qualifies, or even contradicts the poet's speech again remind us that power struggles between male and female voices may be contested and unresolved.

Thus the female voice at times functions very like the other counter-discourses of Petrarchism at their most problematical: in one sense it can reshape the voice of the Italian Narcissus, Petrarch, casting back words in very different form, and yet in another sense it can only, as it were, echo the words of Petrarchism. From one perspective this counterdiscourse rewrites and revises, from another it merely repeats and reenacts. Petrarchan poets, in other words, sometimes literally gender female their own doubts about Petrarchism—and thus gender them transgressive, seductive, at once dangerously empowered and powerless.

Recognizing the many different approaches to women's voices in English Petrarchism suggests some protocols for approaching that issue elsewhere in Tudor and Stuart culture, though a detailed discussion is outside my scope now. Female silence should be read less as hegemonic ideology than as one of several conflicting and conflicted norms. Like other cultural norms, it bears a complex and variable relationship to behavior. This is not to deny that in many ways women were denied a voice in sixteenth- and seventeenth-century England. But neither the ideology nor the practice of

---

[72]I cite Klawitter, *Richard Barnfield*.

silencing women was any more consistent or monolithic than, say, the institution of marriage. In the culture as a whole, as within the sonnet tradition, contestation, contradiction, and variety are manifest in constructions of the female voice, and sometimes the subaltern does indeed speak— and speak forcefully.

Petrarchism, as its deployments of the story of Echo remind us yet again, works out its own strategies for controlling many of the anxieties associated with gender in its culture; indeed those strategies are not the least source of its appeal. For example, just as the female voice may be controlled, so the hostility that it and other female characteristics excited may be deflected onto Cupid. Yet, as I suggested, a number of the problems related to gender remain unresolved within mainstream Petrarchism. As with other problems in that discourse, they are variously minimized and mirrored in the three principal counterdiscourses traced in this chapter.

The counterdiscourse that trades youthful error for mature spirituality on one level erases the anxieties associated with gender by erasing gender itself. Loving one's God, as Barnes reminds us in the opening lyric of *A Divine Centurie of Spirituall Sonnets,* is preferable to loving one's Laura. But that poem also reminds us that eschewing the hostility that English Petrarchism often associates with sexuality is almost as difficult as eschewing sexuality itself. Might not Barnes's lengthy attack on the type of poetry he used to write—"[Cupid's] quenchlesse Torch foreshowes hell's quenchles fire, / Kindling mens wits with lustfull laies of sinne" (9–10)—both conceal and deflect an attack on the women to whom that poetry was addressed?

The counterdiscourse that emphasizes fulfilled erotic desire celebrates a different type of consummation: it transforms the threatened conflation of male and female into an ecstatic physical union. Other problems of Petrarchism, however, do not lend themselves to so easy a solution. Poems in this category remind us, if one needed any reminding, just how complicated the relationship between aggression and desire can be. Barnes's fifth sestina, for example, clearly exhibits the fusion of the aggressive drive with the sexual one. In Sonnet 13 of *Chloris,* Smith's fantasy of sexual consummation seemingly effects a radically different response, for the hostility that he elsewhere addresses to his disdainful lady is missing. In lieu of the poet attacking her verbally, the satyr attacks her physically. But that is, of course, the very point. For the priapic creature whom the poet clubs serves as the symbol not only of his desires but also of his own potential anger towards the victimized nymph whom he rescues. Or, from another perspective, the vanquished satyr also serves as the repository for hostility that the poet might otherwise direct elsewhere. He is attempting to rescue the nymph both from that assailant and from his own potential anger—

which makes it all the more telling that his fantasy of rescue proves to be only that—an unrealized fantasy.

But it is the counterdiscourse attacking other Petrarchan poetry that effects the most intriguing solutions—or apparent solutions—to the problems in question. On one level these poems, like their spiritual siblings, simply finesse such dilemmas, focusing not on desire for a woman but on disdain for other poets. But again women and the issues they raise about gender may well be most present where their presence is most repressed. To what extent is the hostility directed towards male poets redirected from its more customary target? These lyrics attempt to criticize and control the voice of those poets, a process not unlike the way English sonneteers sometimes approach the voice of the Petrarchan mistress. Anti-Petrarchists of this bent assert that representation is inadequate in conventional Petrarchism—"My mistress' eyes are nothing like the sun" (Shakespeare, 130.1)[73]—and woman, as the French feminists among others have reminded us, is associated with problems in representation.[74] This counterdiscourse accuses the poets it targets of writing without true emotion—of being, in other words, as hard-hearted, as rocklike, as a Petrarchan mistress. The parallel is not exact but close enough to invite further speculation about the subterranean impulses behind diacritical desire.

Even formulated that cautiously, however, such speculation immediately demands a proviso. My point is not that hostility towards male poets simply screens hostility towards Petrarchan mistresses or that lyrics that appear to be about the poetic are really about the erotic. Anti-Petrarchan poets are genuinely, intensely concerned about what they conceive of or construct as bad poetry; at the same time, that concern may be ignited or intensified or both by what bad poetry may represent, notably the issues at hand about gender.

VII

Who so list to hounte I know where is an hynde;
But as for me, helas, I may no more:
The vayne travaill hath weried me so sore,

[73]The citation is to Stephen Booth, ed., *Shakespeare's Sonnets* (New Haven: Yale University Press, 1977).

[74]The gendering of representation is, of course, a large and multifaceted subject. Among the most influential introductions to it is Luce Irigaray, "The Sex Which Is Not One," in *New French Feminisms: An Anthology*, ed. Elaine Marks and Isabelle de Courtivron (New York: Schocken, 1981).

I ame of theim that farthest cometh behinde;
Yet may I by no meanes my weried mynde
Drawe from the Diere: but as she fleeth afore
Faynting I folowe; I leve of therefore,
Sithens in a nett I seke to hold the wynde.
Who list her hount I put him owte of dowbte,
As well as I may spend his tyme in vain:
And graven with Diamondes in letters plain
There is written her faier neck rounde abowte:
"Noli me tangere for Cesars I ame,
And wylde for to hold though I seme tame."[75]

For all the self-consciousness of Wyatt's reactions against Petrarch here, attempts to label this lyric anti-Petrarchan are problematical. Petrarch himself attempts to give up love, as Donald L. Guss among others reminds us when discussing this text.[76] We observed earlier that elements in this lyric which seem anti- or at least un-Petrarchan may be traced to Petrarch's commentators or his Continental imitators. Indeed, because literary imitation is so often a process of reinterpretation, Wyatt's versions of Petrarch encapsulate all the problems of trying to decide when the label "anti-Petrarchan" is apt. But in a different sense, I suggest, this poem not only participates in but also analyzes the counterdiscourses of Petrarchism. Whether or not it refers to Anne Boleyn, on one important level it can fruitfully be read as a study of the problems of abandoning a particular hunt and a particular lady—and also the entire Petrarchan tradition. Thus it provides a summary of and gloss on many of the issues I have chased in this chapter.

The text both enacts and explores the two contradictory drives that I argue are at the very core of Petrarchism: the compulsion to imitate and the pressure to differentiate. The lyric is, of course, an interpretation of Petrarch's "Una candida cerva," Sonnet 190 in the *Rime sparse*, which self-consciously draws attention to its deviations from its models, proffering an alternative model for writing and loving in the ways that Thomas M. Greene has brilliantly analyzed.[77] The decision, announced but not achieved, no longer to hunt demonstrates the complexity of the poet's

---

[75]Wyatt is quoted from Kenneth Muir and Patricia Thomson, eds., *Collected Poems of Sir Thomas Wyatt* (Liverpool: Liverpool University Press, 1969).

[76]Donald L. Guss, "Wyatt's Petrarchism: An Instance of Creative Imitation in the Renaissance," *HLQ*, 29 (1965), 1–2.

[77]Greene, *The Light in Troy*, pp. 261–262. Anthony LaBranche's observations about Wyatt's "oscillating" (316) reactions to Petrarch, though brief, are also illuminating ("Imitation: Getting in Touch," *MLQ*, 31 [1970], 311–316).

responses to Petrarchism: the discourse, no less than the deer, draws him against his will. For this poem, as much as any other in the tradition, is about diacritical desire. Wyatt's speaker wants to differentiate himself from lovers who may pursue this vain hunt, from Petrarch, and from Petrarchism; he wishes to avoid both the idealizations of his Italian model and the delusions of the fictive lover he evokes. Thus "faynting I folowe" (7) refers not only to the spatial movement of the hunt but also to the process of following a model. Stephen Greenblatt has argued that Wyatt's previous critics erred in their assumption that he could or did achieve independence from literary and social conventions;[78] I argue that the possibility of that independence is thematized, questioned, and reinterpreted in the poem at hand.

Different texts and codes are played against one another throughout this lyric: Petrarch's version of the whole poem against Wyatt's, one version of the inscription against another, and Latin against English. Or, to put it another way, the struggle between imitating and differentiating is enacted through a series of purloined letters. The poem contains an intriguing series of them, enough to discourage even Lacan from ending a seminar or therapeutic session on the subject before the full fifty minutes. Signifiers are eroded and meanings destabilized throughout Wyatt's canon, as Thomas M. Greene has demonstrated,[79] so in a sense in this lyric as elsewhere language itself is purloined. Of course, the poem is borrowed from Petrarch. And much as Petrarch himself borrows and changes the collars of Roman deers that read "Caesaris sum" ("I am Caesar's") to " 'Libera farmi al mio Cesare parve' " (11; " 'It has pleased my Caesar to make me free' "),[80] so Wyatt steals Petrarch's collar and reinscribes a version of the original message. But in another sense he is also purloining the collar from the deer, because he too is announcing both the control exercised by the author of the *Rime sparse,* his Italian Caesar, and his wildness, his refusal to be held in check by the tradition.[81]

The paradoxes of anti-Petrarchan autonomy are realized by that collar itself. As readers have recognized, the relationship of line fourteen to line thirteen is problematical: does the wildness in question refer to the deer's

---

[78]Greenblatt, *Renaissance Self-Fashioning,* chap. 3, esp. p. 120.

[79]Greene, *The Light in Troy,* esp. p. 258.

[80]See *Petrarch's Lyric Poems: The "Rime sparse" and Other Lyrics,* ed. Robert M. Durling (Cambridge: Harvard University Press, 1976), p. 336.

[81]In "Becoming the Other/The Other Becoming in Wyatt's Poetry" (*ELH,* 51 [1984], 431–445), Barbara L. Estrin traces the elision between the speaker and the lady in several of Wyatt's poems, though she discovers that process in some passages where I myself do not find it.

response even to Caesar? Is the second line itself wild, itself a wild card, undercutting the meaning of the first and allowing the deer's own voice to emerge?[82] If so, there is no better example in the entire language of the workings of what Elaine Showalter, adapting the work of the social scientist Edwin Ardener, terms *double-voiced discourse*, the language of a subordinate group that both overlaps with and separates itself from that of the dominant group. It is not entirely a coincidence, in fact, that Showalter, adopting Ardener's terminology, describes the muted group as living in a "wild zone."[83]

The problems of adjudicating among these interpretations of the collar are confounded by the difficulty of determining whether we should read "wyld" (14) in the obvious sense of "not under, or not submitting to, control or restraint" or as meaning "shy; *esp.* of game, afraid of or avoiding the pursuer . . . having a timid expression like a wild animal."[84] The first suggests a rebellion against the collar and perhaps against moral standards as well, and the second, a timidity that conforms to patriarchal norms of female submission. All this is relevant if we interpret the collar as concerning the poet as well as (though certainly not rather than) the deer: as we have seen, the counterdiscourses of Petrarchism in effect attempt to reject the first line of the collar in favor of the second in asserting their own freedom from the collars and leashes of Petrarchan convention. But the reading of line fourteen which announces such freedom is fragile and unstable, much as the counterdiscourses themselves strive for an autonomy from the original which they often achieve only imperfectly and intermittently.

This collar, then, is as resonant with meaning as is Herbert's. If it represents the volatile admixture of submission and autonomy in the lady, it also stands for that admixture within the poet's own approach to Petrarchism, thus linking his rebellions and hers and again inviting us to inquire to what extent and in what ways the female voice in the sonnet tradition resembles the counterdiscourses we have been examining. To engage that question and to supplement the broad overview of this chapter with more detailed analyses, we need to turn to Sidney, Shakespeare, and Wroth.

[82]I am indebted to my graduate students in English 760 for several useful discussions of this and related problems.

[83]Elaine Showalter, "Feminist Criticism in the Wilderness," in Elizabeth Abel, ed., *Writing and Sexual Difference* (Chicago: University of Chicago Press, 1982), 29–31.

[84]*OED*, s.v. "wild." Also cf. the discussion of the word in Alastair Fowler, *Conceitful Thought: The Interpretation of English Renaissance Poems* (Edinburgh: Edinburgh University Press, 1975), p. 6.

CHAPTER FOUR

PETRARCHAN EXECUTORS:
SIDNEY, SHAKESPEARE, WROTH

I

> I First adventure, with fool-hardie might
> To tread the steps of perilous despight:
> I first adventure: follow me who list,
> And be the second English Satyrist.
> (*Virgidemiae*, I, Prologue, 1–4)[1]

Thus Joseph Hall introduces his pioneering contribution to formal verse satire. Sir Philip Sidney, however, scripts literary history and his own role within it very differently:

> Oft turning others' leaves, to see if thence would flow
> Some fresh and fruitfull showers upon my sunne-burn'd braine.
> (*Astrophil and Stella*, 1.7–8)[2]

Both poets could stake a contested yet plausible claim to the titles of harbinger and progenitor. Some previous writers had composed formal verse satires and sonnets; nonetheless, Hall and Sidney, unlike their native predecessors, fashioned entire collections of poems in their chosen genres and in so doing introduced many innovations. Neither writer, however, offers a balanced evaluation of his relationship to his forebears and putative successors. On the one hand, Hall dubiously appropriates the title of first

---

[1]Hall is quoted from Arnold Davenport, ed., *The Collected Poems of Joseph Hall* (Liverpool: Liverpool University Press, 1949).
[2]All citations from Sidney are to William A. Ringler Jr., ed., *The Poems of Sir Philip Sidney* (Oxford: Clarendon, 1962).

English satirist and constructs himself as the explorer, confidently striding forth, while on the other, Sidney presents himself as variously stumbling over and rejecting the feet of others. Hall looks forward with confidence, even cockiness, whereas Sidney claims, though with a wit that under-mines that claim, that he is nervously looking back over his shoulder. Hall fashions himself as potential patriarch, and Sidney as rebellious son. Why, then, is Sidney so concerned to define himself against and distin-guish himself from other poets? Or, to put it another way, why is his se-quence one of the most intense and hence most suggestive instances of diacritical desire in English Petrarchism? The answers to those questions are rooted both in his attitudes to Petrarchism and in the nexus of social, political, and aesthetic problems which informs *Astrophil and Stella*.

A more detailed examination of the two opening sonnets adumbrates many of those answers. These poems have been explicated so often that they may appear translucent at this point, but in fact some of their most significant lines have generally received only cursory or partial readings. Additional transgressive implications slide back and forth along the polished surfaces of those lines or hover in their depths, demonstrating in particular Sidney's ambivalence about poesy, his preoccupation with the slippery con-nections between success and failure, and the relationship of those issues to gender.

Loving in truth, and faine in verse my love to show,
That the deare She might take some pleasure of my paine:
Pleasure might cause her reade, reading might make her know,
Knowledge might pitie winne, and pitie grace obtaine,
    I sought fit words to paint the blackest face of woe,
Studying inventions fine, her wits to entertaine:
Oft turning others' leaves, to see if thence would flow
Some fresh and fruitfull showers upon my sunne-burn'd braine.
    But words came halting forth, wanting Invention's stay,
Invention, Nature's child, fled step-dame Studie's blowes,
And others' feete still seem'd but strangers in my way.
Thus great with child to speake, and helplesse in my throwes,
    Biting my trewand pen, beating my selfe for spite,
    "Foole," said my Muse to me, "looke in thy heart and write."

In interpreting this poem we confront two methodological problems that are repeatedly posed by *Astrophil and Stella*. First, in reading the interplay between success and failure in this and other lyrics in the sequence, should one assume a close bond between Astrophil and Philip Sidney? Sidney, according to some critics, diagnoses and demonstrates in Astrophil, his "speaking picture," faults of which he himself should not stand accused.[3] Thus whether or not one agrees with the scholars who find in the sequence a Christian rebuttal the speaker's cupiditas,[4] one could make a case that Sidney does not suffer from that sin. Yet that argument is undermined by the sequence itself: much as *Astrophil and Stella* anticipates the questions a reader might raise about the paradox of grounding success in narrating one's failures, so it speaks to the interpretive problem of the relationship between poet and persona. For when the extraordinary Eighth Song collapses the third- and first-person pronouns—"Leaving him so passion rent, . . . That therewith my song is broken" (102–104)—Sidney is hinting again at the implication embedded in the very name "Astrophil": his attempts to distinguish himself from his speaker are at best limited. To be sure, he tries with partial success to create a critical distance between himself and Astrophil—yet another instance of the agenda of externalization and bifurcation which operates on so many other levels throughout the sequence—but his own emotions interfere with that agenda. In short, here, as in the sequences examined in Chapter 3, speaker and poet are certainly distinct, and yet the boundaries between them are once again as unstable as those between Petrarchism and anti-Petrarchism.

Second, should the reader interpret the interplay of success and failure in this and subsequent sonnets in the sequence as merely a sign of Astrophil's canniness? Perhaps, as some critics have asserted, Astrophil's repeated laments about his own limitations are simply feints in the game of winning Stella.[5] This reading, which emphasizes male power and dominance, is attractive given the intense training in rhetorical strategies which Sidney, like many of his contemporaries, had received. But it is surely significant that those strategies for wooing Stella do not succeed: their laments of defeat are self-fulfilling prophecies. Indeed, as Pyrocles's cross-dressing re-

---

[3]See, e.g., James J. Scanlon, "Sidney's *Astrophil and Stella*: 'See what it is to Love' Sensually!" *SEL*, 16 (1976), 65–74; and Andrew D. Weiner, "Structure and 'Fore Conceit' in *Astrophil and Stella*," *TSLL*, 16 (1974), 1–25.

[4]The most detailed presentation of this case appears in two studies by Thomas P. Roche Jr., "*Astrophil and Stella*: A Radical Reading," in *Sir Philip Sidney: An Anthology of Modern Criticism*, ed. Dennis Kay (Oxford: Clarendon, 1987); and *Petrarch and the English Sonnet Sequences* (New York: AMS Press, 1989), chap. 4.

[5]See esp. Jacqueline T. Miller, " 'Love doth hold my hand': Writing and Wooing in the Sonnets of Sidney and Spenser," *ELH*, 46 (1979), 541–558; and Maureen Quilligan, "Sidney and His Queen," in *The Historical Renaissance: New Essays on Tudor and Stuart Literature and Culture*, ed. Heather Dubrow and Richard Strier (Chicago: University of Chicago Press, 1988), esp. p. 189.

minds us, Sidney understands as well as any writer how readily the mask becomes the face, how frequently we turn into what we pretend to be. Hence it is more precise to argue that Sidney attempts to deploy admissions of failure in some spheres to win victories in others, but with only partial and limited success. For finally neither the reader nor the speaker can distinguish rhetorical pretenses of inadequacy from demonstrations of it, much as observers cannot readily distinguish Pyrocles from Zelmane when he assumes that identity.

However one resolves these two interpretive problems, the opening sonnet clearly exemplifies many of the strengths of the sequence that will follow. A reading that aims to untangle the knotty ambivalences hidden in the texture of this poem, as mine will do, must first emphasize that on the whole it is woven with sophistication and skill. The carefully wrought gradatio in the opening lines, for example, fulfills the very goal it establishes, that is, bringing pleasure to a reader. Yet if the sonnet illustrates its author's command of rhetoric, it also embodies his, or his speaker's, emotional instability: the abrupt reversal in the final line, like the similar reversals in Sonnet 5, Sonnet 71, and others, mimes the abruptness of love and desire. For Sidney's swerving and skidding conclusions enact syntactically and structurally the way an unexpected encounter with the beloved, even an unexpected glance or memory, can jolt and delight. The whole earth may move only three times for lovers, but the ground beneath our feet shakes far more often, and Sidney's anticlosural reversals aptly evoke that very process.[6]

This text is unstable in other, less familiar ways as well. "I sought fit words to paint the blackest face of woe" (5) is a more complex assertion than it might appear. Although *paint* may merely signify the process of representation, in the sixteenth century as today it also carried meanings such as "to give a false colouring or complexion to" and "to feign,"[7] denotations activated in this context by the adjoining word "face" and consequent associations with the controversial subject of cosmetics. Hence the line introduces unresolved questions about art that conceals and deceives and art that disguises pain, questions to which Sidney shortly returns, as will we. But for now we may wonder in what way words that disguise

[6]Compare Marion Campbell's assertion that the sequence as a whole creates yet frustrates our anticipation of closure ("Unending Desire: Sidney's Reinvention of Petrarchan Form in *Astrophil and Stella*," in *Sir Philip Sidney and the Interpretation of Renaissance Culture: The Poet in His Time and in Ours*, ed. Gary F. Waller and Michael D. Moore [London and Totowa, N.J.: Croom Helm and Barnes and Noble, 1984], p. 92).

[7]*OED*, s.v. "paint."

and cover over are "fit" (5) and what relationship art bears to nature when it "paints" in this sense.

The poem concludes on an apparently closural answer that is craftily painted in all these senses.[8] A generation of Sidney scholars has warned us to read the final line—" 'Foole,' said my Muse to me, 'looke in thy heart and write' "—as an allusion not to romantic emotion but to the image of Stella within Astrophil's heart,[9] an interpretation that Neil L. Rudenstine nuances with the reminder that it does not preclude some reference to genuine emotion.[10] Fair enough. But, as the puns on "touch" in Sonnet 9 and similar wordplay in many other sonnets remind us, antanaclasis is one of Sidney's favorite kinswomen.[11] Given that affinity and the fact that the prevocalic h was apparently sometimes silent in Elizabethan England,[12] surely a play on "art" and "heart" is present.[13] In one sense it represents a logical culmination to the rest of the poem. Thus, since the phrase includes yet another trochaic inversion ("thy art"; emphasis added) in a line already packed with metrical variation, the line seems to suggest a contrast between Sidney's art and that of other poets and hence an anticipation of the interest in diacritical desire and innovation which characterizes his anti-Petrarchan poems. Similarly, the aural identification of Stella's image and Sidney's art intensifies the compliment to Stella which is overtly expressed in the line: she is not merely the Muse inspiring his art but also its embodiment.

On another level, however, this same pun deconstructs the very opposition that Sidney has apparently been concerned to establish, here and elsewhere in his canon, between art and that best representative of nature, Stella herself. If the seat of her image is equated with his art, the seemingly stable boundary between deriving inspiration from Stella and from aesthetic strategies collapses; the writer whose *Apology for Poetry* praises Antonius and Crassus for the art that conceals art here conceals "art" within his own

---

[8]Patricia Fumerton argues from a different perspective that the poem undercuts its claim to present pure, unmediated feeling; she notes that the Muse speaks for Sidney in the final line (*Cultural Aesthetics: Renaissance Literature and the Practice of Social Ornament* [Chicago: University of Chicago Press, 1992], pp. 102–103).

[9]See, e.g., Ringler, *Poems of Sir Philip Sidney*, p. 459.

[10]Neil L. Rudenstine, *Sidney's Poetic Development* (Cambridge: Harvard University Press, 1967), p. 200.

[11]On Sidney's propensity for punning, see Alan Sinfield, "Sexual Puns in 'Astrophil and Stella,' " *EIC*, 24 (1974), 341–355.

[12]On the controversial and vexed issue of the pronunciation of h, see Fausto Cercignani, *Shakespeare's Works and Elizabethan Pronunciation* (Oxford: Clarendon, 1981), pp. 332–343.

[13]In *The "Inward" Language: Sonnets of Wyatt, Sidney, Shakespeare, Donne* (Chicago: University of Chicago Press, 1983), chap. 4, Anne Ferry discusses Sidney's preoccupation with the heart from a different perspective, arguing that he and Shakespeare manifest a new preoccupation with the inability of language to express inner being.

heart, here hides his craft, "bravely maskt" (3.2) as Stella. My point is not
that the pun in question is a primary meaning—it remains elusive at best—
but that its presence, however flickering and fleeting, undercuts the stability
of language and the sincerity of its manipulators. Moreover, it implicitly
equates ostensibly unmediated personal emotion with the mediations of art
and thus also calls into question the stability of the subject. "I am not I"
(45.14) indeed, and poststructuralism could have taught Sidney nothing he
did not already know and manifest here about threats to subjectivity.[14]

Allusions to children and other family members recur throughout the
sequence, but nowhere are they more tantalizing than in the poem at hand.
We should, as critics have pointed out, trace "sunne-burn'd" (8) not only
to Sidney's darker redaction of Thomas Wilson's trope for imitation but
also to a pun on the term for a male child.[15] The sonnet also describes
invention as "Nature's child" (10), implicitly alludes to· a schoolboy in
"trewand" (13), and evokes a stepmother and a woman in labor. Cristina
Malcolmson, adducing object relations theory, argues that Sidney defines
desire as in part familial and thus relates the development of the self to
disillusionment with the mother.[16] Certainly the repeated allusions to familial roles, here and elsewhere in Sidney's canon, justify psychoanalytic
inquiries. In this instance, however, the family romance is complicated by
ambivalence towards not only the maternal role but also the artistic role
that Sidney is assuming. The anxiety of influence that distinguishes his
poem from Hall's is, I would argue, deflected here from literary fathers to
a stepmother, a figure often assigned the role of whipping boy.[17] The stepmother may represent both Sidney's threatening progenitors and Sidney
himself. Doubts about the legitimacy of his literary undertaking, grounded
in the many reservations expressed in the *Apology for Poetry* about poesy in

[14]Compare Gary F. Waller's argument that both Petrarchism and Protestantism involve
decentered selves ("The Rewriting of Petrarch: Sidney and the Languages of Sixteenth–
Century Poetry," in *Sidney and the Interpretation of Renaissance Culture*, ed. Waller and Moore).

[15]On the echo of Wilson, see Russell M. Brown, "Sidney's *Astrophil and Stella*, 1," *Explicator*, 32 (1973), item 21; and David Kalstone, *Sidney's Poetry: Contexts and Interpretations*
(Cambridge: Harvard University Press, 1965), pp. 127–128. On familial references
throughout the sequence, see Cristina Malcolmson, "Politics and Psychoanalysis: Sidney's
Imagery of the Child," unpublished paper delivered at the 1990 Modern Language Association convention, Chicago. Similarly, in her unpublished essay "From Canticles to Edmund
Spenser's *Amoretti*," Theresa Krier traces the influence of maternal/filial relations on Spenser's
sequence. I thank Cristina Malcolmson and Theresa Krier for making their work available
to me.

[16]Malcolmson, "Politics and Psychoanalysis."

[17]On using stepmothers to express aggression originally intended for mothers, see Bruno
Bettelheim, *The Uses of Enchantment: The Meaning and Importance of Fairy Tales* (New York:
Alfred A. Knopf, 1976), esp. pp. 66–73.

general and lyric in particular, may spur him to evoke a figure who is doubly dubious: a stepmother is female and is often seen as a familial usurper. To Sidney and other members of his generation, who had witnessed the loss and replacement of mothers in the wake of the mortality crisis of 1557–1559, such references to stepmothers must have been especially resonant.

Having identified with the errant schoolboy, he proceeds almost immediately to construct himself as the woman in labor, an abrupt shift that foreshadows the shifts in other kinds of power relationships which recur throughout the sequence. In one sense, this merely continues the deflection present in the reference to the "step-dame Studie" (10): resentful of powerful literary progenitors and ambivalent about expressing that resentment, he rechannels tensions about paternal figures towards a less powerful but perhaps more threatening maternal authority and then diminishes that authority by presenting her as "helplesse" (12).[18] Thus the regendering facilitates delimiting the power he fears. At the same time, however, may not the shift from the schoolboy to the obstetrical patient enact an autobiographical allegory about this moment in Sidney's own career? Having started out in texts such as *Certaine Sonnets* as the "sunne-burn'd" pupil, he is now ready to assume the role of creator by composing a major sonnet sequence, but his anxiety about doing so leads him to present himself as suffering mother-to-be, not confident father. In short, then, rather than simply segueing from a playful yet painful description of the poet's failures to a tribute to Stella, the poem introduces into the sequence anxieties that are not definitively resolved by the final line, particularly those about the failures that art may represent in more than one sense of that verb.

Indeed, the succeeding sonnet expresses entrapment not only in love but also in and by art and thus draws our attention to the connection between those dilemmas. Its opening, as many readers have observed, demonstrates Sidney's independence from the conventions of love at first sight. Admitting his subservience and associating loss of social position with loss of national identity, he compares himself to a "slave-borne *Muscovite*" (10). Sidney proceeds to introduce a preoccupation that is to recur throughout the sequence: the shame involved in both experiencing and, even worse, accepting enslavement.

It is telling, however, that Sidney focuses here on the process of describing—or painting—that tyranny: "I *call it* praise to suffer Tyrannie" (11;

---

[18]Richard C. McCoy, however, argues that this image represents a further regression (*Sir Philip Sidney: Rebellion in Arcadia* [New Brunswick, N.J.: Rutgers University Press, 1979], p. 76).

emphasis added). This allusion prepares us for the focus on self-deception and the deception of others on which the poem concludes:

> And now employ the remnant of my wit,
> To make my selfe beleeve, that all is well,
> While with a feeling skill I paint my hell.
>
> (12–14)

The final line of this poem, like the comparable allusion to painting in the previous sonnet, on one level refers merely to mimetic representation but on another level suggests the process of fairing the foul that Shakespeare was to find so threatening. That line, again like its counterparts in Shakespeare's sonnets, also suggests the slippage between deceiving oneself and others. These parallels anticipate the somewhat different reference to hell at the end of Shakespeare's Sonnet 129 ("To shun the heav'n that leads men to this hell" [14])[19] and in so doing invite us to ask whether Sidney's hell might in some way allude to its source, the heavenly Stella, whose name is repeatedly echoed in the sounds of the couplet?[20] The respect with which most of the other poems describe her immediately enjoins us to consider that reading unlikely—yet the very fact that it seems so unlikely may be another version of painting a hell so that it appears heavenly.

The opening two sonnets, then, introduce queries about the relationship of success and failure, the perils of art, and the connections of those problems to gender which will arise throughout the sequence. That relationship between success and failure is, as I have been arguing, at the core of the Petrarchan tradition: all sequences pivot on the poet's attempts to succeed in the sense of winning the lady and the consequences of his failure to do so. But no other English sequence is quite as involved with these two terms as is Sidney's, perhaps in part because of his keen awareness of his own "great expectations" and of how they had been destroyed by the marriage of the earl of Leicester in 1578 and the subsequent birth of his son.[21] Having opened on a poem that focuses on failure, he proceeds later

[19]All citations from Shakespeare's sonnets are to Stephen Booth, ed., *Shakespeare's Sonnets* (New Haven: Yale University Press, 1977).

[20]I am indebted to Nona Fienberg for the observation that Stella's name is inscribed in these lines.

[21]On the consequences of this marriage, see Katherine Duncan-Jones, *Sir Philip Sidney: Courtier Poet* (New Haven: Yale University Press, 1991), esp. pp. 156–157 and chap. 9. In "Turning Others' Leaves: Astrophil's Untimely Defeat," *Spenser Studies*, 10 (1992), 197–212, Christopher Martin notes the emphasis on waste, delay, and defeat in the sequence; his observation that Sidney often attacks others for his own faults also parallels my argument, though from a different perspective.

in the sequence to present his own verse as a source and symbol of both his power (his verbal agility comes to represent sexual ability, as Margreta de Grazia among others points out)[22] and his powerlessness. According to the traditional rhetorical analyses of the suasive force of poesy, Astrophil yields a mighty weapon and yields it with consummate skill. At the same time, the sequence repeatedly reminds us of his failures as both a poet and a lover.[23] In addition, these poems draw attention to many other arenas in which contestants, literal or figurative, struggle for success—tournaments, courtly politics, and so on.

In Shakespeare's *Sonnets*, as in Petrarch's poetry, narrativity is implicated in those struggles. But here, unlike Petrarch's poetry, its role is the straight-forward one critics of nineteenth- and twentieth-century texts have generally assigned to it: the ability to narrate both represents and produces other forms of mastery. Thus Sidney repeatedly uses mythological narratives etiologically: in the eighth sonnet, for example, his ability to craft an urbane story about love's emigration from Greece to Stella's face suggests his own detachment and power, even while he is admitting that he himself is now Cupid's hotel room. The panache of his narrative skills enables and justifies the culmination of the poem, in which he transforms his own love wound into an injury experienced by Cupid—"He burnt unwares his wings, and cannot fly away" (14)—a deflection that anticipates patterns elsewhere in the sequence. Similarly, in Sonnet 17, when narrating the story of his falling in love, he constructs Cupid as an unhappy child, revising his source, a neo-Latin epigram by Pontano, to play up the god's childishness and dependency.[24] In short, Sidney deploys narratives about his own failure to achieve a kind of success. Yet, characteristically, rather than denying that paradox, he draws attention to it. In particular, Sonnet 34 renders what must have been internal doubts about such narratives into an externalized dramatic dialogue: " 'Art not asham'd to publish thy disease?' / Nay, that may breed my fame, it is so rare" (5–6).

The dynamics of success and failure in the sequence are also manifest in the power struggles around which it is structured.[25] The obvious, overt

[22]On connections between desire and writing in the sequence, see, e.g., Campbell, "Unending Desire," p. 86; and Margreta de Grazia, "Lost Potential in Grammar and Nature: Sidney's *Astrophil and Stella*," *SEL*, 21 (1981), 32.

[23]On his failures as a poet, cf. Martin, "Turning Others' Leaves," esp. pp. 207–208.

[24]For a different but not incompatible analysis of Sidney's revision of this source, see J. W. Lever, *The Elizabethan Love Sonnet*, 2d. ed. (London: Methuen, 1966), p. 62.

[25]See esp. Nona Fienberg, "The Emergence of Stella in *Astrophil and Stella*," *SEL*, 25 (1985), 5–19; Clark Hulse, "Stella's Wit: Penelope Rich as Reader of Sidney's Sonnets," in *Rewriting the Renaissance: The Discourses of Sexual Difference in Early Modern Europe*, ed. Mar-

one, the contest between Stella and Astrophil, is refracted in battles between Astrophil and the court wits or between Cupid and his mother.
These struggles are characterized above all by their volatility and unpre-
dictability—victories are often Pyrrhic, and apparent conquests are limited
and temporary. Many different and conflicting types of power and arenas
for winning it are uneasily juxtaposed. Thus in Sonnet 49 Sidney plays the
equestrian paradigm for passion, a commonplace that can be traced back
to Plato, against the tale of himself as victorious rider:

> I on my horse, and *Love* on me doth trie
> Our horsmanships, while by strange worke I prove
> A horsman to my horse, a horse to *Love*.
>
> (1–3)

As Clark Hulse aptly observes, the sequence is based on a "complex and
pluralistic transaction" among varied power centers.[26] Or, to return to an
earlier debate, to privilege the "act of public mastery" in these poems over
the poet's portrayal of himself "as humble suitor to a dominating lady" is
to privilege certain contemporary assumptions about hegemony over the
more indeterminate and dynamic workings of power in late sixteenth-
century England.[27]

Those contemporary assumptions do, however, help us to interpret the
politics of Sidney's interplay between success and failure and power and
powerlessness by directing our attention to his preoccupation with dependence, which at its outer limits descends to total helplessness. Richard
C. McCoy, extending his valuable analysis of submissiveness and authority
in Sidney's prose, has emphasized Astrophil's submission to Stella.[28] More
precisely, however, that is but part of a larger pattern in the sequence which
can better be evaluated as dependence than submissiveness. Sidney depends
on rhetorical authorities and on the image of Stella, chides other writers
for their dependence on their forebears ("*Pindare's* Apes" [3.3]), mocks
Cupid for his boyish dependence, and repeatedly evokes images of dependent children. Whether or not the Fifth Song was originally written

---

garet W. Ferguson, Maureen Quilligan, and Nancy J. Vickers (Chicago: University of Chicago Press, 1986); and Miller, " 'Love doth hold my hand.' "

[26]Hulse, "Stella's Wit," p. 286.

[27]Ann Rosalind Jones and Peter Stallybrass, "The Politics of *Astrophil and Stella*," *SEL*,
24 (1984), 54.

[28]McCoy, *Sir Philip Sidney*, chap. 3.

for *Astrophil and Stella*,[29] its connections between dependency, threatening, and being threatened recur throughout the sequence (as well as in the texts by Lady Mary Wroth, Sidney's niece, to which we will turn shortly, and in the "ugly beauty" poems we will examine in Chapter 5). Again, some critics have attempted to dismiss allusions to dependence as a clever game that in fact ensures domination,[30] and once more that explanation is only partially true. For one thing, it ignores an even more ominous agenda: acknowledging dependence on Stella entails not only complimenting her overtly but also blaming her covertly for the demands of the infected (and erected) will. More to our purposes, to the extent that admissions of dependency are a game, neither Sidney nor Astrophil wins it completely. Associating dependency with the court, the queen, and his literary predecessors, Sidney expresses fears of it throughout his career and nowhere more than in his sonnet sequence. He variously parlays those fears into a modicum of reassurance by presenting them as a comic turn in the first sonnet and deflecting them onto Cupid, who is constructed as a helpless, dependent child in such poems as Sonnet 17, or onto other lovers, who are labeled "babes" in Sonnet 16 (7). And he crafts a counterdiscourse that allows him to rewrite the dependence that he controls only imperfectly elsewhere in the sequence.

Just as the preoccupations with failure and dependency in Sonnet 1 recur throughout the sequence, so too do the aesthetic questions raised there reappear in many later poems. If Sidney's *Apology for Poetry* explicitly defends lyric from its critics, it implicitly incorporates its author's own reservations and anxieties (notice, for example, the curious negative syntax in the observation "Other sorts of Poetry almost have we none, but that lyrical kind of songs and sonnets,"[31] a peculiar prologue to a sentence that goes on to defend spiritual uses of "that lyrical kind"). Equally telling is how Sidney defends lyric from the charge of "effeminate wantonness" (p. 129) in the *Apology*: he argues that this accusation could not be relevant to a society in which women were shared—without suggesting that lyric would necessarily be innocent of it under other circumstances. Similarly, *Astrophil and Stella* repeatedly dwells on the fear that the languages of love are deceptive and destructive. Sidney frames that question in terms of interest to

[29]On the interpretive problems posed by this poem, see James Finn Cotter, "The Songs in *Astrophil and Stella*," SP, 67 (1970), 186–190; and Roche, "*Astrophil and Stella*," pp. 207–208.

[30]See, e.g., Quilligan, "Sidney and His Queen."

[31]Sir Philip Sidney, *An Apology for Poetry or The Defence of Poesy*, ed. Geoffrey Shepherd (London: Nelson, 1965), p. 137. Further page references to this edition will appear in the text.

contemporary pragmatists, for, as we have already seen, one measure of the deceptiveness of language is that even the act of identifying and attacking its strategies may be implicated in those strategies—"while with a feeling skill I paint my hell" (2.14). This propensity of language is yet another reason why reading Sidney's admissions of failure and doubt as a game does not establish him as its victor.

Sidney's mode of anti-Petrarchism seeks to mediate conflicts about success and failure, dependence and independence, power and powerlessness, and in addition it addresses his concerns about the deceptiveness of art. It is no accident that our two touchstones, Sonnets 1 and 2, are followed sequentially by the first of Sidney's anti-Petrarchan sonnets, for that pattern enacts structurally the intimate relationship between the problematics introduced in those first two texts and the counterdiscourses of Petrarchism.

As many readers have uneasily recognized, Astrophil's Petrarchism is seemingly not free of the faults chronicled in his anti-Petrarchan poems: he appears to commit the very errors he condemns, raiding Petrarchism in more sense than one of the verb. Denying this problem, certain scholars have asserted that Astrophil attacks only the abuses of Petrarchism, which he himself avoids, not the uses of the tradition that his own work exemplifies.[32] Others have argued instead that the anti-Petrarchism is merely another of Sidney's ploys, a ruse that creates a useful impression of forthrightness and trustworthiness.[33] But the best analysis of this issue, like so many others raised by Sidney's poetry, is David Kalstone's assertion that Astrophil's comments on style represent "a series of rather troubled and self-conscious gestures" rather than systematic suggestions for reform. "His straining after sincerity," Kalstone continues, "suggests an uncertainty about the inherited vocabulary of love poetry."[34] My analysis, building on yet rebuilding that perception, attempts to redefine the etiology of Sidney's uncertainty about love and several other issues.

Samples from Sonnets 15 and 55 provide the clearest introduction to these and other questions about Sidney's anti-Petrarchism.

> You that do search for everie purling spring,
>   Which from the ribs of old *Parnassus* flowes,
>   And everie floure, not sweet perhaps, which growes
> Neare therabout, into your Poesie wring;

---

[32] See, e.g., Robert L. Montgomery Jr., *Symmetry and Sense: The Poetry of Sir Philip Sidney* (Austin: University of Texas Press, 1961), p. 109.

[33] See, e.g., Jean Robertson, "Sir Philip Sidney and His Poetry," in *Elizabethan Poetry*, Stratford–upon–Avon Studies 2 (London: Edward Arnold, 1960).

[34] Kalstone, *Sidney's Poetry*, p. 130.

> You that do Dictionarie's methode bring
> Into your rimes, running in ratling rowes:
> You that poore *Petrarch's* long deceased woes,
> With new-borne sighes and denisend wit do sing;
> You take wrong waies, those far-fet helpes be such,
> As do bewray a want of inward tuch.
>
> (15.1–10)

It is telling that this poem attacks not only Petrarchists but also other literary practitioners, such as addicts of alliteration: just as Sidney's doubts about Petrarchism are intertwined with broader aesthetic concerns, so he deploys the counterdiscourses of Petrarchism to attempt to resolve a number of literary problems only tangentially connected to the sonnet tradition. The same scope is manifest in his references to "far-fet helpes" (9) and "deni-send wit" (8), which implicitly ally his literary program with nationalism. In fact, although William A. Ringler Jr. persuasively interprets "inward tuch" (10) as "natural capacity,"[35] surely the sixteenth-century denotation of "inward" as "pertaining to the country or place itself; domestic" is relevant as well.[36]

Structured around the *then/now* opposition that we have traced in so many other Petrarchan poems, Sonnet 55 contrasts the way its speaker used to love with how he does so now:

> Muses, I oft invoked your holy ayde,
> With choisest flowers my speech to engarland so;
> . . . .
> But now I meane no more your helpe to trie,
> Nor other sugring of my speech to prove,
> But on her name incessantly to crie.
>
> (1–2, 9–11)

Here, as in Sonnet 15, Sidney raises broader literary issues of which conventional Petrarchism is but one manifestation. In this poem, however, Sidney transforms the spatial contrasts of Sonnet 15 into temporal dichotomies. Fashioning yet another version of narrative displacement, he declares that once he loved the wrong way, but now, inspired by Stella, he has seen the light.

Both texts, then, direct our attention to the metonymic thrust of Sidney's counterdiscourse. He repeatedly deflects concerns about his art onto the

---

[35] Ringler, *Poems of Sir Philip Sidney*, p. 466.
[36] *OED*, s.v. "inward."

practices of other poets or onto his literary past, and he variously displaces
faults in English poesy in general onto foreign practices or Petrarchism in
particular. Such patterns of deflection are evident when Sidney focuses on
stylistic issues, which he does most notably in Sonnets 3, 6, and 15. Like
many other anti-Petrarchan lyrics, these texts attack the practices of re-
hashing tired conventions and phrases and borrowing foreign traditions. In
so doing, as we have already seen, Sidney alludes not only to the faults of
Petrarchism but also to flaws in several other styles and genres, so that
Sonnet 6, for example, refers explicitly to the "shepheard's pipe" (7).[37] In
one sense Petrarchism interests him less than it interests other sonneteers
because in another sense it interests him more: that is, it synecdochically
represents faults manifest in those other modes of writing too.[38]

When these poems are read in relationship to the anxieties about art
expressed in their author's *Apology for Poetry*, however, it is clear that he is
narrowing his lens as well as widening it. For the poet who elsewhere
expresses broader concerns about the corruptions of language and its practitioners,[39] who fears that our infected will makes us prone to misuse the
very faculty that distinguishes us from the beasts, here implies that only
certain schools and styles are at fault. Criticizing Petrarchism and selected
other stylistic modes allows him to localize the dangers he apprehends, to
contain the contagion, thus implying that other forms of language, whether
they be the honest speech of native poets or the way he now writes in
contrast to the way he once did, are uncontaminated by those dangers.
Similarly, it is no accident that reliance on other writers is, as the phrase
"*Pindare's* Apes" (3.3) reminds us,[40] one of his most frequent charges: the
fear of dependence that runs throughout his canon is, as we saw when
examining Sonnet 15, deflected onto the imitative verse of other poets.
And once again the problematics of dependence may conceal and reveal
the perils of gender: might not his fear of the excesses of his own sexuality
partly explain his condemnation of the rhetorical excesses of those poets?

---

[37]Compare A. E. Voss, "The 'Right Poet' in *Astrophil and Stella*," *Unisa English Studies*,
24 (1986), 9.

[38]Many critics have observed Sidney's preoccupation with the dangers of art; see, e.g.,
Ronald Levao, "Sidney's Feigned *Apology*," *PMLA*, 94 (1979), 223–233.

[39]Compare Levao; and Jacqueline Miller, " 'What May Words Say': The Limits of Language in *Astrophil and Stella*," in *Sidney and the Interpretation of Renaissance Culture*, ed. Waller
and Moore.

[40]On the possibility that Sidney alludes to Pindar's Second Pythian Ode, see E. J. Dev-
ereux, "A Possible Source for 'Pindare's Apes' in Sonnet 3 of 'Astrophil and Stella,' " *NQ*,
24 (1977), 521.

We have, after all, already observed that he repeatedly connects modes of writing with modes of desiring.[41]

Sidney's anti-Petrarchan poems, then, mediate his preoccupations with social behavior as well as his concerns about literary style. In some of his sonnets he works out his ambivalences about authority and dependence through the figure of Cupid, variously dramatizing Venus's son as a helpless or rebellious child and at times addressing that mythological character from a position of knowing authority that he himself assumes. Lady Mary Wroth was to deploy Cupid very differently in her own struggles with autonomy.

Anti-Petrarchism permits a related solution to Sidney's concerns about dependence. Attributing to sonneteers an unseemly reliance on the work of others, he implies that they, like Cupid, are submissive children, displacing his own putative loss of autonomy onto them. In so doing he has it both ways, implicitly assuming multiple roles. Like Pyrocles and Musidorus, the poet who opens his sequence by characterizing himself as "sunne-burn'd" (1.8) reacts against the paternal authority of Petrarch and Pindar. And yet, like Euarchus, at the same time he establishes himself as an authority, indeed as a judge: it is he who will establish the faults in bad poesy and lead the way to its alternative. And it is he who is a success, not least because of his ability to uncover the failures of other poets.

In uncovering those failures, however, he complicates the displacement we are analyzing—and compromises some common modes of anatomizing the anxiety of influence. "Pindare's Apes" (3.3) may well refer to Ronsard,[42] whom Sidney is likely to have seen as a member of an older generation; but many other attacks in Astrophil and Stella are directed to poets who, rather than being paternal figures, are in or close to Sidney's own age cohort. Such passages warn us to interpret allusions to poetic competition, whether in Sidney's poems or in those of other writers, with great care: as I have suggested, the power of ostensibly rejected Freudian models is manifest in many critics' tendency to assume that rivalries among brothers merely disguise the primary Oedipal conflicts, but for many writers they may be equally powerful in their own right, especially given the repercussions of the mortality crises which I discussed in Chapter 1.

Despite—or because of—Sidney's strategies for addressing both inter- and intragenerational tensions, some of the aesthetic problems behind the sequence are not completely resolved. In particular, he remains ambivalent about both ornate rhetoric and one of its chief exemplars, the Petrarchan

---

[41]Compare de Grazia, "Lost Potential in Grammar and Nature," p. 32.

[42]See Anne Lake Prescott, French Poets and the English Renaissance: Studies in Fame and Transformation (New Haven: Yale University Press, 1978), p. 110.

tradition itself. The contradictions between his aesthetic pronouncements and his own practices should not be explained away with the claim that he is merely rebuking those who misuse rhetoric: Sonnets 3, 6, and 15 do not clearly distinguish its uses from its abuses. The best analyses of his style, notably the studies by Kalstone and Rudenstine,[43] replace the notion that Sidney gradually abandoned a courtly, highly ornamented mode of writing for a simpler one with the recognition that throughout his short career he was attracted to and skilled in many different modes of writing. Nor was he entirely comfortable with the apparent alternative to ornateness, that is, simple, straightforward language. Like Shakespeare, he at times violates his own allegiance to it.[44] And it is telling that he parodies such rhetoric in Sonnet 74, showing that it readily descends to the wooden and naïve.[45] Sidney, then, is conscious that all levels of style are liable to abuse, and he certainly does not consider simple diction a ready alternative to the tricks of *"Pindare's* Apes" (3.3) and other members of their menagerie.

If he cannot completely resolve these problems, however, he does effect a strategy for sidestepping them. While declaring that Stella is the answer to all aesthetic dilemmas allows Sidney economically to dovetail courtly compliment and literary critique, it also permits him to finesse the dilemma of offering a more precise alternative to the literary faults he criticizes. Claiming that writing about Stella will solve one's aesthetic problems is an urbane and clever solution for a poet intensely aware of how intractable some of those problems really are. He responds, in short, to the aesthetic and other confusions that Kalstone diagnoses in part by deflecting those confusions onto other poets and in part by localizing their solution in Stella herself.

But if Stella is part of the solution to the faults of Petrarchism, she is also, of course, part of the challenge to those faults; if she is constructed as the decisive rejoinder to those who condemn that discourse, she repeatedly condemns it herself. Just as Sidney's internal conflicts about a range of aesthetic and social issues are deflected onto dramatic encounters between Astrophil and court wits or Astrophil and other poets, so they are projected onto the interplay between Stella and Astrophil. Her voice in the sequence,

---

[43]Kalstone, *Sidney's Poetry*, esp. chap. 5; and Rudenstine, *Sidney's Poetic Development*.

[44]Compare Ferry, *"Inward" Language*, esp. pp. 176–178, 202.

[45]On this curious sonnet, see Ann Romayne Howe, *"Astrophel and Stella*: 'Why and How,'" *SP*, 61 (1964), 155–156; and Richard B. Young, "English Petrarke: A Study of Sidney's *Astrophel and Stella*," in *Three Studies in the Renaissance: Sidney, Jonson, and Milton* (New Haven: Yale University Press, 1958), pp. 7–8. Young's discussion includes the passing observation that Sidney characteristically defines himself through contrasts (p. 8), a point very germane to my arguments.

like that of Petrarch's Laura, assumes multiple and contradictory roles but is often positioned as the counterdiscourse that criticizes not only Astrophil in particular but also Petrarchism in general. In so doing, it provides one of the clearest examples in the English Petrarchan tradition of the workings of female speech—and of the dangers of reducing that complex phenomenon to broad generalizations about silencing.[46]

Not only does Stella speak, but the power and significance of her speech are also emphasized at several points in the sequence. In Sonnet 77, for example, Sidney apportions one characteristic of Stella to each of the first seven lines—but devotes the next six lines to her speech and its consequences, celebrating the "high comforts" (10) of her conversation. Sonnet 62 stresses her exhortations to virtue. In the Eighth Song her words silence his.

Stella's words, like those of Laura and some of the Echo figures examined in Chapter 3, assume multiple and contradictory functions. These contradictions are further destabilized because Sidney cannot produce narrative displacement as Petrarch does: he cannot, that is, sort out conflicting perspectives on his lady's speech and assign them respectively to "in vita" and "in morte" sonnets. Stella's language is indubitably associated with the erotic; both words and kisses can issue from her "swelling lip" (1), Sonnet 80 reminds us. Yet the same text contains the phrase "wisedome's beautifier" (6), thus once again creating a connection between the aesthetic and moral functions of female speech. With all due respect to some common generalizations about objectification, "beautifier" does not necessarily diminish "wisedome" or demean the speech in question. As I have argued, sixteenth-century readers would surely have recognized that aesthetic beauty can be a source and even a condition for rhetorical power; delighting and instructing are, of course, closely connected achievements, according to Horace's *Ars Poetica* (99–100, 333–346) and many other texts of classical rhetoric as well. The relationship between wisdom and beauty is more ambiguous in another tribute to Stella's language, however: "*Stella,* whose voice when it speakes, / Senses all asunder breakes" (Eighth Song, 37–38). Although the primary meaning of the words is that her voice is powerful and beautiful enough to overwhelm the listener, a hint that its force destroys "sense" as well as "senses" clings to the lines.

Yet the power of Stella's voice is frequently limited, thus reminding us that in certain cases the conventional wisdom on the silencing of women

---

[46]Nona Fienberg is one of the few other critics to draw attention to the fact that Stella speaks; her argument differs from mine, however, in her contention that nonetheless Stella is silenced as the sequence draws towards a close ("The Emergence of Stella.").

needs to be refined, not rejected. One aim of that voice is to criticize Petrarchism; like that of Spenser's lady, which it resembles in many ways,[47] it often functions as the kind of counterdiscourse which offers an ethical and spiritual alternative to the yearnings of Petrarchism. Stella can teach and delight as she propounds her counterdiscourse; she cannot, however, move Astrophil to abandon love for higher pursuits. In that regard her voice is as impotent as Astrophil's own; neither of them realizes their respective contradictory goals of moral education and seduction. Similarly, in the Third Song, for example, she is compared to Orpheus, a mythological role the Petrarchan lover often assumes; in the Fourth Song she is enchained in repetitiveness, a rhetorical pattern that often entraps the Petrarchan lover.

The Fourth and Eighth Songs body forth these and other characteristics of Stella's voice particularly dramatically. Although some readers have claimed that in the first of those poems Stella's final "No, no, no, no, my Deare, let be" signals her yielding to him,[48] it is hard to believe that in a sequence as carefully written as this one, other signs of that event would not be manifest in some form, however coded, in adjoining poems. When that interpretation is abandoned, it becomes clear that the poem plays the power—and the impotence—of the two voices against each other and in so doing demonstrates, as Petrarchism and its counterdiscourses so often do, the variety of forms that power may assume. Her repetitiveness at once signals the limitations of her speech (a new avatar of Echo, she is condemned to rehearse her own words) and also its unyielding firmness. It signals, too, further parallels and elisions between the male and female figures in the sequence: repetition is, we have noted, the primary symptom of the pathologies of Petrarchism. Astrophil himself expresses but does not achieve the aim often ascribed to Petrarchan poets, mastering the lady and her body: "Write, but first let me endite" (40), with a witty and disturbing suggestion that her body will be his parchment, is his unrealized plea. It is telling, too, that even while arguing for the chronological primacy of his own writing, he figures her as a type of writer, though of letters rather than sonnets; the relationship of their voices is contestatory, as that of Petrarchism and anti-Petrarchism so often is.

In the Eighth Song, the use of the definite article and of third-person

---

[47]For a different but compatible analysis of how Spenser's lady opposes his Petrarchan statements, see William J. Kennedy, *Authorizing Petrarch* (Ithaca: Cornell University Press, 1994), chap. 5.

[48]See, e.g., Russell M. Brown, "Sidney's *Astrophil and Stella,* Fourth Song," *Explicator,* 29 (1971), item 48.

plural pronouns once again links those voices and renders them temporarily indistinguishable:

> *Their* eares hungry of each word,
> Which *the* deere tongue would afford,
> . . . .
> But when *their* tongues could not speake,
> Love it selfe did silence breake.
>
> (21–22, 25–26; emphasis added)

In the speech by Astrophil which follows, his claim to be speechless may indeed be a feint, especially since he follows it almost immediately with the familiar ploys of a persuasion poem. In response to those maneuvers, however, Stella delivers a moral counterdiscourse that silences not only the song but also the pretense on which it is grounded of separating Astrophil and Philip:

> Therewithall away she went,
> Leaving him so passion rent,
> With what she had done and spoken,
> That therewith my song is broken.
>
> (101–104)

The fact that Astrophil is not permanently silenced warns us against overestimating the power of Stella's words; the fact that throughout the sequence he is periodically troubled by the doubts Stella's words express and permanently unable to overcome their objections warns us against underestimating their power.

Stella's voice, then, encapsulates many patterns that recur in the counterdiscourses of Petrarchism in general and one manifestation of those counterdiscourses, the female voice, in particular. Contradictory cultural attitudes towards female speech are suggested by the contradictory realizations of it in the sonnet tradition; one is once again reminded that silence is only one of several conflicting norms for woman's speech in sixteenth-century England. Sidney's sequence also reminds us of the varied forms of power to which speech may aspire: Stella's words delight and instruct Astrophil, Astrophil's words delight the reader whether or not they do the same for Stella, but neither character can move the other to adopt her or his perspective on love. Thus Stella's words both participate in unresolved gendered tensions and externalize tensions within Astrophil and Sidney about literary and social practices.

The sequence can also direct our attention to two problems in our own critical practices: our approaches to aesthetic issues and to social status in sixteenth-century England. *Astrophil and Stella* demonstrates the dangers of either analyzing Sidney's style at the expense of studying his position at court, as an earlier generation of critics was prone to do, or, alternatively, reversing those priorities as contemporary critics typically do. Those arenas, the aesthetic and the politic, are entwined in the workings of his anti-Petrarchism and should be entwined in our analyses.

Sidney, master of masking that he was, delights in jumping between roles, and frequently, as we saw when reading Sonnet 1, they are roles with very different degrees of social status.[49] These predilections, like many of the other characteristics of *Astrophil and Stella*, at once encourage biographical analysis and draw attention to its potential dangers. In particular, in assessing Sidney's social standing, an issue of considerable concern in the contemporary literary climate, scholars sometimes err both in focusing only on his position at court and in oversimplifying even that issue. Concerned to demonstrate his inferior standing in a class system within which his father was merely a knight and to chronicle his tensions with the earl of Oxford and the queen, they neglect how multifarious and varied social rankings were at the end of the sixteenth century. Sidney's status was low enough to make him liable to insults from Oxford. And yet a poem composed after his death attributes to him the sentiment that he might have had a queen as an aunt, a claim that could in fact be variously justified by noting that the earl of Leicester might have married either Elizabeth or Mary Queen of Scots, that his uncle the earl of Huntingdon was considered in some quarters to have a claim to be monarch, and that Lady Jane Grey was, however briefly and tragically, queen.[50] Furthermore, the court was not the only arena in which social status was determined: one must consider as well the distinction enjoyed by the Sidney family in Kent. To neglect the provinces by focusing only on the court is itself a form of provinciality. Neither did class rankings necessarily coincide with political power, an alternative source of status. Thus if his father's title was a recent and relatively insignificant one, he nonetheless enjoyed considerable power as a civil servant, another version of rank which was manifest in his elaborate

---

[49]On Sidney's predilection for role–playing, cf. Richard A. Lanham, "*Astrophil and Stella*: Pure and Impure Persuasion," *ELR*, 2 (1972), esp. 107–109; Levao, "Sidney's Feigned Apology," esp. 144; Miller, " 'What May Words Say,' " esp. p. 106; and Rudenstine, *Sidney's Poetic Development*, p. 204.

[50]On that claim, see Duncan–Jones, *Sir Philip Sidney: Coutier Poet*, pp. 5–15. Her entire book provides valuable biographical information that subverts the common oversimplifications of Sidney's social status.

and costly funeral. Sidney's propensity for variously constructing himself as truant schoolboy, laboring expectant mother, authoritative literary critic, and so on no doubt has many sources, but one may well be his awareness of how many different rankings he could lay claim to in his culture. His critics, too, need to be aware that its status systems were as plural and contested as were Sidney's responses to Petrarchism.

Sidney, then, deploys the counterdiscourses of Petrarchism to address not merely the aesthetic issues raised by Petrarchan poetry but also the concerns about success and failure and dependence and autonomy which are germane to both that mode of writing about love and the social practices of his day. His responses to these problems, as we have seen, repeatedly involve establishing an unresolved and complex dialogue between Stella and Astrophil. They involve, too, distinguishing himself from other figures much as he first does in Sonnet 1 and thus addressing a range of questions about art in the most specific sense as well as the arts of social behavior. Divisive, derisory, and above all diacritical, Sir Philip Sidney's allusions to other Petrarchan sonneteers variously reveal and conceal the central agendas of *Astrophil and Stella*.

II

Shakespeare criticism has long been recognized as a touchstone to shifts in our critical discourses. Witness the popularity that *The Taming of the Shrew* and *Henry V*, texts that demand and reward feminist and new historicist inquiry respectively, have achieved in recent decades. Consider, too, the denigration in many quarters of three methodologies that were once staples of Shakespeare scholarship: genre studies, literary history, and formalist analyses. Instances of those three earlier methods risk at worst being condemned as irrelevant and outdated. And at best the first two methods court the label *solid*, a term that itself embodies telling shifts in our critical registers, for in the United States (though not, interestingly, in England or Canada) *solid* is currently prone to be translated as "dull." But Shakespeare's sonnets, engaged as they are in challenging binary divisions between fair and foul, male and female, and so on, also challenge the binary divide between traditional and contemporary criticism. For these poems (and, as I have argued elsewhere, many other texts as well)[51] invite us to adduce traditional critical approaches, notably the questions about genre

[51]Heather Dubrow, *A Happier Eden: The Politics of Marriage in the Stuart Epithalamium* (Ithaca: Cornell University Press, 1990), pp. 265–270.

and literary history involved in studying the sonnet tradition, to elucidate the most contemporary critical issues about gender and power.

The influence of Petrarch and Petrarchism on these lyrics has not, of course, been ignored. Thomas P. Roche Jr., for example, argues that Shakespeare shares with Petrarch an acute awareness of the dangers of human love.[52] In Joel Fineman's judgment the sequence is shaped by its reinterpretation of an exhausted tradition of praise, notably Petrarchan praise.[53] Despite these and other commentaries, however, many critics (including myself in earlier studies) are still prone to stress what is unique about this sequence at the expense of fully analyzing its Petrarchan elements.[54] Or, alternatively, readers stress its distinctive qualities by allying Shakespeare with one or two other poets and then contrasting the resulting pair or group with more typical sonneteers.[55]

Admittedly, the texts offer some support for such readings; in the complexity of the relationship between the poet and the Friend, for example, these poems are certainly unusual. But interpretations that stress what is atypical about them at the expense of fully acknowledging their intimate relationship to Petrarchan norms also again manifest the dangers of circular reasoning: oversimplifying both Petrarchism and anti-Petrarchism through

[52]See two texts by Thomas P. Roche Jr.: "How Petrarchan Is Shakespeare?" *Proceedings of the Comparative Literature Symposium, Texas Tech University,* 12 (1981), 147–164; and *Petrarch and the English Sonnet Sequences,* esp. chap. 8.

[53]Joel Fineman, *Shakespeare's Perjured Eye: The Invention of Poetic Subjectivity in the Sonnets* (Berkeley: University of California Press, 1986); developed throughout the book, this argument is encapsulated on pp. 1–2. John D. Bernard argues that Shakespeare, though drawing on certain Petrarchan elements, rejects conventional Petrarchism and transforms its assumptions to produce a sacramental vision of the poetry of praise (" 'To Constancie Confin'de': The Poetics of Shakespeare's Sonnets," *PMLA,* 94 [1979], 77–90). On other parallels between Shakespeare and Petrarch, see, e.g., J. B. Leishman, *Themes and Variations in Shakespeare's Sonnets,* 2d ed. (London: Hutchinson, 1963), pp. 44–57. Shakespeare's adoption of the Petrarchan octet–sestet division has often been noted (see, e.g., Philip C. McGuire, "Shakespeare's Non–Shakespearean Sonnets," *SQ,* 38 [1987], 306).

[54]See, e.g., Sandra L. Bermann, *The Sonnet over Time: A Study in the Sonnets of Petrarch, Shakespeare, and Baudelaire* (Chapel Hill: University of North Carolina Press, 1988), esp. pp. 61–62, 73–77; and J. W. Lever, *The Elizabethan Love Sonnet,* 2d ed. (London: Methuen, 1966), esp. pp. 165–168. The theses of Fineman's *Shakespeare's Perjured Eye* are rooted in the differences between the sequence in question and others. In *Shakespeare's Sonnets: Self, Love, and Art* (Cambridge: Cambridge University Press, 1972), pp. 83–84, J. M. Martin maintains that Shakespeare is often "heedless" (p. 83) of Petrarchism but nonetheless writes poems that both participate in it and criticize it. As even this brief sample may indicate, the distinctiveness of Shakespeare's sequence is often emphasized, but the resulting arguments vary in their focus and persuasiveness.

[55]See, e.g., Ferry, *"Inward" Language,* esp. chap. 4. Joan Grundy claims that only Shakespeare, Sidney, and occasionally Drayton question Petrarchism ("Shakespeare's Sonnets and the Elizabethan Sonneteers," *Shakespeare Survey,* 15 [1962], 46–48).

our choice of representative examples clearly encourages us to dismiss the
range of poems that do not fit our definitions as sports. Behind the drive
to read Shakespeare's sonnets as sui generis rather than relating them more
closely to Petrarchism may also lie the bardolatry that several studies have
chronicled.[56] And might not critics' anxiety about one possible contrast
between this sequence and others, the difference whose name many scholars still dare not speak, be deflected into a concern about other distinctions?

In any event, these sonnets are deeply engaged with their primary tradition and source: they are at once intensely Petrarchan and insistently anti-
Petrarchan. If, as Stephen Booth observes, "the most important thing about
a sonnet is that it is a sonnet,"[57] certainly one of the most important things
about Shakespeare's contributions to that genre is that they are variously
and on occasion simultaneously Petrarchan and anti-Petrarchan sonnets. It
is precisely by writing about, within, and against Petrarchism that Shakespeare writes about so much else as well.[58] And it is precisely by raising
questions about source, genre, and linguistic nuances that we can understand many of the questions that Shakespeare himself raises about the
construction of gender, the gendering of empowerment, and the empowering—and disempowering—of language.

Answering these and many other questions, however, depends on arriving at a sound position on three of the critical conundrums the sonnets
involve. The shifts in critical practice to which I referred earlier are also
manifest in discussions of the first of these problems: the nature of the
relationship between the poet and the Friend. Assurances that it exemplifies
asexual friendship have been challenged by studies that assume homoeroticism, most notably Bruce R. Smith's judicious *Homosexual Desire in Shakespeare's England*.[59] Such analyses have provided a valuable corrective; there
is no question but that the relationship to the young man has an intensity
that undermines bland generalizations about the workings of Renaissance
friendship. But students of early modern literature currently risk allowing

[56]For example, Michael D. Bristol, *Shakespeare's America, America's Shakespeare* (London:
Routledge, 1990); and Leah S. Marcus, *Puzzling Shakespeare: Local Reading and Its Discontents*
(Berkeley: University of California Press, 1988).
[57]Stephen Booth, *An Essay on Shakespeare's Sonnets* (New Haven: Yale University Press,
1969), p. 29.
[58]Compare Rosalie L. Colie's emphasis on the process by which each Renaissance writer
"newly [creates] out of and against his tradition" (*Shakespeare's Living Art* [Princeton: Princeton University Press, 1974], p. 5).
[59]See esp. the pioneering though flawed statement of this case by Joseph Pequigney, *Such
Is My Love: A Study of Shakespeare's Sonnets* (Chicago: University of Chicago Press, 1985);
also cf. Bruce R. Smith, *Homosexual Desire in Shakespeare's England: A Cultural Poetics* (Chicago: University of Chicago Press, 1991), chap. 7.

the pendulum to swing too far: if the assertion that these poems are indubitably heterosexual is too dogmatic (as defensive observations so often are), so too is the assertion that they are unquestionably the product of a homoerotic relationship. After all, Sonnet 20 both hints at and denies homoeroticism,[60] and urging one's beloved to produce children with someone else is at the least unusual behavior.[61] Donne provides the best gloss on the relevant passages in this text and elsewhere in the sequence: "Doubt wisely."[62] That stance need not, however, preclude hypotheses rooted in the possibility of a homoerotic reading. In particular, might the conventions of Petrarchism synecdochically represent for Shakespeare the norms of all socially sanctioned love, and might his ambivalences towards Petrarchism and its counterdiscourses both express and repress his ambivalences about those norms?

In any event, not the least reason a critic cannot with certainty adjudicate the homoerotic interpretations that have been proposed for the sequence is that one cannot determine the addressee of many of the poems.[63] The division of these texts into two groups is the second critical conundrum that complicates our interpretations of not only their sexual orientation but their ethical, psychological, and literary orientations too. Most critics simply assume that, with the exception of Sonnets 40 through 42, the first 126 poems refer to the male Friend, whereas the subsequent texts describe the Dark Lady. To be sure, that conventional wisdom has occasionally been challenged. Hilton Landry, for example, briefly calls into question the model of two groups, though he proceeds to accept it implicitly.[64] But the power of the more customary readings of the sonnets is manifest in the fact that trenchant arguments like his have had so little influence.

I am not maintaining that the claim that Shakespeare's poems fall into two distinct groups with different addressees is definitely fallacious. It is, however, grounded on shaky evidence. After all, as Margreta de Grazia

[60]See esp. the notes on this poem in Booth, *Shakespeare's Sonnets*, pp. 163–165.

[61]I thank Michael Stapleton for useful comments on this and other issues.

[62]Compare the trenchantly skeptical statements in Booth, *Shakespeare's Sonnets*, pp. 431–432, 548–549; and Barbara Herrnstein Smith, ed., *Sonnets* (New York: New York University Press, 1969), pp. 23–24.

[63]For a more detailed exposition of this argument, cf. the paper I delivered at the 1992 Shakespeare Association of America conference, " 'Incertainties now crown themselves assured': The Politics of Plotting *Shakespeare's Sonnets*," Kansas City, Mo.

[64]Hilton Landry, *Interpretations in Shakespeare's Sonnets* (Berkeley: University of California Press, 1963), pp. 4–5. Also cf. C. L. Barber, "An Essay on the Sonnets," in William Shakespeare, *The Sonnets*, ed. Charles Jasper Sisson, The Laurel Shakespeare (New York: Dell, 1960), p. 8; Barber notes that the poems might have been written to more than one young man.

notes, the addressee of many of the sonnets is not explicitly gendered.[65] Moreover, the stanzaic irregularities of Sonnet 126 do not irrefutably mark it as a turning point, as many critics have asserted; Sonnet 99 has what might be described as a similar irregularity—fifteen lines—and in a sequence that includes a repeated couplet and several pairs in which one may well be a draft of the second, it is risky to assign thematic significance to the fact that Sonnet 126 is incomplete. Similarly, Katherine Duncan-Jones's claim that the 1609 edition was not pirated and that the sequence enjoys an integrity and structural unity is compromised by the sonnets that are evidently imperfect and the sets that seem to be versions of the same lyric.[66] Above all, the assertion that the first 126 poems consistently apply to the Friend and the next group to the Dark Lady is a classic illustration of circular reasoning: one chooses a few poems to establish the truism that the Friend is generally fair and the Dark Lady incessantly evil and then deploys that assumption to gender the addressee of other sonnets.

If, then, we acknowledge that we do not definitively know the direction of address of many sonnets, we need at least to entertain the possibility that not only Sonnets 40 to 42 but also a number of the others in the first 126 poems describe the Dark Lady. And perhaps a few of the subsequent lyrics refer not to her but to the Friend. This supposition of course complicates many conventional interpretations of the sequence and generates a range of alternatives. For example, if some poems, such as Sonnet 128, that are usually read in reference to the Dark Lady are addressed to the Friend, the sequence might be more overtly homoerotic than we usually believe. And if one destabilizes the direction of address of many poems, one cannot assume that the sonnets to the Friend typically represent an idealized Petrarchism and those addressed to the Dark Lady a virulent anti-Petrarchism.

That recognition gestures towards our third conundrum: the recurrent difficulty of defining what Petrarchism and anti-Petrarchism are in this sequence. Many of its elements comfortably fit into one or the other of those categories. But in some instances the line between them, like so many other boundaries, blurs. Thus, as Fineman among others has shown, in certain respects the Dark Lady is the prototypical Petrarchan mistress, and yet in other respects so too is the Friend.[67] And the problem of determining

---

[65]Margreta de Grazia, "The Scandal of Shakespeare's Sonnets," *Shakespeare Survey*, 46 (1994), 40–41.

[66]Katherine Duncan-Jones, "Was the 1609 *Shake-speares Sonnets* Really Unauthorized?" *RES*, 34 (1983), 151–171.

[67]Fineman, *Shakespeare's Perjured Eye*, esp. pp. 169–170, 251. On Petrarchan elements in the sonnets to the Friend, see also Carol Thomas Neely, "The Structure of English Renaissance Sonnet Sequences," *ELH*, 45 (1978), 374.

whether allusions to blackness are Petrarchan or anti-Petrarchan is clearly posed by poems such as Sonnet 127.[68] The sequence is certainly loaded with more Petrarchan motifs and conventions than readers preoccupied with its unique qualities have acknowledged. Shakespeare refers repeatedly to immortalization and the dangers of praise; poems such as Sonnet 98 emphasize absence; Sonnet 43 among others describes seeing the beloved in a dream; Sonnet 66 offers social satire; and Sonnet 86 credits the beloved with inspiring the poet's verse. For all the originality and idiosyncrasy of Sonnet 94, its famous observation that the figures it anatomizes "are themselves as stone" (3)[69] recalls Dante's *rime petrose* and their lineal descendants, the many sonnets by Petrarch which describe the lady or her poet as stonelike. Other Petrarchan tropes pepper the sequence too—love is compared to a ship, to tyranny and idolatry, and so forth.[70] Sonnet 104 echoes Petrarch's signature poems, the anniversary lyrics (though with a telling shift in emphasis, Shakespeare's intensified focus on the passage of time rather than the originary moment or the possibility of recalling that moment). Recognizing these overt Petrarchan elements prepares us to acknowledge that although the procreation sonnets differ from conventional Petrarchism, if taken out of context some of them would read like wholly standard carpe diem poems within that tradition. Consider, for example, Sonnet 4:

> Unthrifty loveliness, why dost thou spend
> Upon thyself thy beauty's legacy?
> Nature's bequest gives nothing but doth lend,
> And being frank she lends to those are free.
> . . . .
> Thy unused beauty must be tombed with thee,
> Which used lives th' executor to be.
>
> (1–4, 13–14)

Above all, however, Shakespeare's sonnets are Petrarchan in a more subtle way: their speaker's subjectivity is shaped and often misshaped by precisely the issues about agency and authority which we traced in Chapter 2. Although his skids between asserting the immortalizing power of his own verse and denying that power may well manifest his ambivalence

---

[68]See the reading of this lyric in Heather Dubrow, *Captive Victors: Shakespeare's Narrative Poems and Sonnets* (Ithaca: Cornell University Prerss, 1987), pp. 237–239.

[69]All citations from the sonnets are to Booth, *Shakespeare's Sonnets*.

[70]On Shakespeare's references to tyranny and slavery, see the useful comments in Ferry, *"Inward" Language*, pp. 207–208.

about the object of praise, as Anne Ferry persuasively demonstrates,[71] in addition they show his uncertainty over his own agency. Notice the characteristic grammatical structure that at once celebrates that agency and undercuts it: "O none, unless this miracle have might / That in black ink my love may still shine bright" (65.13–14). Indeed, throughout these lyrics he repeatedly draws attention to his own inadequacies.[72]

In a sequence that obsessively returns to binary contrasts and equally obsessively undercuts them, those inadequacies are frequently played against the potency of the Friend and the Dark Lady. "They that have *pow'r* to hurt, and will do none" (94.1; emphasis added) is the revealing opening of one of the most famous—and most notorious—sonnets in the sequence. The fact that neither the Friend nor the Dark Lady speaks does not testify to limitations in their power; indeed, the negatives in the subsequent lines of Sonnet 94, which describe behavior that is in a sense the physical equivalent of speechlessness, associate that behavior with a kind of power:

> That do not do the thing they most do show,
> Who moving others are themselves as stone,
> Unmovèd, cold, and to temptation slow.
>
> (2–4)

Similarly, the characters in Shakespeare's plays sometimes assert their power by refusing to act when others expect them to—witness Coriolanus and his wounds.

One of the primary arenas for the speaker's battles between power and its absence is, however, in a sense formal. Here, as in other sequences, those struggles are waged in terms of the conflict between narrative and lyric. Yet once again narrative does not represent the speaker's achieved and assured male power, as the conventional gendering of narrativity or its role in *Astrophil and Stella* might lead us to expect. At times it represents instead a threat to his relationship with the beloved, as in many of Petrarch's poems, whereas elsewhere it is a source and symbol of the power for which he strives, often in vain.

The tension between narrative and antinarrative elements which characterizes Petrarchism in general occurs in intensified and heightened form

---

[71]Ferry, *All in War with Time: Love Poetry of Shakespeare, Donne, Jonson, Marvell* (Cambridge: Harvard University Press, 1975), chap. 1.

[72]Some critics have asserted that doing so is a rhetorical ploy. See Gerald Hammond, *The Reader and Shakespeare's Young Man Sonnets* (Totowa, N.J.: Barnes and Noble, 1981); and John Klause, "Shakespeare's *Sonnets*: Age in Love and the Goring of Thoughts," *SP*, 80 (1983), 300–324.

in Shakespeare's lyrics in part because both the drive to narrate and the
fear of that drive or incapacity to fulfill it are more intense than in most
other sequences. The desire to immortalize by praising the beloved as well
as by telling stories (including stories about immortalization) impels narrativity in these texts, and the concern to trace the effects of time generates
an attraction to narrative, the mode rooted in temporality.[73] On the other
hand, these sonnets also variously manifest a fear and a rejection of storytelling. Here, as in Petrarch, that activity is often associated with the threatening passage of time. Thus Sonnet 73, a meditation on temporality, is in
a sense itself suspended in an imperiled lyric instant.

> That time of year thou mayst in me behold,
> When yellow leaves, or none, or few, do hang
> Upon those boughs which shake against the cold,
> Bare ruined choirs, where late the sweet birds sang.
> In me thou seest the twilight of such day,
> As after sunset fadeth in the west,
> Which by and by black night doth take away,
> Death's second self, that seals up all in rest.
> In me thou seest the glowing of such fire,
> That on the ashes of his youth doth lie,
> As on the death-bed whereon it must expire,
> Consumed with that which it was nourished by.
>
> (1–12)

The text focuses not on process but on the moment before it and the
fearful anticipation of it: "whereon it *must* expire" (11; emphasis added).
Or, to put it another way, it presents the fear of narrativity in the sense of
temporal change by rooting itself in beleaguered lyric stasis. Notice that
even line two ("yellow leaves, or none, or few") displaces yet draws attention to the diachronic by transforming it into a series of synchronic
alternatives. Here narrativity is in a sense the enemy at the gates. In other
sonnets, however, narrativity threatens the speaker of these poems in a very
different way: if narrative is, as Barthes among many others has claimed,
the product of the drive to know, Shakespeare's sonnets demonstrate the
fear of that drive ("Suspect I may, yet not directly tell" [144.10]).

More to our purposes, Shakespeare also sometimes eschews narrative
because of a lack, real or perceived, of the authority and control involved
in shaping stories; if one is directed, even constructed, by the will of others,

[73]Many critics have analyzed the treatment of time in these poems. See esp. Ferry, *All in
War with Time*, chap. 1.

if it is hard or even impossible to assume control over the story of one's own life, other types of narrative may be rendered problematical as well. (Compare Ariel, whose powerlessness is manifest not in the inability to tell stories but in the imperative to repeat tales dictated by others: "Where was she born? / Speak. Tell me" [*Tempest*, I.ii.259–260].)[74] Storytelling is further complicated, though not necessarily precluded, in this sequence by its approach to human agency. For yet another way the poems avoid making definitive statements about the action they concern is by deflecting or even denying its source. For example, Sonnet 87 laments "So thy great gift, upon misprision growing, / Comes home again, on better judgement making" (11–12), thus deflecting agency to the gift and obscuring the action of the person who calls it home and makes the seemingly better judgment.

Hence it is not surprising that these poems generally avoid many of the types of narrativity that figure so prominently in certain other sequences—descriptions of events that befall the lovers like *Astrophil and Stella* 41, allegorical tales like *Amoretti* 75, detailed rehearsals of the first sight of the beloved. But rather than eschewing narrative completely, as I argued in a previous study,[75] Shakespeare's sonnets respond to an ambivalence about narrativity by delimiting it and displacing it in three arenas: syntactical formulas such as *when/then*, Anacreontic stories, and accounts of the future. Like the displacement and condensation involved in dreamwork, which they resemble in many ways, these strategies typically try to control the anxieties associated with storytelling. And, like that displacement, the three techniques are at best only partly successful in their attempt to restore agency to the speaker and narrative order to his sequence. In short, these poems repeatedly problematize the narrative impulse that the conventional wisdom so unproblematically assigns to them.

The third mode, narratives of the future, is most germane here because of both its connection with the modalities of the *Canzoniere* and its relevance to the poet's subjectivity. Many students of narrative devote little or no attention to this category—Tzvetan Todorov, for example, has an entire chapter on primitive narratives, of which only two and one-half pages concern what he terms *prophetic narratives*[76]—but the process of telling stories about the future would repay further attention. Such a project could

---

[74]I cite G. Blakemore, Evans, ed., *The Riverside Shakespeare* (Boston: Houghton Mifflin, 1974).

[75]Dubrow, *Captive Victors*, pp. 171–190. See also the earlier version of this argument, "Shakespeare's Undramatic Monologues: Toward a Reading of the Sonnets," *SQ*, 32 (1981), 55–68 (reprinted in *Shakespearean Criticism*, 10 [Gale, 1990]).

[76]Tzvetan Todorov, *The Poetics of Prose*, trans. Richard Howard (Ithaca: Cornell University Press, 1977), pp. 63–65.

fruitfully start by examining prophecy in the sixth book of the *Aeneid*, where its ambivalences are bifurcated and gendered into the frenzied darkness of the Sibyl and the genealogical reassurances of Anchises, the first of whom represents agency compromised and complicated by the god within, whereas the second both embodies agency and strengthens that of his son.[77]

Shakespeare's sonnets inhabit a different type of underworld, but prophecies of the future are as important here as in the *Aeneid*, raising similar issues about agency. Sometimes these texts tell a story of an ideal future, projecting onto that moment a return of the ideal, idyllic past or a fantasy of untroubled union which apparently cannot be realized in the present. Or they may deploy a monitory narrative about the future to encourage the addressee to change the plot that she or he has scripted for the present; witness the predictions in the procreation sequence, notably Sonnet 12.

Other sonnets project what has happened or may happen onto what will happen, attributing to the future a fulfillment of fears about the present. In Shakespeare's Sonnet 71 the act of commanding the addressee not to love him in the future might displace fears that he is not loved now. As this instance suggests, however, even the most disturbed and disturbing narratives about the future involve some assertion of control: announcing that one can predict treachery and betrayal, that one will not be surprised by them, suggests at least a measure of mastery.

But the most intriguing narratives about the future are those in which two narrators struggle for possession of it, thus rendering its events even more cloudy. By alluding to time's "ántique pen" in Sonnet 19 (10), Shakespeare reminds us that he and Time are plotting alternative narratives about the future. In Sonnet 7 the speaker, once again using a version of the when/then formula and thus suggesting inevitability, crafts a metaphor that indicates that the addressee, like the sun, will "[reel] from the day" (10). Yet the couplet invites that addressee to unlink tenor and vehicle, to disprove the inevitability, to write his own alternative narrative: "So thou, thyself outgoing in thy noon, / Unlooked on diest unless thou get a son." The so-called Rival Poet is not the only rival narrator in this sequence. And in another group of poems, which includes Sonnet 2 and several other lyrics in the procreation sequence, the speaker writes alternative narratives between which the addressee must choose, thus once again on the one hand demonstrating his power (it is he who crafts the narratives) and on the other hand signaling his powerlessness (it is the addressee who must select one of the stories and delete the other file, no matter how much the poet attempts to guide his choice). Thus narratives about the future, de-

---

[77] I am indebted to Howard Weinbrot for suggesting the relevance of the *Aeneid*.

signed in no small part to assure the agency of their teller, may mark the threats to that agency as clearly as his difficulty with narrativity elsewhere in the sequence does.

As these instances suggest, by displacing narrativity onto the future Shakespeare struggles to achieve the types of certainty and mastery that many other sonneteers are more able than he to achieve when they tell stories in the present tense. In so doing, however, he often merely replicates the threats to that mastery which recur elsewhere in the sequence. Indeed, narrative in Shakespeare's sonnets is typically a process of struggle—struggle between rival narrators, rival endings to the same story, and rival models for sonneteering.

These analyses of one central Petrarchan element in the sonnets, the problematics of agency, suggest the relationship of these poems not only to the traditions of Petrarchism but also to the work of Petrarch specifically. Admittedly, some blatant differences distinguish the two poets. In particular, although the sequence contains political sonnets and poems addressed to Petrarch's friends, Petrarch and Laura often appear isolated both from each other and from the rest of the world. In contrast, although Peter Greenaway's extraordinary film *Prospero's Books* in many ways violates the play it purports to represent, in one relevant respect its spirit is curiously close to that of the sonnets: their isle, too, is full of noises, of the dissonant mutterings and constant movements of shadowy figures ("every alien pen" [78.3], "lest the world should task you" [72.1]) who impinge on the speaker even, or especially, when he appears to be most alone.[78] Despite differences like this, however, the sonnets of Petrarch and Shakespeare share an obsessive fear of impending harm and a slippage between success and failure which, though far from unique to these poems, is more rapid and dramatic than its analogues in many other sequences. And the structural function of Shakespeare's couplets, which so often unsettle the very closure they seemingly establish, is strikingly similar to that of the final poem in the *Rime sparse*. Both poets establish a formal pattern that apparently builds to resolution, in the one instance the rhyme scheme of the so-called Shakespearean sonnet, and in the other a narrative culminating in a climactic union with Laura's alternative and alter ego, the Virgin Mary. And both poets proceed to undermine that resolution in ways that also undermine their power.

[78]Many critics have analyzed the presence of the social world in Shakespeare's sequence. For two different interpretations of its pressures, see Lars Engle, "Afloat in Thick Deeps: Shakespeare's Sonnets on Certainty," *PMLA*, 104 (1989), 832–843; and Hallett Smith, *The Tension of the Lyre: Poetry in Shakespeare's Sonnets* (San Marino, Calif.: Huntington Library, 1981), p. 68.

I have argued at some length for the Petrarchan elements in the sonnets because their presence helps to explain the intensity and variety of their counterdiscourses. It is precisely because Petrarchism is always a major force in this sequence and often a menacing one that these texts react against it. In his dramatic as well as his nondramatic works, Shakespeare typically sees conflict in terms of rivalry, which is one of many reasons the best of the psychoanalytic Shakespeareans have so often hit the mark. And in the case of the sonnets, not the least of the many rivalries that construct the geometry of this triangulated sequence are those among conflicting discourses: Petrarchism versus anti-Petrarchism and one version of anti-Petrarchism against another.

First, then, these poems participate in one of the most common modes of anti-Petrarchism, the stylistic critique. Like many other poets, Shakespeare assails Petrarchism for strained comparisons and unoriginal rhetoric. The simple, straightforward, and constant style that his poems represent and recommend is played against a more duplicitous language.

> So is it not with me as with that muse,
> Stirred by a painted beauty to his verse,
> Who heav'n itself for ornament doth use,
> And every fair with his fair doth rehearse—
> ....
> O let me true in love but truly write.
>
> (21.1–4, 9)

"A painted beauty" (2) may, of course, refer either to someone else's art or to a woman wearing cosmetics;[79] the body of the text and of the mistress elide, a pattern we will encounter again in Chapter 5. Similarly, although it alludes less explicitly to Petrarchism, Sonnet 76 raises related aesthetic issues.

> Why is my verse so barren of new pride,
> So far from variation or quick change?
> Why with the time do I not glance aside
> To new-found methods, and to compounds strange?
> ....
> O know, sweet love, I always write of you,
> And you and love are still my argument.
> So all my best is dressing old words new.
>
> (1–4, 9–11)

---

[79]Compare Booth, *Shakespeare's Sonnets*, p. 166.

Here, in establishing the norm of constancy, Shakespeare is not only rejecting Petrarchism but also reinterpreting one of its characteristics in a way
that makes it more acceptable: the repetitions associated with it (as well as
with other literary styles, of course) become a sign of ethical probity, not
literary or psychological weakness. So in the very process of condemning
doubleness, Shakespeare pursues his own double agenda.

Stylistic critiques like these are the core of the anti-Petrarchism in many
other sequences. Here, however, they are but one battle, and neither the
most fierce nor the most interesting, in the war against Petrarchism. The
principal linkages between Petrarch and Shakespeare which I have traced
involve losses and failures, and so it is not surprising that many of Shakespeare's attacks on Petrarchism represent attempts to reassert the power of
the speaker.

In particular, we should read the procreation sonnets as an implicit counterdiscourse among whose agendas is that reassertion. Two practitioners of
gay and lesbian criticism, Joseph Pequigney and Bruce R. Smith, have
found in these poems a denial of desire which is played against its admission, in more than one sense of that word, in Sonnet 20.[80] Whether or not
one accepts those readings, the procreation poems represent another form
of denial. If they echo the carpe diem topos that is so common in Petrarchan and other forms of love poetry, they also establish a series of contrasts
with Petrarchism. Against sexuality as blind and blinding desire, they play
sexuality as the means of procreation. Against love as narcissistic drive, they
play love as the opposite pole to narcissism: the fulfillment of social obligations. It is telling that Sonnet 9 repeats "the world" no fewer than five
times:

> Ah, if thou issueless shalt hap to die,
> The world will wail thee like a makeless wife;
> The world will be thy widow and still weep,
> . . . .
> Look what an unthrift in the world doth spend
> Shifts but his place, for still the world enjoys it;
> But beauty's waste hath in the world an end.
>
> (3–5, 9–11)

The world, which elsewhere is represented as gossiping tongues and dis-
approving eyes, here stands instead for the obligations that the young man

[80]Pequigney, *Such Is My Love*, esp. chaps. 2, 3; and Bruce R. Smith, *Homosexual Desire
in Shakespeare's England*, esp. pp. 248–251.

is enjoined to fulfill. And that process of enjoining suggests the most central contrast with Petrarchism: against the role of sophistic and self-serving lover is played that of apparently disinterested and detached mentor, who himself represents the very sense of responsibility which he is advocating. In a few sonnets, of course, he admits his own emotional involvement ("Make thee another self for love of me" [10.13]). But even this involvement seems less intense and more rational than the emotions found in subsequent lyrics, and in any event it does not seriously challenge the stance of objective adviser. Thus the procreation sonnets constitute a counterdiscourse in one of the most important senses that we have defined: they represent an alternative mode of love and of writing about it that is repeatedly if implicitly contrasted with Petrarchism. The speaker assumes the high ground—a high ground that in other sonnets will be buffeted by tornadoes and drowned by tidal waves.

Many though not all the sonnets usually assumed to be addressed to the Friend also seem to represent an alternative to Petrarchan love. The contrast has been variously defined by students of these poems: friendship versus love, fidelity versus deceit, and so on. Shakespeare himself appears to establish and then gloss this dichotomy when he enumerates his "two loves . . . of comfort and despair" (144.1). But, as that poem itself demonstrates, such contrasts are at once as fascinating and fragile as a mirage. Fascinating because, like other mirages, they reveal the thirsts of the poet and the critics who support them. And fragile because they dissolve when one approaches them. The Friend is graced—or ostensibly so—with some of the qualities often associated with the Petrarchan lady, such as beauty and constancy.[81] Moreover, the reader often does not know for sure, I have argued, whether a given sonnet refers to the Friend or the Dark Lady, and so the assertion that one represents an un-Petrarchan reliability ("not acquainted / With shifting change, as is false women's fashion" [20.3–4]) is problematical. Above all, however, the contrast between the two breaks down because of the parallels between them; in particular, in both Friend and Dark Lady the relationship between show and substance, outer form and inner being, is dubious and duplicitous.

Even if one questions the division of the sonnets into two groups, it is clear that the central attacks on Petrarchism occur in the poems between 127 and 154.[82] These texts are a virtual anthology of the many counter-discourses of Petrarchism: they include the famous parody of Petrarchan

---

[81]Compare Fineman, *Shakespeare's Perjured Eye*, p. 251.

[82]For a lengthier discussion of this group of poems, see Dubrow, *Captive Victors*, pp. 232–245. The current analysis, however, differs from the earlier one in a few ways, notably the suggestion that Sonnet 130 need not have been inspired by the Dark Lady.

compliment in Sonnet 130, the exaggerations of Petrarchan complaint in Sonnets 131 and 133, the moral repudiation of erotic love in poems like Sonnet 129, and the discussions of blackness that run throughout this group. Critics generally assume that Sonnet 130 was inspired by the Dark Lady. The caveats I raised earlier (as well as the broader problems of referentiality) suggest one should question even that assumption: the poem could conceivably have originated as an exercise in anti-Petrarchism written before any encounter with a particular woman, perhaps a coda to the debates about blackness in *Love's Labour's Lost*. Whatever its genesis, this text cleverly rebuts many Petrarchan clichés:

> My mistress' eyes are nothing like the sun—
> Coral is far more red than her lips' red—
> If snow be white, why then her breasts are dun—
> If hairs be wires, black wires grow on her head:
> I have seen roses damasked, red and white,
> But no such roses see I in her cheeks,
> And in some pérfumes is there more delight
> Than in the breath that from my mistress reeks.
> I love to hear her speak, yet well I know
> That music hath a far more pleasing sound.
> I grant I never saw a goddess go;
> My mistress when she walks treads on the ground.
>   And yet by heav'n I think my love as rare
>   As any she belied with false compare.

The straightforward declarative syntax and the prevalence of monosyllables in the opening lines exemplify the plain-speaking that the author has elsewhere advocated and hence implicitly offer an alternative to the poems being mocked. Notice, too, how the precision of *"some pérfumes"* (7; emphasis added) suggests the reliability of the poet. The tone of the poem, however, is not completely straightforward. Stephen Booth, hardly one to gloss over ambiguities and dissonances, categorizes it as "a winsome trifle."[83] Fair enough, but one exception introduces more troubling issues into the text and thus foreshadows the complications that arise when this poem is read in relation to the others that surround it. *Reeks* primarily means "to emanate"—but its negative connotations may have been available to poet and reader in the 1590s.[84] Therefore this lyric raises questions,

---

[83]Booth, *Shakespeare's Sonnets*, p. 452.
[84]*OED*, s.v. "reek," locates the first negative usage in the eighteenth century, but cf. Booth, *Shakespeare's Sonnets*, p. 454.

however ambiguously and briefly, about what failings in both poet and lady may lurk beneath the dappled surfaces of an apparently urbane and balanced counterdiscourse.

Those questions arise in surrounding texts as well: Sonnet 130 must also be read in the context of the other poems about black wires, black brows, and black morals, and these texts render the witty surfaces of Shakespeare's most famous lyric on blackness more suspect. Whether or not Sonnet 130 was inspired by the figure we call the Dark Lady, all these poems indubitably concern the process of celebrating blackness. The playful assertions in Sonnet 130 that black is really fair are countered by pained acknowledgments in other sonnets that it is evil, as is the process of praising it: "In nothing art thou black save in thy deeds" (131.13). Indeed, as I have argued elsewhere,[85] the poems on blackness play several types of counterdiscourse against one another and in so doing raise questions about not merely Petrarchism but also the poet's challenges to it. Thus while several of the other poets who celebrate their own dark ladies mock the deceptions suffered by others, Shakespeare's texts pivot on self-deception.[86]

In short, in attempting to find our way within what Martin Green aptly termed the labyrinth of Shakespeare's sonnets,[87] we may be guided by some of the threads that we have followed elsewhere in this study. Once again we recognize the variety that characterizes both Petrarchism and its counterdiscourses despite all their conventions. Once again we see that the role of Petrarchan lover—or anti-Petrarchan satirist—does not guarantee power, or at least not unchallenged power. Nor does the silence of the Friend and the Dark Lady signal their powerlessness. And once again we acknowledge that the counterdiscourses of English Petrarchism cannot be defused by calling them a game: Shakespeare's sonnets enact the attempt to do so and display its sorry consequences.

III

Lady Mary Wroth's sonnets, too, are labyrinthine. Not only do they explicitly invoke the image of a labyrinth, but they mime one as well in their knotty syntax, refusal of a linear plot, evocation of psychic entrap-

[85]Dubrow, *Captive Victors*, pp. 232–245.

[86]Many critics have discussed self–deception in Shakespeare's sequence. See, e.g., Michael Cameron Andrews, "Sincerity and Subterfuge in Three Shakespearean Sonnet Groups," *SQ*, 33 (1982), 314–327.

[87]Martin Green, *The Labyrinth of Shakespeare's Sonnets: An Examination of Sexual Elements in Shakespeare's Language* (London: Charles Skelton, 1974).

ment, and, above all, the critical conundrums they pose for their readers. To trace the relationship between autonomy and subjection in *Pamphilia to Amphilanthus* is to enter a maze signposted with clear but conflicting directions from previous critics. How does one reconcile Wroth's choice of the Sidney family arms and Sidney family genres with the independence she lays claim to as a female author?[88] How does one connect the passivity that, as I will demonstrate shortly, distinguishes the opening of her sonnet sequence from many of its counterparts with the agency she so triumphantly asserts elsewhere in that sequence? How does one explain the connection between constancy as a sign of heroic, proud female subjectivity and constancy as a value patriarchy ascribes to women for its own ends?[89] The final sonnet in *Pamphilia to Amphilanthus* raises such questions in particularly pointed form: does the sequence culminate in Pamphilia's freedom from love and the sonnet tradition, or is her achievement of that state incomplete, much as both the folio and the manuscript continuation of the *Urania* break off in midsentence?[90] These problems are embedded in an issue especially germane to this study: Mary Wroth's juxtaposition of the most conventional Petrarchism with its most rebellious counterdiscourses.

Feminist criticism, especially as practiced by students of nineteenth- and twentieth-century texts, proffers a number of possible models for resolving these paradoxes about freedom and its absence. Some paradigms invite us to approach Wroth's apparent loss of freedom as a politic feint testifying to the latent or realized power of suppressed groups; others encourage us instead to interpret that loss as yet another sign of the power against which such groups struggle in vain. For example, the theory of masquerade developed in film studies by Mary Ann Doane maintains that women deliberately adopt in exaggerated form characteristics assigned to them by men, such as passivity, to reveal such traits as dubious cultural constructions.[91] Articulated by Elaine Showalter, the concept of the double-voiced dis-

[88]On Wroth's retention of the Sidney arms, see Margaret P. Hannay, *Philip's Phoenix: Mary Sidney, Countess of Pembroke* (New York: Oxford University Press, 1990), p. 188.

[89]For the argument that Wroth develops—and questions—a "heroics of constancy," see Mary Ellen Lamb, *Gender and Authorship in the Sidney Circle* (Madison: University of Wisconsin Press, 1990), chap. 4; also cf. Elaine V. Beilin, *Redeeming Eve: Women Writers of the English Renaissance* (Princeton: Princeton University Press, 1987), chap. 8, on Wroth's concept of "heroic virtue."

[90]A number of critics have commented on the ending of the *Urania*; Lamb, for instance, maintains that the incompleteness is deliberate (*Gender and Authorship in the Sidney Circle*, p. 148).

[91]On masquerade, a widely debated concept in contemporary film studies, see Mary Ann Doane, *Femmes Fatales: Feminism, Film Theory, Psychoanalysis* (New York: Routledge, 1991), chaps. 1 and 2. The first of those chapters is reprinted from *Screen*, 23 (1982), 74–87, and the second from *Discourse*, 11 (1988–1989), 42–54.

course situates members of a muted group in a cultural space that overlaps with but is not completely contained by the dominant culture, as we saw earlier;[92] this model, which emphasizes that the muted must express their values within constraints, might well explain the double-voiced responses to independence in Wroth. In addition, many students of early modern England have discussed how women in Tudor and Stuart England internalize cultural images of themselves, and so one should hardly be surprised to find a considerable component of ambivalence in a woman who challenges those images. Can the subaltern subvert? Yes, according to this interpretation, but only with an ambivalence that itself subverts subversion. The career of Lady Mary Wroth provides a good test case for these theories.

Previous critics of Wroth also offer a range of possible interpretations on the subject of her independence. Although some earlier students of her work, such as Janet MacArthur and May Nelson Paulissen, emphasize her indebtedness to generic and familial traditions and her participation in a coterie of writers,[93] Gary Waller depicts a more conflicted struggle against various father figures.[94] Ann Rosalind Jones attributes signs of meekness in Wroth to a politic desire to regain her position at court.[95] Other critics emphasize the triumphant achievement of autonomy despite the pressures Waller chronicles. Barbara Kiefer Lewalski, for example, argues for Wroth's independent reinterpretation of the literary traditions she inherited. The apparent contradiction to that independence, her espousal of the stereotypically feminine virtue constancy, is briefly but suggestively read as a kind of knowing camouflage (the parallel with the cinematic masquerade, though not asserted, is telling); thus Lewalski maintains that Wroth's espousal of constancy could serve to distract readers from the radical innovations of Wroth's sonnet sequence.[96]

The seemingly conflicting approaches enumerated above all have more than a grain of truth, but they need variously to be revised and reconciled

[92]Elaine Showalter, "Feminist Criticism in the Wilderness," in *Writing and Sexual Difference*, ed. Elizabeth Abel (Chicago: University of Chicago Press, 1982), pp. 29–30.

[93]Janet MacArthur, " 'A Sydney, though un–named': Lady Mary Wroth and Her Poetical Progenitors," *English Studies in Canada*, 15 (1989), 12–20; and May Nelson Paulissen, *The Love Sonnets of Lady Mary Wroth: A Critical Introduction*, Salzburg Studies in English Literature (Salzburg: Institut für Anglistik und Amerikanistik, 1982), esp. chap. 2.

[94]Gary Waller, "Mother/Son, Father/Daughter, Brother/Sister, Cousins: The Sidney Family Romance," *MP*, 88 (1991), esp. 408–409.

[95]Ann Rosalind Jones, *The Currency of Eros: Women's Love Lyric in Europe, 1540–1620* (Bloomington: Indiana University Press, 1990), chap. 4. Jones's otherwise incisive reading of Wroth should be qualified by the reminder that the evidence for her disgrace at court is debatable (cf. Barbara Kiefer Lewalski, *Writing Women in Jacobean England* [Cambridge: Harvard University Press, 1993], pp. 248–249).

[96]Lewalski, *Writing Women in Jacobean England*, p. 263.

before they can be properly applied to Wroth. In her stance towards male authorities of all types, literary tradition in general, and Petrarchism in particular, she, like certain Continental women writers,[97] does indeed manifest both dependence and independence. Critics should not, in response to the very pressures that impelled some first-generation Shakespearean feminists to focus unduly on Shakespeare's strong heroines, obscure the surrender of power which coexists so uneasily with Wroth's assertion of it. Their amalgam, though it illuminates other women writers and women's writing, is in an important sense idiosyncratic, or at least local: the paradoxical characteristics that I have already identified in Wroth can be traced in part to certain models that inspired her quest for autonomy. In particular, Petrarchism was both a source of and a stage for that quest; hence examining the relationship between Petrarchism and its counterdiscourses helps us to understand Wroth's connection to those literary traditions and also her conflicting and conflicted approach to autonomy in general.

Dismayed by the early studies that dismissed Wroth's poetry as boilerplate Petrarchism,[98] inspired by the feminist analyses that demonstrate the distinctive gendering of genres, many scholars have focused on the idiosyncratic characteristics of *Pamphilia to Amphilanthus* and especially on how they reform or deform the Petrarchan tradition, not how they embrace it. No sensible critic would advocate a return to classifying these poems as mechanical Petrarchan imitations. But neither should studying how they reinterpret that tradition preclude emphasizing their extensive debts to it: acknowledging and anatomizing the Petrarchan elements in *Pamphilia to Amphilanthus* allows us to understand more about the characteristics of that literary mode, the ways it negotiates gender, and its author's travails and travels in those two neighboring labyrinths that mirror each other's structure, Petrarchism and its counterdiscourses.

The opening sonnet in the sequence, a poem that has not received as much scrutiny as it deserves, introduces its author's approach to both Petrarchism and anti-Petrarchism.

> When nights black mantle could most darknes prove,
> And sleepe deaths Image did my senceses hiere
> From knowledg of my self, then thoughts did move
> Swifter then those most swiftnes need require:

[97]See Jones's argument about dialogic writing in the work of Pernette du Guillet and Tullia d'Aragona (*Currency of Eros*, chap. 3).

[98]See, e.g., MacArthur's argument that though the poems stage a conflict between female difference and the desire to emulate Petrarchism, the latter wins, producing a sequence that subscribes to the Law of the Father (" 'A Sydney,' " esp. pp. 17–18).

In sleepe, a Chariot drawne by wing'd desire
I sawe: wher sate bright Venus Queene of love,
And att her feete her sonne, still adding fire
To burning hearts which she did hold above,

Butt one hart flaming more then all the rest
The goddess held, and putt itt to my brest,
Deare sonne, now shutt sayd she: thus must wee winn;

Hee her obay'd, and martir'd my poore hart,
I, waking hop'd as dreames itt would depart
Yet since: O mee: a lover I have binn.[99]

This lyric flags its indebtedness to a whole range of literary and icono-
graphic traditions. The murdered heart is a convention of Petrarchism, and,
in addition, Mary Wroth borrows from Petrarch's *Trionfi,* part of which
her aunt had translated. Indeed, in alluding to the *Trionfi* at the beginning
of a sonnet sequence, Wroth plays one Petrarch against another—which is
itself a characteristically Petrarchan maneuver, as the opening lyric in the
Rime sparse reminds us. As Nona Fienberg has demonstrated, Wroth also
invokes the *Vita Nuova*,[100] practices emblemmatic writing, and deploys the
dream vision. The lyric is, in short, intensely, even insistently Petrarchan,
and its other debts are unabashed too.

But this sonnet also differs from many of its sources and in so doing
signals the agendas of the entire sequence. Wroth transforms literary conventions in ways that direct our attention to both the power of gender and
the gendering of power. The dream vision is itself a norm of Petrarchism,
in which it generally permits forms of wish fulfillment, as Freud asserts
dreams typically do:[101] the chaste mistress may be embraced in one's dreams,
the threatening satyr killed. Mary Wroth, in contrast, dreams of the origins
of an unfulfilled love, of loss and pain, a deviation from other sequences
which prepares us for the exceptionally melancholy tone of her sonnets.
In most Petrarchan cycles, two radically different modes of consciousness,

[99]All citations are to Josephine A. Roberts, ed., *The Poems of Lady Mary Wroth* (Baton
Rouge: Louisiana State University Press, 1983).

[100]On the connections with Dante, see Nona Fienberg, "Mary Wroth and the Invention
of Female Poetic Subjectivity," in *Reading Mary Wroth: Representing Alternatives in Early Modern England,* ed. Naomi J. Miller and Gary Waller (Knoxville: University of Tennessee Press,
1991), p. 185.

[101]See esp. Sigmund Freud, *The Standard Edition of the Complete Psychological Works of
Sigmund Freud,* trans. James Strachey et al. (London: Hogarth Press and Institute of Psychoanalysis, 1955), 4:122–133.

sleep and waking, are played against each other in narratives of a dream, but here Wroth presents not change but stasis. For the speaker's desire that "as dreames itt would depart" (13), like so many of her desires later in the sequence, is unfulfilled, another harbinger of the monochromatic tone of many of these sonnets and of their refusal to sustain the types of transformation for which the speaker strives elsewhere in the sequence, notably in the crown poems.

Above all, the emphasis on dreaming places her in a singularly passive position. If one plot of the sonnet, her encounter with Venus and Cupid, casts her as the object of actions performed by others ("and martir'd my poore hart" [12]), its overarching plot, the dream vision, intensifies that loss of agency. Her absence of agency distinguishes her from the speakers in some comparable poems. In *Idea* 2, Drayton deploys the conceit of the murdered heart to seek revenge against his lady; he is remarkably feisty, if not downright nasty, for a man whose heart was slain. And in *Astrophil and Stella* 20, Astrophil speaks with real energy when he urges his friends to fly because of his "death wound" (1). Similarly, Sidney opens his sequence on action attempted though frustrated; in the first poem of *Pamphilia to Amphilanthus*, in contrast, the speaker created by his niece does not even attempt to act. The poem that concludes the sequence echoes P1 in many ways, not least its emphasis on passivity ["Sleepe in the quiett of a faithfull love" (2)], though here the speaker chooses passivity rather than having it imposed on her.

Pamphilia's loss of agency in P1 is also manifest through narrativity. Telling this story does not assure the kind of mastery narratologists sometimes associate with the act of recounting a tale: it is a story of failure like so many of Shakespeare's, and its epistemological status as a dream further plays down the act of shaping it. Thus Wroth's approach to narrative at the beginning of *Pamphilia to Amphilanthus*, like some other traits of her writing, allies her more closely with her literary forebear Shakespeare than with her blood relative Sir Philip Sidney.

Other deviations from models and sources are equally telling. Mary Wroth recasts the narrative she tells to structure it around a binary, gendered conflict. The description in the *Trionfi* focuses on Cupid, with Venus making a cameo appearance as one of his victims, and in the third chapter of the *Vita Nuova*, Love feeds Dante's heart to his beloved, who was herself asleep until that event. Here, however, Wroth stages a scene between Venus and Cupid (her speaker, though present, does not assume an active role in this particular drama), thus introducing the predilection for pairs of characters and binary formulations which will recur throughout. More specifically, she introduces a pair including a male character into a sequence that erases the male who appears within its title, but she does not erase possible avatars and reincarnations of him.

Indeed, the role of gender in the encounter between Venus and Cupid prepares us for its workings throughout this cycle. Given his prominence later in the sequence, it is all the more surprising and all the more telling that Cupid is here reduced to a subservient position. His literal lowliness— he sits at his mother's feet—is matched by his role as her minion: he follows her orders throughout, adding fire to a heart she holds. Thus the lyric evokes a hierarchical relationship between a male and a female character; the potential conflict between them (Venus and Cupid are at odds later in the sequence, as in so many of the Anacreontic poems that help to shape it) is averted, and the dominant adult woman controls her young son. Or, to put it another way, the female is bifurcated into two figures, the wholly passive speaker and the active and powerful goddess of love—a divide that manifests Wroth's own divided responses to female power and probably more specifically to the forms of it evident in writing sonnets. Whereas Sidney expresses his ambivalence about poesy at the beginning of *Astrophil and Stella* by variously identifying Astrophil with a child and with a woman struggling through a difficult labor, Wroth expresses many of her ambivalences by evoking two very different female figures.

In so doing, she also hints at her preference for assuming multiple roles. As Naomi J. Miller has argued, Wroth typically constructs multiple and at times contradictory subjectivities.[102] In the poem at hand she is, of course, primarily figured as Pamphilia. But as a writer undertaking a bold generic experiment, she may well identify, or at least attempt to identify, with Venus's confident mastery as well.[103] And as the child of Robert Sidney and niece of Philip Sidney, is she perhaps in a role of pupil which may even ally her, however tangentially, with Venus's son? Luce Irigaray among others has pointed out that subject and object often reverse places in a dream;[104] this may be one of the many reasons that form of narrative appeals to Wroth. These speculations about her identification with all three personages are necessarily tentative, but they gain some credence from the

---

[102]Naomi J. Miller, "Changing the Subject: Mary Wroth and the Formations of Gender in Early Modern England," chap. 2, forthcoming. I am indebted to the author for sharing this work before it was published, as well as for a number of useful suggestions about Wroth; I regret that I read her manuscript only after this chapter was substantially complete.

[103]In her unpublished paper "Mary Wroth's Poetics of the Self in the Petrarchan Tradition," Nona Fienberg suggests that Wroth identifies with Venus elsewhere in the sequence. I am grateful to the author for making her article available to me.

[104]Luce Irigaray, *Speculum of the Other Woman*, trans. Gillian C. Gill (Ithaca: Cornell University Press, 1985), p. 138.

juxtaposition of multiple roles and the elision of gender boundaries elsewhere in the sequence.

Pamphilia to Amphilanthus opens, then, on many of the issues I will trace throughout this section: Wroth's skilled reinterpretation of generic traditions inherited from a range of writers besides Philip and Robert Sidney, her deflection of issues about gender from the main plot to other stories, her predilection for both creating and blurring binary formulations, and her ambivalence about her own power and authority. But these problems, the material of contemporary feminist and new historicist inquiry, are expressed not only within but also in terms of a question of interest to traditional literary historians, Mary Wroth's relationship to Petrarchism and its counterdiscourses.

Pamphilia to Amphilanthus is festooned with and impelled by Petrarchan conventions. Witness its subject matter: the difficulties of night, the beauty of eyes, the resemblances between the beloved and the stars. Observe, too, its tropes: storm-tossed crafts careen through this sequence, the lover freezes and burns, her sighs might well drown Donne's merchant ships. And note its diction: Song 2 deploys the refrain "Ay mee," and "pain" is a recurrent rhyme word. P33 localizes many of these characteristics and draws attention to their prevalence elsewhere, for this lyric orders joy to fly away, compares the beloved to a sun, laments his absence, and refers to "fires of love" (14).

The sequence also resembles other Petrarchan collections in the juxtaposition of narrative and lyric elements and the fragility of the types of control and authority often connected with the former. Despite the presence of narrativity in a set of mythological stories, it is rarely associated with the kinds of authority that Astrophil achieves through his storytelling: P1 exemplifies the paradoxical links between storytelling and absence of agency which are more subtly present throughout the sequence, and the fact that almost all narratives are located in a mythological realm may suggest that she cannot achieve narrativity in other worlds. Certainly her typically Petrarchan emphasis on entrapment in a static, obsessive state of mind testifies to what threatens the very possibility of narrative in those worlds. Perhaps Mary Wroth is attracted to concatentio, the repetitive enchaining that she deploys in her crown sequence, partly because it incorporates some narrative qualities in what is predominantly a lyric sequence.

But the connections between this sequence and Petrarchism go far deeper than the mannerisms of style and choices of mode I have enumerated so far. Whether or not family loyalty rendered that discourse attractive to Mary Wroth, as MacArthur has argued,[105] it appealed to her because of

[105]MacArthur, " 'A Sydney,' " esp. p. 13. Also cf. Josephine Roberts's suggestion that

deep connections between its assumptions and her own. Certainly the Petrarchan ambivalence about poesy in general and love poetry in particular
was congenial to her. Mary Wroth, like many Petrarchan poets, repeatedly
draws attention to the inadequacies and dangers of what she at one point
terms "that Divell speach" (P52.10) and her command of it; yet in assuming
the name "Pamphilia" she allies herself with a distinguished female poet.[106]
Her *Urania*, as Mary Ellen Lamb among others has argued, demonstrates a
comparable ambivalence.[107] Similarly, the passivity in P1 is a version,
though intensified, of the typical helplessness of the Petrarchan speaker, a
point to which we will return.

Petrarchism is the genre that always looks back over its shoulder—at
footprints of its lost beloved, traces of its speaker's lost youth, poems by
earlier writers. Mary Wroth, too, is preoccupied with what is past and what
may be lost: her sonnet sequence manifests the customary nostalgia of Petrarchism and in so doing also signals her consciousness of the achievements
of a dead father, a dead uncle, and a genre that many of her contemporaries
considered moribund. Her interest in pastoral and romance has sometimes
been linked with her uncle's work in both those literary forms. Quite
possibly, but it is no accident that those modes, like the Petrarchan sonnet,
look backward. Nor is it an accident that her *Urania* quite literally fulfills
the romance's agenda of "finding what was lost" by opening on the title
character, whose disappearance was lamented in the opening of Sidney's
Arcadia.

This anatomy of Mary Wroth's Petrarchism in turn invites a genealogy.
Not surprisingly, many critics, assuming an overlap between her biological
and literary genetic pools, have focused on her debts to Philip and Robert
Sidney.[108] Certainly the influence of her uncle is clear not only in poems

---

Wroth may have stayed close to Petrarchism out of a desire to perpetuate a family tradition
in an age turning against it (*The Poems of Lady Mary Wroth*, p. 59).

[106]On the significance of that name, see Josephine A. Roberts, introduction to *The Poems
of Lady Mary Wroth*, p. 42, and an earlier version of some of the same material, "The
Biographical Problem of *Pamphilia to Amphilanthus*," *Tulsa Studies in Women's Literature*, 1
(1982), 44.

[107]Lamb, *Gender and Authorship in the Sidney Circle*, esp. pp. 159–162. See also Lewalski's
suggestion that Wroth's prose romance contrasts characters representing good and bad artists
(*Writing Women in Jacobean England*, pp. 280–281).

[108]See esp. the very useful notes in Roberts, *The Poems of Lady Mary Wroth*; and Maureen
Quilligan, "The Constant Subject: Instability and Female Authority in Wroth's *Urania* Poems," in *Soliciting Interpretation: Literary Theory and Seventeenth–Century English Poetry*, ed.
Elizabeth D. Harvey and Katharine Eisaman Maus (Chicago: University of Chicago Press,
1990). In addition to tracing parallels with the Sidneys, Paulissen has noted a wide range of
other influences, notably Jonson, Donne, Neo–Platonic writers, and the Italian *capitoli* tradition (*Love Sonnets of Lady Mary Wroth*, chaps. 2, 3).

that echo his (P16, for example, bears unmistakable traces of *Astrophil and Stella* 47) but also in recurrent stylistic mannerisms. Thus, despite the predilection for lyric that I noted, when Mary Wroth does compose a narrative she develops its dramatic potential. Moschus's First Idyll merely mentions that Cupid must be tied up lest he escape, whereas in P70 Wroth refashions those events into a conflict between the errant god of love and a group of nymphs, a point to which we will return. And, like both her uncle and her father, Wroth delights in technical experimentation, deploying more stanzaic variations than are found in *Astrophil and Stella*.[109] Her concern with subservience and autonomy also recalls her uncle, and it is no accident that P16, one of the poems that is closest to *Astrophil and Stella*, explores that very issue. Similarly, the rapid shifts in power in Philip Sidney's sonnets find their analogue in lines such as Wroth's "Yett this Sir God, your boyship I dispise" (P8.13). (The origins of that particular line are, however, more complex than they may appear. Wroth's editor adduces an apostrophe by Sidney, " 'What now sir foole' " *[Astrophil and Stella* 53.7] as its antecedent,[110] but as is so often the case, a lesser sonneteer deserves more credit than he has received. Bartholomew Griffin's generally undistinguished sequence *Fidessa* includes a splendid line that provides a far closer source for Wroth: "I hope sir boy you'll tell me news tomorrow" [14.12].)[111]

Acknowledging the parallels between Wroth and her uncle and father allows us to question critical assumptions that are sometimes unthinkingly deployed. In their seminal *Madwoman in the Attic*, Sandra Gilbert and Susan Gubar assume that women writers are not likely to feel the Bloomian anxiety of influence because they are estranged from male literary traditions.[112] This hypothesis is too often baldly repeated in less thoughtful studies, and it finds its analogue in the film criticism that argues that the woman viewer cannot replicate the gaze of the male spectator—a position that is in important ways analogous to the authorial—or can do so only at the price of a kind of androgyny.[113] Influential though these and many

[109]Roberts, *The Poems of Lady Mary Wroth*, p. 47.

[110]Roberts, *The Poems of Lady Mary Wroth*, p. 90.

[111]Bartholomew Griffin, *Fidessa, More Chaste then Kinde* (London, 1596).

[112]Sandra Gilbert and Susan Gubar, *The Madwoman in the Attic: The Woman Writer and the Nineteenth-Century Literary Imagination* (New Haven: Yale University Press, 1979).

[113]For a useful summary of the extensive debates on this issue, see Robert Lapsley and Michael Westlake, *Film Theory: An Introduction* (1988; rpt., Manchester: Manchester University Press, 1989), pp. 95–104. Important studies in the debate include Doane, *Femmes Fatales*, chaps. 1 and 2; Tania Modleski, "Hitchcock, Feminism, and the Patriarchal Unconscious," in *Issues in Feminist Film Criticism*, ed. Patricia Erens (Bloomington: Indiana University Press, 1990); and two essays by Laura Mulvey, "Visual Pleasure and Narrative Cinema," *Screen*,

cognate theories have proved, they err in their assumption that gender is necessarily the overriding determinant of subjectivity. When Mary Wroth approaches the sonnet, her status as a Sidney may well be as important as her status as a woman. While this particular instance may at first seem so idiosyncratic as to be irrelevant to other women, I would argue that it is only an extreme case of the multiple forms of identity and identification which may challenge gender for primacy. More to the point, these alternative forms also interact complexly with gender, as Ann Rosalind Jones has shown in her important study of social, economic, and geographical conditions, such as the status of the cities of Lyon and Venice, that facilitated the writing of English and Continental women.[114] In any event, the relationship among the components of subjectivity is a dynamic one, for identification should be seen more as a process than an act: at a specific moment in writing a text or, analogously, seeing a film, a previously subsidiary factor may assume new importance or the members of a group of formerly harmonious vectors may initiate a struggle for supremacy. In particular, many critics have grown accustomed to emphasizing three issues— race, class, and gender—but one needs to look not only at times those categories conflict rather than overlapping (race, class, *or* gender) but also at other modes of classification that may on occasion be equally important. Our own politics, in other words, should not constrain our reading of identity politics. When a woman from New York watches a film set in that city, at some points at least might not her geographical affiliations permit a spectatorship close to that often attributed to the male viewer rather than ensuring her identification with the passive object of desire? When a female professor analyzes a film for her class, might not her professional affiliation help to produce the kinds of distance that many film theorists consider necessary for the gaze but inaccessible to women because of their identification with the maternal body?[115] Once again my concern is not to deny the profound significance of gender but to emphasize its complex interactions with other components of identity and identification,

---

16 (1975), 6–18, and "Afterthoughts on 'Visual Pleasure and Narrative Cinema' Inspired by *Duel in the Sun*," *Framework*, 10 (1979), 3–10.

[114]Jones, *The Currency of Eros*; Lyon and Venice are discussed in chap. 5.

[115]Some film critics have perceptively discussed the complexity of identification, though from perspectives different from my own; see, e.g., Tania Modleski, *Loving with a Vengeance: Mass–Produced Fantasies for Women* (1982; rpt., London: Routledge, 1990), and Gaylin Studlar, *In the Realm of Pleasure: Von Sternberg, Dietrich, and the Masochistic Aesthetic* (Urbana: University of Illinois Press, 1988). An overview of Studlar's argument may be found in an earlier article, "Masochism and the Perverse Pleasures of the Cinema," *Quarterly Review of Film Studies*, 9 (1984), 267–282.

an agenda encouraged by enumerating the connections between Wroth's poetry and that of her uncle and father.

Yet such enumerations also risk distracting attention from the principal analogue to her sequence. Many of Wroth's critics have been barking up the wrong family tree, for in a number of respects Wroth's closest connections are with Shakespeare, not Robert or Philip Sidney. The aim of this parallel, needless to say, is not to lend respectability to Wroth by drawing on the reserves of bardolatry which survive in our culture and even our profession despite repeated attacks. Rather, it is only by acknowledging the extraordinary affinities between Wroth and Shakespeare that one can understand both her Petrarchism and her reactions against it.[116]

In both its diction and sentiments, P24 sounds remarkably like Shakespeare's sonnets.

> When last I saw thee, I did nott thee see,
> Itt was thine Image, which in my thoughts lay
> Soe lively figur'd, as noe times delay
> Could suffer mee in hart to parted bee;
> . . . .
> Pitty my loving, nay of consience give
> Reward to mee in whom thy self doth live.
>
> (1–4, 13–14)

Behind these connections lie the similarities that unite the two sequences. Sonneteers typically express doubts about their own poetic achievements, but these expressions, as we have seen, are especially intense in the two writers in question. Sonneteers generally establish a complex relationship to narrativity, but it is especially fraught in the texts of Wroth and Shakespeare: they structure their sequences in terms of groups rather than as a linear narrative, and their apparent sorties into linearity, such as the state Pamphilia seemingly realizes at the end of her crown sequence, are undermined. Having juxtaposed two contrasting forms of love (the Friend versus the Dark Lady, the Anacreontic versus the magisterial Cupid), both unsettle those binary models. "From contraries I seeke to runn Ay mee; / But contraries I can nott shunn Ay mee" (P14.9–10), Wroth writes, and Shakespeare would second both the sentiment and the lamentation it provokes.

[116]In "Changing the Subject," chap. 2, Naomi J. Miller also notes some parallels between Wroth and Shakespeare, and some similarities between Wroth and Shakespeare are briefly listed by Paulissen (*Love Sonnets by Lady Mary Wroth*, pp. 65–69); most of the characteristics these critics identify, however, differ from the ones I discuss.

Many sonnet sequences are peopled with courtiers and friends; despite all Shakespeare's references to the world's judgments, his poems seldom present human characters like those. Wroth herself subsists in a curiously isolated world; the darkness to which she so often refers is a diurnal physical analogue.[117] Thus, for example, whereas *Astrophil and Stella* 47 pivots on the entrance of Stella, its equivalent in Mary Wroth's sequence, P16, is marked by the absence of the beloved and, indeed, of any other human contact. Sometimes, as we have seen, she does recast her source as a more dramatic encounter—but its personages are typically mythological figures. These predilections, like several of the other similarities we have noted, may be connected to the ways both poets sometimes saw, or constructed, themselves as outsiders, whether because of gender in one case or because of class in the other.

In both Shakespeare and Wroth, the obsessive ideation that characterizes Petrarchism typically assumes the form of jealousy and suspicion. Wroth, like Shakespeare, is preoccupied, perhaps even obsessed, with betrayal.[118] Witness, for example, P65 and P66, which chronicle the workings of "cruell suspition" (P66.1). As the brooding anxieties in these texts would suggest, both Wroth and Shakespeare are intensely aware of the dangers of their own imaginations. "Thou suff'rest faulsest shapes my soule t'affright" (P18.5), Wroth accuses sleep, and it is no accident that she writes so often of fancy. (That interest is manifest in the *Urania* too: its prose often recounts the distortions wrought by the imagination, and the term recurs in its poetry ["Phantsie's butt phantastiks skill" (N18.3)]). And in both Shakespeare and Wroth the alternative to suspicion is an ideal of constancy, an ideal that is problematized as often as it is invoked. Shakespeare localizes constancy in his dark Friend and his own love for that problematical being, and Wroth, in her approach to love.

This alternative genealogy clarifies Wroth's attraction to Petrarchism and anti-Petrarchism. Like Shakespeare, she is drawn to the discourse inspired by the *Rime sparse* partly because several of its characteristics conform so closely to her own subjectivity—which, of course, they may also have helped to form. Hence when she reacts against it, she, like Shakespeare, above all is rejecting not merely a series of literary mannerisms but rather one side of herself. And she, like Shakespeare and so many other writers,

[117]Wroth's isolation is discussed by Gary Waller in *The Sidney Family Romance: Mary Wroth, William Herbert, and the Early Modern Construction of Gender* (Detroit: Wayne State University Press, 1993), esp. pp. 204–206. I regret that this study appeared after I had finished my work on Wroth.

[118]Her interest in betrayal is also noted in Roberts, *The Poems of Lady Mary Wroth*, p. 46.

struggles to achieve an anti-Petrarchan stance that proves no more stable than Petrarchism.

To stress the connections between Wroth and Shakespeare, however, is not to deny the distinctive role gender plays in her Petrarchism and anti-Petrarchism—distinctive, but also nuanced in ways that demand a qualified and cautious critical response. Although many feminist studies of the relationship between gender and genre have been incisive, the less successful ones exemplify the by now familiar dangers of essentialism, positing as they do a monolithic female version of the genre in question. Often, too, they assume it is more skillful and appealing than its antitype, the monolithic male version, thus understandably but unfortunately offering a reversed analogue to patriarchal condescension, much as some of the less trenchant versions of gay and lesbian criticism sometimes present heterosexual love as an imperfect version of its alternative.

In this case, critics who assess the relationship of gender and genre need to beware not only of subscribing to these oversimplifications but also of labeling as distinctively female those qualities that are also gendered male in Petrarchism. In particular, as we have already observed, Mary Wroth's sonnets often express doubts about her ability to write or the value of her compositions. Thus in P45 she laments,

> Nor can I as those pleasant witts injoy
> My owne fram'd words, which I account the dross
> Of purer thoughts.
>
> (5–7)

"Fram'd" refers primarily to the process of composition (a usage that just might have been sparked by the unusual density of what were known as "timber-framed" houses in the county of Kent, where Penshurst is situated), but it could also mean "to adapt, adjust, fit," and in fact Wroth's writing involves a series of adaptations.[119] More to our purposes now, however, the lines denigrate her verse. Similarly, in Song 1 she evokes a shepherdess, clearly an alter ego for Pamphilia, who writes on bark and whose poetry will be preserved only "if some such lover come . . . And place them on my tombe" (42, 44). (In the Urania, Pamphilia carves a poem, which appears in the standard modern edition of Wroth's poetry as U5, onto a tree.) This denigration of artistic achievement might be seen simply as a gendered response—until one acknowledges how common those doubts are in poems by male sonneteers. Similarly, although composing sonnets is

---

[119]OED, s.v. "frame," "framed."

certainly a transgressive act for a woman, *The Apology for Poetry* reminds us that choosing love lyrics over religious hymns could be interpreted as transgressive for a male as well.

The argument that qualities sometimes labeled female are in fact gendered more ambiguously serves once again to redefine, not deny, the significance of gender. I have suggested that in some instances the counterdiscourses of Petrarchism are gendered female, and in the case at hand, Wroth's position as a woman may well have intensified the doubts and guilt already connected with the genre.[120] Indeed, it is quite possible that she was attracted to Petrarchism in part because its ambivalence about writing appealed to her and allowed her at once to express and to deflect her ambivalences under the cover of generic convention. (The same potentialities are realized in her responses to the passivity of the Petrarchan lover.) Mary Wroth's hesitancy about writing is overdetermined, with gender an important but by no means exclusive factor.

Similarly, discussions of gender and genre often emphasize that a female writer destabilizes gender within the text itself. Fair enough, and in this instance the absence of physical descriptions of Amphilanthus draws attention to such shifts. At the same time, however, the first three chapters of this study impel us to admit that the destabilization in question is different in degree, not kind, from what is customarily effected in sonnets.[121] For if the positions of male and female so often elide even in male-authored sonnets, if the sonneteer and his lady bear equally fraught relationships to speech and engage in an often unresolved struggle for power, then the changes brought about when a woman writes sonnets will be more subtle than literary studies sometimes assume, though no less significant.

What, then, are those changes in the case of Wroth in addition to those problematical issues of guilt about writing and destabilized gender? The presence of images of birth and miscarriage is striking and has been noted by Naomi J. Miller among others.[122] Some other thought-provoking pos-

---

[120]For a different but not incompatible analysis, see Jones, *The Currency of Eros*, p. 149; she finds in the claims of poetic failure a "false modesty" about lyrics that in fact demonstrate their author's constancy and virtuosity.

[121]In the unpublished paper "More I Still Undoe: Louise Labé, Mary Wroth, and the Petrarchan Discourse," Roger Kuin offers perceptive insights into how the absence of pronouns in Wroth reveals our presuppositions about gender; my argument qualifies his by suggesting that other Petrarchan sequences typically destabilize gender as well. I thank the author for making his work available to me.

[122]Naomi J. Miller, "Rewriting Lyric Fictions: The Role of the Lady in Lady Mary Wroth's *Pamphilia to Amphilanthus*," in *The Renaissance Englishwoman in Print: Counterbalancing the Canon*, ed. Anne M. Haselkorn and Betty S. Travitsky (Amherst: University of Massachusetts Press, 1990), p. 303.

sibilities necessarily remain more speculative. Wroth repeatedly evokes encounters between male and female mythological characters, as we have
already observed; in addition to recasting the sources of P1 in those terms,
in P70 she reshapes her sources to emphasize the nymphs' clash with the
god of love. Similarly, in P58 she displaces Pamphilia's power struggles
with Amphilanthus, always covert at best in this sequence, onto Venus's
conflicts with Cupid.[123] Surely this attraction to mythological narratives
manifests not only her uncle's interest in dramatic confrontations but also
her own concern with clashes between men and women. The point is not
that Amphilanthus is absent from the collection but that he is, as it were,
distanced, dispersed among many characters, dismembered so that he can
be less painfully remembered. On one level this dispersal exemplifies the
deflection that is so characteristic of the Petrarchan mode. On another level,
however, the strategy is gendered, for Wroth's response to the betrayal that
is a dark undercurrent in this sequence and a central plot line in *Urania* is,
like that of so many members of subordinated groups, passive aggressive:
rather than attacking Amphilanthus directly, she diminishes him by implicitly associating him with the boyish Cupid and punishes him by covertly
linking him with the Cupid who suffers for his trickery.

Yet Wroth's Cupid is often victorious, and his triumphs direct our attention to another way gender may affect Wroth's Petrarchism and anti-
Petrarchism. In rejecting one version of Cupid, Mary Wroth eagerly turns
to—and does obeisance to—another. Although the notion of Cupid as a
powerful monarch is hardly unique to this sequence, Wroth's emphasis on
it and on her own subservience is striking. Notice, for example, how appositive phrases draw attention to Cupid's role as monarch:

> To thee then lord commander of all harts,
> Ruller of owr affections kinde, and just
> Great King of Love.
>
> (P89.9–11)

In other words, whereas many versions of Petrarchan counterdiscourses
stress the lover's newfound freedom, the love Wroth espouses is associated
with being the loyal subject of Cupid. In P8 she addresses Love, lamenting,
"I ame thy subject, conquer'd, bound to stand" (6); in the crown sequence
she delightedly accepts subjection to a different version of the god of love.
Thus, as I suggested earlier, Wroth figures her escape from the labyrinth
of Petrarchism not as a reassertion of autonomy but as an acceptance of

[123]Compare Miller, "Rewriting Lyric Fictions," pp. 298–299.

submission to a higher, better authority. In this respect, then, her discourse is double-voiced in Showalter's sense, and despite all the independence Wroth achieves in other ways, she draws attention to her acceptance of hierarchical power. Wroth may well be attracted to the common rendition of Cupid as powerful monarch in part because of her own history: perhaps unease about her deviation from social norms, whether as debtor, mother of one or more illegitimate children, or poet, encourages her to uphold political norms by emphasizing Pamphilia's willing subvervience to a powerful king.

To Petrarch and Petrarchism, however, neither Wroth nor Pamphilia is willingly subservient. Indeed, the sequence includes not one but a group of successive attempts to dethrone those monarchs, thus recalling Mark Twain's observation that giving up smoking could not be difficult, for he had done it so often. First, then, P46 contrasts false and true love:

> Itt is nott love which you poore fooles do deeme
> That doth apeare by fond, and outward showes
> Of kissing, toying, or by swearings glose,
> O noe thes are farr off from loves esteeme;

> Alas they ar nott such that can redeeme
> Love lost, or wining keepe those chosen blowes
> Though oft with face, and lookes love overthrowse
> Yett soe slight conquest doth nott him beeseeme,

> 'T'is nott a showe of sighes, or teares can prove
> Who loves indeed which blasts of fained love
> Increase, or dy as favors from them slide;

> Butt in the soule true love in safety lies
> Guarded by faith which to desart still hies,
> And yett kinde lookes doe many blessings hide.

Wroth's emphasis on sighs and tears, those staples of Petrarchism, encourages us to number that discourse among the adversaries being attacked. Yet this lyric immediately recalls Shakespeare's counterdiscourses in the breadth of its targets: clearly the love made of "fond, and outward showes" (2) has multiple referents, and thus this sonnet, like so many of Shakespeare's, casts its net widely and in so doing associates Petrarchism with many modes of behavior. The type of love being attacked, then, relies on specious appearances in contrast to the "inward language" about which Anne Ferry has written so well.[124] *Toying* no doubt has its sixteenth- and seventeenth-century meaning of "amorous dalliance" in this context, but an allusion to children's playthings, which would serve to connect this lyric with Wroth's `Anacreontic renditions of Cupid as mischievous child, may be present as well.[125] The reference to "glose[d]," or deceptive, "swearings" (3) associates Petrarchism with misleading language, language that both testifies to the Fall and tempts further falls. Against this deceived and deceptive love the poem plays the true love described in the last three lines. Notice how for all the emphasis on its safety the allusion to a guardian also reminds us that such safety may be imperiled, even besieged. That siege was to be enacted in Wroth's more extensive treatment of anti-Petrarchism, her crown sonnets. And notice, too, how Wroth's characteristic obscurity generates a final line that may complicate the binary contrast she establishes. Is the suggestion that faith is not enough, for love needs "kinde lookes" (14) as well? Do those looks contrast with the "outward showes" (2) condemned earlier or modulate that condemnation? And, in particular, might "hide" (14) uneasily recall earlier suggestions of deceit?

The issues adumbrated in P46 are developed at length in the crown poems. Here too Wroth sets up a contrast between the love she condemns, which encompasses Petrarchism among many other related targets, and a safer and surer love. And once again the high ground from which Pamphilia speaks proves unstable, crumbling away in the course of this series of lyrics.

The crown is preceded by a kind of palinode: in P76 the speaker asks pardon for having appeared to question Cupid's power, surely a curious introduction to a counterdiscourse. The paradox is apparently resolved by the fact that Wroth plays two different Cupids against each other, but the reader's initial unease anticipates the recognition at the end of the sequence that her attempt to establish this neat contrast has failed. In any event, in P76 the juxtaposition of political ("For treason never lodged in my mind" [3]) and religious ("thy endless prayse . . . thy glory" [12, 13]) language establishes the coordinates by which the beneficent Cupid will be mapped.

The prosodic structure of the crown sequence prepares us for the complexity of that mapping. An Italian poetic form in which the final line of one poem or stanza recurs in the first line of the next, the crown had attracted a number of poets before, including Wroth's father and uncle. She might also have known Donne's "La Corona," especially if the scholars who argue that a copy of it was sent to Magdalen Herbert are correct.[126]

[124]Ferry, *"Inward" Language.*
[125]*OED*, s.v. "toy," "toying."
[126]On the possibility that "La Corona" was sent to Magdalen Herbert, see Herbert J. C. Grierson, ed., *The Poems of John Donne*, 2 vols. (Oxford: Oxford University Press, 1912), 2:

Robert Sidney left his own crown incomplete—is Wroth in a sense attempting to complete it and thus to achieve not only spiritual resolution but also an analogue to it in poetic closure?[127] If so, the indeterminate ending of her crown is all the more telling. In any event, in choosing the form Wroth overtly puns on its association with monarchy ("And give a crowne unto thy endless prayse" [P76.12]), thus justifying her decision to crown Cupid poetically. In all these ways she implicitly contrasts false love and false poesy with the latest improved model. And yet in selecting a form grounded in repetition, she also recalls the repetitiveness of Petrarchism and the propensity of its counterdiscourses for reenacting what they aim to reject.

Subterranean though they may be, these implications of Wroth's prosody become overt in the sequence itself. "In this strang labourinth how shall I turne?" (P77.1) refers to Petrarchism inter alia, especially because Petrarch himself fashions the image of a labyrinth of love.[128] (The spelling of "labourinth" may also contain a punning reminder of how much work is involved in either of the two types of love Wroth evokes: both her concern with that travail and her wordplay in expressing it suggest that in *Pamphilia to Amphilanthus*, like the *Urania*,[129] she is Spenser's heir as well as Sidney's and Shakespeare's.)

The reference in P78 to "idle phant'sie" (4), one of Wroth's most recurrent antagonists, further helps us to define the behavior that the crown sonnets eschew. The overlapping and often indistinguishable terms *fancy* and *fantasy* were of considerable interest in the seventeenth century, as the lengthy discussions of them in Hobbes's *Leviathan* and in Davenant's "Preface to Gondibert" and Hobbes's answer to it would suggest. *Imagination* and *fancy* were often used as synonyms in the period, and Hobbes's treatment manifests a deep suspicion of fancy unrestrained by judgment. In Wroth's case, the term involves distortions of the imagination; some sug-

---

228–229; and John Donne, *The Divine Poems*, ed. Helen Gardner (Oxford: Clarendon, 1952), pp. 55–56. To the best of my knowledge, however, a close connection between Magdalen Herbert and Wroth has not been established. Wroth may have gained access to that or another manuscript of the sequence through another route: Hannay (*Philip's Phoenix*, p. 184) points out that Donne was one of the writers whom the third earl of Pembroke encouraged. Other connections between Donne and Wroth are suggested in Naomi J. Miller, "Changing the Subject," chap. 2.

[127]Compare the thoughtful arguments in Naomi J. Miller, "Rewriting Lyric Fictions," pp. 300–304, on differences between Wroth's crown and those of her father and uncle.

[128]On the significance of the labyrinth in Petrarchism, see Roberts's notes on this poem (*The Poems of Lady Mary Wroth*, p. 128).

[129]On the influence of Spenser on the *Urania*, see Lewalski, *Writing Women in Jacobean England*, pp. 268, 269.

gestion of the distortions effected in and by literary discourses may well be present as well, again directing her attacks at least in part against Petrarchism. Paradoxically, however, the type of love celebrated in the crown sonnets enables her to become a successful artist—"Love will a painter make you" (P83.9)—as Lewalski points out.[130] And given the Neo-Stoic resonances of her emphasis on constancy, should one not also adduce the Neo-Stoic concept of opinion in interpreting fancy? Opinion, according to Justus Lipsius, "is vaine, uncertaine, deceitfull, evill in counsell, evill in judgement. It depriveth the mind of Constancie and veritie. To day it desireth a thing, to morrowe it defieth the same."[131] Surely this is an apt gloss on "idle phant'sie" as presented in P78 and elsewhere in the sequence.

If P78 aids us in understanding the type of love Wroth eschews in the crown, it also clearly spells out the alternative values she espouses, which may explain why it is accompanied in the manuscript with the note "This showld be first."[132]

> When chaste thoughts guide us then owr minds ar bent
>   To take that good which ills from us remove,
>   Light of true love, brings fruite which none repent
>   Butt constant lovers seeke, and wish to prove;
>
> Love is the shining starr of blessings light;
>   The fervent fire of zeale, the roote of peace,
>   The lasting lampe fed with the oyle of right;
>   Image of fayth, and wombe for joyes increase.
>
> Love is true vertu, and his ends delight;
>   His flames ar joyes, his bands true lovers might.
>   (5–14)

The emphasis on "chaste thoughts" (5) signals both the rejection of lust and the focus on the internal, on the mind of the lover rather than the relationship between lovers, that characterizes the whole sequence. The religious language throughout emphasizes that Wroth is writing about a spiritual love and the heightened spiritual peace it brings—but not, interestingly, turning away from human love in favor of the worship of God, as Barnes and others did.

---

[130]Lewalski, *Writing Women in Jacobean England*, p. 260.

[131]Justus Lipsius, *Two Bookes of Constancie . . . Englished by Sir John Stradling*, ed. Rudolf Kirk (New Brunswick, N.J.: Rutgers University Press, 1939), p. 82.

[132]See Roberts, *The Poems of Lady Mary Wroth*, p. 129.

Wroth's characteristic preoccupation with constancy emerges in line eight of this poem. Given the obvious resonance of this ideal in the realm of love, many critics have slighted its grounding in the Neo-Stoicism that was enjoying such a vogue in the early seventeenth century. Constancy, Seneca emphasizes throughout "De Constantia Sapientis," shields us from both injuries and insults, which is very much the role Wroth assigns it in her own city of dreadful night. Perhaps her observations and experiences of courtly gossip, manifest in her decision to cast *Urania* as a roman à clef, attracted her to the promise of freedom from insults; perhaps her interest in the poetry of Donne and Jonson, both of whom were influenced by Stoicism, intensified her interest in the school. And, given other signs of her independence, she may well have been challenged to appropriate for her own purposes the author who opens his essay "De Constantia Sapientis" on the observation that the relationship between Stoics and other philosophers resembles that between men and women in that the first was born to command, and the second to obey (1.1)—and proceeds to declare that some men are mad enough to assume that even a woman could insult them (14.1).

Later sonnets within the crown further elucidate and develop Wroth's values. As many other critics have noted, she implicitly contrasts the mischievous Anacreontic Cupid evoked in many of her other sonnets with the majestic god of love celebrated here. Thus she draws on traditions contrasting two Cupids, or Cupid and his brother Anteros, whose tangled roots include a putative reference in Plato, an emblem by Alciati, and poems by several members of the Pléiade.[133] It is quite possible that Mary Wroth, a female poet working in a male tradition, was cognizant of and intrigued by Marguerite de Navarre's treatment of the idea. In any event, her deployment of the two Cupids once again establishes her predilection for binaries and echoes the contrast between another binary set, the unreliable Venus and the trustworthy Cupid evoked in P85.

But seventeenth-century English monarchs were not strong candidates for life insurance policies, and Wroth's Cupid is no exception. As some other critics have recognized, the values espoused in the crown do not survive intact at its conclusion.[134]

---

[133]On this tradition see Robert V. Merrill, "Eros and Anteros," *Speculum*, 19 (1944), 265–284.

[134]For example, Jones (*The Currency of Eros*, p. 152) argues that the end of the series "calls Pamphilia's knowledge of true love into question" but traces this and other contradictions to the expiatory motives that she finds in the sequence. In two studies, Roberts finds in the crown poems an unsuccessful attempt at idealization (*The Poems of Lady Mary Wroth*, p. 45, and "The Biographical Problem of *Pamphilia to Amphilanthus*," p. 50).

> Yett other mischiefs faile nott to attend,
> As enimies to you, my foes must bee;
> Curst jealousie doth all her forces bend
> To my undoing; thus my harmes I see.
>
> Soe though in Love I fervently doe burne,
> In this strange labourinth how shall I turne?
> (P90.9–14)

Admittedly, the enemies are not granted a clear-cut victory; but surely the mode of love they attack is at least imperiled. The labyrinth here comes to represent, in addition to the tangled meanings it assumed earlier in the sequence, the confused struggle between the norms Wroth has established and the "mischiefs" (9) that threaten them. The verb "attend" (9) perhaps gestures towards courtly attendance and hence the court as a site of the threats in question. In addition to these resonances, in "mischiefs" the once illuminating, now shopworn new historicist attraction to the term *re-present* acquires new vitality, for the many other mischiefs towards which the passage gestures re-present Petrarchism itself in all the senses of that verb. Thus the repetition of the opening lines of the sequence, the recurrence of blind turnings within the maze, and the return of the Petrarchan image of that labyrinth all signal the appearance once again of the dilemmas of Petrarchism—a discourse grounded in repetition, a discourse that inspires counterdiscourses based on reenactment.

Those counterdiscourses repeatedly attempt to distance themselves from the Petrarchan dilemmas they instead often replicate, and Mary Wroth's sequence is no exception: the crown is followed by other poems that record the effort to abandon a destructive love for a purer, more constant alternative.[135] In particular, the sequence ends on a lyric that apparently fulfills the compromised aims of the crown poems and in so doing again stages a conflict between a love of inconstant "phant'sies" (3) on the one hand and a love of constancy and peace on the other.

> My muse now hapy, lay thy self to rest,
> Sleepe in the quiett of a faithfull love,
> Write you noe more, butt lett thes phant'sies move
> Some other harts, wake nott to new unrest,

---

[135]Beilin claims unpersuasively that the sonnets after the crown sequence refer covertly to divine love (*Redeeming Eve*, pp. 240–241); I maintain that that ideal is as elusive and unstable as the attacks on Petrarchism in many earlier sequences.

Butt if you study, bee those thoughts adrest
To truth, which shall eternall goodnes prove;
Injoying of true joye, the most, and best,
The endles gaine which never will remove;

Leave the discource of Venus, and her sunn
To young beeginers, and theyr brains inspire
With storys of great love, and from that fire
Gett heat to write the fortunes they have wunn,

And thus leave off, what's past showes you can love,
Now lett your constancy your honor prove,
                                        Pamphilia.

The poem also recalls earlier lyrics in its emphasis on writing as a prime symptom—and perhaps even a prime source—of the illness of love: the connections between established modes of writing and of loving elsewhere in the sequence encourage us to attach to "discource" (9) the full Foucauldian senses. However one interprets the word, lines nine to twelve, and especially the phrase "storys of great love" (11), do suggest some lingering attraction to "the discource of Venus."

And, indeed, this is not the only trace of a lingering attraction. To be sure, in most respects the poem is firmly committed to both signaling and supporting the abandonment of destructive love.[136] The references to sleep and to Venus and Cupid clearly link this lyric to the opening one, providing a cyclical thematic repetition not unlike the repetitions in the crown itself; the closural force of the poem is intensified by both those allusions to rest and words suggesting finality ("noe more" [3], "endles" [8], "leave off" [13]). Yet this text is not quite as definitive as some critics have assumed.[137] Much as a refrain establishes closure and undermines it by raising the possibility of yet another refrain, so this poem cannot help but remind us of Wroth's previous assays at subscribing to a purer, more serene love. We know that Wroth generally composed carefully, structuring the first part of the sequence around groups of six lyrics followed by a song;[138] and

[136]Compare Naomi J. Miller's observation that the speaker gives up the helpless dreaming in which she was engaged at the beginning of the sequence ("Rewriting Lyric Fictions," p. 304); she notes other connections with the opening sonnet as well.

[137]Beilin, for example, finds in the poem a more definitive farewell to passion (*Redeeming Eve*, pp. 241–242).

[138]See Roberts, *The Poems of Lady Mary Wroth*, p. 63. Beilin acutely observes that "the regular ordering of the sonnets is ironic, belying the disorder of Pamphilia's mind" (*Redeeming Eve*, p. 234).

we know that she rearranged the sonnets from an earlier version of *Pamphilia to Amphilanthus*.[139] Hence if she had wanted to evoke steady and successful progress towards "the quiett of a faithfull love" (2), she surely would have placed P46 and the crown sonnets immediately before the culmination of the sequence; by not doing so, she encourages us to feel uneasy about its conclusion.

Throughout *Pamphilia to Amphilanthus*, then, Wroth plays two types of love against each other, a conflict that encompasses but is by no means confined to the dialogue between Petrarchism and anti-Petrarchism. The negative alternative is associated with psychic instability and its interpersonal source and symptom, inconstancy—or, to put it another way, it is associated with restless movement of many types. In contrast, here as in the *Urania* Wroth proffers the ideal of constancy and spirituality; in emphasizing these values and associating them with stasis, she again reminds us to list prominently not only Shakespeare but also Spenser when diagramming her inheritance.

But why, especially given her general preference for lyric rather than narrative, does Wroth so often stage the conflict between two loves as a clash between two personages? We have already considered some explanations: an attraction, perhaps familial, to dramatic encounters; a desire to deflect conflicts within herself, or between Pamphilia and Amphilanthus, onto a safer site. Lamb has argued persuasively for a similar pattern of deflection in the *Urania*.[140] Probably it is also significant that Venus sometimes represents lustful, irresponsible love, whereas her son symbolizes the more desirable alternative. And it may be telling that, as Lord Denny's satirical poem about her testifies,[141] Wroth herself was sometimes associated with the very qualities she attributes to Venus. In other words, Wroth may well be at once denying guilt for sexual licentiousness by displacing it onto her mythological creatures and admitting or at least acknowledging guilt by displacing it onto a woman, not a man. The retreat to political norms which lies behind her loyal enthronement of Cupid finds its analogue in this acceptance of the conventional gendering of desire.

The presentation of Venus, then, circles back to the problems about autonomy on which this study of Wroth opened, and we are now in a position to address two issues. First, how can a woman writer create a voice within the Petrarchan tradition, given that it is generally interpreted as deeply masculine and even masculinist? This question resembles the con-

---

[139]On that revision, see Roberts, *The Poems of Lady Mary Wroth*, pp. 63–64.

[140]See esp. Lamb's argument about Antissia (*Gender and Authorship in the Sidney Circle*, pp. 162–169).

[141]On the poem, see Roberts, *The Poems of Lady Mary Wroth*, pp. 32–35.

troversial problem in film studies to which I alluded earlier: can the female viewer achieve any position other than masochistic identification with the feminine in the film, which is typically denied agency and constructed as the object of the gaze? And, second, how do we reconcile the autonomy Wroth apparently achieves by reshaping her genre or the freedom Pamphilia seemingly achieves by virtually erasing her lover, with evidence of continuing servitude to Petrarchan conventions, to familial practices, and to Cupid himself? In this strange labourinth how shall we turne?

Following a thread woven earlier in this study helps guide us through the maze of the first question, the problem of creating a female voice within a male genre. Generalizations about the masculinity of Petrarchism again need to be modulated not only by the activities of women poets on the Continent but also by the workings of that tradition in England and elsewhere, especially its tendency to elide gender boundaries. Petrarch himself is associated with the veil and footprints he elsewhere assigns to Laura. The agency connected with speech is sometimes denied to the Petrarchan poet and bestowed on his lady. And in important senses that poet is the object of his mistress's gaze. These characteristics of Petrarchism neither deny the anomaly of having an Englishwoman write sonnets nor lessen Wroth's achievement in doing so, but they cast that anomaly as an acknowledgment and heightening of patterns already in the tradition: Wroth is responsible not for introducing the erosion of boundaries but for intensifying an ongoing process. In particular, while some critics have rightly assumed that her constancy is a patriarchal ideal for women, it is also true that the Petrarchan poet is often presented as constant in his devotion for all his desire to escape it—obsessively constant. Moreover, we observed that in ascribing this ideal to the Stoic wise man, Seneca explicitly emphasizes its inaccessibility to, as it were, Cato's sister. A number of seventeenth-century women do express interest in Senecanism;[142] but doing so may well have been seen as transgressive in light of Seneca's injunctions. If so, Pamphilia's constancy, far from simply reverting to patriarchal definitions of the feminine, further obscures the boundaries between male and female, a process also enacted in different ways in many male-authored sequences.

That process may help us to describe, but cannot help us to explain, the contours of our second labyrinth, the apparent juxtaposition of the originality celebrated by some critics with the subservience lamented by others. The mythological tale in P1, in which the passive, dreaming Pamphilia watches her female alter ego give directions to Cupid and also perhaps identifies with Cupid, encourages us to look for our answers by identifying

---

[142]See, e.g., Lamb, *Gender and Authorship in the Sidney Circle*, pp. 126–127.

the multiple roles Pamphilia. and Wroth play and by seeking the sources of that script. Yet another reason Wroth creates not one but two Cupids and bifurcates Cupid's role between himself and Venus in that opening poem is that she is projecting onto her mythological characters the multiple and often contradictory roles she herself assumes. If she is a cross-dresser in the sense defined in the paragraph above, she is an actor in doubled parts as well.

To begin with, she is undoubtedly the forceful innovator, appropriating a genre to her own ends. Indeed, in so doing she sometimes achieves the types of autonomy for which the authors of other counterdiscourses struggle in vain. Delighting in the revision of previously drafted scripts, whether written by herself or her predecessors, Wroth is particularly adept at transforming a potential liability of Petrarchism into a strength. In one scenario common to love poetry, the passivity of the Petrarchan lover is a sign of weakness and failure; in Wroth's revised scenario, by adducing the concept of constancy, she turns that passivity into a positive value. In one script of Petrarchism the woman is an object to be investigated; Wroth rewrites this situation to investigate her own emotions and thus wrest agency from objectification. And in the most common Petrarchan plot the lover loses the beloved; Wroth plots, as it were, to renounce him, thus again achieving agency.

At the same time, as we have seen, the transformations are not wholly successful or consistent; she repeatedly denies that agency even in circumstances where she could easily lay claim to it. Her poetry is figured not as an endless monument to herself or the immortalized beloved but rather as scribblings on tree bark that might or might not be saved by a passerby. Her freedom from the Anacreontic Cupid is expressed through her submission to his majestic alter ego.

Given the achievements of feminist criticism, explanations for why a woman writer might skid between announcing her independence from a lover or a literary tradition on the one hand and manifesting signs of submission on the other might seem at best unnecessary, at worst fatuous. Poststructuralist interpretations of divided and unstable subjectivity also present such slippages as predictable, even inevitable (indeed, Freudian explanations of personality, too often oversimplified dismissively by literary critics, do not necessarily posit the sort of stable and unitary ego their antagonists attribute to them). But in fact further explanations are called for: both the cinematic theory of the twentieth century and the intellectual and literary history of the Renaissance can add nuances to our assumptions about Wroth's ambivalence.

Critics might adapt the cinematic theory of the masquerade and posit an intensification of femininity which aims to expose its artificiality. Or, alternatively, we could maintain instead that Wroth's behavior is a feint to disguise her true subversiveness. Both arguments assume skillful role-playing, but the first involves an agenda of exposure, and the second, one of concealment. I suggest that an inhabitant of the court such as Wroth is likely to try to do both, hoping at once to communicate her rebelliousness to sympathizers and to conceal it from antagonists. Yet these theories, however applicable to Wroth, need to be modulated with the recognition that Petrarchism inherently involves these elisions of gender; Wroth is playing on a generic tradition as well as playing against it. And, above all, they need to be bracketed with the reminder that the best laid plans of Petrarchan authors, no less than cinematic auteurs, full often go astray, once again activating that seesaw between success and failure. For the theories of masquerade and camouflage both assume that Wroth and Pamphilia retain control over their strategies. But, as we saw when reading Sidney, a masquerade may become a mask one cannot peel away. Not the least of the parallels between Wroth and Shakespeare is their knowledge of the dyer's hand. In other words, in orchestrating masquerade and camouflage to explain Wroth, we need to posit a more dynamic and more troubling instrumentality in which the actor gets carried away with the lines and is herself half persuaded of her submission to a social or literary convention or to a male figure. I am arguing, then, not for a consistent and unitary interpretation but for one that recognizes a volatile admixture of control and contradiction, strategy and self-deception.

The sources of that admixture include not only the biographical and cultural pressures to which feminism and new historicism rightly direct our attention but also Wroth's intellectual and poetic models: they intersect and interact in Wroth's texts as they should do in our criticism. Like many other students of Tudor and Stuart literature, I have noted that translation is a mode of writing often associated with women in that tradition, and Wroth would have been especially aware of that connection because of her aunt. Though, as her critics often emphasize, Wroth eschewed the role in question, translation might well have provided a metaphor for the varied and shifting ways she, as it were, translates the conventions of Petrarchism and the gendered assumptions of her culture. For some translators are far more concerned with literal fidelity than others. And a given practitioner of that art often does not have a consistent relationship to her or his text: some passages may strive to follow the original closely, others to interpret and reinterpret its complexities. (It is no accident that twentieth-century professionals in the field are variously assigned two significantly different titles, translator and interpreter.) In addition, her sequence may well be shaped by Stoicism in yet another respect. That school, Herschel Baker reminds us, is clouded by a paradox: "Of all forms of Renaissance neopaganism worked into the fabric of Christianity it advocated the most ruthless individualism; yet it also put man's freedom under the severest check. The Neo-Stoics could urge the utmost liberty for man's conscience and conduct precisely because they could not conceive of freedom without law."[143] Might not Neo-Stoicism have appealed to Wroth in part because it stages the very paradox of constrained autonomy on which her sequence pivots? And might it then not have provided a model for her own explorations of that paradox, with the beneficent Cupid of the crown assuming the role of law?

Above all, however, Petrarchism and anti-Petrarchism provide the most significant model for Wroth's relationship to autonomy and submission. Petrarchan discourses define themselves diacritically, through contrast with other writers and other selves—and yet so frequently incorporate that which they reject within themselves. The counterdiscourses of Petrarchism, as we have seen, struggle for autonomy, struggle to dethrone conventions of writing and loving—and yet so often acknowledge that Petrarch's Cupid remains their deity. Thus they offer a blueprint both for the slippage between success and failure or power and powerlessness in male subjectivity and for the situation of a woman attempting to achieve freedom from a man and a convention and to appropriate a genre that both is and is not her birthright. The counterdiscourses of Petrarchism, then, can mime the problematics of female subjectivity as well as male, and Wroth is attracted to the sonnet not only as the genre of her male relatives but also as a potential model for her own subjectivity.

That attraction generates poetry that variously manifests interpellations and effects new interpretations, poetry that variously reinterprets and reenacts problems that had appeared to be solved earlier. Both the reinterpretation and the reenactment ally Wroth with other, male speakers of the Petrarchan discourse and counterdiscourse—and at the same time establish a distinctively female idiolect. Play it again, Pamphilia.

[143]Herschel Baker, *The Dignity of Man: Studies in the Persistence of an Idea* (Cambridge: Harvard University Press, 1947), p. 309.

CHAPTER FIVE

FOREIGN CURRENCIES:
JOHN COLLOP AND THE "UGLY
BEAUTY" TRADITION

I

Sir John Davies praises a prostitute. Thomas Carew and Lord Herbert of Cherbury both celebrate women suffering from the "green-sickness."[1] Their less well known contemporary John Collop renders the currency of love poetry as unstable as the literal currency of Henrican England by repeatedly lauding women with what he terms "golden skin." As we have observed, the diacritical drive at the core of anti-Petrarchism can take many different forms: writers mock other poets for insincerity, parody Petrarchan language, substitute spiritual values for erotic imperatives, and so on. In the poems explored in this chapter, however, the process of differentiation is even more central, constituting the primary drive behind them and often the global speech act within them. Under what circumstances and for what reasons, then, does the diacritical impulse of anti-Petrarchism generate a diacritical response to the Petrarchan lady—that is, the ironic praise of a woman who is, or who seems to be, her opposite?

Widely though misleadingly termed the *ugly beauty* or *deformed mistress* tradition, the mode in question comprises poems that describe, generally in ostensibly favorable terms, a woman with qualities that are seldom the subject of praise.[2] Instances range from texts that satirize indubitably neg-

---

[1]For a seventeenth-century discussion of this condition, see Nicholas Culpeper, *Culpeper's Directory for Midwives: or, A Guide for Women. The Second Part* (London, 1662), pp. 100–106. This text must be distinguished from one with a similar title, *A Directory for Midwives*, which Culpeper published in 1651.

[2]Critics have devoted little attention to these poems. The best discussion is the brief but suggestive introduction in Conrad Hilberry, ed., *The Poems of John Collop* (Madison: University of Wisconsin Press, 1962), pp. 19–26.

ative characteristics, such as Davies's epigrammatic description of a prostitute, to ones that focus on a trait sometimes coded as negative by the culture at large but seemingly not by the poet at hand, such as Lord Herbert's apparently unironic praise of a woman with what he calls brown skin, to the many poems that occupy a contested and mined territory between praise and dispraise, such as "One Enamour'd on a Black-moor" by the minor seventeenth-century poet Eldred Revett. Often, as in Carew's "On Mistris N. to the Greene Sicknesse," it is almost impossible to determine whether the thrust of the lyric is ironic. In some instances, such as Shakespeare's Sonnet 130, the poem focuses on traits that render the woman more human; frequently, however, they render her unappealing, even disgusting, with certain texts portraying an aging or ill body and others reversing characteristics so that she has, say, red eyes and bluish lips rather than blue eyes and red lips. In one subdivision of the tradition, a type of poem that is Cavalier in several senses of the word, the poet celebrates his ability to love women with a wide range of appearances, including some generally considered unattractive.

If ugly beauty poems vary in their portrayal of the woman, they vary, too, in genre, some borrowing the sonnet form, others adopting epigrammatic characteristics, and yet others combining elements of sonnet and epigram and thus reminding us of Rosalie L. Colie's emphasis on the frequent twinning and overlapping of those types.[3] Members of this third, hybrid group, such as Sidney's poem on Mopsa, may shift the generic balance of Petrarchism by playing up the epigrammatic elements subordinated in more straightforward sonnets, hence making what had been minor or latent more prominent, much as they accord dominance to the subversive, anti-Petrarchan strains that are often latent even in apparently conventional Petrarchism. In short, the lyrics that describe women who are marginal to the culture because of their skin color and other traits or women who unsettle cultural standards of beauty often occupy marginalized spaces in a generic system that itself was prone both to establish and to flout generic standards. In so doing, they may implicitly comment on the norms of the sonnet, demonstrating once again that the counterdiscourses of Petrarchism allow poets to practice genre criticism by example rather than precept.

Even this brief introduction suggests the problem of labeling such texts. Although I adopt for convenience the term used by most critics, *ugly beauty*, that phrase (like its French analogue, *jolie laideur*) ignores the fact that some

---

[3] Rosalie L. Colie, *Shakespeare's Living Art* (Princeton: Princeton University Press, 1974), chap. 2.

of the women are not ugly according to prevailing cultural norms. And, more to the point, that oxymoron accepts the very cultural standards that these poems are at pains to undermine.[4] Some poems do so directly, by arguing that, say, the racial Other is attractive. And in the very act of describing an unambiguously unattractive woman and distinguishing her from attractive ones, certain lyrics unmoor the categories on which they depend—ugliness and beauty—thus rendering problematical the oxymoron that customarily labels their tradition. Hence they also slide between satiric and epideictic modes, confounding those categories too. In skidding between literary types and tones, as in so many other ways, the poems enact generically the processes of disguise, equivocation, and transformation which they perform rhetorically.

As an instance of the paradoxical encomium, the ugly beauty tradition traces its ancestry to classical versions of that literary type.[5] The paradoxical encomium, a popular and varied form, was apparently deployed as a school exercise in Greece and Rome. Gorgias, Isocrates, Lucian, and Plato, among other authors, write paradoxical encomia, while classical commentaries both anatomize and advocate them. In a passage particularly germane to the English tradition, Ovid ironically suggests that rather than reproaching women with their faults, one should reinterpret those failings as strengths: "Nominibus mollire licet mala: fusca vocetur, / Nigrior Illyrica cui pice sanguis erit" (*Ars Amatoria* 2.657–658, "With names you can soften shortcomings; let her be called swarthy, whose blood is blacker than Illyrian pitch").[6] Notice that the subject of gendered transgressions generates an example of what might today be viewed as racial ones and that *malum*, the word translated as "shortcomings," could also be read as "evil" or "calamity."[7] Medieval instances of paradoxical encomia, though scanty, include the mock blazon in the *Nun's Priest's Tale*.[8] In both the Continental and the English Renaissance, the paradoxical encomium flourished, as did the

---

[4]My omission of quotation marks around "ugly beauty" does not imply my acceptance of the implications behind the phrase. I thank Amy Ling for useful insights into this and several other issues in this chapter.

[5]On the tradition, see Theodore C. Burgess, *Epideictic Literature* (Chicago: University of Chicago Press, 1902); Rosalie L. Colie, *Paradoxia Epidemica: The Renaissance Tradition of Paradox* (Princeton: Princeton University Press, 1966); J. B. Leishman, *The Monarch of Wit: An Analytical and Comparative Study of the Poetry of John Donne* (London: Hutchinson, 1951), pp. 74–81; Henry Knight Miller, "The Paradoxical Encomium with Special Reference to Its Vogue in England, 1600–1800," *MP*, 53 (1956), 145–178; and Arthur Stanley Pease, "Things without Honor," *Classical Philology*, 21 (1926), 27–42.

[6]The citation to Ovid is from *The Art of Love and Other Poems*, trans. J. H. Mozley (London and Cambridge: William Heinemann and Harvard University Press, 1957).

[7]Charlton T. Lewis, *A Latin Dictionary*, rev. ed. (Oxford: Clarendon, 1980), s.v. "malum."

[8]I am indebted to Alger N. Doane for helpful suggestions about medieval and other texts.

version of it which praises unattractive women; especially relevant to the English tradition is Francesco Berni's "Chiome d'argento fine." As this influential text reminds us, such poems of praise were hardly unique to early modern England, but they interacted in distinctive ways with the distinctive chemistry of that culture.

Among the ugly beauty poems in Tudor and Stuart England are two little known poems by Gascoigne, the ninth and thirteenth lyrics in his *Devises of Sundrie Gentlemen;* the tribute to Mopsa in the third chapter of the *New Arcadia;* the mock encomium in Lyly's *Endymion;* Davies's epigram "In Gellam" ("Gella, if thou dost"); Barnes's Sonnet 13; Shakespeare's Sonnet 130 and some of the other Dark Lady poems; three of Donne's elegies; and lyrics by Drayton, Carew, Herrick, and Suckling. Less well known authors also contributed to the tradition: *Poems,* a collection that Eldred Revett published in 1657, includes a few texts about black women, and the most prolific writer in the tradition is the seventeenth-century poet and doctor John Collop.

Members of the English ugly beauty tradition sport complex and differing intellectual and literary genealogies. They are all heirs and assigns of the classical paradoxical encomium, but they may variously participate as well in Restoration satire, Platonism, and iconographical traditions of *vanitas.*[9] Although Petrarchism is the primary target of texts like Sidney's, it is a more subsidiary antagonist in lyrics like Lord Herbert of Cherbury's descriptions of women with atypical skin colors. Nonetheless, the ugly beauty tradition remains one of the most significant and most suggestive instances of our counterdiscourses. These poems are the epicenter of the eruptions that shake English Petrarchism.

II

What rhetorical strategies recur even in these seemingly dissimilar texts, and what do they suggest about the agendas that impel the ugly beauty tradition? Because many of its poems are unfamiliar and because their significance often resides in nuances of tone, addressing these problems calls for detailed textual analyses.

> What length of verse can serve brave *Mopsa's* good to show,
> Whose vertues strange, and beuties such, as no man them may know?

[9] On their Platonic elements, see Peter Ure, "The 'Deformed Mistress' Theme and the Platonic Convention," *NQ,* 193 (1948), 269–270.

Thus shrewdly burdned then, how can my Muse escape?
The gods must help, and pretious things must serve to shew her shape.
Like great god *Saturn* faire, and like faire *Venus* chaste:
As smooth as *Pan*, as *Juno* milde, like goddesse *Isis* faste.
With *Cupid* she fore-sees, and goes god *Vulcan's* pace:
And for a tast of all these gifts, she borowes *Momus'* grace.
Her forhead jacinth like, her cheekes of opall hue,
Her twinkling eies bedeckt with pearle, her lips of Saphir blew:
Her haire pure Crapal-stone; her mouth O heavenly wyde;
Her skin like burnisht gold, her hands like silver ure untryde.
As for those parts unknowne, which hidden sure are best:
Happie be they which well beleeve, and never seeke the rest.[10]

Appearing in book 1, chapter 3 of Sidney's *New Arcadia,* this sonnet exemplifies many of the rhetorical devices and techniques most frequently used in the tradition. It exemplifies, too, one end of that spectrum, straightforward satire. But in many respects it is far from straightforward, and the prose passages surrounding it, as well as the lyric itself, reveal through their equivocations that their author's motives extend far beyond satirizing a grossly unattractive character.

Not only does the poem itself represent a paradigmatic instance of its tradition, but Sidney also projects the impulses and anxieties behind that tradition onto the seemingly unrelated plot immediately surrounding the poem. In other words, he displaces the tensions that are usually embedded within or hidden beneath poems in praise of ugly women by turning them into narrative, thus exemplifying the deflection that is itself so characteristic of the tradition. In this instance, the passage pivots on one particularly significant form of saying and unsaying: the expression and then denial of hostility towards women.

Gender is not, however, the only locus of antagonism in this or several other beauty poems. Mopsa, like some of Collop's women, is a lower-class character, which reminds us that social tensions may lurk behind the aesthetic valuations of the ugly beauty tradition. These tensions, too, figure in the narrative surrounding the poem, for one sign that Basilius's behavior is foolhardy is that he has entrusted his daughter Pamela to her irresponsible social inferiors Dametas and Miso, Mopsa's parents.

The drive both to express and to erase the hostility behind an ugly beauty poem is proleptically introduced earlier in the passage by the description of that odd couple Basilius and Gynecia. Basilius has abandoned his king-

[10] I cite William A. Ringler Jr., ed., *The Poems of Sir Philip Sidney* (Oxford: Clarendon, 1962).

dom, a threatening situation that anticipates the significance of threats both elsewhere in this passage and in the entire ugly beauty tradition. As for Gynecia, the ostensible praise of her lends credence to the excavators who have discovered a dark maternal subtext beneath the romance:[11] she is, the reader is informed, "in truth of more princely virtues than her husband . . . but of so working a mind and so vehement spirits as a man may say it was happy she took a good course, for otherwise it would have been terrible" (p. 76).[12] Notice how "as a man may say" distances the speaker from his judgments, a pattern that recurs throughout the passage.

The succeeding introduction of the princesses marshals other strategies for at once introducing and denying gendered hostility. These exemplary women prove, Sidney's character Kalander tells us, that "nature is no stepmother to that sex, how much soever some men . . . have sought to disgrace them" (p. 76). Distancing anxiety about maternity by deflecting it onto the stepmother, these lines near the beginning of Sidney's romance may remind us that early in the first sonnet of *Astrophil and Stella*, he displaces anxiety about creativity onto that same family member. More to our purposes here, Kalander proceeds to deflect a broader attack on women onto "some men" and in so doing denies his own criticism. Sidney then offers a description of Pamela and Philoclea which casts its praise of these princesses in terms of competitive comparisons—"more sweetness in Philoclea but more majesty in Pamela" (p. 76).[13]

Cognate forms of distancing and denial are again enacted in the lines that immediately precede the hostile ugly beauty sonnet that mocks Mopsa. "But because a pleasant fellow of my acquaintance set forth her praises in verse," Kalander explains, "I will only repeat them and spare mine own tongue, since she goes for a woman. The verses are these, which I have so often caused to be sung that I have them without book" (p. 77). "Goes for a woman" performs that process of both establishing and eliding distinctions: while protecting the category of woman by suggesting Mopsa doesn't really fit in it (much as the stepmother figure may permit the

<hr>

[11]On that subtext, see esp. Barbara J. Bono, " 'The Chief Knot of All the Discourse': The Maternal Subtext Tying Sidney's *Arcadia* to Shakespeare's *King Lear*," in *Gloriana's Face: Women, Public and Private, in the English Renaissance*, ed. S. P. Cerasano and Marion Wynne-Davies (New York: Harvester Wheatsheaf, 1992). I thank the author for making her work available in manuscript and for other valuable assistance with this book.

[12]Quoted from Sir Philip Sidney, *The Countess of Pembroke's Arcadia*, ed. Maurice Evans (Harmondsworth, Eng.: Penguin, 1977). Page references to this work and to the *Old Arcadia* appear in my text.

[13]Nancy Lindheim also notes these antitheses but relates them to Sidney's other contrasting descriptions of the princesses (*The Structures of Sidney's "Arcadia"* [Toronto: University of Toronto Press, 1982], p. 31).

idealization of maternity), the phrase also reminds us that Mopsa is in fact a woman. Such equivocations are writ large in Kalander's introduction of the song. He did not write it, yet he repeats it; he claims to spare his own tongue even while deploying it; he doesn't sing the poem but causes it to be sung; and despite his reservations about it, he has done so often enough to know it by heart. Similarly, in book 1 of the *Old Arcadia* the narrator is at pains to attribute the song to one Alethes. Here too he stresses that the song is not his own ("I will only repeat them and spare mine own pen").[14] But the fact that he devotes less space to the process of both explaining and disavowing his connection to the poem suggests that on the subject of transgressive women and his responses to them, as on many other issues, Sidney's anxieties intensified when he rewrote his romance.

Despite these forms of distancing, Kalander does deploy this sonnet as a counter in his relationship with Musidorus. The poem does not serve to advance the narrative; rather, the younger man is invited to appreciate its wit. Within this text, as in the text of Renaissance culture, ugly beauty poems seem designed in part to strengthen the bonds between men.

The poem itself is typical in many ways of a subdivision of the ugly beauty tradition, the unabashedly satirical poem.[15] Sidney opens on a parody of the inexpressibility conceit: "What length of verse can serve brave *Mopsa's* good to show, / Whose vertues strange, and beuties such, as no man them may know?" (1–2). By playing on "length," he gestures towards his use of poulter's measure, an ungainly meter for an ungainly subject. Though light-hearted mockery of Mopsa is his overt agenda in the opening lines, these references to what cannot be said foreshadow the darker allusions to both poetic and physiological concealment at the conclusion of the poem.

Sidney then incorporates twisted versions of Petrarchan praise. The Other, Mopsa, both is and is not like the normative Petrarchan mistress, much as this sonnet both resembles and rejects generic norms. In particular, its author parodies mythological comparisons, informing us that this prize is as fair as Saturn and as chaste as Venus. He proceeds to describe Mopsa through the anagram, a strategy very common in the ugly beauty tradition. Qualities are reversed, so that her eyes rather than her mouth are "bedeckt with pearle" (10), and her mouth rather than her eyes are blue. This game, memorably developed by Berni, was also to be played in many later English poems. In such anagrams, a kind of demonic parody of Petrarch's reordering of the letters in

---

[14]The citation is to *The Countess of Pembroke's Arcadia (The Old Arcadia)*, ed. Jean Robertson (Oxford: Clarendon, 1973).

[15]Sidney's poem was to be closely imitated in a Restoration satire attributed to John Mennes and James Smith, "In Imitation of Sir Philip Sydnie's Encomium of Mopsa" (in [John Mennes, James Smith et al.], *Wit Restor'd in Severall Select Poems* [London, 1658]).

"Laureta," the blazon itself is reordered. "Her skin like burnisht gold" (12), Sidney then proceeds to declare, thus introducing a comparison that also recurs in several poems in the tradition. As Collop's poems will demonstrate, such comparisons at once stabilize and unsettle valuation: if they remind us of the norm, such as pearly teeth, they also question that norm by raising the possibility that pearls are less valuable than they might appear, for they can figure repulsive secretions in addition to beautiful teeth.

The most significant part of the poem, however, is its conclusion: "As for those parts unknowne, which hidden sure are best: / Happie be they which well beleeve, and never seeke the rest" (13–14). Thus the sonnet continues its game of equivocation, in one sense revealing the very parts that it conceals and advocates concealing. How is the desire to describe Mopsa's lips or cheeks related to the drive to conceal yet hint at her genitals? The answer, we will discover, lies in the imbricated gynephobic hostility and gynecological anxiety manifest not only in this poem but throughout its literary tradition.

If Sidney's tribute to Mopsa exemplifies the overtly hostile reaches of the tradition, one of Thomas Carew's poems as aptly represents the many poems that are on a fulcrum between repulsion and admiration.

On Mistris N. to the Greene Sicknesse

Stay coward blood, and doe not yield
To thy pale sister, beauties field,
Who there displaying round her white
Ensignes, hath usurp'd thy right;
Invading thy peculiar throne,
The lip, where thou shouldst rule alone;
And on the cheeke, where natures care
Allotted each an equall share,
Her spreading Lilly only growes,
Whose milky deluge drownes thy Rose.
    Quit not the field faint blood, nor rush
In the short salley of a blush,
Upon thy sister foe, but strive
To keepe an endlesse warre alive;
Though peace doe petty States maintaine,
Here warre alone makes beauty raigne.[16]

---

[16] All citations from Carew are to Rhodes Dunlap, ed., *The Poems of Thomas Carew* (Oxford: Clarendon, 1957).

The poem delights in witty paradoxes. Blood, normally associated with strength, is here apostrophized as "coward blood" (1), a reversal that Lord Herbert of Cherbury also uses in one of his two poems on the greensickness, "The Green-Sickness Beauty."[17] The concluding line, "Here warre alone makes beauty raigne," is epigrammatic enough to recall one of its ancestors, the "point" on which epigrams often terminate. In analyzing its darker tonalities, one should not forget that in one sense it is a playful tour de force.

But neither should one ignore the tensions behind its playfulness. Notice that rather than being predominantly pale, the woman is the arena for an unresolved conflict between the two colors. Hence her appearance is another version of blurred boundaries in a literary type that focuses on marginal states of all kinds. And by emphasizing that she too sports the Petrarchan red and white rather than merely emphasizing her paleness, Carew creates an Other whose relationship to the norm is as volatile and contested as her complexion. Moreover, the apparently playful war between red and white calls into question other social norms: because some Renaissance medical tracts, following Hippocrates, advocate sexual activity as a cure for the green-sickness,[18] the battle between the colors may be interpreted as a struggle between virginity and its loss.

The poem proceeds to describe that conflict between red and white in terms that variously emphasize and deny its abnormality. If on the one hand this text quite literally naturalizes the customary Petrarchan amalgam of white and red ("where natures care / Allotted each an equall share" [7–8]), on the other hand it also naturalizes the lady's disturbed constitution. For if paleness can be seen as the blooming of lilies, her condition itself is transformed into a botanical bounty. At the same time, however, the notion of drowning in a "milky deluge" (10) hints at an element of threat. (The adjective "milky" may recall the maternal subtext of Sidney; these resonances remain merely a troubling undercurrent in this text, but they urge us to keep asking how anxieties about maternity relate to the ugly beauty tradition.) Carew's tropes, then, make it hard to determine to what extent, if at all, the woman who violates the Petrarchan norms is being described as unappealing. That determination is further confounded by the final line, which does seem to attribute beauty to this woman. On one level, her unattractiveness is purged; on another level, the witty jokes draw attention

[17]Lord Herbert has two poems of that title; the one in question opens, "From thy pale look."

[18]See, e.g., Culpeper, *Culpeper's Directory for Midwives*, pp. 105–106.

to just how undesirable she really is. Thus the tone of the poem is unstable and elusive.

That tone is further complicated by Carew's mechanisms for distancing his lyric from its apparent addressee, Mistress N. Witness the curious reversal of prepositions in the title, "On Mistris N. to the Greene Sicknesse." Although one cannot rule out the possibility of a simple error on the part of the author or compositor, that reversal might serve to direct attention away from the subjectivity of the woman, a pattern common in the straightforward Petrarchan lyrics too.

In a sense, however, the title describes not only a woman but its own ugly beauty tradition in general and this poem in particular. Mistress N.'s face, like the poem itself, is comprised of Petrarchan elements—but in a skewed relationship that makes them hard to evaluate. And, much as that face is a battlefield for a struggle that is emphatically unresolved, so the text is an arena for unresolved wars between praise and dispraise, conventional and transgressive attitudes towards beauty. These parallels between a woman's body and a male writer's poem, parallels found in many other lyrics in the tradition, exemplify two recurrent characteristics of the counterdiscourses of Petrarchism. Explicitly gendered female in some other texts, such as Wyatt's "Whoso List To Hunt," here, too these counterdiscourses are associated with women, though in this case more implicitly. And as a result the boundaries between male and female again blur, as they do so often in Petrarchism.

Several of Lord Herbert of Cherbury's ugly beauty poems involve neither the open satire of Sidney's sonnet to Mopsa nor the ambivalent praise of Carew's lyric but virtually unqualified celebration. The title "La Gialletta Gallante, or, The Sun-burn'd Exotique Beauty" emphasizes the foreignness of the woman through the foreignness of its own language as well as the epithet "exotique." "Sun-burn'd" may hint at the atypical, even abnormal, but at the same time by making the sun the source of the lady's skin color, Lord Herbert, like Carew, naturalizes what might otherwise appear unnatural.[19]

The first stanza focuses again on the sun by opening on the apostrophe "Child of the Sun" (1).[20] In so doing, it reminds us of the Petrarchan commonplace of comparing the mistress to the sun: once more this counterdiscourse does not so much ignore or reject Petrarchan rhetoric as ap-

[19]Juliet Fleming has suggested to me that "sun-burn'd" may also encode a secondary reference to the anxiety of influence: the author of the Petrarchan counterdiscourse is a son burned by the patriarchal power of the sun.

[20]Lord Herbert is quoted from G. C. Moore Smith, ed., *The Poems English and Latin of Edward, Lord Herbert of Cherbury* (Oxford: Clarendon, 1923).

propriate and reinterpret it. The stanza proceeds to declare that if the woman's dark skin is natural in one sense, in another it transcends nature because it is immune from peril:

> What need'st thou fear
> The injury of Air, and change of Clime,
> When thy exalted form is so sublime,
> As to transcend all power of change or time?
>
> (3–6)

An American poet, John Josselyn, was to make the same point by ending his lyric "Verses Made Sometime Since Upon the Picture of a Young and Handsome Gypsie" with the declaration "and such perfection here appears / It neither Wind nor Sun-shine fears" (19–20).[21] Such lines add another problem to the agenda of this chapter: how and why does the same tradition that sometimes focuses on conditions like the green-sickness or on pathological symptoms like jaundice in other instances praise women precisely for their immunity to mutability of all types?

Lord Herbert proceeds with the witty reversals that are so characteristic of ugly beauty poetry, overturning the hierarchy that would rank Englishwomen with golden hair over this golden-skinned woman:

> How proud are they that in their hair but show
> Some part of thee, thinking therein they ow
> The greatest beauty Nature can bestow!
> When thou art so much fairer to the sight,
>
> (7–10)

Notice that again he declares the Other's un-Petrarchan complexion not merely natural but also an improved version of Petrarchan beauty. Thus the distinction between this woman and normative beauties is simultaneously asserted and undermined. The poem then continues its ploy of demonstrating her superiority by suggesting that she is "cordial" (13; yet another passing allusion to disease and health) and that "rare fruit[s]" (14) circulate within her (another suggestion that she is natural yet exotic). The lyric concludes by emphasizing her foreignness and inviting her to enter and in a sense even invade and conquer England, much as Lord Herbert's reinterpretation of tropes like the comparison between the lady

---

[21]The citation is to Harrison T. Meserole, ed., *Seventeenth-Century American Poetry*, Stuart Editions (New York: New York University Press, 1968). I thank Emory Elliott for bringing this poem to my attention.

and the sun has invaded and conquered English Petrarchan discourse. A concern with the abnormal in the form of disease reappears, though here transferred from the woman whose skin color might have led to the accusation of jaundice to those whose skin color would seem most normative and least jaundiced.

> Leave then thy Country Soil, and Mothers home,
> Wander a Planet this way, till thou come
> To give our Lovers here their fatal doom;
>   While if our beauties scorn to envy thine,
>   It will be just they to a Jaundise pine
>   And by thy Gold shew like some Copper-
>   mine.
>
>   (25–30)

John Collop was to develop Lord Herbert's concern with gold skin, foreignness, and disease in ways that help us to understand the relationship of the ugly beauty tradition to both the counterdiscourses of Petrarchism and the culture of Tudor and Stuart England.

III

Four rhetorical patterns—antitheses, the erosion of such antitheses, equivocations, and threats—recur not only in the poems by Sidney, Carew, and Lord Herbert of Cherbury which we examined but also throughout the ugly beauty tradition. Poems of this type are generally structured in terms of competing and often conflicting alternatives, though that competition may assume forms ranging from a dialogue between opposites to a pitched battle. The contrasts on which Sidney's sonnet pivots (blue eyes versus blue lips, Mopsa's ugly beauty versus the genuine loveliness of the princesses) are manifest as well in the surrounding prose, which dwells on distinctions between Pamela and Philoclea. Many other texts contrast straight Petrarchan language with their own—"My mistress' eyes are nothing like the sun" (Shakespeare, Sonnet 130.1)[22]—and standard Petrarchan beauties with their own object, as Lord Herbert does when he declares that his brown beauty is more attractive than women with either white or black skin. Or this emphasis on difference and conflict may be displaced

---

[22]I quote from Stephen Booth, ed., *Shakespeare's Sonnets* (New Haven: Yale University Press, 1977).

onto narrative elements, as when Carew describes the green-sickness of a woman as a battle between those Petrarchan colors red and white. The focus on alternatives is also manifest syntactically and rhetorically, with various tropes of antithesis and negative and privative constructions. Many poems deploy antithesis in its most straightforward form, the trope sometimes called antitheton: "Thy Cheeke, now flush with Roses, sunke, and leane" (Drayton, *Idea* 8.9).[23] Or the comparison of opposites may take the form of antimetabole, the syntactical mirroring that, as Quintilian himself stresses, is a type of antithesis: "One like none, and lik'd of none" (Donne, "The Anagram," 55).[24] Thus poems based on conflicting and conflicted responses to gender and the female body inscribe conflicts on the body of the text or, to put it another way, deflect conflicts from one body to the other. And in so doing they project the diacritical drive of Petrarchism onto their own rhetoric.

Though these modes of antithesis imply distinction and contrast, these poems are also concerned to elide those distinctions. Like the anamorphic art and other baroque experiments that flourished in the seventeenth century, they may remind us that our perspective determines what we see. As we will observe, Collop's black woman Nigrina is, paradoxically, praised for the whiteness of her teeth. Often the reader cannot be sure if the woman in question is an antithesis to the Petrarchan woman or merely a new and improved model. Or these texts may describe a form of beauty which depends on the elision of distinctions, as when Lord Herbert of Cherbury asserts in "The Brown Beauty" that a brown-skinned woman breaks down the contrast between black and white skin. Above all, though, it is the anagram form, memorably developed by Berni and exemplified by Sidney's tribute to Mopsa, that most effectively and most disturbingly erodes distinctions. Claiming that the woman has all the qualities of beautiful women but in an unusual order ("Marry, and love thy *Flavia*, for, shee / Hath all things, whereby others beautious be" [Donne, "The Anagram," 1–2]), these poems twist the normative blazon into a kaleidoscope. "Though her eyes be small, her mouth is great," Donne proceeds to observe (3). Similarly, Sidney asserts that his Mopsa has not the customary pearly teeth but rather pearls in her eyes, presumably some discharge. Hence these anagrammatic poems perform on the blazon the process of antithetical reversal which, as we have just seen, is staged rhetorically through antimetabole in Donne's lyric "The Anagram" and elsewhere:

[23]All citations from Drayton are to J. William Hebel, Bernard H. Newdigate, and Kathleen Tillotson, eds., *The Works of Michael Drayton*, 5 vols. (Oxford: Basil Blackwell, 1931–1941).

[24]The citation to Donne is from Helen Gardner, ed., *The Elegies and The Songs and Sonnets* (Oxford: Clarendon, 1965).

"One like none, and lik'd of none" (55). Thus if such poems establish distinctions through the implicit contrast with the normative woman who has red cheeks rather than red hair, they simultaneously undermine those distinctions with the reminder that the women have, after all, comparable coloring. And if they enshrine cultural norms by reminding us of the standards from which this woman deviates, they unsettle those norms by questioning both the valuation on which they are based (are pearls really so precious if they can be shanghaied to represent not white teeth but runny eyes?) and the stability of our judgments (if the ugly beauty in question is really a version of the beautiful woman, is that beauty in fact volatile and frangible?) The anagram formula transforms beauty from a stable and fixed norm to a fragile point within an erratic volatile process of valuation in which colors may switch their place on a face and pearls careen between value and worthlessness.

As these elisions would suggest, ugly beauty poems, like other forms of the paradoxical encomium, typically both disguise and shift their own aims and strategies. In this as so many other ways, representation is called into question. Nowhere is Colie's observation about the equivocations of the paradox more clearly demonstrated than in the poems in this tradition.[25] Ironic and evasive, they are engaged in saying and unsaying, asserting and denying, praising and dispraising. Many of them, of course, are parodic. If they evoke women who are on the boundary between fair and foul, black and white, pale and ruddy, young and antique, rhetorically they themselves, as we have already seen, occupy contested and shifting borders.

Anxieties involving gender are often at once the result and the source of threats, and nowhere is this pattern more revealingly enacted than in the ugly beauty tradition. Most obviously, in Collop's "To Aureola" the speaker threatens to inflict degrading descriptions on the woman if she does not yield to him. He is the bad cop who will harm her and the good cop who offers a way out. Lurking just beneath the surface of many other ugly beauty poems is the threat of a more pejorative description, a slippage into a more antagonistic poem in a genre that involves slippages of so many other sorts. Thus when Donne distinguishes his aging woman from one who is more elderly ("But name not Winter-faces," ["The Autumnall," 37]) or when he rejects a more negative portrayal of his subject ("Call not these wrinkles, graves" ["The Autumnall," 13], he is introducing only to disown, disowning only to introduce. Similarly, as we saw earlier, in declaring that his mistress's breath "reeks" (Sonnet 130.8), Shakespeare is invoking a word that might have negative connotations and thus reminding

[25]Colie, *Paradoxia Epidemica*, esp. pp. 5–6.

us of the more critical poem that could be written about a woman with black wires on her head.[26] Such alternative poems are the alter ego, the demonic shadow, of Sonnet 130.

Threats such as these destabilize language in two ways. First, they often either express or assume a conditional, as in Collop's "To Aureola," which pivots on this threat: if you will not be mine, I will defame you. Iago, that master of equivocation, delights in conditionals for the very reason they are significant here: they seesaw between a firm commitment (I will defame you) and a proviso that limits that commitment. But fully to understand the presence of threats in this tradition, critics need to rediscover speech act theory. Often scorned by literary critics as positivistic and ahistorical, linguistics, including this branch of it, can illuminate many issues of concern to students of literary and cultural studies.[27] In particular, speech act theory can be redirected to show how both power and authority are not only manifested but also, more to the point, generated in discourse. In this instance, speech act theory helps us to understand why threats occupy a central if often subterranean position in ugly beauty poems. For through the threat the speaker asserts power and agency—but they are never tested, never realized. So the poems effect yet another form of equivocation: the reader is never quite sure how seriously the threat is meant or to what extent, if at all, the poet would be able to fulfill it. The dynamic interplay between threatening and being threatened is central to the issue on which this chapter focuses: how and why the diacritical imperative of Petrarchism is so often interpreted as a diacritical contrast between the Petrarchan mistress and her twin and rival, the ugly beauty. Sa semblable—sa soeur.

IV

Frustrating in their syntactical obscurities, unsettling in their vituperative prejudices, disturbed and disturbing in their racial and sexual fantasies, the poems of John Collop exemplify many of the characteristics we traced in the ugly beauty tradition. In so doing they reveal its etiologies, its genealogies, and its pathologies better than any other texts in English. Collop, a writer and a doctor who lived from 1625 until sometime after 1676,

---

[26]See Booth, *Shakespeare's Sonnets*, pp. 454–455.

[27]The continuing relevance of speech act theory is also discussed in Susanne Wofford's unpublished manuscript, "Theatrical Power: The Politics of Representation on the Shakespearean Stage," esp. chap. 1. I thank the author for making her research available to me. See also my earlier discussion in *A Happier Eden: The Politics of Marriage in the Stuart Epithalamium* (Ithaca: Cornell University Press, 1990), pp. 142–148, 266–267.

published a prose tract attacking sectarian strife and arguing for religious toleration,[28] which appeared under the alternative titles *Medici Catholicon* and *Charity Commended,* and *Itur Satyricum,* a royalist poem welcoming Charles II back to London.[29] His main work, however, is the collection entitled *Poesis Rediviva* (1656). Typically epigrammatic in their genre and variously metaphysical and Cavalier in their style, these poems encompass a range of subject matter. The volume includes yet more texts lamenting religious controversy and supporting royalism, a series of epigrams on medical issues, some Latinate misogynistic epigrams, and, more to our purposes, some dozen lyrics about women with qualities including what he calls golden skin, black skin,[30] a hunchback, and one eye.

One of his most significant contributions to the ugly beauty tradition is "To Aureola, or The Yellow Skin'd Lady; Asking Who Could Love a Fancy":

Who could a Fancy love? who Fancy have.
None e're love wit, whom nature no wit gave.
Some say my Fancy's rich, you'l love it sure;
My Fancy's you, can you your self endure?
Most fancy gold, and I a golden skin:
Who's gold without, is she not rich within?
I from thy skin did make the break of day;
The Moon made pale you took her light away.
To yellow skin the *Indies* I'd confine;
Give every part the riches of a Mine,
Scorn but my fancy, thou again art poor;
Horses with Yellows shall be valued more.
I'le say the Yellow Jaundies doth thee die;
Beggers with lice shall bear thee company.
Or yellow Oaker thus thee colour'd tell,

[28]On Collop's religious writing, see the brief references in W. K. Jordan, *The Development of Religious Toleration in England: Attainment of the Theory and Accommodations in Thought and Institutions (1640–1660)* (Cambridge: Harvard University Press, 1940), pp. 83, 89, 90.

[29]Collop's life and works have received very little attention. See two essays by Conrad Hilberry, introduction to *The Poems of John Collop,* ed. Hilberry, and "Medical Poems from John Collop's *Poesis Rediviva* (1656)," *Journal of the History of Medicine,* 11 (1956), 384–385.

[30]Several scholars have drawn attention to connections between the Petrarchan palette and developing ideas of race. See, e.g., Roland Greene, " 'For Love of *Pau-Brasil*': Petrarchan Experience and the Colonial Americas," paper delivered at the English Institute, Cambridge, Mass., August 1990; Kim Hall, " 'I would rather wish to be a Blackamoor': Race, Colonialism, and the Female Subject," paper delivered at the Renaissance Society of America conference, Stanford, Calif., April 1992; and Linda Woodbridge, "Black and White and Red All Over: The Sonnet Mistress amongst the Ndembu," *RQ,* 40 (1987), 247–297.

And send thee Customers such as Oaker sell,
An unlick'd Calf came into th' world with dung;
Which yellow ever since about you hung,
Or with Childes cack thou since wer't yellow'd o're,
'Cause shitten luck is good, hast suiters store.
I made thee gold, 'tis I can make thee brasse,
Currant with Tinkers thou shalt onely passe:
Yet while thy flesh such company draw near,
Like th' Cynicks gold, you may grow pale by fear.
You must be mine if you would golden be;
Know that a golden Angel is my fee.[31]

In response to the question in its title, the poem apparently proceeds to justify its speaker's attraction to Aureola. In so doing, however, it in fact threatens her with pejorative descriptions—and then insists that she yield to him to avoid that infamy ("You must be mine if you would golden be" [25]). Thus the poet whose poem "To A Lady of Pleasure" describes an erection as the swelling from a snake bite here projects the transgressiveness that he seems to associate with sexual desire and his own critique of that desire onto a woman who transgresses normal standards of beauty, much as Carew projects onto her face the literary and psychic battles behind praising a woman with green-sickness.

The title is intriguing for many reasons, not least that Martial, whom Collop clearly knew well, refers to a Roman gold coin as an "aureolus" in 5.19 and again in 12.36. Notice too that this title, adopting the usual epigrammatic strategy of assigning a fictive name, reduces the woman to a single quality, an analogue to the dismemberment that has interested so many students of Petrarchism. The syntax is ambiguous, as is often the case with Collop, but he may well be attributing to Aureola herself a query about the attractiveness of so-called yellow-skinned women; certainly other lyrics by Collop respond to questions and complaints by the woman herself. This discursive pattern yet again complicates our usual equation between speech and power on the one hand and silence and powerlessness on the other. In any event, though the title may attribute speech to Aureola, in another sense she appears to be neither speaking nor listening: here, as in the *Arcadia*, the witty misogyny of the text seems addressed more to young gallants than to women. Collop, the royalist outsider, here constructs himself as insider in a circle of men. Thus the rivalries that often shape diacritical desire may also be mediated.

---

[31]All citations from Collop are to Hilberry, *The Poems of John Collop.*

In line nine of "To Aureola" the text connects its eponymous subject, doubly alien in her gender and her skin color, with an exotic country, while in the next line it describes her in terms of "the riches of a Mine." Seemingly praising her, this trope anticipates the blend of dirt and wealth which the poem associates with that other mine, the female body. And it offers a literal, physical image of descent which anticipates the metaphorical social descent that will ensue. Thus sexuality, wealth, filth, and challenges to social hierarchy are juxtaposed in this lyric, an amalgam that often recurs when the female body is minted.

In lines eleven to twenty allusions to several types of social and bodily degradation and dysfunction—the jaundice, the lice-infested beggars, the newborn calf with feces—provide a textbook enumeration of the tensions associated with both Aureola's gender and her race and also recall Freud's observations about connections among gynecological functions, money, and excrement.[32] Those connections, pathological fantasies for the poet and his culture, are represented instead as verbal options that he has the choice of exercising in describing the woman; thus Collop again asserts his agency, transforming himself from the object of threatening fears about the feminine to a subject who can use them to threaten others. That assertion of agency is manifest in how these ten lines shift between two types of speech act. Some statements threaten a depreciative description ("I'le say the Yellow Jaundies" [13]), reminding us again that threats are intriguing speech acts because they, like conditional statements, can both do and undo, inflict and withhold harm. Other passages, in contrast, simply consist of such descriptions ("An unlick'd Calf came into th' world with dung; / Which yellow ever since about you hung" [17–18]), performatively demonstrating the poet's power to fulfill his threats, for in such lines he actually transforms her into whatever he wants.

But perhaps the best approach to this disturbing list of potential and realized insults is generic: this list suggests that alternative poems lurk behind the surface of the ones in this tradition, with their alternative genres and subgenres representing roads not taken. As Colie reminds us, epigrams could be classified in terms of foeditas, or vileness; mel, or honey (that is, amatory epigrams); acetum, or vinegar; and so on.[33] Collop, who deploys many of these subgenres elsewhere in his canon, here asserts his control

---

[32]See Freud, *The Standard Edition of the Complete Psychological Works of Sigmund Freud*, trans. James Strachey et al., vol. 1 (London: Hogarth Press and Institute of Psycho-analysis, 1966), p. 243; vol. 9 (London: Hogarth Press and Institute of Psycho-analysis, 1959), pp. 168, 173–174; and vol. 10 (London: Hogarth Press and Institute of Psycho-analysis, 1955), esp. pp. 213–217.

[33]Colie, *Shakespeare's Living Art*, pp. 86–87.

over a potentially dangerous Other by brandishing his power to insert her into a literary version of the Other, the foeditas subgenre.

The vitriolic enumeration of insults in lines eleven to twenty culminates in a solipsistic assertion that aptly explains both this passage and all Collop's other poems in the ugly beauty tradition: "I made thee gold, 'tis I can make thee brasse" (21). Like the trochaic inversion that stresses the pronoun in line seven ("*I* from thy skin"; emphasis added), this line emphasizes the power of the poet to determine her value. But in this poem, as in others in Collop's ugly beauty series, that power is slightly yet significantly destabilized when he refers to the coin known as an angel. While readers in the late twentieth century might at first assume a gold coin is the best possible icon for both stable representation and objective valuation, Collop's original audience, as I will argue shortly, would have interpreted coinage very differently.

In any event, Collop is clearly dealing in a currency that at once elevates and denigrates, credits and discredits his Aureola. Thus although the reference in the final line to "a golden Angel" obviously objectifies the woman by deploying the commonplace pun about the coin called an angel, the line also attributes some potency to her. Because of the association of Petrarchan women with angels, this woman is, however playfully, graced with the magnetism of the Petrarchan mistress. But just as Petrarchism was a long discredited discourse by 1656, so the angel coin was mainly talismanic during Charles I's reign, being used to cure the "king's evil." And it was not issued during the Commonwealth.[34] Thus this allusion gestures towards a link between his political and religious poems on the one hand and his ugly beauty lyrics on the other. The royalist who praised Laud and celebrated the return of Charles as the restoration of a golden age hints here, however fleetingly and ambiguously, at a nostalgic, recuperative vision and yet reminds us that it is indeed out-of-date.

That vision of a golden age is also undercut by a darker subtext that further unsettles the concluding lines. Like earlier passages, the end of Collop's poem implies that Aureola, in one sense herself a golden angel, may in another sense perhaps be a prostitute who receives that angel as her payment. Certainly Collop had precedents both in English and Continental literature for poems that explicitly cited the rates of prostitutes; in the lyric beginning "It is not four years ago," for example, Suckling translates a

---

[34]See George C. Brooke, *English Coins from the Seventh Century to the Present Day*, 3d ed. (London: Methuen, 1950), chaps. 16, 17; and C. H. V. Sutherland, *English Coinage 600–1900* (London: B. T. Batsford, 1973), esp. pp. 164, 171. Johann Sommerville offered valuable assistance on the subject of coinage.

poem by Desportes on that subject.[35] If Collop's own golden lady is indeed a lady of the evening, she is transgressive in her occupation as well as her appearance—and hence the act of praising her itself becomes even more transgressive.

"To Aureola," then, may complicate the process of valuation and the power that derives from controlling that process, but its main agenda is clearly the successful establishment of the poet's power over the currency, as it were, in which he trades. The balance between his agency and that of the woman is more hotly contested, however, in "The Praise of a Yellow Skin: or An Elizabeth in Gold."

> The Sun when he enamels day,
> No other Colour doth display.
> Lillies asham'd thou should'st out-vie,
> Themselves from white to yellow die.
> Thy arms are wax, nay honey too,
> Colour and sweetnesse hath from you.
> But when thy neck doth but appear,
> I think I view an *Indie* there.
> Can passion reason then befool,
> Where such an Emp'ress beareth rule?
> Thy yellow breasts are hills of fire
> To heat, not snow to quench desire.
> Ransack *Peru,* and *Tagus* shore,
> And then vie treasure: thou'lt be poor.
> Let wretches delve for yellow Ore,
> A golden skin I ask, no more.
>
> Sure *Jove* descending in a yellow shower
> To rival me, thus gilt my *Danaë* over.

In this lyric Collop ostensibly praises a yellow-skinned woman—or, significantly enough, a yellow skin—by portraying her in terms of natural objects and the wealth of exotic territories, then proceeding to associate her with the Danaë myth.

Here, as in "To Aureola," the title begins the process of colonization which occurs more explicitly and literally in the poem. This title, like the name "Aureola" in the previous poem, reduces her to one part of her body, her skin. It may also link her to the coins with Elizabeth's portrait

[35]See Anne Lake Prescott, *French Poets and the English Renaissance: Studies in Fame and Transformation* (New Haven: Yale University Press, 1978), pp. 159–160.

(the *Oxford English Dictionary* cites several seventeenth-century instances of calling coins issued by her successors "a Carolus" or "a Jacobus").[36] If these resonances are present, they offer a singularly literal version of the paradigm that women are a currency that can be passed among men. In any event, her subjectivity is unquestionably compromised through the indefinite articles in "a Yellow Skin" and "An Elizabeth"—"your yellow skin," "her yellow skin," or "the Elizabeth in gold" would all have sounded very different. Yet the reference to the monarch once again unsettles what might otherwise seem an unambiguous process of domination. On one level, the disjunctive conjunction "or" signals not synonymous titles but two alternatives, the second of which focuses on and privileges the woman, and thus enacts the way the poem will shift between empowering and disempowering her. On another level, the second title elides boundaries by associating the exotic, the foreign, the subordinate with the ultimate icon of English nationalism and the ultimate symbol of female agency and potency. And value is once more located in a golden age of the past.

Moreover, these juxtaposed allusions to yellow skin and a potent monarch undermine common critical assumptions about dismemberment in love poetry. Joel Altman has written about the body parts in *Henry V* in terms of amplification, not diminishment, and Katherine Rowe has anatomized the paradoxical ascription of agency to fetishized detached hands in *Titus Andronicus*, among other texts.[37] Is it possible, perhaps, that the golden skin, like the detached body parts in Petrarchan sonnets, is not simply diminished, as critics typically assume, but also invested with a potency that the poet then struggles to control anew and without complete success?

Here, as in so many of the related texts currently studied by postcolonialist critics, the foreign woman is associated with unruly passion, with the "hills of fire" (11). Yet this poem, like many other instances of the ugly beauty tradition, proceeds to justify her apparent deviance and regulate the force of her attractiveness by showing that she, like "la gialletta" in Lord Herbert's poem, in fact conforms to accepted standards of beauty—a textbook example of another pattern traced by students of postcolonialism, the denial of difference in the Other.[38] In this case, her seemingly unnatural

---

[36]*OED*, s.v. "carolus," "jacobus." In her unpublished thesis, "The Writing Body/The Body Written: Gender and Sex in Seventeenth-Century Poetry," Jeneva Burroughs offers a different but not incompatible perspective on connections between coinage, wit, and semen.

[37]Joel Altman, " 'Vile Participation': The Amplification of Violence in the Theater of *Henry V*," *SQ*, 42 (1991), 1–32; and Katherine A. Rowe, "Dismembering and Forgetting in *Titus Andronicus*," *SQ*, 45 (1994), 279–303. I am indebted to Katherine Rowe for making her work available to me as well as for a number of useful suggestions about this chapter.

[38]Postcolonial critics have written extensively on this question. See, e.g., two essays by

appearance is quite literally naturalized in lines one and two ("The Sun when he enamels day, / No other Colour doth display") and in several senses her foreignness domesticated in line five ("Thy arms are wax, nay honey too"). But the poet's assertions of his power over her beauty do not go completely unchallenged. If in line eight she is a territory, "an *Indie*," two lines later she becomes the empress who rules over territories, including, apparently, the poet: "Can passion reason then befool, / Where such an Emp'ress beareth rule?" This line reactivates the power associated with the queen in the title.

The concluding couplet further entangles all these complexities. Danaë is confined in a brass tower by her father, who was frightened by a prophecy that her child will destroy him; visited there by Jove in the form of a golden shower, she eventually gives birth to Perseus. It is no accident that the love poetry of Tudor and Stuart England so often refers to this story, for it allows that culture to bifurcate and narrativize its conflicting attractions to the figures of the father who immures the threatening woman to control her sexuality and the lover who penetrates her prison. (Rendered as dramatic comedy, in contrast, a similar plot channels the sympathy of the male audience away from the father and towards the young lover.) Or, to put it another way, this bifurcation corresponds to the workings of displacement in Petrarchism, though in this instance not the chronological version that I have termed narrative displacement but rather a form that might be called dramatic displacement. The contradictions among interpretations of the myth of Danaë, which variously emphasize the chastity and the venality of its heroine, also conveniently correspond to ambivalences about women in sixteenth- and seventeenth-century England.[39] This narrative is appealing, too, in that it resolves tensions rather than just mirroring them: it serves to acknowledge the threats the woman represents, then reassuringly deprives her of agency while stressing both the agency and potency of Jove. Queen and empress earlier in the poem, at its conclusion she is minted anew as a daughter who needs to be locked up lest her behavior harm her father.

Equally important for our purposes—and for Collop's—is the myth's emphasis on gold. The subversive sexuality that her father feared in her and Jove's subversive intrusion into the tower are turned into precious

---

Homi K. Bhabha, "The Other Question—the Stereotype and Colonial Discourse," *Screen*, 24 (1983), 17–36; and "Representation and the Colonial Text: A Critical Exploration of Some Forms of Mimeticism," in *The Theory of Reading*, ed. Frank Gloversmith (Sussex, Eng.: Harvester Press, 1984).

[39] On these contradictions in the iconographical treatment of Danaë, see Madlyn Millner Kahr, "Danaë: Virtuous, Voluptuous, Venal Woman," *Art Bulletin*, 60 (1978), 43–55.

metal.[40] And yet not quite—the final phrase of the poem, "gilt my *Danaë* over" (18), like the proleptic enameling in the first line, suggests the superficiality of her gold coating. This point would have been resonant in seventeenth-century England because, as we will shortly see, coins were prone to adulteration and other forms of corruption in both that period and the sixteenth century. In any event, it is Jove who performs here the alchemy on which all Collop's ugly beauty poems are based—or, as Collop puts it in "To Aureola," "I made thee gold" (21). Thus the poet's role mimes Jove's, and on one level he is associating himself with that god's potency and agency. Similarly, in the twentieth poem of the first book of his *Amours de Cassandre,* Ronsard expresses the wish that he, like Jove, might descend in a shower of gold into his lady's lap.

But rather than accepting that empowering allegory, as Ronsard does, Collop undermines it by scripting a narrative of rivalry: "Sure *Jove* descending in a yellow shower / To rival me" (17–18). He then proceeds to reclaim the woman from his rival through the pronoun in "my *Danaë*" (18), a telling contrast with his earlier indefinite articles. He is deflecting onto his putative relationship with Jove his unresolved power struggle with the woman who is at once empress and territory, much as more conventional Petrarchan poets project onto their relationship with men the differentiation that they cannot reliably achieve in gendered relationships.

"Of the Black Lady with Grey Eyes and White Teeth" demonstrates further ways race inflects the struggles for mastery and control present in Collop's other texts.

> Like to the grey-ey'd Morn, your sparkling eyes
> Dart lustre, while a sable clothes the skies.
> And your white teeth resemble th' milky way,
> The glory of the night, and th' shame of day,
> Complain not then *Nigrina* of thy white,
> Since stars shine brightest in the blackest night.

Collop distances himself from the object of desire, the potential source of that arousing snake's venom, by deploying in his title the preposition "Of" rather than "To." If in other ugly beauty poems anxieties about gender generate both a drive to express hostility and an impulse to deflect or suppress it, here anxieties about race effect the same sort of equivocation. In one sense the similes of this poem, like the figures in "The Praise of a

---

[40]Several scholars have examined artistic renditions of the coins in this myth; see esp. Leonard Barkan, *The Gods Made Flesh: Metamorphosis and the Pursuit of Paganism* (New Haven: Yale University Press, 1986), pp. 189–195; and Kahr, "Danaë."

Yellow Skin" and in the poems by Carew and Lord Herbert of Cherbury which we examined, render this putatively unnatural beauty natural by comparing it to physical phenomena. Moreover, while ascribing to the woman a name that emphasizes her blackness, Collop praises her whiteness, a literal instance of making the Other like oneself. Similarly, in the ninth poem in *The Devises of Sundrie Gentlemen,* Gascoigne declares that Cleopatra's skin was a foil to her white teeth.

Yet Collop's text remains equivocal in many ways, establishing neat contrasts between black and white, powerless and powerful, and then blurring them. In particular, her eyes, emphasized by their position in the title, complicate such contrasts. Gray is, of course, literally a midpoint between black and white, though the term may in fact refer to a gray-blue color.[41] In any event, her eyes may suggest that the woman is of mixed race and hence represents such a midpoint.[42]

Collop's predilection for transforming difference into sameness, a staple of postcolonialist analysis, is both compounded and confounded in the final lines. Nigrina's complaint about her whiteness suggests that she herself does not accept the standards of beauty through which the poem is appropriating her; her putative condemnation of her white teeth reverses the rebuke a white person might offer about her blackness, thus effecting what Homi K. Bhabha describes as the colonial mimicry of the colonized.[43] Yet the ending of the poem can be read as either an affirmation or a rejection of the standards of the poet's culture. On one level Collop declares that black is indeed beautiful, that Nigrina is more lovely than women whose teeth and eyes are set off against Caucasian skin. Yet on another and primary level black is beautiful only because it serves the ends of white, making white look better—servant and object, the color black itself assumes precisely the role that would so often be assigned to the subaltern who bears it. In other words, much as the battles waged on the face of Carew's lady figure the struggles of Petrarchism and its counterdiscourses, so the relationship between the colors in Collop's final line glosses the very impulse behind the text: using Nigrina to enhance the status of the poet who ostensibly celebrates her and the culture he represents. In this sense, just as the black skin literally, visually disappears in serving as a foil for her white teeth, so the threatening Otherness that her blackness represents is erased as well.

[41]For this reading of "gray," see the gloss in William Shakespeare, *Romeo and Juliet,* ed. G. Blakemore Evans (Cambridge: Cambridge University Press, 1984), II.iii.1.
[42]I am indebted to Lisa Woolfork for suggesting the possibility of mixed race.
[43]See esp. Homi K. Bhabha, "Of Mimicry and Man: The Ambivalence of Colonial Discourse," *October,* 28 (1984), 125–133.

One of the best ways of summarizing Collop's approach to the ugly beauty tradition is to ask why he, like other writers in that tradition, celebrates women with gold skin in four poems, whereas other atypical characteristics, such as a hunchback, merit only one poem and black skin only two. Gold skin is a version of elided boundaries which fits well into a genre that so often erases the very distinctions it might seem to erect. But Collop is interested not merely in gold in general but in its incarnation as coinage. His witty allusion to that subject in his prose tract *Charity Commended* suggests that his concern for currency extends beyond its aptness for describing women and may involve as well its propensity for adulteration: "And no coyne can be so adulterate as not to passe currant, if it bee but stamp'd with the face of Religion. I would not act high treason against heav'n by adulterating my Kings Coyne, or by an uncharitable clipping of it take away the Crowne."[44] The primary explanations for the references to coinage in Collop's ugly beauty poems, however, lie in the status of money in general and gold in particular. These subjects have been extensively scrutinized by students of medieval, nineteenth-century, and modern literature, notably Kurt Heinzelman, Walter Benn Michaels, Marc Shell, and R. A. Shoaf.[45] One of the most influential discussions of coinage in early modern England is Foucault's analysis in *The Order of Things*, in which he characteristically both exaggerates the difference between the sixteenth and seventeenth centuries and elides the distinction between England and other countries. Yet in so doing he draws our attention to some important subtexts of coinage, notably representation.[46] Though not totally neglected by other critics of Tudor and Stuart England,[47] coinage deserves much more attention than it has yet received: it is through this subject that English culture both expressed and repressed concerns about not only gender but also the power of the monarch and the stability of the nation itself.[48]

[44]John Collop, *Charity Commended* (London, 1667), sig. A5–A5ᵛ.

[45]Kurt Heinzelman, *The Economics of the Imagination* (Amherst: University of Massachusetts Press, 1980); Walter Benn Michaels, *The Gold Standard and the Logic of Naturalism: American Literature at the Turn of the Century* (Berkeley: University of California Press, 1987); Marc Shell, *Money, Language, and Thought: Literary and Philosophical Economics from the Medieval to the Modern Era* (Berkeley: University of California Press, 1982); and R. A. Shoaf, *Dante, Chaucer, and the Currency of the Word: Money, Images, and Reference in Late Medieval Poetry* (Norman, Okla.: Pilgrim Books, 1983).

[46]Michel Foucault, *The Order of Things: An Archaeology of the Human Sciences* (New York: Pantheon, 1970), pp. 166–174.

[47]See, e.g., the useful glossary of Renaissance terminology for money by Sandra K. Fischer, *Econolingua: A Glossary of Coins and Economic Language in Renaissance Drama* (Newark and London: University of Delaware Press and Associated University Presses, 1985).

[48]On the history of coinage in England, see Brooke, *English Coins*; C. E. Challis, *The Tudor*

The norm in Tudor and Stuart England was a correspondence between face value and intrinsic value—in other words, a coin worth a shilling should contain a shilling's worth of silver. But that norm could be threatened in many ways: it was as vulnerable and variable as norms associated with gender. Because silver and gold could not be readily used for coins of very low denomination, certain monarchs issued coins, sometimes known as "tokens" or "pledges" (both words are suggestive), whose face value and intrinsic value did not coincide. Versions of such coins were also illicitly issued by merchants, who needed them to trade in. Bimetallism, the term for a monetary system relying on both gold and silver, created further problems, especially the difficulty of stabilizing the relationship between the value of the two metals, a relationship that differed from one country to the next. Moreover, changes in the supply of bullion, counterfeiting, even normal wear and tear could result in coinage whose face value and intrinsic value did not coincide.

"Whereas in the beginning of our reign, to the great honour and profit of us and all our people," the draft of an Elizabethan proclamation opens, "we did restore and reduce the monies of our realm from dross and base matter unto fine gold and fine silver."[49] Behind this nationalistic linkage of the Elizabethan golden age and the purity of gold lies the history of Tudor coinage. Despite coinage reforms earlier effected by Wolsey, under Henry VIII the English currency system was very unstable. External pressures included the introduction of precious metals from the Americas. But Henry himself was responsible for much of the instability: to raise money, during the period between 1542 and 1547 he debased coins by calling them in and reminting them into coins with the same face value but less silver, thus bringing about a serious inflation. Elizabeth, in contrast, attempted to restore stability to the monetary system through a package of major reforms: she called in old money, which included many debased and otherwise unreliable coins, and reminted it so that on the whole face value and intrinsic value coincided. The Stuarts resisted proposals for debasing the currency, but they did introduce some base tokens, that is, coins made of a

Coinage (Manchester and New York: Manchester University Press and Barnes and Noble, 1978); E. E. Rich and C. H. Wilson, eds., The Economy of Expanding Europe in the Sixteenth and Seventeenth Centuries, vol. 4 of The Cambridge Economic History of Europe (Cambridge: Cambridge University Press, 1967), pp. 378–391; B. E. Supple, Commercial Crisis and Change in England, 1600–1642: A Study in the Instability of a Mercantile Economy (Cambridge: Cambridge University Press, 1964); and Sutherland, English Coinage.

[49]Joan Thirsk and J. P. Cooper, eds., Seventeenth-Century Economic Documents (Oxford: Clarendon, 1972), p. 599.

metal other than silver or gold whose face and intrinsic value were far apart.

Although this history can be narrated according to teleological patterns that were very popular in the period, with earlier unrest culminating in Elizabethan stability, it can instead be scripted as a cyclical struggle and slippage between stable and debased coinage. But in any event that struggle was staged synchronically in addition to diachronically. In other words, even in periods of relatively stable currency, such as the years after Elizabeth's major recoinage, the sources of instability to which I referred earlier remained. For example, the valuation of the foreign coins circulating in England was often complicated, as Donne indicates in "The Bracelet" when he jokes about debased French crowns. Bimetallism was relatively unproblematical if the value of both metals remained constant, but when the supplies of either changed, as was the case in both the fifteenth and the sixteenth centuries, the ratio of the relative value of gold and silver would be interrupted.

All this is germane to Collop's poems, then, in that he not only refers explicitly to currency but also constructs female beauty in precisely the ways that denizens of Tudor and Stuart England constructed the significance of gold: both represent at once an apparently stable norm and the ever present possibility of forgery and decay, and both raise questions about representation that in the Stuart period coincide, not by chance, with the popularity of anamorphic paintings.[50] And over both the poet attempts to assert his control by, as it were, assuming the monarch's prerogative of revaluing coins. More specifically, the foreignness of women with black and golden skins is suggestively related to how foreignness functioned in monetary exchanges. Might not the fear that foreign coinage was contaminating the English system while English coinage was being drained abroad figure the fears of contamination and loss that construct xenophobia? To what extent were early fears of miscegenation, as well as longer-standing fears of class conflict, staged in the struggle between "fine," or unalloyed, and base coins? Indeed, the many royal proclamations that declare foreign currency legal tender in England and then proceed to regulate its value attempt to control the transgressive invader in much the same way that Collop does in his own cross-cultural encounters.[51]

His poems are, however, a product not only of cultural tensions that recur throughout the sixteenth and seventeenth centuries but also of his

[50]Compare Michaels, *Gold Standard and the Logic of Naturalism*, pp. 161–165, on connections between American trompe l'oeil art and monetary issues.

[51]See, e.g., James F. Larkin, ed., *Royal Proclamations of King Charles I, 1625–1646*, vol. 2 of *Stuart Royal Proclamations* (Oxford: Clarendon, 1983), proclamation no. 69.

particular historical moment. Our limited knowledge of Collop—the biographical facts are scanty, the texts relatively short and sometimes syntactically obscure—precludes definitive pronouncements but permits speculations. If, as Thomas M. Corns persuasively argues in relation to Cavalier lyrics, the very act of writing libertine love poetry can be read as a royalist rebellion against Puritan morality,[52] surely composing such verse in praise of a woman normally considered undesirable intensifies that rebelliousness. Thus in the poems invoking Elizabeth, Collop not only looks back nostalgically to a golden age but also glosses the impulse to do so with an implicit critique of the leaden morality of the Commonwealth. But Collop's ugly beauty poems reflect his antagonisms as well as his anxieties. A fear of schism, for example, emerges in poems like "On the Master's of the Science of Defense in Controversie" and "The Polemick Protestant D." Given that his original audience had lived through the Civil War and the Commonwealth, many of them must have shared that fear. Collop's ugly beauty poems both replicate and eradicate tensions about schism: their ladies threaten a breach in cultural norms of beauty, and yet Collop repeatedly reassures us that such women do in fact conform to those standards. One wonders, too, if Collop, who writes poems in praise of both Laud and Charles II, was painfully conscious of being an outsider during the Commonwealth. If so, the stance offered by the ugly beauty tradition, that of the sophisticate instructing a coterie of male friends, may have been especially appealing to him. The historical ramifications of these poems, then, testify to the dangers of an unremittingly synchronic reading of the ugly beauty tradition.

Collop's lyrics, however, also share many characteristics with earlier poems in that tradition. They too stage a scenario in which the poet attempts to assert agency and authority over a deviant body by at once contrasting it with and connecting it to cultural norms. He variously relates that body to the alien and the national, to the exploited and the exploiter, to disease and gold. And in so doing he helps us to understand the popularity of the ugly beauty tradition in Tudor and Stuart England.

V

In tracing the attraction of that mode of writing, one should avoid the contemporary move of discounting traditional literary explanations. The

---

[52]Thomas M. Corns, *Uncloistered Virtue: English Political Literature, 1640–1660* (Oxford: Clarendon, 1992), esp. pp. 75–76, 247.

respective norms of the epigram and sonnet surely help to explain some of formal devices that recur in such texts; a delight in rhetorical display, fostered by an educational system that characteristically focused on the tropes in a small passage rather than the work as a whole, explains other devices.[53] But these literary explanations are not as antithetical to more contemporary cultural ones as each of those warring camps sometimes termed traditionalists and theorists would assert: rhetorical tropes like the antitheses of the ugly beauty lyrics may convey ideologies, and cultural values such as a fear of female attractiveness may be explored through or even represented by generic decisions.

Explicating the popularity of the ugly beauty tradition is complicated for other reasons too. Equivocal and guarded in their strategies, these poems demand equivocal and guarded explanations: as their variety would suggest, they appealed in a range of ways to a range of readers and writers. In some instances the sheer delight in playing a witty game was no doubt the principal motivation for writing these poems. Nonetheless, one apparent instance of that variety—the contrast between Collop's suggestion that one of his ugly beauties is liable to disease and Lord Herbert of Cherbury's boast that his subject is free from all peril and change—in fact gestures towards the shared agenda that unites these and other poems in the tradition. Hidden female organs impel that hidden agenda: anxieties not merely about the female body in general, not merely or mainly about the mortality threatened by pregnancy, but rather specifically about gynecological diseases and obstetrical traumas help to explain both the appeal of this tradition and its complex relationship to mainstream Petrarchism. My aim is not the tempting but reductive move of establishing these maladies as the sole explanation for the tradition or even the primary explanation that other genealogies encode: as I suggested earlier, no single etiology could encompass the complexity and variety of such texts. But the threat of damage to the female genitals is certainly a central anxiety behind the threats issued by these poems, and it is one that has largely been neglected.

Indeed, students of Tudor and Stuart literature have devoted relatively little attention to the entire question of illness.[54] Curiously, this subject has

[53]On this and other related aspects of Renaissance education, see Mary Thomas Crane, *Framing Authority: Sayings, Self, and Society in Sixteenth-Century England* (Princeton: Princeton University Press, 1993), esp. chaps. 2, 3.

[54]There are some exceptions worth noting, though their approach is different from the one in this chapter. See, e.g., Barbara H. Traister, " 'Matrix and the Pain Thereof': A Sixteenth-Century Gynaecological Essay," *Medical History*, 35 (1991), 436–451. The disfigurement potentially associated with gynecological and obstetrical problems is also briefly noted in two other studies: Gail Kern Paster, *The Body Embarrassed: Drama and the Disciplines of Shame in Early Modern England* (Ithaca: Cornell University Press, 1993), pp. 44–45; and

been of great interest to feminists studying Victorian culture,[55] reminding us of the unfortunate isolation that sometimes separates even practitioners of the same methodology. Gynecological and obstetrical conditions in particular have as yet received less attention than they deserve from students of early modern England.[56] If allusions to sexually transmitted diseases are an exception, this exception proves the rule: observing the frequency of those references may have distracted us from other and equally significant gynecological problems. The female body is often discussed, but its propensity to the gynecological ailments in question seldom adduced. Bakhtin alludes to illness in describing his model of the grotesque body, but many of his followers skirt that issue.[57] Similarly, the incidence of mortality in childbirth is often cited, but the far higher risk of morbidity is less often acknowledged. These lacunae may stem in part from the distinctions between our culture and its sixteenth- and seventeenth-century counterparts: our tendency to see in early modern culture, as that term would suggest, harbingers of our own society may tempt us to devote less attention to problems that are no longer a clear and present danger.

But a clear and present danger they were in sixteenth- and seventeenth-century England. Gynecological manuals, like the conduct books on marriage, testify that the female body was threatening and threatened not

---

Louis Schwartz, " 'Spot of child-bed taint': Seventeenth-Century Obstetrics in Milton's Sonnet 23 and *Paradise Lost* 8.462–78," *Milton Quarterly*, 27 (1993), 104.

[55]See esp. Mary Poovey, *Uneven Developments: The Ideological Work of Gender in Mid-Victorian England* (Chicago: University of Chicago Press, 1988), chap. 2. In addition to books like this, future studies of illness in Tudor and Stuart England might profitably adduce Sander L. Gilman's analysis of connections between the Other and fears of illness in nineteenth- and twentieth-century texts (*Difference and Pathology: Stereotypes of Sexuality, Race, and Madness* [Ithaca: Cornell University Press, 1985]).

[56]Though most literary critics devote little attention to obstetrics and gynecology, scholars in other fields have discussed medical treatises on these subjects at length. The work of Thomas Laqueur, though influential and incisive, is sometimes flawed by his hesitation to acknowledge the variety and inconsistency in the discourse he is studying; see *Making Sex: Body and Gender from the Greeks to Freud* (Cambridge: Harvard University Press, 1990) and "Orgasm, Generation and the Politics of Reproductive Biology," in Catherine Gallagher and Thomas Laqueur, eds., *The Making of the Modern Body: Sexuality and Society in the Nineteenth Century* (Berkeley: University of California Press, 1987). See also Audrey Eccles, *Obstetrics and Gynaecology in Tudor and Stuart England* (Kent, Ohio: Kent State University Press, 1982); Ian Maclean, *The Renaissance Notion of Woman: A Study in the Fortunes of Scholasticism and Medical Science in European Intellectual Life* (Cambridge: Cambridge University Press, 1980), chap. 3; and Hilda Smith, "Gynecology and Ideology in Seventeenth-Century England," in *Liberating Women's History: Theoretical and Critical Essays*, ed. Berenice A. Carroll (Urbana: University of Illinois Press, 1976). I am indebted to Harold Cook and Faye Getz for help with my work on Renaissance medicine.

[57]Mikhail Bakhtin, *Rabelais and His World*, trans. Helene Iswolsky (Cambridge: MIT Press, 1965), chaps. 5 and 6.

merely for the reasons critics usually cite, such as its association with un-controlled sexuality, but also because of its proneness to a range of illnesses. These maladies, I maintain, variously impel, justify, and undermine cultural constructions of gender. For example, although one cannot work out a precise incidence for the prolapsed uterus, a condition in which the womb descends into the vagina or sometimes even emerges externally, the fre-quency with which it is discussed in Renaissance gynecological manuals and the partial though not complete correlation between this condition and numerous pregnancies suggest it was a common problem in early modern England. Many of the remedies advocated in the gynecological manuals were not likely to be successful. Some treatises, for example, assure us that the womb will return to its usual position if attracted by a pleasant smell or repelled by a loathsome one;[58] while this advice may fascinate cultural historians by demonstrating yet again that in a sense the uterus was viewed as an independent animal, it was presumably less than helpful to contem-porary patients. In addition, the pessaries that are recommended in medical treatises may have been palliative, but when inserted without the proper antisepsis, they risked causing infections. When the marriage manuals of the period discuss the ethical dilemmas posed by a partner who was ill, deformed, or incapable of intercourse, they were probably considering the more extreme stages of the prolapsed uterus, among other maladies.

The prolapsed uterus was, however, but one of the many gynecological ailments that could variously render the female body a source of pain and anxiety for women and fear and repulsion for men, particularly in the absence of appropriate treatment. The medical treatises include lengthy discussions of such problems as menorrhagia, a type of pathologically heavy bleeding, and nonsexually transmitted infections; the latter, which presum-ably included uncomfortable though not life-threatening conditions such as moniliasis, trichomoniasis, and bacterial vaginosis, are often classified together as "the whites" because of their discharges.[59]

If the risk of death in childbirth was perhaps lower than scholars sometimes assume (though high enough to justify anxieties on that sub-ject),[60] the risk of illness or injury was higher than students of early modern

[58]On this and other treatments for the prolapsed uterus, see, e.g., two texts by Nicholas Culpeper, *A Directory for Midwives, or, A Guide for Women* (London, 1651), pp. 106–107; and *Culpeper's Directory for Midwives*, pp. 51–53.

[59]On "the whites," see, e.g., Ambrose Parey, *The Workes of that Famous Chirurgion Ambrose Parey* (London, 1634), pp. 953–955.

[60]See Roger Schofield, "Did the Mothers Really Die? Three Centuries of Maternal Mor-tality in 'The World We Have Lost,' " in *The World We Have Gained: Histories of Population and Social Structure*, ed. Lloyd Bonfield, Richard M. Smith, and Keith Wrightson (Oxford: Basil Blackwell, 1986).

literature generally acknowledge. "Many tymes it chanceth that thorowe the greate difficultie and thronges of labor," Roesslin's *Byrth of Mankynde* observes, "the prevye parte and the foundament be come one by reason of rupture and breakynge of the same parte in the delyveraunce of the chylde."[61] Jacques Guillemeau, a French doctor whose obstetrical treatise circulated widely in England, also testifies to this hazard, emphasizing that even with the most skillful care, the pregnant woman's genitals may be damaged during delivery. He proceeds to discuss a case in which he cut away the scar tissue that had formed after a traumatic delivery and sutured the area, only to see it tear again after another delivery.[62] In any event, pregnant women could not be assured of expert attendance, and the medical treatises describe as well the damage caused by midwives themselves. In his dedicatory epistle Culpeper warns members of that profession that they must answer for their work to Jehovah, Jesus and all the angels, and in analyzing the etiology of the prolapsed uterus, he observes that it may be caused "by unskilful drawing out the Child, especially if it be dead, or of the Afterbirth, by MOTHER-CARELESS when she turns MIDWIFE."[63] Rivalries between doctors and midwives might account for some of his fervor, but this and other tracts indicate that unskillful obstetrical care was indeed a danger. When analyzing childbirth, then, students of early modern England need to factor in not only the risk of death but also the far more likely possibility of injuries that would produce chronic pain and disease.[64] Although such ailments were hardly unique to Tudor and Stuart England, the writers who witnessed the mortality crisis of 1557–1559 or its immediate consequences in terms of unsettling families may well have developed an unusually acute fear of illness and hence a heightened consciousness of these gynecological and obstetrical maladies.

Recognizing the high incidence of such conditions invites us to reinterpret the models through which feminists read the female body. For, as I have been arguing, it was liable both to the changes inevitably effected by aging and pregnancy and to a range of illnesses. Hence if one accepts the Bakhtinian distinction between the classical and grotesque bodies,[65] one

[61]Eucharius Roesslin, *The Byrth of Mankynde* (London, 1540), sig. Kiv.
[62]James Guillemeau, *Child-birth or, The Happy Deliverie of Women* (London, 1612), pp. 211–215.
[63]Culpeper, *A Directory for Midwives*, "Epistle Dedicatorie."
[64]Judith Walzer Leavitt observes similar dangers in her studies of childbirth in America: "Under the Shadow of Maternity: American Women's Responses to Death and Debility Fears in Nineteenth-Century Childbirth," *Feminist Studies*, 12 (1986), 129–154; and *Brought to Bed: Childbearing in America, 1750 to 1950* (New York: Oxford University Press, 1986).
[65]Deborah Jacobs has recently drawn attention to the dangers of applying Bakhtin to early modern texts ("Cultural Imperialism and Renaissance Drama: The Case of *The Roaring Girl*,"

may wonder whether the former conception as realized in Petrarchan poetry in particular was a defensive evasion of the fear that seemingly classical bodies were in fact very prone to disease and therefore to many characteristics associated with their apparent opposite, the grotesque body. Indeed, the female body was culturally coded as volatile and vulnerable, a signifier that resisted stable signification and interpretation.

But how is all of this relevant to the ugly beauty tradition? Most obviously, some poems comment directly on illnesses. Collop's "To Aureola" implicitly associates its anti-Petrarchan mistress with childbirth, which is presented in terms of scatological images ("An unlick'd Calf came into th' world with dung" [17], "Or with Childes cack thou since wer't yellow'd o're" [19]).[66] And disease is the threat that impels many of these threatening poems. For, as Sander L. Gilman's study of connections between illness and Otherness in nineteenth- and twentieth-century texts demonstrates, disease intensifies and rationalizes hostilities and fears connected to gender.[67] Ugly beauty poems variously deny that fear through their antithetical contrasts between fair and foul women or display it when they suggest that the boundaries between such women are permeable and unstable. The anagram form enacts this fear of volatility and variability, for it suggests how readily an attractive woman may be transformed into an unattractive one. In other words, in a sense poems in the ugly beauty tradition are less about those unattractive women than about the fear that they represent the ever present potentiality for even the Petrarchan beauty.

These patterns suggest one possible manifestation of the interplay between the semiotics of gender and what academics used to call without embarrassment the facts of social history. Was the fantasy that the female genitals are always deformed both activated and justified by gynecological and obstetrical ailments? Was that fantasy, a hidden response to hidden organs, then projected onto fears of the unattractiveness or abnormality of the visible parts of the body?[68] After describing in detail the grotesqueness of the rest of Mopsa's body, Sidney concludes, "As for those parts unknowne, which hidden sure are best: / Happie be they which well beleeve, and never seeke the rest." Spenser's emphasis on Duessa's deformed genitals

in *Feminism, Bakhtin, and the Dialogic*, ed. Dale M. Bauer and Susan Jaret McKinstry [Albany: State University of New York Press, 1991]); although I disagree with some of her conclusions, her suggestion that the early modern period should be seen as pre-bourgeois rather than bourgeois is a useful corrective.

[66]"Cack" is an obsolete term for excrement (*OED*, s.v. "cack").

[67]Gilman, *Difference and Pathology*.

[68]Compare Achsah Guibbory's observation that Donne's "Anagram" uses the same terminology for the lady's face and genitals (" 'Oh, let mee not serve so': The Politics of Love in Donne's *Elegies*," *ELH*, 57 [1990], 815).

is also germane; lest he be cursed by such witches, the poet in the ugly beauty tradition preemptively curses them.

But I do not intend to erase all other cultural tensions in this corrective emphasis on illness. Quite the contrary. The illnesses that threatened the female body and its representation are significant in part because they provided both metaphors for and literalizations of other cultural fears; illness both constituted and was constitutive of several other issues connected with gender. In particular, the fear that the radiant Petrarchan beauty could be transformed by disease into the anti-Petrarchan hag is closely related to fears of aging; it is no accident that poems in the ugly beauty tradition, notably Drayton's *Idea* 8, often incorporate carpe diem motifs. Similarly, the two modes are closely connected in French poetry; Du Bellay's "O beaux cheveux d'argent" *(Regrets* 91) focuses on aging,[69] and, although it is not strictly speaking an ugly beauty poem, Ronsard's "Quand vous serez bien vieille" *(Sonnets pour Hélène,* II.43) also gestures towards the connection between the traditions. In texts like these, in short, the counterdiscourses of Petrarchism respond both to fears of aging shared by many members of the culture and, more specifically, to the Petrarchan preoccupation with the passage of time.

When writing about the process of growing old, Drayton recasts his Continental models with striking bitterness. In the twelfth poem of the *Rime sparse,* Petrarch envisions Laura's aging as an opportunity for him to express his suffering more frankly and be rewarded with some pity; Ronsard's "Quand vous serez bien vieille" is relatively gentle in its descriptions of the aged woman. The ugly beauty poem that Drayton models on these precedents, however, is more hostile and vengeful in tone. Responses to or memories of the dynastic problems associated with Elizabeth's aging may perhaps lie behind this and other such lyrics, intensifying their bitterness.[70] As usual, though, students of Tudor and Stuart culture should orchestrate the insights of new historicism with observations about family dynamics; if, as I have argued elsewhere, tensions about widows heading families intensified and were intensified by tensions about a queen heading a country,[71] so too concerns about the aging of a wife, a sister, or a mother no

---

[69]These questions are discussed in an unpublished essay by Cathy Yandell, "Carpe Diem and the Ravishing of the Body," and in her "Carpe Diem, Poetic Immortality, and the Gendered Ideology of Time," in Anne R. Larson and Colette H. Winn, eds., *Renaissance Women Writers: French Texts/American Contexts* (Detroit: Wayne State University Press, 1994).

[70]Compare Guibbory, " 'Oh, let mee not serve so,' " esp. pp. 815, 828–829.

[71]See Heather Dubrow, "The Message from Marcade: Parental Loss in Tudor and Stuart England," in *Attending to Women in Early Modern England,* ed. Betty S. Travitsky and Adele S. Seeff (Newark and London: University of Delaware Press and Associated University Presses, 1994).

doubt inflected readings of Elizabeth's face. And, as Cathy Yandell incisively argues, a poet who deploys the carpe diem motif to lament the aging of his mistress really deflects his own fears about growing old.[72]

In any event, the instability of the body that is liable to illness or aging figured the instability of many other issues connected to gender; once again, the female body becomes both an arena and a metaphor for a range of cultural tensions. In particular, the inconsistencies of male discourses about gender are projected onto the female body: the volatility of illness represents and in so doing in a sense represses the volatility of other discursive systems, in somewhat the same way female hysteria is often interpreted as a projection of its male analogue.[73] For, as I argued earlier, in analyzing the source of gendered anxieties in Tudor and Stuart England, many critics have focused too much on the rival theories about the improvement in women's status on the one hand or the unremitting imposition of patriarchal strictures on the other.[74] Rather, many anxieties stemmed from the fact that on this issue as so many others, the culture was far from hegemonic; it was instead an arena for competing and conflicting ideologies about questions ranging from the role of the wife in marriage to the female contribution to procreation to androgyny. A marriage manual such as Gouge's popular Of Domesticall Duties, for example, is peppered with internal contradictions on issues such as the wife's role in marriage. The instability of the body liable to illness figured the changeability of the ideologies of gender.

A concern for illness is not absent from mainstream English Petrarchan poems: Laura's ophthalmological problems are contagious. But the fears excited by illness and especially by the obstetrical and gynecological pathologies on which I am focusing appear in very different form in ugly beauty poems: they are variously more covert and more intense. Or, to put it another way, the poets in the tradition sometimes seem to be responding more pathologically than their mainstream Petrarchan counterparts to conditions that are themselves more seriously pathological. And these contrasts aptly introduce a broader issue, the complex relationship between the ugly beauty tradition and traditional Petrarchism in Tudor and Stuart England. On one level, of course, the ugly beauty poems substitute a hostile image of the woman for an idealized one. But they also rewrite

---

[72]Yandell, "Carpe Diem, Poetic Immortality, and the Gendered Ideology of Time."

[73]The literature on the gendering of hysteria is extensive. See, e.g., Arthur Kroker and Marilouise Kroker, eds., The Hysterical Male: New Feminist Theory (New York: St. Martins, 1991).

[74]See Dubrow, A Happier Eden, chap. 1, as well as Chap. 1 of this book.

many other characteristics of Petrarchism, notably its creation and depiction of male subjectivity.

Indeed, one of the most striking ways the ugly beauty tradition differs from the more common forms of Petrarchism is that it attributes to the poet the very agency, authority, and autonomy for which he often struggles in vain in standard Petrarchan poems.[75] This potentiality helps to explain why many English Petrarchan poets are attracted to this particular discourse at the very time they are writing more straightforward Petrarchan verses. Within the ugly beauty tradition they are seemingly in control of their medium and their women and, indeed, other men as well. In particular, such poets assert authority over the female body, celebrating their ability not only to read that ever changing text but also to write it. In so doing they also assert autonomy over cultural norms and tensions, trumpeting their willingness to love even women deemed unattractive and, through rhetorical tricks, to turn such women into gems of perfection. Or, to put it another way, these poets play a version of fort-da through their poems: they reject the woman only to reinstate her as an empress or queen; they threaten her with insults only to shower her, like Jove, with golden praise. Thus they attempt to grasp the mastery and control often denied them in other types of love poetry and in the patronage system. And so they transform the indecisiveness of Petrarchism into the canny equivocations of this counterdiscourse, a metamorphosis that in more ways than one may remind us of the structure of Donne's "Canonization." Not the leader of the society but the poet himself, they assert, will mint its coins. Not the ravages of illness but the wit of the poet, they claim, will transform the female body.

And transform it they do in ways that lend a new and more literal dimension to the commonplaces about the woman's body as a text. In poems that blur so many other distinctions, the one between the text of her body and the more literal text breaks down too: both are transgressive, both resist interpretation, both inhabit borders and margins. And over both the poet asserts his control. Thus the poet deflects the guilt that he, like Sidney's Kalander, may feel about participating in this genre not onto another male voice as does Sidney's Kalander but onto the woman herself: in mocking her body he mocks his genre, and in defending her he defends, in several senses of the noun, his own craft. Anxieties about both the transgressiveness of desire and the subversiveness of writing these poems

---

[75]Guibbory notes that Donne's elegies, some of which participate in the ugly beauty tradition, often reassert male control over love (" 'Oh, let mee not serve so,' " esp. pp. 819–820).

are deflected onto descriptions of a subversive and transgressive woman. Given that writing love poetry was itself disdained in many quarters, the woman may also represent the infractions of mainstream Petrarchism. In other words, the elision between subject and object, male and female, that sometimes compromises the subjectivity of the poet in Petrarchism here becomes yet another strategy for bolstering it.

But one of the most intriguing strategies of these poems is also one of the most subterranean—their indirect speech act. The direct speech acts encompass descriptions, questions, and so on, with the threat especially prominent. Behind those illocutionary acts, however, lies the riddle.[76] For poems in the tradition implicitly present their reader with a conundrum: How could a woman whose lips are bluish be praised? Or, why is a black woman more fair than a white one? Or, why is illness really attractive? Long studied by students of folklore, the riddle deserves further scrutiny by students of Tudor and Stuart literature as well, for it occupies a central position in many texts of that tradition; notice, for example, how often Shakespeare's plays end on an implicit or explicit riddle. More to our purposes here, the perlocutionary force of the riddle is establishing a hierarchical relationship between, so to speak, riddler and riddlee. That relationship derives from the similarities between the speech act in question and two of its cousins, the joke and the rhetorical question. Tellers of riddles, like tellers of jokes, derive and assert power by transforming a social and linguistic situation from ordinary discourse to a transaction with special rules.[77] And posers of riddles, like posers of rhetorical questions, further enforce their power by reminding us that they, and perhaps they alone, know the answer. (Witness the upheaval when that prerogative is subverted. Guess "Rumpelstiltskin," and Rumpelstiltskin collapses.)

In the course of establishing his power over his listeners, however, the author of ugly beauty poems also cements his relationship with them. Though certain lyrics, such as Lord Herbert of Cherbury's "Gialletta Gallante," do not presuppose an audience of men linked by their mockery of a woman, that situation is, as we have observed, implied by many other

[76]The riddle has been examined by scholars in a range of fields. See, e.g., Northrop Frye, *Anatomy of Criticism: Four Essays* (Princeton: Princeton University Press, 1957), p. 280; Phyllis Gorfain, "Riddles and Reconciliation: Formal Unity in *All's Well That Ends Well*," *Journal of the Folklore Institute*, 13 (1976), 263–281; Johan Huizinga, *Homo Ludens: A Study of the Play-Element in Culture* (London: Routledge and Kegan Paul, 1949), esp. chaps. 6, 7; and W. J. Pepicello and Thomas A. Green, *The Language of Riddles: New Perspectives* (Columbus: Ohio State University Press, 1984).

[77]Michael Riffaterre notes a related but different parallel with the joke, observing that in both the reader cannot go beyond the laugh and the solution (*Semiotics of Poetry* [Bloomington: Indiana University Press, 1978], p. 16).

texts in the tradition. Some instances of English Petrarchism do not assume a community of male friends, but one of its principal counterdiscourses, the ugly beauty tradition, often does, typically projecting a social situation very like the one dramatized in the *Arcadia,* where Kalander shares his rude and ribald description of Mopsa with Musidorus. As Colie points out, the paradox typically permits a writer or orator to show off his cleverness to a sophisticated audience;[78] in this and many other ways, the type of paradoxical poems in question resemble the epyllion and formal verse satire, both of which often pivot on mocking women to impress other men. If diacritical desire in mainstream Petrarchan poems often involves distinguishing oneself from other men because one cannot reliably distinguish oneself from women, here that desire involves differentiating women or apparently doing so, and thus allying oneself with one's own sex.

In short, then, poems in the ugly beauty tradition marshal strategies of denial, domination, and deflection in a number of ways in response to hostilities and anxieties. First, they may deny some of the very threats in which they are grounded. In other words, these poems may claim that the culturally normative beauty can be readily differentiated from her opposite number (an assertion mirrored in the privative and antithetical constructions of their rhetoric). Or, paradoxically, they may claim that the ostensibly transgressive woman in fact represents the stable continuation of traditional values. Thus they both stage and allegorize a contemporary drama: the attempt to incorporate the Other—whether it be defined as a subordinate gender; an atypical race; a subversive political, religious, or aesthetic position; or, as in Collop's case, a female body that represents several of these categories—into a cultural norm.

Second, poets in the ugly beauty tradition may attempt to dominate the transgressive women they evoke, the very systems of valuation that identify transgression, and the emotions that overwhelm their Petrarchan counterparts. These moves, too, are typically signaled by antithetical patterns and by deictics such as *here/there* and *this/that,* which intensify other antithetical structures. Such structures, then, serve to reassert the poet's control over both language and love and thus in some cases to distinguish him from the conventional Petrarchan lover: far from being caught in the labyrinth of an oxymoron or even the stasis of a gaze, he can make a clear and free choice between opposing paths. In Sonnet 13 Barnes glosses this strategy by announcing that he attempted to locate imperfections, such as a mole, so that he could hate his mistress and escape the misery she was causing him. Similarly, whereas the Petrarchan poet is often trapped in recurrent

---

[78]Colie, *Paradoxia Epidemica,* esp. pp. 3, 5.

emotions and familiar literary conventions, his counterpart in this version of anti-Petrarchism attempts to escape repetition through his allegiance to an atypical woman and an unconventional literary type. The masking of hostility in that type is a further way of dominating unruly emotions: by half concealing the bitterness behind these poems, their poet claims that it too is within his control. Anger may, as Kent tells us, have a privilege, but controlled anger has a power. Finally, poems in the ugly beauty tradition may covertly deploy strategies of deflection. Anxieties about the so-called normal and normative body may be deflected onto the atypical bodies being anatomized, as when Collop associates his deviant beauty with childbirth. And, as we have seen, the relationship between the poem and the woman it evokes is above all rooted in deflection.

This is not to say, however, that such strategies are always successful. Quite the contrary. Lacan interprets this version of fort-da more surely than does Freud. As the work of John Collop demonstrates, the poet's triumphant assertions of agency and authority are sometimes undermined in the course of the poem. In the selections we examined in detail, Lord Herbert and Carew achieve the mastery that Collop gains only intermittently. Similarly, if the authors of these lyrics implicitly or at times even explicitly declare their superiority to Petrarchan and other love poets and their command of the very agency the Petrarchan speaker so tenuously and temporarily lays claim to, that declaration is as unreliable as other declarations in this tradition. For these poems at times replicate the struggles for power and autonomy, sometimes successful and sometimes not, which compromise that agency in Petrarchism itself. Under such circumstances they, like mainstream Petrarchan poets, reenact what they attempt to reject. They too skid between success and failure. In this as in so many other ways, the conventions of ugly beauty poems prove to be a currency as volatile and complex, as threatened and as threatening, as the bodies these texts evoke.

CHAPTER SIX

RESIDENT ALIEN: JOHN DONNE

I

MADAME,
Here where by All All Saints invoked are,
'Twere too much schisme to be singular,
And 'gainst a practise generall to warre.

Yet turning to Saincts, should my'humility
To other Sainct then you directed bee,
That were to make my schisme, heresie.
"A Letter to the Lady Carey,
and Mrs Essex Riche," 1–6)[1]

Most students of Donne ignore this verse letter completely; a few comment in passing on its cleverness.[2] Yet the excerpt above, like so many sections of its author's so-called minor poems, deserves not passing praise but intense and sustained scrutiny. For it glosses both Donne's agenda in the epistle that ensues and his approach to Petrarchism and its counterdiscourses throughout his career.

The lines in question associate Donne's compliments to Lady Carey and

---

[1] All citations from Donne's satires, verse letters, and *Metempsychosis* are to Wesley Milgate, ed., *The Satires, Epigrams and Verse Letters* (Oxford: Clarendon, 1967).

[2] See, e.g., Milgate's brief but trenchant observations about how Donne is playing with the image he deploys (*Satires*, p. xxxix) and Margaret Maurer's explanation of how the reference to sainthood excuses flattery ("John Donne's Verse Letters," *MLQ*, 37 [1976], 257–258). Laurence Stapleton less persuasively suggests that Donne "makes amends to the absent patronesses by satirizing the invocation of saints" ("The Theme of Virtue in Donne's Verse Epistles," *SP*, 55 [1958], 199).

her sister with French Catholicism. Yet even in 1611–1612, the period to which Donne's editors assign this poem,[3] this passage would also have recalled the popular Petrarchan convention of comparing the lady to a saint, which Donne himself had used in an early verse letter to his friend Christopher Brooke. Thus Donne invokes not only saints but also a Petrarchan trope. At the same time, however, he hints that the decision to participate in these discourses is not uncontested ("Twere too much schisme to be singular" [2]). And, more to our purposes, he distances himself from this staple of Petrarchan praise by flagging the meaning of sainthood within the Catholic Church and thus relating the conventions of Petrarchism to the suspect ideology of French Catholicism.

Indeed, in this intriguing passage Donne is engaged in participating in Petrarchism while distancing himself from it in a whole range of ways: generically, in that the conventions of sonneteering are deployed in a sphere other than love poetry; grammatically, in that the lines are structured around the instabilities of conditionals ("'Twere," "should," "That were" [2, 4, 6]); and, above all, geographically, in that he emphatically locates himself, his poem, and his hagiography in a foreign country, even going so far as to attach the phrase "From Amyens" onto his title. This is, indeed, but one of many instances in which Donne creates and signals other types of gaps through literal, geographical space. And, like the other poets we have examined, he distances himself diacritically as well, for in the very act of participating in a religious and literary practice, he is concerned to distinguish his version of it from that of the French, who invoke all saints. (Later in the poem he would pursue his diacritical agenda from a Neo-Platonic perspective: "your Beauty wounds not hearts, / As Others, with prophane and sensuall Darts" [43–44].)

In an equally revealing line in another verse letter, Donne writes "Smooth as *thy* mistresse glasse, or what shines there" ("The Calme," 8; emphasis added) rather than "Smooth as *my* mistresse glasse," thus distancing the conceits of love poetry. Holding his Petrarchism at a remove, he deploys similar strategies in this poem addressed to the Lady Carey and Mrs. Essex Rich. Admittedly, many forms of literary imitation involve some detachment from the original, but the sources, methods, and consequences of Donne's approach to Petrarchism are distinctive. In particular, he neither embraces Petrarchism enthusiastically, as some revisionist readers

---

[3] On its dating, see esp. Milgate, *Satires*, p. 274. R. E. Bennett classifies it among other letters Donne wrote during a trip to the Continent ("Donne's Letters from the Continent in 1611–12," *PQ*, 19 [1940], 66–78), and R. C. Bald discusses the dates and addressees of Donne's early letters to male friends ("Donne's Early Verse Letters," *HLQ*, 15 [1952], 283–289).

assert, nor rejects it under the guise of participating in it, as others claim.[4] Rather, complicating—but not canceling—his debt to that tradition, Donne uses modes of distancing here, as he does throughout his canon, to establish himself as both inside and outside Petrarchism, as both "Here" (1) and there. Or, as his own vocabulary suggests, he is a visitor to, perhaps even a temporary resident in, a foreign country, following its customs and talking its language yet never forgetting or allowing us to forget that he is no native.

If critics are sometimes prone to misinterpret Donne's relationship to Petrarchism, they are not prone to neglect it: that topic is an old chestnut, at times even a stale one. In general, until the past few decades many studies of Donne devoted more attention to his reactions against Petrarchism than to its continuing presence in his canon; more recently, revisionist studies have emphasized his debts to that movement. But, inhabiting as we do a critical climate that encourages an oversimplification of the criticism of the past as a convenient strategy for celebrating the present, we should acknowledge that even the apparently straightforward picture I am painting is as shaded as a sixteenth-century Venetian portrait: as is so often the case, many of the observations about Donne's Petrarchism expressed in contemporary revisionist analyses were in fact anticipated considerably earlier. If Mario Praz establishes the rebelliousness of the author of the *Songs and Sonets*, he also draws attention to the affinities between Donne and Petrarch;[5] if Clay Hunt emphasizes Donne's mockery of Petrarchism, he acknowledges as well that Donne borrows virtually all the conventions of that discourse.[6]

In whatever manner one summarizes the positions of earlier critics, it is clear that the past few decades have witnessed renewed attention to the Petrarchan elements in the monarch of anti-Petrarchan wit. Critics disagree, however, as to the extent to which those elements are ultimately rejected. Locating Donne firmly within traditions of Continental Petrarchism, Donald L. Guss, for instance, declares that "the richness of Petrarchism explains

---

[4] One of the most influential studies of his debt to Petrarchism is Donald L. Guss, *John Donne, Petrarchist: Italianate Conceits and Love Theory in "The Songs and Sonets"* (Detroit: Wayne State University Press, 1966). For the argument that he subtly rejects that tradition, see, e.g., Patricia Garland Pinka, *This Dialogue of One: The "Songs and Sonnets" of John Donne* (Tuscaloosa: University of Alabama Press, 1982).

[5] Mario Praz, *The Flaming Heart: Essays on Crashaw, Machiavelli, and Other Studies in the Relations between Italian and English Literature from Chaucer to T. S. Eliot* (New York: Doubleday, 1958), esp. pp. 198, 280–281.

[6] Clay Hunt, *Donne's Poetry: Essays in Literary Analysis* (New Haven: Yale University Press, 1954), esp. p. 7.

the richness of Donne.'"[7] Silvia Ruffo-Fiore presents Donne as refining, not rejecting, his heritage from the author of the *Rime sparse*.[8] Such reactions against our emphasis on Donne's putative anti-Petrarchism were no less predictable—and no less significant—than the reaction against the emphasis on the putative classicism of eighteenth-century writers. On the other hand, N. J. C. Andreasen, among many other critics, also stresses the pervasiveness of that heritage but maintains that Donne criticizes it by associating it with speakers he condemns.[9]

Studies of Donne's relationship to Petrarchism, fruitful though they may be in other respects, have frequently been limited by certain intellectual preconceptions and methodological misprisions. The widespread practice of classifying Donne's poetry by cramming it into a comparatively small set of groups (Platonic versus Petrarchan, for example) risks underestimating the variety that occurs from poem to poem and, above all, within a single lyric, a problem to which we will return. Donne's responses to Petrarchism are as varied and volatile as his responses to women: to vex us, contraries meet in one. Persuasive though it is in other ways, Guss's *John Donne, Petrarchist* does not adequately acknowledge that if Donne participates enthusiastically in certain modes of Petrarchism, he simultaneously reacts against others—and surely would have been perceived by his contemporaries as doing so. Above all, once again it is necessary to focus on short units of time. Donne's attitudes to Petrarchism may well shift within a few years during his career, though those attitudes do not describe the steady trajectory some students of his work have posited. And Petrarchism, I will argue throughout this chapter, meant something very different in England in the early 1590s, when Donne first arrived at the Inns of Court, than it did only a few years later, let alone in the subsequent decade. Historical events are shaped not least by contemporaries' interpretations of the history that preceded them, and in this instance Donne's responses to Petrarchism include and even at times center on his reactions to his own previous involvement with that tradition.

If we bear these caveats in mind, we can more accurately chronicle

---

[7] Guss, *John Donne, Petrarchist*, p. 16.

[8] Silvia Ruffo-Fiore, *Donne's Petrarchism: A Comparative View* (Florence: Grafica Toscana, 1976). For earlier versions of some sections of her argument, see "The Unwanted Heart in Petrarch and Donne," *CL*, 24 (1972), 319–327; and "Donne's 'Parody' of the Petrarchan Lady," *Comparative Literature Studies*, 9 (1972), 392–406.

[9] N. J. C. Andreasen, *John Donne: Conservative Revolutionary* (Princeton: Princeton University Press, 1967). For a similar argument see Pinka, *This Dialogue of One*; also cf. R.W. Hamilton, "John Donne's Petrarchist Poems," *Renaissance and Modern Studies*, 23 (1979), 45–62, who argues that critiques of Petrarchan conventions in some poems that employ them anticipate Donne's subsequent rejection of Petrarchism.

Donne's repeated visits to and incursions into what was both a familiar and an alien territory and the ways he distances himself from that terrain even while dwelling within it. Studying the intersections of cultural and literary history will help us to understand why he constructs the modes of distancing on which this chapter opened; analyzing some lyrics in which the counterdiscourses of Petrarchism are especially intriguing will help us to comprehend how he does so.

II

Donne, I have suggested, presents himself as at once resident and alien in the realms of Petrarchism. In adopting that stance, he transforms a state that was potentially a liability in his own life into a strength in his poetry; that is, he redefines the position of being on the edge of certain cultural institutions, neither quite an insider nor quite an outsider, into a source of power. Turning a perceived or imputed weakness into a strength is very characteristic of Donne: witness, among many other examples, his mockery in "The Will" or how his speaker moves from victim to victimizer in "Satyre I" or "The Funerall." But nowhere does he perform this feat more skillfully than in his approach to Petrarchism.

The poet who so often writes about moments of transition and marginal states (leave-taking, dying, midnight, and so on),[10] the poet who so often speaks a grammar of gerunds, himself dwelt on the cusp, on the edge, even at times on the brink, in many arenas of his life. In some of those arenas, he moved back and forth from one position to the other; in others, he simultaneously occupied both. Most obviously, he was both insider and outsider because of his religious orientation. At one point in his life, conversion—apostasy, if we borrow John Carey's charged term—transformed him from one position to the other;[11] at different points, Richard Strier has argued, his determined intellectual independence established him as an outsider to several traditions.[12] Similarly, the vagaries of the patronage system variously positioned him as insider and outsider at court: he gained

[10] Compare John Carey's related but different observations about Donne's preoccupation with corners in *John Donne: Life, Mind, and Art* (London: Faber and Faber, 1981), esp. chap. 9.

[11] Donne's religious conversion has, of course, been studied extensively. See esp. Carey's controversial arguments about apostasy as a formative experience (*John Donne*, chaps. 1 and 2), and Richard Strier, "John Donne Awry and Squint: The 'Holy Sonnets,' 1608–1610," *MP*, 86 (1989), 357–384.

[12] Richard Strier, "Radical Donne: 'Satire III,' " *ELH*, 60 (1993), 283–322.

certain promising appointments, such as secretary to the lord keeper, but
the consequences of his marriage and of the political problems of Sir Robert
Drury, who had appeared a promising patron, demonstrated the slipperiness
of patronage.[13]

The complexities of Sidney's career warned us against oversimplifying
the class system of early modern England and, in particular, against approaching its stratifications almost as if they had the fixity and clarity widely
attributed to social estates. In fact, even the medieval class system was
neither as simple nor as rigid as students of early modern culture, always
at risk of simplifying the Middle Ages, are wont to assume. Chaucer's great-
great-grandson John, earl of Lincoln, was heir to the throne.[14] Donne's life,
like Sidney's, exemplifies the perils of making similar mistakes about the
early modern period. Not only did late sixteenth- and seventeenth-century
England witness a significant pattern of class mobility, but because status
was multiply determined, even a relatively stable position could be hard to
classify. Thus Donne was the son of an ironmonger, though a prosperous
one, stepson of a doctor who had repeatedly served as president of the
Royal College of Physicians, and the scion on the maternal side of a distinguished and undoubtedly upper-middle-class line.[15] Hence his claims to
gentility, though credible, were by no means assured: in this arena, too,
he was on the edge. Recognizing this leads to speculations that nuance
Arthur F. Marotti's important work on Donne as coterie poet:[16] whether
at Oxford or the Inns or both, he must have been aware not only of being
an insider in certain circles but also of being relegated to the position of
outsider in others because of his paternal lineage. Certainly the Inns were
a microcosm of the social mobility of English culture in the later sixteenth
century, with most of their inhabitants still members of the landed gentry
but a number of merchants' sons present as well.[17] Donne straddled those
two groups, and one wonders if he was conscious of doing so—or was
made to be conscious.

---

[13] For a thorough summary of Donne's struggles in the patronage system, see R. C. Bald,
John Donne: A Life (New York: Oxford University Press, 1970), esp. chaps. 6–11.

[14] On Chaucer's life and social status, see Martin M. Crow and Virginia E. Leland,
"Chaucer's Life," in *The Riverside Chaucer*, ed. Larry D. Benson, 3d ed. (Boston: Houghton
Mifflin, 1987); his great-great-grandson's claim to the throne is discussed on p. xvi.

[15] On Donne's social background, see Bald, *John Donne: A Life*, chaps. 2, 3.

[16] Arthur F. Marotti, *John Donne, Coterie Poet* (Madison: University of Wisconsin Press,
1986).

[17] On the social composition of the Inns, see Philip J. Finkelpearl, *John Marston of the
Middle Temple: An Elizabethan Dramatist in His Social Setting* (Cambridge: Harvard University
Press, 1969), pp. 5–6.

Donne's family background poses other questions, even harder to adjudicate, about the senses in which he was both insider and outsider. His father died when he was four, and the consequences of early parental death in Tudor and Stuart England, as I argued in Chapter 2, are extensive and pervasive. How, if at all, did the role of stepson affect the peculiar amalgam of contiguity and distance so central to Donne?

Though one cannot answer that question decisively, and perhaps not even responsibly, it is clear that the peculiarities of the Inns of Court established Donne and the other members of the Inns as simultaneously insiders and outsiders in other circles of London culture. Skillfully analyzed by Philip J. Finkelpearl and Marotti,[18] the Inns comprised young men who saw themselves, or perhaps merely presented themselves, as engaged in a complex and ambivalent relationship to Elizabethan culture. Considerable evidence suggests that they admired and indeed often created the mainstream sixteenth-century literature that they sometimes professed to scorn.[19] In the generations immediately preceding Donne's, the Inns had been a center for translators, and many authors of the *Mirror for Magistrates* were also associated with that institution; in Donne's day, the revels that were so important a part of the Inns incorporated courtly language, apparently used without parodic intent.[20] Yet members of the Inns, notably Marston, enthusiastically adopted the persona of that ultimate outsider, the formal verse satirist. The Inns, in short, provided Donne yet again with the experience of being both insider and outsider, both contiguous and distant, and also with a ready symbol of that dual state. Such paradoxes should not be difficult for contemporary critics to understand, for the relationship of the young men at the Inns to the court, especially their deployment of the status of powerless outsider to advance their own power, is reminiscent of the workings of our own profession. In particular, critical schools tend to insist on their transgressiveness and exclusion long beyond the point where those and other characteristics have helped to insure them a secure position in the academy.

Finally, in fashioning himself as both insider and outsider, Donne would surely never forget the theological doctrines that constructed him and all mankind as inhabitants of a perilous middle state on this imperiled middle earth. Rehearsing one of the most familiar of those doctrines in his *Devotions,* he observes, "As yet God suspends me between heaven and earth,

[18] Finkelpearl, *John Marston of the Middle Temple*; Marotti, *John Donne, Coterie Poet.*
[19] See Marotti, *John Donne, Coterie Poet,* pp. 82–83.
[20] Finkelpearl, *John Marston of the Middle Temple,* pp. 20–23, 41.

as a meteor; and I am not in heaven because an earthly body clogs me, and I am not in the earth because a heavenly soul sustains me."[21] Students of Tudor and Stuart literature sometimes view the intellectual history favored by an earlier generation of critics as distinct from, if not inimical to, the concerns of the current generation, which in certain instances is quite true: the distinctions between Ficino and Pico, for instance, have relatively little bearing on, say, issues of colonialism. But in the case of Donne, as with many other authors, the methodologies of intellectual and cultural history can and should be deployed together: when he tailored an image of himself as both outsider and insider, a process at the core of new historicist inquiry, the theological doctrine I have cited was surely among his principal patterns.

Studying the interplay of cultural and intellectual history which informs Donne's status as insider and outsider, then, bears on his Petrarchism in two ways. One of his most characteristic maneuvers is restoring his own agency, or that of a speaker, in a situation initially characterized by passivity; in "The Sunne Rising" the sun, previously an unwelcome intruder, is invited to return, and in "The Apparition" the victim of the murderous hate of the Petrarchan lady comes back to terrorize his tormentor. Similarly, in poems such as "A Letter to the Lady Carey, and Mrs. Essex Riche," Donne transforms the position of being on the edge, being an outsider trying to get in or an insider slipping out, into a more positive and more powerful role, that of the poet who chooses to be simultaneously a practitioner of and a critic of Petrarchism. Once again, the point is not that he criticizes that mode under the guise of practicing it by discrediting his speaker but rather that he has it both ways at once.

In the lyric on which this chapter opened, Donne's Petrarchan counterdiscourse is assertively diacritical, and a summary of the arenas in which he was both outsider and insider—and hence in another sense neither outsider nor insider—can also offer yet another perspective on diacritical desire. Donne's culture repeatedly threatened him with exclusion, whether as a Roman Catholic not permitted to take a university degree, as an ironmonger's son whose claim to gentility was problematical, or as a courtier whose search for patronage was often frustrated. In his approach to Petrarchism and anti-Petrarchism, as in so many of his other activities, Donne transforms the base and debasing metal of exclusion into the gold— or, rather, fool's gold—of exclusivity. Born into a religion that cut him off from the Church of England, in this poem he chooses to mock those who

---

[21] John Donne, *Devotions upon Emergent Occasions* (Ann Arbor: University of Michigan Press, 1959), pp. 20–21.

worship all saints at the same time as he celebrates his own, more discriminating mode of worship.

Donne's approach to Petrarchism is shaped, of course, both by his reactions to the imbricated cultural circles of the court, the patronage system,
and the Inns and by his ambivalent responses to his literary milieu and to
the process of imitation. That process clearly touched several nerves, even
nerve centers. Whether one reads his responses to authority as fundamen-
tally absolutist, as Jonathan Goldberg has alleged, or as changing and conflicting, as Marotti among others has argued,[22] they are clearly complex
enough to color literary imitation. Not the least reason for Donne's attraction to the Roman elegy is its opportunities for mocking fathers, occasions he gleefully seizes in such poems as "The Perfume" and "On his
Mistris." Literary imitation clearly offers dangers of subservience as well as
potentialities for rebellious mockery, both the possibility of advancing ambition and of thwarting it by unsuccessful or servile copying.[23] Above all,
literary imitation provides an arena for competitive jousting to a poet no
less preoccupied with rivalry than Shakespeare. Donne is concerned with,
even possessed by, competition in part because of the pressures of patronage,[24] though one suspects multiple etiologies.

But perhaps the best explanation of Donne's ambivalence about literary
imitation is one of his own tropes. Haunted by entrapment, whether it is
engineered by courtly spies or the speaker's own psyche, Donne returns
repeatedly to the image of a net:

> he throwes
> Like nets, or lime-twigs, wheresoere he goes,
> His title'of Barrister.
> ("Satyre II," 45–47)

> Or treacherously poore fish beset,
> With strangling snare, or windowie net:
> ("The Baite," 19–20)[25]

---

[22] Jonathan Goldberg, *James I and the Politics of Literature: Jonson, Shakespeare, Donne, and
Their Contemporaries* (Baltimore: Johns Hopkins University Press, 1983), esp. pp. 107–112,
210–219; and Marotti, *John Donne, Coterie Poet*, esp. pp. 253–254.

[23] For a thought-provoking but controversial argument about Donne's ambitiousness, see
Carey, *John Donne*, chaps. 3 and 4.

[24] Compare Patricia Thomson's argument about the competition between Donne and
John Burges for the patronage of the countess of Bedford ("John Donne and the Countess
of Bedford," *MLR*, 44 [1949], 331–335).

[25] All citations from Donne's elegies and love poems are to Helen Gardner, ed., *The
Elegies and The Songs and Sonnets* (Oxford: Clarendon, 1965).

Man hath weav'd out a net, and this net throwne
Upon the Heavens, and now they are his owne.
(First Anniversarie, 279–280)[26]

He hunts not fish, but as an officer
Stayes in his court, as his owne net.
(Metempsychosis, 321–322)

It would not be difficult to multiply these examples, especially if one combed through *Metempsychosis*, which is crammed with references to nets (perhaps Donne was impelled to write that poem partly because its plot allowed so many opportunities to describe those snares). In any event, as telling as his attraction to the trope is the way he modifies it in "The Baite," where his "windowie net" (20) fascinates him because it represents both a threat and the possibility of escaping it—confinement and distance—a pattern that, as we have already seen, recurs repeatedly in his work. Strier's observation that Donne's love lyrics manifest an "identification of commitment with enthrallment" glosses some of these tropes.[27] More to our purposes now, literary imitation is for Donne the windowy net par excellence, involving as it does both the danger of being entrapped by another writer, another style, and another era and the opportunity of gliding by, victorious, if one tempers one's imitation with innovations or undercuts it with mockery. Or, to put it another way, literary imitation tenders both the threat of being imprisoned in another country and the opportunity of vacationing there in the sunshine, without the obligations of its citizens.

Donne's ambivalence about literary imitation was intensified by the challenges of adapting Petrarchism in particular. Fully to understand the appeal of that discourse for him, one needs to focus on not only its overt qualities, especially its tropes and its adulatory stance, but also the characteristics identified in this study. Donne must have found Petrarch's self-consciousness and self-centeredness congenial, even perhaps uncomfortably familiar, and of course he shared that poet's preoccupation with death as well. The elision of gender that is, as I have argued, so central to Petrarchism would have been equally attractive to the poet whose astronomy includes a "shee Sunne, and a hee Moone" ("An Epithalamion, or Mariage Song on the Lady Elizabeth, and Count Palatine," 85). As central to Petrarchism as the slippage of gender is the slippage between success and

---

[26] Citations from Donne's wedding poems and *Anniversaries* are to Wesley Milgate, ed., *The Epithalamions, Anniversaries, and Epicedes* (Oxford: Clarendon, 1978).
[27] Strier, "Radical Donne," p. 284.

failure, and this all too familiar pattern no doubt further intensified Donne's interest in that mode of writing.

Above all, however, the diacritical drive of Petrarchism conforms to one of the deepest and most recurrent impulses in Donne's writing. The encounter between satiric protagonist and antagonist that is most overt in "Satyre I" but present elsewhere in Donne's formal verse satires is of course diacritical in its origins. The letter to the countess of Bedford that begins "Reason is our Soules" opens on a contrast between two types of love, as does the epistle to Lady Carey and her sister. And throughout Donne's love poetry the speakers engage in distinguishing themselves from others, whether they be the "dull sublunary lovers" (13) of "A Valediction: Forbidding Mourning" or the "prophane men" (22) mentioned in "The Undertaking." The expressions of this diacritical drive in Donne's lyrics may well echo his Petrarchan desire to reject earlier versions of himself, particularly the Catholic and the man-about-town, and in so doing to renounce youthful errors. At the same time, Donne's diacritical impulse is the product of another, equally pressing desire, that competitive urge that so often makes his verse edgy. Finally, yet again one needs to sidestep the temptation to discard intellectual history as irrelevant to the concerns of contemporary criticism. If Donne's diacritical drive is central to issues on the cutting edge of our professional discourse, notably gender, Augustinian doctrine is no less central to that drive. As many critics have demonstrated, Augustine's influence is manifest throughout Donne's canon.[28] Donne himself acknowledges that influence; in *Biathanatos,* for example, he celebrates Augustine's "sharpe insight, and conclusive judgement in exposition of places of Scripture."[29] Diacritical desire in Donne is rooted in the Augustinian distinction between caritas and cupiditas, even though that contrast is transmuted into very different secular forms in several of the poems I cited.

Donne's diacritical drive helps to shape both his Petrarchism and his anti-Petrarchism; many additional pressures and predilections also impel the latter agenda. Most obviously, the adulatory subservience that is at the heart of Petrarchism was deeply uncongenial to him, as many critics have noted; William Kerrigan observes that Donne celebrates an ideal of mutual love that is foreign to Petrarchism, and Achsah Guibbory argues persuasively that his doubts about Petrarchan humility may be traced, at least in part,

---

[28] See, e.g., Patrick Grant, "Augustinian Spirituality and the *Holy Sonnets* of John Donne," *ELH*, 38 (1971), 542–561; and John Klause, "The Montaigneity of Donne's *Metempsychosis*," in *Renaissance Genres: Essays on Theory, History, and Interpretation*, Harvard English Studies 14, ed. Barbara Kiefer Lewalski (Cambridge: Harvard University Press, 1986), esp. pp. 428–429.

[29] John Donne, *Biathanatos,* ed. J. William Hebel (New York: Facsimile Text Society, 1930), p. 98.

to his unease at submission to a female ruler.[30] One of the most recurrent fears in Donne's poetry and so many other texts of sixteenth-and seventeenth-century England—that the woman will betray her lover with another man—is also foreign to Petrarchism. (Although one might maintain that Donne's own preoccupation with that fear can be traced in part to his Ovidian and elegiac sources, that argument begs the question of why he is attracted to those texts; more persuasive is the assertion that he is attracted to them in no small measure because they express the fear in question.) Finally, Donne's concern with rivalry impels his counterdiscourses in two ways: the relative absence of that pressure in Petrarch's own poetry widens the gap he senses between its vision and his own, while writing poetry that is anti-Petrarchan in the several senses of that term is one ploy in his relationship with actual or fictive rivals, particularly in "The Anagram" and "The Comparison."

In listing the distinctions between Donne and Petrarch, however, we need to note how interactive and dynamic their relationship is. The point is not, of course, that Donne, blessed with a stable sense of self, recognized and reacted against uncongenial elements of the *Rime sparse*. Rather, the patterns of Petrarchism influence Donne's self-fashioning and the fashioning of his speakers in that the Petrarchan lover provides both a model to emulate and one to reject. And it is worth reminding ourselves that Petrarchism itself did not enjoy a stable and fixed identity in Tudor and Stuart England or any other culture: both the lyrics in which Donne adapts Petrarchism and those in which he mocks it help to define the nature of Petrarchism for him and his readers.

III

Moving from a synchronic overview of Donne's counterdiscourses to a diachronic study of specific poems immediately poses further methodological problems. Such an analysis will necessarily be selective, for Donne's anti-Petrarchism is a subject more fit for a book than a chapter; I have tried to counterbalance the habit of concentrating on the *Songs and Sonets* to the virtual exclusion of other texts by devoting considerable attention to Donne's less well known poems in genres such as the verse epistle and correspondingly less to his love lyrics. Indeed, it is imperative, not merely

[30] William Kerrigan, "What Was Donne Doing?" *South Central Review*, 4 (1987), 11–12; and Achsah Guibbory, " 'Oh, let mee not serve so': The Politics of Love in Donne's *Elegies*," *ELH*, 57 (1990), esp. 813, 828–829.

advisable, to encompass texts in a range of genres, for Donne himself deploys the act of choosing one literary form over another to comment on Petrarchism. In studying his relationship to Petrarchism, critics also cannot ignore chronology, for his counterdiscourses respond variously to specific moments in his culture and hence shift in important ways over time, though they never assume a simple pattern of moving from acceptance to rejection. In particular, as I will argue, Petrarchism sparked his interest when he was a young man at the Inns, and the bitterness with which he sometimes attacks it when practicing his *acerbo stil nuovo* demonstrates again that the counterdiscourses of Petrarchism are often reactions against an earlier version of oneself. Any chronological examination of Donne's reactions against Petrarchism, however, must also be provisional, for dating his poems is more problematical than some of his critics have admitted.[31]

Petrarchan sentiments, tropes, and situations are pervasive in both Donne's major and minor poems. The *Songs and Sonets* refer repeatedly to sighs and tears, those staples of Petrarchan experience, and they focus on certain moments central to the *Rime sparse* and many of its imitators: leavetaking, the illness or death of the beloved, and the anniversary of the relationship. Whether or not the deflection of Petrarchan conceits from a woman to a young girl should make us hesitate to call the *Anniversaries* Petrarchan, as Barbara Kiefer Lewalski has asserted,[32] those poems certainly adopt the refined adulatory discourse associated with the *Rime sparse* and, of course, also focus on the death of the beloved. Similarly, the praise in the verse letters to patronesses often adapts Petrarchan tropes. Moreover, the conceits long hailed as the hallmark of Donne's poetry themselves express a debt to Petrarchism: Guss rightly reminds us of the connections between Donne's wit and certain modes of Continental Petrarchism, notably the version practiced by Serafino.[33] Such debts have editorial implications as well. The manuscript evidence for excluding "The Token" from the canon is significant though not conclusive; in light of the extent and

---

[31] In particular, the important book by Marotti, *John Donne, Coterie Poet*, is sometimes limited by its reliance on dubious assumptions about dating, a problem occasionally acknowledged (see, e.g., pp. 83, 137) but never resolved.

[32] Barbara Kiefer Lewalski, *Donne's "Anniversaries" and the Poetry of Praise: The Creation of a Symbolic Mode* (Princeton: Princeton University Press, 1973), esp. pp. 12–14. For alternative views of Petrarchan elements in these poems, see O. B. Hardison Jr., *The Enduring Monument: A Study of the Idea of Praise in Renaissance Literary Theory and Practice* (Chapel Hill: University of North Carolina Press, 1962), chap. 7; and John Donne, *The Anniversaries*, ed. Frank Manley (Baltimore: Johns Hopkins University Press, 1963), p. 10.

[33] Guss, *John Donne, Petrarchist*, esp. chap. 5.

range of Donne's Petrarchism, he could well have written an extended love sonnet, so stylistic evidence should not be adduced in support of that exclusion.[34]

Although dating most of Donne's poems is difficult, it is likely that the verse letters to male friends which identify their recipients by initials were composed in the early and mid-1590s and hence constitute some of his earliest texts.[35] These poems are far more indebted to Petrarchism than the old clichés about their author's anti-Petrarchism would even deem possible. Seven of the fifteen texts are fourteen lines long, an eighth consists of two fourteen-line stanzas, and a ninth has two fourteen-line stanzas plus an envoy of four lines.[36] Many of their stances, too, recall Petrarchism, with the speaker petitioning for pity in "To Mr T.W." ("All haile sweet Poet"), describing the recipient as "my pain and pleasure" in "To Mr T.W." ("Hast thee harsh verse," 2), and debasing himself in the course of showering adulation on the addressee in "To Mr R.W." ("Kindly'I envy").

Yet two particularly interesting epistles in the group also participate in and in so doing explicate the counterdiscourses of Petrarchism:

To Mr C.B.

Thy friend, whom thy deserts to thee enchaine,
　Urg'd by this inexcusable occasion,
　Thee and the Saint of his affection
Leaving behinde, doth of both wants complaine;
And let the love I beare to both sustaine
　No blott nor maime by this division,
　Strong is this love which ties our hearts in one,
And strong that love pursu'd with amorous paine;
But though besides thy selfe I leave behind
　Heavens liberall, and earths thrice-fairer Sunne,
　Going to where sterne winter aye doth wonne,
Yet, loves hot fires, which martyr my sad minde,
　Doe send forth scalding sighes, which have the Art
　To melt all Ice, but that which walls her heart.

---

[34] For the argument that it should be excluded on both grounds, see Gardner, *Elegies*, p. xlviii.

[35] On the division of these poems into groups and the characteristics of these early letters, see Milgate, *Satires*, pp. xxxiii–xxxiv. On their dates, see his notes on individual poems.

[36] In arriving at the number fifteen, I include the poem to Rowland Woodward beginning "Like one who'in"; its recipient is identified by initials in some poems and by his full name in others, and the poem itself is transitional in style between the early and more mature letters to male friends. The letters to Henry Wotton are excluded.

To Mr. I.L.

Blest are your North parts, for all this long time
My Sun is with you, cold and darke'is our Clime;
Heavens Sun, which staid so long from us this yeare,
Staid in your North (I thinke) for she was there,
And hether by kinde nature drawne from thence,
Here rages, chafes, and threatens pestilence;
Yet I, as long as shee from hence doth staie,
Thinke this no South, no Sommer, nor no day.
With thee my kinde and unkinde heart is run,
There sacrifice it to that beauteous Sun:
And since thou art in Paradise and need'st crave
No joyes addition, helpe thy friend to save.
So may thy pastures with their flowery feasts,
As suddenly as Lard, fat thy leane beasts;
So may thy woods oft poll'd, yet ever weare
A greene, and when thee list, a golden haire;
So may all thy sheepe bring forth Twins; and so
In chace and race may thy horse all out goe;
So may thy love and courage ne'r be cold;
Thy Sonne ne'r Ward; Thy lov'd wife ne'r seem old;
But maist thou wish great things, and them attaine,
As thou telst her, and none but her, my paine.

These lyrics, textbook instances of the Renaissance fascination with *genera mista*, boast a complex genealogy. Their debt to the Petrarchan sonnet is manifest; Donne variously writes of "amorous paine" ("To Mr C.B.," 8), evokes a saintlike woman and her icy heart, indulges in hyperbole, and focuses on the consequences of absence. The second text contains as well a proto–country house poem, complete with a version of the rhetorical staple of that tradition, the negative formula, as well as the customary allusions to the Fall.

At this point one should not be surprised to learn that both lyrics center on distance and its counterpart, loss. They comment explicitly and repeatedly on the distance from their recipients, a situation that motivates most other verse letters but often remains implicit in them. The sun, too, is distant. Various forms of negatives and privatives ("No blott nor maime" ["To Mr C.B.," 6]; "Thinke this no South, no Sommer, nor no day" ["To Mr I.L.," 8]) enact distance and loss grammatically. And the ladies in question are distanced not only geographically but also rhetorically in that the poet's sentiments are not addressed to them directly but rather filtered through messengers, the addressees of these letters. The second of these letters also includes a pattern of pairing that is rendered explicit in the wish for literal twins: it involves two forms of love, refers to two suns, and pairs words ("kinde and unkinde," 9; "chace and race," 18). And the poet who, when writing an epithalamium for the Somerset-Howard wedding nearly two decades later, was to project two versions of himself under the names "Idios" and "Allophanes,"[37] here asks his friend to speak his words and thus to become his double. These patterns of distance or privation and the pairing that in a sense is the opposite of privatives are not, I suggest, present fortuitously: they enact rhetorically the very agenda of these poems, distancing their speaker and their poet from the discourse he is practicing by pairing the Petrarchan sonnet to a mistress with the verse epistle to a male friend.

On one level that pairing serves to intensify the bond between the male friends. Both loves may be strong, as Donne insists in "To Mr C.B.," but it is telling that the letters are addressed to another man, not to the Petrarchan mistress. In "To Mr I.L." the role of messenger cements the bond between the men. That is, though Donne's speaker is associated with privation and the addressee with plenitude, the relationship between them does not evince the competitiveness that Donne's other poetry would lead us to expect but rather a symbiosis in which the poet depends on his friend to deliver a message and the friend depends on the poet, like his counterpart in the country house poem, for good wishes that culminate on implicit apotropaic threats. (Our expectation of rivalry is not wholly fallacious, however, for it is not so much erased as on the one hand controlled by mutual dependency and on the other displaced onto the competitive horses who appear in line eighteen of "To Mr I.L.") Hence both poems exemplify certain characteristics of homosocial desire: they assert the symmetry between the genders (in one letter mirroring it as well through the other forms of pairing which we traced) while apparently undermining that symmetry by privileging the male addressee and the relationship between him and the speaker.[38] And the erasure of the woman that often results from homosocial desire is thematized in both poems, which focus on the absence of both male friend and mistress yet reinstate the former by addressing him on the subject of the lady, as well as other topics, within the letter. Thus

[37] See my argument about those names in *A Happier Eden: The Politics of Marriage in the Stuart Epithalamium* (Ithaca: Cornell University Press, 1990), pp. 193–195.

[38] The highly influential concept of homosocial desire was introduced by Eve Kosofsky Sedgwick in *Between Men: English Literature and Male Homosocial Desire* (New York: Columbia University Press, 1985). For a summary of some of its characteristics, see pp. 47–48.

the Petrarchan mistress seemingly serves mainly to enable a relationship between men, a relationship that negotiates some distance from both Petrarchism and the Petrarchan lady.

The verse letters in question, then, might appear to provide a textbook example of homosocial desire. Perhaps. Certainly that model usefully directs our attention to the triangulation of the participants and the focus on the friend throughout much of both letters. Yet in making assumptions about the erasure of the woman, we need to acknowledge a countervailing factor, the radiant force she represents in these lyrics. Indeed, "To Mr C.B." concludes by contrasting the powerlessness of the poet's verse and the power of the lady's disdain: "scalding sighes, which have the Art / To melt all Ice, but that which walls her heart." Moreover, as these lines remind us, at their climactic final couplets both poems swerve from the relationship beween the men to that between the poet and lady; this shift is all the more startling because it is all the more abrupt in "To Mr I.L.," where the evocation of the addressee's rural retreat has distracted us from the pains of Petrarchan love. Mr. I.L. himself enables the return to that love in that, like the poem itself, he is enjoined to bear the poet's message. And if the construction of a Petrarchan situation has facilitated a link between two men, the link between those men has facilitated the Petrarchan situation inasmuch as Donne apparently feels more comfortable with Petrarchism when it is distanced by being filtered through an intermediary— or, in this case, two intermediaries, the customarily un-Petrarchan genre of the verse letter and the male friend onto whom the Petrarchan message of adulation is displaced. Thus Donne simultaneously speaks the discourse of Petrarchism and one version of a counterdiscourse as well. And in so doing he invites us to refine the paradigm of homosocial desire which has recently proved so influential. Might one find instances in other writers as well where the primacy of male bonds represents but one stage of a continuing, circular process that moves back and forth between homosocial and heterosocial relationships? In particular, should one think not simply of the erasure of the female in the service of male bonding but also of an even more unstable circular pattern in which that male bonding is then redeployed, possibly in response to homophobic anxieties, in the service of a heterosexual relationship, which may then generate further homosocial bonding, and so on?

However those questions are answered, Donne's early verse letters impel us to return to the specifics of chronology. If these poems testify to his status as resident alien in the domain of Petrarchism, his readers need to examine as precisely as possible the dates at which his visa was granted. Donne was admitted to Lincoln's Inn from Thavies Inn on May 6, 1592, paying the reduced fee for entrants who had been members of one of the Inns of Chancery associated with Lincoln's Inn for at least a year.[39] Hence he was at the Inns when Sidney's *Astrophil and Stella* appeared in 1591.

Though the consequences of this chronology are necessarily speculative, several suggestive possibilities present themselves. Sidney's sequence is in many ways not only a poet's poem but a young man's poem, and it is likely that the members of the Inns, like many other participants in London literary culture, were excited with its wit, its technical virtuosity, and its sophisticated, knowing enactment of desire. At the same time, they may well have felt some competitive unease, perhaps fearing that their own great expectations as men of letters would be hampered or at least threatened by the adulation Sidney was receiving posthumously. In any event, later in the decade many members of the Inns reacted virulently against the stylistic abuses of Petrarchism: that movement is a recurrent target in formal verse satire, and in my concluding chapter I argue that the Ovidian epyllion, another genre that proved popular at the Inns, should be read as one of the counterdiscourses of Petrarchism. If *Astrophil and Stella* engendered interest and even enthusiasm in the authors of formal verse satires early in the 1590s, that reaction may help to explain the intense repudiation within those satires of what Joseph Hall terms "patched *Sonettings*" *(Virgidemiae,* I.vii.11);[40] once again the counterdiscourses of Petrarchism disown their authors' previous interest or participation in that movement.

Ontogeny recapitulates phylogeny. We may also hypothesize with some conviction that Donne shared the excitement generated by *Astrophil and Stella* and wanted his circle at the Inns to know that he shared it: witness the extensive Petrarchism in the verse letters to young men. At the same time, for all the reasons we have traced, he probably shared as well the reservations about Petrarchism that may have been present at the Inns in the early 1590s and are indubitably manifest in some of the verse letters he composed during the 1590s. Hence the distancing devices in the poems to Christopher Brooke and "I.L." and at least some of the violence with which he mocks Petrarchism later in his career. Donne is reacting against his earlier experiments in that mode, an earlier version of his literary culture, an earlier self. Obsessed with betrayal in so many other arenas,[41] he is likely to have felt betrayed by Petrarchism—and by his own earlier attraction to it. A proverb he adduces in one of his prose letters both excuses

---

[39] See Bald, *John Donne: A Life*, pp. 54–55.

[40] Arnold Davenport, ed., *The Collected Poems of Joseph Hall* (Liverpool: Liverpool University Press, 1949).

[41] Compare Carey's arguments about how apostasy affected Donne's preoccupation with betrayal (*John Donne*, esp. pp. 37–38).

and explicates that dual betrayal—"The Spanish proverb informes me, that he is a fool which cannot make one Sonnet, and he is mad which makes two"[42]—and his uneasy identification with the literary movement he is rejecting helps to explain why the sonneteer whom he mocks in "Satyre II" is a lawyer.

The difficulty of dating most of the *Songs and Sonets* in and of itself undermines any notion that Donne moved from youthful Petrarchism, his own *giovenile errore*, to Platonism.[43] It is more than possible that when he wrote love poetry during the final decade of the sixteenth century, Donne, like many other members of his culture, was simultaneously penning the discourses and the counterdiscourses of Petrarchism. Indeed, the *Songs and Sonets* also reminds us of the misconceptions that survive in our literary histories despite frequent disavowals of them. The notion of a neat movement from sixteenth-century lyricism to seventeenth-century realism and cynicism is as problematical as comparable mappings of Donne's career, for hardly more reason exists to define the 1590s as the decade of Petrarchan love sonnets and *The Faerie Queene* than to see it as the period of formal verse satire, the epyllion, and Donne's own amoral love poems. It is only narrative displacement that tempts us to say otherwise.

However the story of literary history is told, that tale will include the many ways Donne reacts against Petrarchism in his *Songs and Sonets*. Some poems, of course, straightforwardly satirize or rebut Petrarchism; self-consciously reversing Petrarchan assumptions and in so doing calling attention to their ideology, these lyrics announce themselves as a counterdiscourse. "The Indifferent" and "Communitie," for example, position their amoral naturalism against the idealistic assumptions of the Petrarchan discourse.[44] Similarly, the open eroticism of "The Good Morrow" stands in self-conscious contrast to the frustrations of the Petrarchan lover. As Kerrigan points out, in "Loves Diet" the figure of Love attempts to establish a Petrarchan vision that the speaker resists.[45] If, as seems likely, many of Donne's love poems were written during the 1590s, their original readers were inundated by Petrarchan sequences and hence intensely con-

---

[42] John Donne, *Letters to Severall Persons of Honour (1651)*, ed. M. Thomas Hester (New York: Scholars' Facsimiles and Reprints, 1977), pp. 103–104.

[43] The chronology of these poems is a complicated issue largely outside the scope of this chapter. For an influential but unpersuasive argument that many of them can be dated with some certainty, see Gardner, *Elegies*, pp. lvii–lxii; on the problems of dating them, see esp. J. B. Leishman, *The Monarch of Wit: An Analytical and Comparative Study of the Poetry of John Donne*, 6th ed. (New York: Harper and Row, 1966), pp. 185–187.

[44] On Donne's attack on Petrarchism in this poem, see, e.g., Hunt, *Donne's Poetry*, pp. 1–15.

[45] Kerrigan, "What Was Donne Doing?" pp. 8–9.

scious of such contrasts. Thus the stance of poems like "The Indifferent" must have seemed to readers during that period—and to the poet himself— as not merely a reversal but also a rebuttal of Petrarchan idealizations.

In general, however, Donne effects a more complex relationship to Petrarchism in his *Songs and Sonets*. In certain lyrics, as many critics have noted, he pushes the conceits of Petrarchism to an extreme, often by taking them literally. Thus "The Apparition" translates the lament that the Petrarchan mistress is killing her lover into a narrative that presupposes his actual death. Guss asserts that readers should see this text, as well as many of Donne's other poems, as Petrarchan, not anti-Petrarchan, in that they have close analogues in texts by Continental followers of Petrarch.[46] Donne's original audience, I suggest, would have seen them as both at once: they follow certain Petrarchan models but in so doing distance themselves from other such models by exaggerating their statements and hence adding an "as it were." To this predilection, too, we will return, but for now we can observe that it is almost impossible to separate the discourses and counterdiscourses of Petrarchism in such instances. As Donne himself might have put it were he writing in the 1990s rather than some four hundred years earlier, if they be two, they are two so, as the sides of a Möbius strip are two.

Similarly, "The Anniversarie" cannot be readily categorized as either Petrarchan or anti-Petrarchan. Its debts are as profound as its critiques, and one could make a case for reading the poem as adapting Petrarchism as all innovative imitation is wont to do or challenging some of its fundamental presuppositions. Certainly the lyric determinedly signals its participation in some conventions of Petrarchism: not only is the speaker marking the anniversary of his love, he is festooning that occasion with Petrarchan tears and, like Petrarch, both bemoaning the passage of time and transcending it. One of his deviations from Petrarchism, however, conveniently exemplifies a familiar distinction between the author of the *Rime sparse* and the poet who composed the *Songs and Sonets*: Donne focuses not on the first sight of the woman—indeed, not on the woman at all—but on the relationship between the lovers and his speaker's reaction to it. Contrast his "When thou and I first one another saw" (5) with Petrarch's customary emphasis on his initial vision of Laura. Moreover, Petrarch constructs the anniversary as the culmination of the repetitiveness that characterizes Petrarchan love: if the occasion marks the continuation of their love, it also involves entrapment in a never-ending, never-changing pattern:

---

[46] Guss, *John Donne, Petrarchist*, esp. pp. 53–60.

et d'antichi desir lagrime nove
provan com' io son pur quel ch' i' mi soglio,
né per mille rivolte ancor son mosso.

(118.12–14; and new tears for old desires show me to be still what I used to be, nor for a thousand turnings about have I yet moved.)[47]

Shakespeare, as we saw, reads anniversaries as signs of the unrelenting passage of time. Donne, in contrast to both these writers, depicts the anniversary as short time's endless monument: haunted throughout both his poetic and his prose works by inconstancy, mutability, and decay, here he celebrates their antithesis:

> All other things, to their destruction draw,
>   Only our love hath no decay;
> This, no tomorrow hath, nor yesterday.
>
> (6–8)

"The Canonization," one of Donne's best known poems, also bridges Petrarchism and anti-Petrarchism. In this text he again pushes conventional tropes to an extreme in deploying the Petrarchan conceit that the woman is a saint; at the same time, by suggesting that both lovers, not just the mistress, are candidates for canonization, he rejects the humility and worshipful distance that are among the other trademarks of Petrarchism. Similarly, "Loves Deitie" apparently opens on the prototypically Petrarchan speaker—the lover devoted to a lady who does not return his affection—but culminates in the prototypically un-Petrarchan declaration that the worst possible fate would be her loving him after all, given that she loves someone else. In "A Valediction: Forbidding Mourning" the evocation of absence, the emphasis on the refinement of love, and the diacritical response to inferior lovers are all reminiscent of Petrarchism. Yet the line "No teare-floods, nor sigh-tempests move" (6) encompasses not only its literal injunction about controlling emotion but also implicit commands to avoid both the hyberbole that "teare-floods" metaphorically represent and the Petrarchism that hyperbole synecdochically represents.

Often, of course, Donne's rebukes to Petrarchan assumptions are more explicit and extensive. Thus "The Dreame," as many readers have noted, invokes the Petrarchan dream vision, going so far as to term the lady an

---

[47] I cite Robert Durling, trans. and ed., *Petrarch's Lyric Poems: The "Rime sparse" and Other Lyrics* (Cambridge: Harvard University Press, 1976).

angel.[48] But the poem signals its differences in several ways. By associating her eyes with the light of tapers rather than that of the sun, Donne draws attention to the erotic nocturnal setting of his lyric. And this prepares us for his principal revision of his model. Whereas awakening represents a sorry end to the eroticism that Petrarch can achieve only in sleep, for Donne's speaker it permits the highly erotic enactment of the dream.

That much is apparent. On another level, however, "The Dreame" invites us to read it as not merely an instance but also an allegory of its author's contested relationship to Petrarchism. For in a sense he awakens from Petrarchism itself, shifting from a world in which the woman can be available only when she is not available, only in a dream, into a world where consummation is possible. The language of his dream is the Petrarchan discourse; awakened, he speaks its counterdiscourse.

"The Baite" does not present itself as the most obvious candidate for inclusion in a study of Donne's anti-Petrarchism: the lyric vision that it both evokes and undermines draws primarily on pastoral traditions in general and poems in that mode by Marlowe and Sannazaro in particular.[49] Yet this text does contain a few traces of Petrarchism: the woman's eyes are compared to the sun, the roles of hunter and hunted are reversed in the course of the poem, and perhaps reminiscences of the Actaeon myth, so central a narrative in the *Rime sparse,* lie behind "If thou, to be so seene, beest loath, / By Sunne, or Moone, thou darknest both" (13–14). And, more important, "The Baite" illuminates approaches to the *Rime sparse* and its heirs that recur throughout the *Songs and Sonets.* Like "The Dreame," it even comments on that tradition, encouraging us, paradoxically, to classify it less as Petrarchan or anti-Petrarchan than as meta-Petrarchan.

The most revealing section of the poem occurs shortly after the lines I just quoted, when it abruptly skids from lyrical reverie to a lower register:

> Let others freeze with angling reeds,
> And cut their legges, with shells and weeds,
> Or treacherously poore fish beset,
> With strangling snare, or windowie net:
>
> Let coarse bold hands, from slimy nest
> The bedded fish in banks out-wrest,

---

[48] Many critics have commented on this genealogy. See, e.g., Praz, *Flaming Heart,* pp. 186–191.

[49] See my article "John Donne's Versions of Pastoral," *Durham University Journal,* 37 (1976), 33–37.

> Or curious traitors, sleave-silke flies
> Bewitch poore fishes wandring eyes.
>   (17–24)

The best parallel to this passage, curiously, comes from a poem in a different genre, Donne's "Epithalamion made at Lincolnes Inne," which slashes into its celebration of the wedding with an infamous evocation of violence:

> And at the Bridegroomes wished approach doth lye.
> Like an appointed lambe, when tenderly
> The priest comes on his knees t'embowell her.
>   (88–90)

Without erasing the many other resonances of these passages, I suggest that they too are allegories for the poet's complex, contested relationship to the styles he adopts, with the abrupt intrusion of these lines into the poems at once enacting and countering the intrusion of his anxieties about those styles. In both poems Donne is both a helpless fish and a coarse fisherman, sacrificial priest and sacrificed lamb. For these passages result in part from his fear of being seduced, entrapped, and violated by a style about which he is at best ambivalent: the title "The Baite" includes an allusion to the snare of a sensuous, lyrical pastoralism or, more broadly, to the trap represented by other styles as well, including Petrarchism. Donne is characteristically concerned to be victimizer as well as victim, and in the fantasy that impels these passages, he is also the destroyer of the vision represented by the glittering fish and innocent lamb—which is, indeed, precisely the role he performs as a poet when he intrudes passages of such a different, such an inimical tonality into his evocations of that vision and thus reveals it as the product of a suspect ideology. In other words, his fear of being violated leads him to construct himself as violator, and thus here, as in *Astrophil and Stella*, the problems of literary style and of desire are intimately, inseparably connected. Such arguments are, of course, necessarily speculative, but surely it is not mere coincidence that the two poems in which Donne is singularly close to literary models about which he clearly felt some ambivalence, the lyricism of the Spenserian wedding poem and the Renaissance pastoral, both contain—or in another sense fail to contain—descriptions of a violent attack, explicitly sexual in one case and implicitly so in the other.

In some sixteenth- and seventeenth-century English poems, as we have observed, the counterdiscourses of Petrarchism are gendered female. In "The Baite" a related type of counterdiscourse is associated with a male figure who is violent and violating. This variety in gendering reminds us again of other types of variety in Donne's challenges to Petrarchism: his *Songs and Sonets* alone range from poems where it is hard to separate or even identify Petrarchan and anti-Petrarchan elements to ones where he figures his own relationship to literary tradition as contestory, even cruel. Contiguity and distance coexist in the collection as a whole and often within a single lyric.

In one important sense, Donne's *Holy Sonnets* evidently represents another type of counterdiscourse: as the poems examined in Chapter 3 demonstrate, the very act of casting a religious lyric in the form of a sonnet can on occasion challenge the values of Petrarchism.[50] Activating and intensifying that challenge, Donne repeatedly contrasts earthly and spiritual love, sometimes explicitly and sometimes implicitly, and in so doing frequently adduces Petrarchism as a model for the former. In particular, given that they appear within sonnets, Donne's references to idolatry—"They see idolatrous lovers weepe and mourne" (8.9), "but as in my idolatrie / I said to all my profane mistresses" (13.9–10), and "In my Idolatry what showres of raine / Mine eyes did waste?" (3.5–6)[51]—specifically recall Petrarch's own fear that his love for Laura is a form of idolatry. The terminal couplet of the poem beginning "Oh my blacke Soule!" more subtly evokes Petrarchism in order to rebuke it: "Or wash thee in Christs blood, which hath this might / That being red, it dyes red soules to white" (IV.13–14). Again, the verse form activates a comparison with Petrarchism, and the poem as a whole plays the Christian iconography of red and white against its Petrarchan counterpart in which in many senses the red is not dyed out.[52] This poem and other lyrics in the series reverse Petrarchan traditions in another way as well: as John N. Wall Jr. points out, whereas in the love

---

[50] For a different but not incompatible explanation of Donne's choice of the sonnet, see Antony F. Bellette, " 'Little Worlds Made Cunningly': Significant Form in Donne's 'Holy Sonnets' and 'Goodfriday, 1613,' " *SP*, 72 (1975), 322–347; he argues that Donne is interested in both threats to the orderliness of the sonnet form and the resolution of those threats through accepting Christ.

[51] I cite Helen Gardner, ed., *The Divine Poems* (Oxford: Clarendon, 1952). My numbering of the poems is, however, based on the system used by Grierson and others rather than Gardner's division into distinct groups (on that division, see *Divine Poems*, pp. xxxvii–lv).

[52] For discussions of the couplet from the perspective of Donne's theology and the agency of his speaker, see Douglas L. Peterson, "Donne's *Holy Sonnets* and the Anglican Doctrine of Contrition," *SP*, 56 (1959), 504–518; Strier, "John Donne Awry and Squint," pp. 371–372; and Stephenie Yearwood, "Donne's *Holy Sonnets*: The Theology of Conversion," *TSLL*, 24 (1982), 213.

sonnet the lady's resistance must be overcome, here it is the speaker's resistance to God that has to be vanquished.[53]

The footprints of Petrarchism are more unsettling in Donne's renowned
poem on the death of a woman generally assumed to be his wife.[54]

> Since she whome I lovd, hath payd her last debt
> To Nature, and to hers, and my good is dead,
> And her soule early into heaven ravished,
> Wholy in heavenly things my mind is sett.
> Here the admyring her my mind did whett
> To seeke thee God;
> . . . .
> And dost not only feare least I allow
> My love to saints and Angels, things divine,
> But in thy tender jealosy dost doubt
> Least the World, fleshe, yea Devill putt thee out.
>
> (17.1–6, 11–14)

Most obviously, the poem clearly recalls Petrarch's own lyrics on the death
of Laura and specifically her position as intercessor, a role often associated
with the *donna angelicata*. But Donne's evocation of that role, like comparable passages by Petrarch, is ambiguous, as readers have acknowledged.[55]
Whereas lines five and six explicitly state that earthly love has inspired its
spiritual counterpart, the preceding quatrain may perhaps hint at the opposite. It leads us to wonder whether Donne, much like Wyatt in "Whoso
List To Hunt," is attempting to present an ongoing struggle as an achieved
victory. Introducing his preoccupation with competition even—or especially—into his religious poems, Donne confounds these interpretive problems when he acknowledges God's jealousy at the end of the sonnet. Does
"saints and Angels" (12) refer to lesser heavenly beings (as the phrase
"things divine" [12]) might well encourage us to believe) or to the woman
herself, who is constructed as saint and angel in the Petrarchan discourse
this poem both imitates and opposes, or in another sense to that discourse

---

[53] John N. Wall Jr., "Donne's Wit of Redemption: The Drama of Prayer in the *Holy
Sonnets*," *SP*, 73 (1976), 200.

[54] For a reading that argues for an unproblematical acceptance of divine love, see, e.g.,
Andreasen, *Donne: Conservative Revolutionary*, pp. 234–236. Critics who find unresolved ten-
sions in the sonnet include John Stachniewski, "John Donne: The Despair of the 'Holy
Sonnets,' " *ELH*, 48 (1981), 677–705, and Wall, "Donne's Wit of Redemption."

[55] See, e.g., M. E. Grenander, "Holy Sonnets VIII and XVII: John Donne," *Boston University Studies in English*, 4 (1960), 100–105.

itself?[56] These readings are not, of course, mutually exclusive, but the tension among them stages the tensions that the poem itself concerns. The second and third interpretations would electrify the otherwise bland appositive "things divine" (12), suggesting that Donne is enacting the very confusion between the spiritual and the secular which he claims to have renounced. As the possibility of these variant glosses suggests, the poem at once establishes its speaker's distance from the world of Petrarchan love and hints that he may attempt to sneak back, at night, over its borders.

On one level, then, Donne's religious poems synecdochically criticize the secular world by calling into question one of its literary discourses. Thus Petrarchism serves as a metaphor for the values these lyrics reject, and the poems exemplify the workings of one type of counterdiscourse. Yet their relationship to that tradition is, predictably, more complex. Louis L. Martz has demonstrated an affinity between the structure of the Petrarchan sonnet and meditative practices.[57] And on another level Donne's religious poetry poses yet again the problem of distinguishing Petrarchism and its counterdiscourses, for, as we have observed before, Petrarch's own struggles between caritas and cupiditas make it risky to describe poetry that eschews the erotic for the spiritual as anti-Petrarchan. Characteristically, in writing his most devout poems, Donne again performs a Möbius strip tease.

The verse letters he composed for noblewomen between about 1605 and 1612[58] are also deeply implicated in both Petrarchism and its counterdiscourses,[59] but they merge the two with an assurance and urbanity lacking in the early epistles to men. Chronology again provides an explanation—and again hedges that answer with its own problems. Because Petrarchism was less central to Donne and his culture at the time he composed these poems than when he wrote his early epistles to male friends,

---

[56] Critics disagree on the referent of the phrase, though to the best of my knowledge it has not been previously read synecdochically for Petrarchism itself. Despite the plural, Gardner assumes that it refers to Donne's wife (*Divine Poems*, p. 79); Stachniewski interprets it as "the objects of his aberrant youthful devotion" ("Donne: Despair," p. 687); Barbara Kiefer Lewalski adopts the meaning signaled by the appositive phrase, holy creatures including saints, angels, and his wife (*Protestant Poetics and the Seventeenth-Century Religious Lyric* [Princeton: Princeton University Press, 1979], p. 273).

[57] Louis L. Martz, *The Poetry of Meditation: A Study in English Religious Literature of the Seventeenth Century*, rev. ed. (New Haven: Yale University Press, 1962), p. 49.

[58] The dating of most of these poems is speculative; see the notes on individual texts in Milgate, *Satires*.

[59] Barbara L. DeStefano has argued, however, that these letters are rooted neither in Petrarchism nor Platonism but rather in the medieval religious lyric and that this perspective absolves their author from the charge of hypocrisy. Her alternative genealogy is a useful supplement to our interpretations but does not preclude the presence of Petrarchan elements as well ("Evolution of Extravagant Praise in Donne's Verse Epistles," *SP*, 81 [1984], 75–93).

the anxieties he brings to that discourse and its counterdiscourses in his earlier epistles are less intense. The vogue for Petrarchism was waning during the first two decades of the Jacobean period: it was neither a promising new opportunity for English poetry, as it may well have seemed when Donne arrived at the Inns, nor a clear and present danger. And although scholars cannot definitively date either the *Songs and Sonets* or the letters to noblewomen, it is more than likely that by the time Donne composed his verse epistles to patronesses, he had written enough innovative love poetry to feel less threatened by Petrarchism.

But these generalizations, like most generalizations about literary history, need to be further nuanced. Donne's critics should discriminate within the group of poems under consideration: Petrarchism was less significant around 1612, when Donne was writing the later letters in this group, than around 1605, when he may have composed the earliest ones, simply because more time had elapsed since its vogue. More important, as the historian J. H. Hexter reminds us, the events of a pennant race may not appear the same retrospectively as they did to contemporary observers.[60] Lacking the benefit of hindsight, Donne and his contemporaries are likely to have interpreted the history of Petrarchism very differently from how many critics do today: whereas they could have perceived at the beginning of the seventeenth century that it was waning, they were not in a position to consider it passé or even to assert with assurance that its decline was not temporary. For though it was apparent at the beginning of the seventeenth century that love sonnets were no longer flooding the market, some sequences were still being reprinted and others being published in revised form. *Astrophil and Stella*, the Short-Title Catalogue testifies, reappeared in 1605 and again in 1613; an edition of Daniel's works came out in 1601, followed by another issue the next year and a new edition in 1623; Drayton's love poetry was reissued repeatedly in revised form during the first two decades of the seventeenth century. Other forms of Elizabethan verse remained popular too, with *The Shepheardes Calendar* being republished twice in the first two decades of the seventeenth century.[61] Jacobean observers may well have felt that the jury was still out on the relationship of their literary milieu to Elizabethan poetry and, in particular, on the long-term prognosis of the Petrarchan love sonnet. If they did not see that form as an immediate threat, neither could they confidently classify it as a mere relic of the past.

[60] J. H. Hexter, *Doing History* (Bloomington: Indiana University Press, 1971), pp. 38–39.

[61] On the publication history of all these texts, see A. W. Pollard et al., *A Short-Title Catalogue of Books Printed in England, Scotland, Ireland, 1475–1640*, 3 vols., 2d ed. (London: Bibliographical Society, 1986–1991).

In his epistles to patronesses, Donne responds to—and helps to create—
the complex status of Petrarchism in his culture by once again establishing
himself as a resident alien. Many of its conventions he freely deploys. Indeed, as Herbert J. C. Grierson observes, it is precisely those conventions
that provide a means for negotiating the complex friendship enjoyed by
Donne and the countess of Bedford.[62] In any event, he repeatedly adduces
them when writing both to her and to other noblewomen. Thus he compares the recipients of these poems to suns: "Your radiation can all clouds
subdue" ("To the Countesse of Bedford" ["Honour is so sublime perfection"], 20). By using terza rima in the passage just quoted, he also recalls
the Dantean tradition of the donna angelicata which lies behind Petrarch's
poetry. In other poems in this group, indeed, Donne casts the recipient in
the position of intercessor, a role associated with the donna angelicata and
hence with Petrarch: "Since you are then Gods masterpeece, and so / His
Factor for our loves" ("To the Countesse of Bedford" ["Reason is our
Soules"], 33–34). And he borrows the humility associated with the Petrarchan lover to express the subservience expected by a patron: "yet they will
doubt how I, / One corne of one low anthills dust, and lesse" ("To the
Countesse of Bedford at New-yeares Tide," 27–28).

In one of his poems to the countess of Salisbury, Donne cleverly defines
his relationship with Petrarchism, establishing himself as a consummately
skilled insider deploying its conventions of epideictic hyperbole and as an
outsider rejecting and reversing those conventions:

> Since now your beauty shines, now when the Sunne
> Growne stale, is to so low a value runne,
> That his disshevel'd beames and scatter'd fires
> Serve but for Ladies Periwigs and Tyres
> In lovers Sonnets: you come to repaire
> Gods booke of creatures, teaching what is faire.
> ("To the Countesse of Salisbury"
> ["Faire, great, and good"], 3–8)

Like other Petrarchan poets, Donne asserts here that his lady not merely
imitates but also exceeds the sun; unlike them, he distances himself from
such assertions by observing that the sun's loss of power is signaled by its

[62] Herbert J. C. Grierson, *The Poems of John Donne*, 2 vols. (London: Oxford University
Press, 1912), 2: xxiii.

conscription into service in Petrarchan sonnets. In so doing, he implicitly contrasts his own genre with the sonnets he dismisses. One is associated with the frankness and moderation of Horace and the other with the excesses of Petrarch; one permits the poet to assume the role of moral tutor, whereas the other forces him into the position of subservient admirer.[63] Hence the tropes of the sun in the letter to the countess of Salisbury, like similar images we have examined, may allude covertly to, or at least be inspired by, Donne's own poetic agendas: is he hinting that just as his lady is superior to other suns (and presumably the Petrarchan mistresses they customarily represent), so his trope, like her beauty, shines brighter than its counterparts in conventional Petrarchan sonnets? And is he implying that his poesy repairs Petrarchan creativity much as the lady repairs God's creatures?

However one interprets this passage, Donne develops a range of strategies to distance himself from Petrarchan conventions in the very process of invoking them, as the verse epistle on which this chapter opened would lead us to expect. Reminding us that he is not applying those conventions to their usual vehicle, romantic poetry, he again determinedly distinguishes himself from lovers and his verse from love poetry:

> Yet neither will I vexe your eyes to see
> A sighing Ode, nor crosse-arm'd Elegie.
> I come not to call pitty from your heart.
> ("To the Countesse of Huntington"
> ["That unripe side of earth"], 21–23)[64]

While the reference to "pitty" surely encodes a critique of Petrarchism, the rest of the passage includes related targets as well. "Satyre II" incorporates similar attacks on sonneteering, but there they are reinforced by a literary form that is in many ways the countergenre of the sonnet; writing in a genre that lacks that inherent distinction from the sonnet, Donne is at pains to establish his distance in the epistle to the countess of Huntington. In other letters to noble women, he distances himself from Petrarchan

---

[63] Many critics have noted these characteristics of the epistle and their appeal to Donne; see, e.g., Gary P. Storhoff, "Social Mode and Poetic Strategies: Donne's Verse Letters to His Friends," *Essays in Literature*, 4 (1977), 11–18. Though he focuses mainly on the later epistles to male friends, Allen Barry Cameron comments usefully on the genre in "Donne's Deliberative Verse Epistles," *ELR*, 6 (1976), 369–403.

[64] The authorship of this poem has been questioned; for a persuasive defense of his attribution to Donne, see Milgate, *Satires*, Appendix D.

praise by moving perilously close to insult.[65] Donne often delights in taking risks, whether they be metrical, moral, or otherwise: had he lived in a later age, he might well have been a frequenter of car and horse races as well as theaters, or possibly even a race-car driver. But the chances he takes in these poems are still unsettling, at least to academic readers accustomed to confining their high-risk behavior to gambling on getting a parking space in the most convenient campus lot. The poem to the countess of Huntingdon [sic] which opens "Man to Gods image" focuses on the failings of women in no fewer than four of its eighteen stanzas, including in them such observations as "Then we might feare that vertue, since she fell / So low as woman, should be neare her end" (19–20). Similarly, "To the Countesse of Bedford" ("T'have written then") encompasses sharp attacks on women among its satiric targets.

Passages like these, however distasteful they may and should appear to modern readers, demonstrate how Donne adeptly satisfies the epideictic requirements of the patronage system at the same time as he negotiates a series of tensions. The process of writing epistles to patronesses no doubt engendered some hostilities in Donne and intensified others—hostilities towards the demands of patronage in general and of the particular patron at hand, towards the failings associated with her gender, and towards the conventions of Petrarchism. In "To the Countesse of Huntingdon" ("Man to Gods image"), he contrives to marry epideictic praise and satiric hostility, a common pairing in the epistolary tradition, through the diacritical strategy of distinguishing the lady at hand from less worthy representatives of her sex, a point to which we will return. In so doing, he intensifies his praise by distinguishing her from other women. And he controls his hostility by channeling it towards a single target. Joining another misogynistic satirist, he too announces, Frailty, thy name is woman. This is, of course, hardly a unique instance of gendered scapegoating, either in the poetry of Tudor and Stuart England or in Donne's own canon.

A particularly skillful passage from one of his letters to the countess of Bedford ("Reason is our Soules") helps us to understand how diacritical strategies inform such scapegoating:

> for you are here
> The first good Angell, since the worlds frame stood,
> That ever did in woman's shape appeare.
>
> (30–32)

---

[65] Compare Carey's similar suggestion about insult in "The Autumnall" (*John Donne*, p. 82).

The lines serve not only to celebrate the countess by stressing her uniqueness but also to distinguish Donne and his poetry from the poets, Petrarchan and otherwise, who, like Uriel, mistake bad angels for good ones and then waste their energies praising those transgressive masqueraders. And thus it allows us to summarize some of the ways Donne scripts the counterdiscourses of Petrarchism within this group of poems. First, he explicitly differentiates himself from the writers of love poems whom he might ostensibly resemble. Deploying genre as a metaphor for those distinctions, he reinforces them by implicitly contrasting the frankness and morality of the epistolary tradition with the empty hyperboles of love poetry. His praise, Donne thus suggests, is reliable currency, not the debased metal he associated with the debased sun and its "Tyres / In lovers Sonnets" ("To the Countesse of Salisbury," 6–7). And, above all, he also constructs his patronesses diacritically, a pattern that recurs in his contributions to the ugly beauty tradition, poems that are as disturbing as they are intriguing.

IV

"The Autumnall," "The Anagram," and "The Comparison" are in some respects catalogues of the characteristics of the ugly beauty tradition, even though the third poem deviates significantly from it in not actually praising its unappetizing heroine. The cultural pressures behind that tradition, especially anxieties about gender and mutability, are strikingly prominent in Donne's texts. The rhetorical strategies most typical of ugly beauty poems also recur throughout these three poems: we find many examples of antitheses, of their erosion, of equivocations, and above all of threats. Here, as elsewhere in his canon, Donne typically responds to receiving threats by issuing them. This maneuver is the global speech act around which "The Curse" is organized, the direct speech act on which "Womans Constancy" culminates, an indirect speech act in poems ranging from "Satyre I" to "The Message"—but nowhere are threats more significant than in Donne's poems about so-called ugly beauties. Despite these and other similarities, however, Donne's elegies also diverge from the patterns traced in Chapter 5 in the emphasis on male rivalry which is latent in "The Anagram" and explicit, even emphatic, in "The Comparison." Thus these texts help us further to understand both the conventions in question and Donne's own status as resident alien.

Written to an aging woman generally assumed to be Magdalen Herbert,[66]

---

[66] Marotti (*John Donne, Coterie Poet*, pp. 51–52) notes, however, that the evidence for

"The Autumnall" has received a little more critical attention than most of its author's so-called minor poems. Yet many of its oddities remain in need of explication: troubling issues such as his description of "Winter-faces" (37) in a poem ostensibly devoted to flattery have not been fully explored. Though the praise of the beauty of mature women had classical precedents, including an epigram in the Greek Anthology,[67] Donne's approach to that subject, like his approach to the ugly beauty tradition as a whole, remains idiosyncratic and unsettling.

Opening on the declaration, "No *Spring*, nor *Summer* Beauty hath such grace, / As I have seen in one *Autumnall* face" (1–2), the poem allies itself with other members of the ugly beauty tradition in its emphasis on comparisons and contrasts. Donne proceeds to describe the appealing moderation of his subject's attractions ("This is her tolerable Tropique clyme" [10]), thus demonstrating that, for all its tensions, the poem represents a warm and urbane tribute on one important level. He is, however, also at pains to rule out of court—and and therefore to introduce into the courtroom—alternative modes of description and alternative types of women with whom his lady might be confused: "Call not these wrinkles, graves" (13), or "But name not Winter-faces, whose skin's slacke; / Lanke, as an unthrifts purse; but a soules sacke" (37–38). Ending on the promise, "I shall ebbe on with them, who home-ward goe" (50), he identifies his state with that of autumnal beauties, thus anticipating more disturbing identifications between men and their mistresses in "The Comparison."

On one level, then, "The Autumnall" exemplifies the distancing devices traced throughout this chapter: in the course of distinguishing his subject from younger, more conventionally attractive women, Donne differentiates himself from the poets, Petrarchan and otherwise, who praise them. But at the same time, this poem, like others by Donne, is concerned not merely with distance but also with edges, margins, or brinks. The lady is repeatedly constructed as between other states. She is positioned chronologically between the spring and summer to which line one refers and the winter mentioned in line thirty-seven, just as the description of her is structurally located within the poem itself between those points. Similarly, "Here, where still Evening is; not noone, nor night" (21) paradoxically associates her with the peacefulness of evening (a peacefulness intensified if, responding to Donne's pun, one reads "still" adverbially) and yet reminds us of the time of day which evening follows and, more to the point, the period

---

assuming it was addressed to her is problematical; although a lengthy discussion of that problem is outside my scope in this chapter, cf. the discussion of biographical readings at the end of the chapter.

[67] For a summary of this background, see Gardner, *Elegies*, p. 147.

that will shortly ensue. Once again the subject of the poem mimes the text itself, for "The Autumnall" locates itself on the margins of bitterness and satire without ever crossing over into them.

Its own position on the verge stems from Donne's attempts, largely successful, to control a series of anxieties and threats. Like other poets in the tradition, he is clearly preoccupied with the fear of the loss of beauty. And, not surprisingly, he is preoccupied as well with the fear of the loss of life: though the poem seemingly addresses itself to autumn, its references to graves, resurrection, and "living Deaths-heads" (43) suggest that it is really more concerned with winter, with death itself. The text, after all, concludes on an allusion to the poet's own demise, reminding us of Cathy Yandell's observation that in French Renaissance poems, the carpe diem tradition may encode the poet's fears of his own mortality.[68]

Donne tries to control these and other fears through his usual linguistic games:

> If we love things long sought, Age is a thing
> Which we are fifty years in compassing.
> If transitory things, which soone decay,
> Age must be lovelyest at the latest day.
>
> (33–36)

The playfulness of these compressed syllogisms as well as the lack of firmness behind the if/then formula in effect bracket these statements. Above all, though, Donne protects the subject of his poem—and his own claim to be bestowing praise rather than drawing on the satiric potentialities of the epistle—through the kind of diacritical maneuver he performs in all three poems. That is, not only is the lady distinguished from younger beauties and his poem distinguished from the more conventional lyrics, Petrarchan and otherwise, that praise them, but he also repeatedly differentiates the subject of the lyric from the less attractive women with whom she might be confused—and whom she will in time become. Thus "name not Winter-faces" (37) reminds us that they could be named and that an honest poem addressed to this same woman some years later might well feel compelled to name them. Here, as in the phrase "Call not these wrinkles, graves" (13), the emphasis on the speech acts of naming and calling reminds us that the poet himself is engaged in such acts, with his ability to

[68] Cathy Yandell, "Carpe Diem, Poetic Immortality, and the Gendered Ideology of Time," in Anne R. Larson and Colette H. Winn, eds., *Renaissance Women Writers: French Texts/American Contexts* (Detroit: Wayne State University Press, 1994).

name and call, rather than any objective assessment, determining how this autumnal beauty is viewed. In these lines, so reminiscent of similar strategies elsewhere in the ugly beauty tradition, Donne at once expresses and contains anxieties that an autumnal beauty is in fact, or will shortly become, wintry—and does so by drawing attention to his own ability to construct that beauty as he pleases.

"The Anagram" is based on several sources, most notably Berni and Tasso.[69] Like Donne's two other ugly beauty poems, it also plays on the paradox, a form that clearly interested Donne. Building on such precedents and models, he declares that Flavia merely reverses the usual criteria for beauty: "though her eyes be small, her mouth is great" (3). But for the monochromatic mood that characterizes some other poems in the ugly beauty tradition, such as Sidney's sonnet on Mopsa, Donne substitutes a startling, unsettling range of emotions and tonalities. We move from obvious, even crude mockery ("Give her thine, and she hath a maydenhead" [8]) to a melancholy meditation on the loss, actual or feared, of beauty (" 'Tis lesse griefe to be foule, then to'have beene faire" [32]) to a down-to-earth assessment of the advantages of not being attractive ("in long journeyes, cloth, and leather use" [34]) and back to crude jokes ("Whom Dildoes, Bedstaves, and her Velvet Glasse / Would be as loath to touch as Joseph was" [53–54]). The final quotation, incidentally, refers to the loyal Joseph's refusal to be seduced by his master Potiphar's wife, a story told in Gen. 39, and thus introduces yet another transgressive woman into a poem whose male author is engaged in transgressing against epideictic norms.

The range of tone in "The Anagram" stems from the range of agendas Donne pursues. As always, one should not neglect the element of play; Donne, whose own verse delights in reversals and puzzles, constructs a woman who is herself an anagram. Thus once again, the poet's verse and the woman it describes are allied; and once again the light-hearted hint of that similarity gestures towards deeper and more troubling elisions of gender, which remain subterranean here but emerge in full force in "The Comparison." But if playful wit is one impetus behind "The Anagram," the author of the "The Autumnall" and the *Devotions* is, predictably, impelled as well by the fear of mutability and its vice-regent disease that so often drives the ugly beauty tradition. As he observes within this poem, "Love built on beauty, soone as beauty, dies, / Chuse this face, chang'd by no deformities" (27–28). In expressing these anxieties about deformity,

[69] See Donald L. Guss, "Donne's 'The Anagram': Sources and Analogues," *HLQ*, 28 (1964), 79–82; and Leishman, *Monarch of Wit*, pp. 77–84.

he wittily deforms a trope associated with Petrarchism in particular and with Elizabethan love poetry in general:

> Women are all like Angels; the faire be
> Like those which fell to worse; but such as shee,
> Like to good Angels, nothing can impaire.
>
> (29–31)

Thus the genuinely angelic women of conventional love poetry become fallen angels, whereas Donne's foul angel becomes a good one, and the boundaries between normative women and their transgressive sisters are again called into question, though in the less threatening guise of a game.

The poem is impelled by anxieties about both literal disease and decay and the moral decay that Donne genders female. Marrying a foul woman, he explains, ensures a faithful wife. In making this argument, Donne reveals a section of the genetic code of this literary type more clearly than do any of the poems we studied earlier. The fear of infidelity is at the roots of a general misogyny that, as Donne's love lyrics suggest, encompasses women in general; the ugly beauty tradition allows Donne at once to express that misogyny and to localize it by attacking one, presumably fictive, woman. He thus transmutes a potential defensiveness in the face of the mutability associated with Dame Nature and the infidelity associated with earthly women into a posture that is once again offensive in both senses. In so doing, Donne indulges and denies his hostility, a pattern we have encountered in his epistles to noblewomen and in ugly beauty poems by other writers.

But this elegy differs from its counterparts in the tradition in one important respect. "Marry, and love thy *Flavia,*" Donne declares in the first line of the lyric, through his pronoun associating the woman with a male addressee, the shadowy figure that we are permitted to forget for much of the poem. He reemerges, however, in a few lines, notably "Oh what a soveraigne Plaister will shee bee, / If thy past sinnes have taught thee jealousie" (37–38). To interpret the presence of this male figure we need to turn to "The Comparison," in which his equivalent is not an extra with a walk-on part but a central character.

"The Comparison" is in many ways the most interesting of Donne's three poems in the ugly beauty tradition. Written by a poet who often genders duplicity female, it opens by establishing a complex and perhaps even duplicitous relationship to literary tradition. It twists Petrarchan tropes; and it appears to be a familiar version of the ugly beauty convention, only to slide into the misogynistic satire that is the road not taken in that tradition, its dark underside. The elegy begins on an apparently admiring description of the first woman's pearl-like perspiration:

> As the sweet sweat of Roses in a Still,
> As that from which chaf'd muscats pores doth twill,
> As the Almighty Balme of th'early East,
> Such are the sweat drops on my Mistris breast.
>
> (1–4)

Thus the lyric invokes staples of the most conventional love poetry, notably tropes deploying flowers and dawn, to perform the decidedly unconventional task of celebrating perspiration. In so doing it seemingly positions itself among the type of ugly beauty poems whose tone we cannot determine with certainty, such as Carew's tribute to the mole. For the contemporary reader is not completely persuaded by this paean to perspiration, this song of sweat, and I think an early modern reader would also be made uneasy by Donne's hyperboles, even though perspiration was no doubt more acceptable in that culture than in our own. From another perspective, Donne is establishing an uneasy relationship to Petrarchism as well. The reference to pearls at once participates in and mocks that discourse, for whether or not Laura lacks pity, she apparently lacks perspiration glands, even when seen under the midday sun of Italy.

Donne abruptly shifts, however, to a different mode of comparison and a different literary model. For he proceeds to contrast his speaker's lady, perspiring but inspiring, with the indubitably repulsive mistress of that other man. As a result his poem assumes a version of a chiasmic structure, playing the ideal Petrarchan mistress against the speaker's lady and then that lady against the far from ideal mistress of another man. Thus Donne also plays two literary forms against each other, the epideictic mode of the ugly beauty tradition versus satire. And thus he deflects from the speaker's lady onto her ostensible opposite number ambivalent or even negative responses to her perspiration and perhaps indirectly to her other bodily functions as well. The contrast between the two women and between the two literary types dramatizes the poet's bifurcated responses to a single woman or to the construction of woman.[70]

Proceeding to elaborate the contrast between the two women, Donne crams his lyric with a series of images that seem odd even when one

---

[70] Compare Guibbory, " 'Oh, let mee not serve so,' " p. 817, on the ambivalence towards the speaker's lady.

considers their author and their roots in that odd convention, the praise of ugly beauty. Each woman is associated with a version of androgyny. First, he plays his mistress's balm against the "spermatique issue of ripe menstrous boiles" (8) produced by the other woman. *Spermatique*, to be sure, could be defined in ways that would not unsettle gender: it might refer to seed in general, which Galen and many later authorities believed that women produce.[71] The *Oxford English Dictionary* assures us that the term may merely mean "generative, productive."[72] These glosses are not, however, unproblematical: whether women produced seed remained debatable during the late sixteenth and seventeenth centuries, and the denotation of *spermatique* as "generative" was rare in that period. The alternative denotation of the adjective, an allusion to male seed in particular, is surely at least latent in the phrase and is activated by the other references in the poem to androgyny. Thus the line links images of male and female fluids, making gender itself more fluid, a point to which we will return. Moreover, the passage associates the male emission with reproductive vigor, whereas the female counterpart is linked to disease, which again demonstrates the connections between the ugly beauty tradition and a misogyny generated by and expressed through bodily dysfunction.

Donne proceeds to describe the genitals of the apparently attractive woman in equally androgynous terms:

> Then like the Chymicks masculine equall fire,
> Which in the Lymbecks warme wombe doth inspire
> Into th'earths worthlesse durt a soule of gold,
> Such cherishing heat her best lov'd part doth hold.
>
> (35–38)

Thus Donne's peculiar alchemy of love virtually transforms the woman's "best lov'd part" (38) into the best loved part of a man. The doctrine of sexual homology cannot wholly explain this passage, not least because that doctrine itself neglects the variety and inconsistency of anatomical descriptions in Renaissance medical tracts.[73] Gender is further confounded by a

---

[71] On the debate about this issue, see Ian Maclean, *The Renaissance Notion of Woman: A Study in the Fortunes of Scholasticism and Medical Science in European Intellectual Life* (Cambridge: Cambridge University Press, 1980), pp. 35–37.

[72] *OED*, s.v. "spermatic."

[73] The argument about homology was established in Thomas Laqueur's influential article "Orgasm, Generation, and the Politics of Reproductive Biology," *Representations*, no. 14 (1986), 1–41, and in his *Making Sex: Body and Gender from the Greeks to Freud* (Cambridge: Harvard University Press, 1990). For attacks on it see Janet Adelman, "Suffocating Mothers:

series of pronouns which identifies the unattractive woman with the speaker's male antagonist: *"Thy* head" . . . *"Thine's* like worme eaten trunkes" . . . *"thy* tann'd skins" (19, 25, 32; emphasis added). While on one level such phrases merely assume the presence of an elided word ("thy mistress' head" and so forth), on another level the referent of the pronouns is the male listener, thus equated with his mistress. (Consistently relying on the third-person pronoun for his speaker's lady, Donne does not identify that pair of lovers with each other in the same way, thereby preserving yet another form of distance.)

If the androgyny of the poem is odd, so too are the seemingly appealing tropes associated with the speaker's mistress. Her head's ideal roundness, we are told, recalls the apple in Eden and the golden apple that inspired the fateful rivalry between Juno, Venus, and Minerva—both tropes that do more to intensify the preoccupation with evil and competitiveness in the poem than to persuade us of the lady's charms. And these ambivalent images culminate in the extraordinary opposition—or apparent opposition—between the experiences of making love to each of these women:

> Are not your kisses then as filthy,'and more,
> As a worme sucking an invenom'd sore?
> Doth not thy fearefull hand in feeling quake,
> As one which gath'ring flowers, still fear'd a snake?
> Is not your last act harsh, and violent,
> As when a Plough a stony ground doth rent?
> So kisse good Turtles, so devoutly nice
> Are Priests in handling reverent sacrifice,
> And such in searching wounds the Surgeon is
> As wee, when wee embrace, or touch, or kisse.
>
> (43–52)

Notice yet again the emphasis on disease, with its implication that the phallic worm is feeding off a sore that is gendered female.

Why, then, does this poem end on so ambivalent a description of a sexuality that is ostensibly presented positively? Given that the tradition of ugly beauty poems regularly involves so many other forms of antithesis,

---

Galen, Hysteria, and the Discourse of the Maternal Body in—and out of—*King Lear*," paper delivered at the Shakespeare Association of America conference, Vancouver, Canada, March 1991; Katharine Park and Robert A. Nye, "Destiny Is Anatomy," review of *Making Sex* by Thomas Laqueur, *New Republic*, February 18, 1991, pp. 53–57; and my article "Navel Battles: Interpreting Renaissance Gynecological Manuals," *American Notes and Queries*, n.s. 5 (1992), 68–69.

including an often implicit contrast between the woman in question and a normative beauty, why does Donne add another antithetical pattern, his dramatized conflict between two opposed men? And why does he identify one of those men with the repulsive mistress, in that and other ways eliding gender categories?

Some answers emerge promptly when we recall the threats we previously identified in the ugly beauty tradition and in Donne's own contributions to it; other responses provide a new perspective on that tradition. Most obviously, this poem, like lyrics in praise of ugly beauty, is rooted in concerns about both poetic and more personal rivalries. By establishing a competitive relationship with another male, Donne characteristically deflects onto that unfortunate lover his antagonisms towards Petrarch and other earlier love poets, thus countering the anxiety of influence. At the same time, this lyric, like other members of its tradition, transforms its male readers from potential rivals, the role in which Donne so often casts other men, into participants in misogynistic jokes. The poem thus rewrites the competitiveness that Donne subdues in his early verse epistles by refocusing a whole series of other tensions on a single male antagonist.

Other threats, of course, involve gender. The pronouns that identify the rival male with his lady clarify a tension latent in other poems in the ugly beauty tradition: these pronouns not only signal but also enact the assumption that a man is judged by the women with whom he is associated to the point where they may virtually be equated: "And like a bunch of ragged carrets stand / The short swolne fingers of *thy* gouty hand" (33–34; emphasis added). Twentieth-century journalists may have invented the term *trophy wife*, but they could have taught Donne and other members of his culture nothing they did not already know about the mirror image of that phenomenon, the denigration of a man because of the unattractive or unfaithful woman with whom he is associated. That denigration is also threatening because it may stage and intensify the broader cultural fear that has recently been studied by many critics: the anxiety that male and female cannot be readily distinguished.[74] Once again the counterdiscourses of English Petrarchism both respond to and replicate the erosion of gender distinctions.

Of course, the lyric draws our attention as well to another tension associated with gender. If other poems in the ugly beauty tradition are grounded in anxieties about the changes that aging and gynecological or obstetrical problems could wreak on the bodies of beautiful women, this

[74] See, e.g., Phyllis Rackin, "Androgyny, Mimesis, and the Marriage of the Boy Heroine on the English Renaissance Stage," *PMLA*, 102 (1987), 29–41.

one testifies to a different but cognate anxiety. As Swift might have put it, "Can *Chloe*, heavenly *Chloe*, smell?" Donne's elegy "The Perfume" demonstrates his own consciousness of both pleasant and repellent smells, but "The Comparison" also invites speculations about the cultural construction of odor in Tudor and Stuart culture. Perhaps critics have thus far devoted so little attention to the subject because it makes us uneasy: in many academic forums it appears to be more acceptable to discuss sexualities— including one's own—than sweat.

Donne, as we have already seen, again responds to all these tensions through a series of deflections. Misogynistic antagonism towards all women is channeled towards the ugly beauty of this poem; if other poets in the tradition praise such a woman to shelter other women, or their images of them, from comparable attack, Donne renders that pattern explicit by actually juxtaposing two mistresses in the lyric. Similarly, potential rivalries with male companions are deflected onto a single target, the unfortunate lover in the poem, with other men implicitly invited to share in misogynistic jokes. And poetic rivalries are transformed into the rivalry between the two men. In short, like so many other poets in the ugly beauty tradition, Donne creates a series of diacritical oppositions to distance himself from what threatens him, whether it be the inanity of conventional Petrarchism, the vulnerability of conventional beauties, or the pugnacity of relationships between men.

Donne's misogynistic antagonism is, then, not suppressed but simply redirected, and its continuing presence helps to explain the extraordinary image of sex on which the poem culminates. I have argued elsewhere that the reference to the violating priest in the "Epithalamion made at Lincolnes Inne" ("Like an appointed lambe, when tenderly / The priest comes on his knees t'embowell her" [89–90]) stems from the author's guilt about his own drive to dominate and violate: in response, he mystifies and sanctifies violence.[75] The same dynamic impels the contrast between two modes of sexuality at the conclusion of this poem.

But much as the line between Petrarchism and anti-Petrarchism is erased in so many other ugly beauty poems, here both that contrast and several other distinctions break down: the poem undermines the very diacritical structures it erects. The line between male and female repeatedly disappears, as we have observed. And while the contrast between the beautiful and repulsive mistresses does not totally disappear, it is certainly blurred. The narrative of the golden apple pivots, after all, on a beauty contest determined not by the intrinsic loveliness of the contenders but by the suasive-

---

[75] See Dubrow, *A Happier Eden*, pp. 162–163.

ness of their bribes, a plot that renders problematical the seemingly objective and clear-cut beauty contest enacted in this poem. Donne's evocation of this myth is all the more telling when one recalls how seldom he draws on mythology.[76] Alerted by its presence and by the adjoining association of the attractive mistress with the Fall, readers may well speculate about whether lovely and loathsome women can be distinguished as easily as this poem insists, a question provoked as well by "The Anagram," "The Autumnall," and many other texts in their tradition. And is the man who loves and praises the beautiful one really so separate from his foolish opposite number?[77]

Such questions raise another: is Donne skillfully manipulating these ironies and contradictions, as literary curators who see poetry as a well-wrought urn might argue, or is he a victim of them, as those who see poetry as another shard of a warring culture might maintain? The first reading would suggest an ironic critique of his speaker, and the second, entanglement in the problems of the ugly beauty tradition, in a net whose windows have been sealed. These questions resemble the debate about the purposiveness of the contradictions and confusions in the *Holy Sonnets*.[78] In neither case is the issue a simple one, but in the instance of "The Comparison," Donne's conclusion—"Leave her, and I will leave comparing thus, / She, and comparisons are odious" (53–54)—favors the second interpretive strategy. He is, I suggest, sheltering behind the old proverb about comparisons to reveal his own unease with the divided aims and divided results of his own comparisons. He characteristically concludes the poem by deflecting some of his unease about that subject onto the male rival whom he has attacked all along.

"The Comparison," like "The Autumnall" and "The Anagram," testifies to some of the reasons he found that counterdiscourse singularly congenial. The poet who saw the skeleton beneath the skin—and also saw the viruses beneath it and the perspiration on it, though he would have assigned different names to the former—found a tradition rooted in fears of bodily mutability and decay attractive. The poet who is so often diacritical was attracted to the literary form that is so as well—attracted to the possibility of rechanneling the diacritical agenda of that form to pursue his more

[76] On his neglect of mythology, cf. Hunt, *Donne's Poetry*, p. 210 n. 23; Leishman, *Monarch of Wit*, p. 119.

[77] Compare Guibbory's observation that "The Anagram" and "The Comparison" draw attention to connections between the grotesque body and the beautiful one (" 'Oh, let mee not serve so,' " pp. 815–817).

[78] For a particularly thoughtful commentary on that debate, see Strier, "John Donne Awry and Squint," pp. 381–382.

idiosyncratic preoccupation with rivalry. And the poet who was both resident and alien in so many areas of his life was drawn to the literary tradition that is at once inside and outside the norms of love poetry.

V

In the academy today, as in the Amiens of which Donne writes in his poem to Lady Carey and Mrs. Essex Rich, certain saints are frequently invoked. Donne's approaches to the counterdiscourses of Petrarchism simultaneously direct our attention to the achievements of more recent criticism and urge some apostasy. Our salutary contemporary emphasis on the political, for example, has helped us to see that even Donne's responses to Petrarchism are implicated in the dynamics of his culture; in particular, his position as both insider and outsider in relation to Petrarchism should be interpreted in light of his comparable position in the patronage system. Yet, as Guibbory shrewdly demonstrates in her evaluation of Marotti's political interpretations of Donne,[79] it is dangerous to assume that his poems are really about something other than their stated subject and, in particular, that concerns about love are merely the vehicle of metaphors for the political sphere.[80] Studying Donne's responses to Petrarchism reinforces and broadens her caveat. Donne writes about many other things when writing about love, the beloved, and love poetry; but those subjects are complicated, not erased, by the additional resonances, political and otherwise, that accrue to them.

The greatest dangers that threaten Donne's interpreters, however, center on issues of chronology and temporality. In particular, this chapter has demonstrated that critics need to question the common assumption that Petrarchism was an early stage in Donne's career, soon to be rejected for his mature anti-Petrarchism and its expression in the alternative Platonic philosophy that characterizes poems inspired by and written to his wife.[81] Though this scenario differs from the theory that Donne rejects his Petrarchan lovers by undercutting them, both readings underestimate the extent of his interest in Petrarchism—and the complexity of his attacks on it.

[79] Guibbory, " 'Oh, let mee not serve so,' " pp. 811–812. See also the discussion of this issue in Chapter 1 of this book.

[80] Equally dangerous, though less germane to the current climate, is Carey's assumption that references to love encode anxieties about religion (see, e.g., John Donne, p. 38).

[81] These assumptions are widespread; for one of the most influential presentations of them, see Gardner, Elegies, pp. xlvii–lxii.

The hypothesis of linear development is dangerous for other reasons as well: an exemplum of the stagist narratives scholars so often bring to bear on the career of Donne and other poets, it indicates some of the interpretive problems that inform and deform such narratives. In the case of Donne, three presuppositions commonly underlie the plot in question: his poems can easily be divided into groups; those groups correspond to chronological changes in his work; and biographical events impel or even determine such shifts and are manifest in the poems. All these assumptions are as problematical as the comparable arguments deployed when interpreting Spenser's 1595 volume.[82] In the case of Donne, the presupposition about groups is undermined by various critics' placement of the same poem in different categories. "The Apparition," firmly labeled Petrarchan by many critics, is classified as Ovidian by one proponent of grouping, whereas another stresses the influence of Horace and Propertius as well.[83] Donne's delight in juxtaposing discourses within a single poem and in challenging a given discourse without totally rejecting it render such classifications of his lyrics unstable at best.

More important, the assumptions about biography that underlie the paradigm of linear development are also tenuous. The notion that biographical incidents typically had a direct and immediate impact on Donne's poetry has been attacked by certain students of Donne: J. B. Leishman, for example, warns against exaggerating the presence of autobiographical references in Donne's texts.[84] I would add that when such references do appear in these or other poems, often it is only after they have been significantly reinterpreted, merged with fictive occurrences, or mediated by a series of subsequent events in intervening years. Above all, to assume that the poems where Donne treats love as mutual and assured were necessarily written to his wife is surely to endorse to an idealized view of marriage—and a curiously circumscribed view of relationships outside it. Yet the strength and longevity of the biographical assumptions Leishman attacks are exemplified by his willingness, however hedged and partial, to subscribe to them in part: "It is . . . sufficient to recognize the existence of these new qualities

[82] Carey also observes the dangers of separating Jack Donne and Dr. Donne, though from different perspectives than mine (see *John Donne*, esp. pp. 10–11).

[83] On Ovidian elements, see Hamilton, "Donne's Petrarchist Poems," p. 47; for the argument that the poem combines elements from Horace, Propertius, and Ovid, see Leishman, *Monarch of Wit*, pp. 159–160. Frank Kermode also comments on the dangers of dividing Donne's poems into groups but does not pursue the point (*Shakespeare, Spenser, Donne* [London: Routledge and Kegan Paul, 1971], p. 127).

[84] Leishman, *Monarch of Wit*, esp. pp. 170–171, 185–186, 191–193. Also cf. Guss's brief but useful warning against assuming that all the poems about licentious love were written before the most idealistic poems (*John Donne, Petrarchist*, p. 146).

and of what, however sceptical one may be about the possibility of auto-biographical interpretation, one cannot but regard as a development or a progress, or avoid explaining to some extent in terms of the entrance into Donne's life of Ann More."[85] Notice how the word "progress" not only assumes a chronological pattern but privileges its later stages.

Of course, I do not deny that Donne developed, changed, and, yes, grew intellectually, stylistically, and ethically in some respects. His later verse letters are more complex in their moral values than the earlier ones, his later epithalamia more skilled in their rhetoric than the first one. But acknowledging these changes should not involve assuming that autobiographical events impelled the changes and are expressed within them; in particular, as I have suggested, the assumption that Donne's love for his wife—as opposed to a relationship with another woman or women or intellectual and ethical considerations unaffected by his own romantic experience—propelled him from cynicism about love to mature mutuality is at best a sentimental hypothesis. Nor should one assume that the developments in question are steady and consistent. And, above all, one should not maintain on the basis of very limited evidence that the poems whose stance the critic finds most congenial succeeded earlier, less congenial ones, representing a change of heart which their author enthusiastically endorsed.

Why, then, does the notion survive that Donne's marriage inspired a linear progression from immature versions of love to their opposite? Like Donne's own attempt to distinguish Jack Donne and Dr. Donne when presenting a manuscript of *Biathanatos* to his friend Sir Robert Ker,[86] that scenario reveals more about the motives of the critics who subscribe to it than about the poet's own career. Those motives are not unique to students of early modern England. They include, among other factors, an attraction to the idea of progress which generates similar assumptions about, say, Chaucer's career or the development of our own discipline. Despite—or because of—the contemporary distrust of liberalism and the resulting disdain for progress models, certain concepts often survive in subterranean forms. So far as Donne is concerned, the narrative of maturation is attractive to certain critics because it allows them to limit their discomfort with Donne's misogyny by confining it to an early stage in his life which he himself repudiated.[87] That narrative is no doubt also appealing to those who wish to limit Donne's transgressiveness. His amoral sexuality becomes

---

[85] Leishman, *Monarch of Wit*, p. 193.

[86] See Bald, *John Donne: A Life*, p. 201.

[87] Compare Guibbory's different but compatible description of critical responses to that misogyny (" 'Oh, let mee not serve so,' " pp. 812–813).

less threatening if we can believe it was unseated by a mature commitment to love—and better yet, married love. Once he was Jack Donne; now he is the John Donnes.

But if certain temporal patterns can distort our interpretations of Donne, others can help us read him more incisively. As I have argued throughout this chapter, generalizations about early modern England should be nuanced both by adducing shorter temporal units (Petrarchism meant something different in 1591 than in 1594) and by acknowledging the historical perspective of people who experience the events (the history of English Petrarchism and anti-Petrarchism would be described very differently in, say, 1605 than in 1995).

Despite the significant year-to-year shifts within Donne's own career and his culture, his approach to the counterdiscourses of Petrarchism admits of some generalizations. He is resident and alien. He does not reject the tradition completely, subscribe to it wholeheartedly, or condemn it under the guise of participation—but rather establishes his status as both insider and outsider at once.

Could one encapsulate that stance by labeling it ironic, a term so often applied to the author of the *Songs and Sonets?* No, definitely not, if we use irony in its customary sense, which privileges one meaning and dismisses another as a decoy. The usual interpretation of irony, that is, would confirm the assumption that when Donne's speakers appear to be expressing Petrarchan sentiments, the poem really discredits Petrarchism. Yet irony, as Linda Hutcheon argues, should be seen instead as inclusive in the sense that both meanings are experienced, as is the third meaning that is formed by the relationship between them. Defending that interpretation, she observes, "Irony would then share with puns a simultaneity . . . and a superimposition of meanings. . . . To think of irony as a playing together of two or more semantic notes to produce a third has at least one advantage over the related image of irony as a photographic double exposure . . . : it suggests more than simply the overdetermined space of superimposition by implying a notion of action and interaction in the creation of a third—the actual ironic—meaning."[88]

It would not be surprising to uncover in Donne, that master of antanaclasis, a strategy analogous to puns. And in fact his Petrarchan counterdiscourses are often ironic in exactly Hutcheon's sense. Deploying what she calls a both/and model, they invite the reader to accept and discredit

[88] Linda Hutcheon, *Irony's Edge: The Theory and Politics of Irony* (London: Routledge, 1994), p. 60. I am indebted to the author for making her work available to me before publication.

Petrarchism and to do both at once in a way that vests meaning in the simultaneity of those responses. The habit of invoking saints, the poem reminds us, is both foolish and entirely appropriate. In other words, these counterdiscourses produce in the reader a reaction that accords to the amalgam of distance and contiguity which is at the heart of Donne's stance towards Petrarchism.

For Donne does not simply reject Petrarchism as a *giovenile errore* but rather continues to forge a complex and varying relationship with it throughout his career. In so doing, he approaches Petrarchism much as many of his speakers approach women: a desire to embrace coexists with a drive to distance. That coexistence is most typically negotiated neither by simply satirizing Petrarchism nor by assigning Petrarchan sentiments to a discredited speaker but rather by putting them in quotation marks in a very different sense. That is, he both expresses such sentiments and holds them at a remove, flagging them with the equivalent of defusing and distancing phrases like "as it were" or "so to speak." Or, to put it another way, it is true that Donne committed Petrarchism. But that, as his letter to the Lady Carey and Mrs. Essex Rich so sedulously reminds us, was in another country.

CHAPTER SEVEN

CONCLUSION: CRITICISM IN THE
TIME OF CHOLER

I

If Ovid's Echo has lost the power of speech, Thomas Watson's Echo, the figure on whom this book opened many footnotes ago, has in a sense lost the power to be heard. Her words are not erased within the poem, but much of what she represents has been erased within the academy. Silenced by the canonicity that thrives even in a critical culture dedicated to attacking it, she may aptly stand for the many less known sonneteers deserving our attention. More to our purposes now, a number of critics are still prone to misread both English Petrarchism and its counterdiscourses by ignoring the complexities that are bodied forth by the disembodied Echo. In particular, while her relationship with the speaker whom Watson labels Author is an ambiguous and continuous struggle for power, students of the sonnet tradition often oversimplify that struggle by subscribing to either of two alternative positions. The first emphasizes the power and agency of the male speaker and of the sonneteer who creates him; protestations of weakness, according to this reading, are merely a feint deployed during the process of subjugating and even erasing the mistress.[1] Reversing that first approach to the sonnet tradition, the second schema maintains that the mistress corresponds to the patron, the sonneteer to the importunate and frustrated suitor.[2]

These two positions have inspired some incisive analyses—and yet both of them, I have maintained, are liable to generate misinterpretations

[1] For an influential statement of this position, see Ann Rosalind Jones and Peter Stallybrass, "The Politics of *Astrophil and Stella*," *SEL*, 24 (1984), esp. 54.
[2] See, e.g., Arthur F. Marotti, " 'Love is not love': Elizabethan Sonnet Sequences and the Social Order," *ELH*, 49 (1982), 396–428.

of Petrarchism. First, they may underestimate the instability of power and success within it. The sonnet mistress has more agency and potency than the readings that stress the efficacy of her lover would suggest and less than the expositions that identify her with the patron would assert—but even more important, her relationship to power is radically unstable, shifting from sequence to sequence, from poem to poem within a sequence, and from line to line within a given sonnet. Similarly, the Petrarchan speaker and the male poet behind him typically lurch between success and failure.

That lurching movement helps to explain the misogyny that is often latent and sometimes overt in Petrarchism: failure, whether realized or anticipated, contributes to the antagonism that is manifest even, or especially, in such sequences as the often worshipful *Amoretti*. And such shifts between success and failure, like related transitions between power and impotence or agency and passivity, also help to explain the popularity of the sonnet tradition in Tudor and Stuart England. For these changes correspond to a range of uncertainties about social standing and achievement in that culture, especially the instability, exemplified by the instances of Sidney and Donne, that resulted from multiple and often conflicting determinants of status. Critical generalizations about class and other forms of status, I have argued, should direct more attention to these complexities.

Neither do the two interpretations in question adequately acknowledge the confusion of gender boundaries, which may be as fluid as the boundaries between Petrarchism and anti-Petrarchism. Often one cannot talk with confidence about a powerful male poet and subservient mistress, or vice versa, because those two figures so frequently appear to merge, to dissolve in each other's subjectivity, even though they never achieve sexual union. This confusion of gender, too, helps us to understand the popularity of Petrarchism in its culture: that discourse reenacts the failed differentiation that I have traced in part to the effects of death on family structure, though it also offers an alternative to that lack through its modes of diacritical desire. These elisions and dissolutions of the boundaries between male and female are, of course, closely related to the movement between success and failure which is so characteristic of the sonnet tradition. If Echo represents the speechlessness that sometimes, though by no means always, threatens the Petrarchan mistress, she also stages threats to the subjectivity of the male sonneteer, not least by challenging when she merely seems to be repeating. Readers of Echo poems in the sonnet tradition often attribute power merely to the person being echoed, but one need only observe young children, who so often torment their peers simply by repeating words, to begin to suspect that that process can be deeply disturbing for the speakers whose utterances are mimed, subverting their autonomy as it does. Witness not only Watson's Echo but Percy's as well.

In English Petrarchism, all these and other complex relationships are expressed through characteristic rhetorical and structural patterns. Diacritical devices, such as comparisons with other poets, are as common in Petrarchism as in its counterdiscourses. Equally common is repetition, whose avatars range from the recurrence of the quatrain in the Shakespearean sonnet to the concatentio in such poets as Daniel to Wyatt's inability to abandon the hunt he has ostensibly renounced. Repetition does, of course, serve many functions in Petrarchism, but in the case of that discourse and its counterdiscourses, it is most frequently the equivalent and expression of the process of reenactment. Denied mastery of Laura and ultimately of their own subjectivity, Petrarchan poets keep revising the scenario in the forever frustrated hope of sometime, some day, achieving a different ending. For this reason among others, the term *cycle* is a far more appropriate label for most groups of sonnets than the more common term *sequence*. Or, as Drayton puts it in *Idea*, "When first I Ended, then I first Began" (62.1).[3] For if romance is the genre of finding what is lost, the sonnet is the genre of seeking what is lost, forever lost, forever irretrievable. The ensuing repetitions, as we saw, accord to a preoccupation in Tudor and Stuart culture with many types of recurrence, ranging from the doctrine of original sin to the practice of revenge.

The instance of repetition exemplifies the relationship of Petrarchism to that culture. By demonstrating the ways that discourse both constitutes and is constituted by a particular era in English history, this book supports the new historicist model of an interactive dynamic between the literary text and what used to be called its context. But certain new historicist studies are still prone to see a culture as a smoothly running machine, oiled by institutions and texts that dutifully perform their cultural work. Petrarchism demonstrates the dangers of that model. Sometimes, admittedly, it does serve the ends of ideologies of gender; for example, Petrarchism responds to uncertainties about women's behavior with an image of an unchanging female chastity. In other respects, however, this discourse intensifies cultural tensions rather than stilling or manipulating them in the interests of patriarchy; for instance, the voice of the Petrarchan mistress may on occasion challenge the formulations of the poet and his Petrarchan discourse. Thus the same poem may fulfill many and contradictory roles in its culture, as the issue of Wroth's both achieved and violated autonomy would indicate.

---

[3] J. William Hebel, Bernard H. Newdigate, and Kathleen Tillotson, eds., *The Works of Michael Drayton*, 5 vols. (Oxford: Basil Blackwell, 1931–1941).

And its performance of those roles is typically by no means as smooth or consistent as that mechanistic model of a smoothly running culture would lead us to expect. For, as Wroth's sequence reminds us, cultural work, like women's work, is never done.

This brief anatomy of Petrarchism helps us to summarize the roles of its counterdiscourses. Both traditions are varied enough to resist such overviews, and I have argued throughout this book for the need to acknowledge both multiple Petrarchisms and multiple, subjective interpretations of them. Positing an orthodox and monolithic Petrarchan discourse against which poets rebel is as tempting and misleading as the assumption of a stable and unitary tradition of praise in Joel Fineman's otherwise trenchant analyses of Shakespeare's rebellions against that tradition[4]—or the assumption of stable and unitary orthodoxies in the body politic of Tudor and Stuart England. If presupposing a monolithic Petrarchan discourse is misleading, a similar assumption about its counterdiscourses would be even more so: they range from Donne's libertine celebration of infidelity to Collop's praise of ugly beauty to Barnes's spiritual recantations.

Nonetheless, the counterdiscourses explored in this study do lend themselves to certain overarching generalizations. By and large they try to counter the many slippages of Petrarchism—male and female, subject and object, success and failure, agency and impotence—with a male voice that is clearly different from its female analogue and clearly in control of the situation, the discourse, and the mistress. In the erotic counterdiscourses, the speaker achieves the consummation of which his counterpart in Petrarchism can, quite literally, only dream; in the discourses within the ugly beauty convention, he achieves an agency ("I made thee gold, 'tis I can make thee brasse" [Collop, "To Aureola, or the Yellow Skin'd Lady; Asking Who Could Love a Fancy," 21])[5] that Petrarchism promises its poets but so often snatches away. The spiritual rejections of Petrarchism, in contrast, generally cast their speakers as humble suppliants, thus echoing one position of Petrarchism even as they renounce others. On the whole, however, the counterdiscourses of Petrarchism replicate other attempts in the culture to regain the authority and certainty that were variously being challenged in families headed by a widow, a state led by a queen, and a culture divided by conflicting paradigms of gender. In this sense anti-Petrarchism can be the last refuge of a male chauvinist.

If the speaker in the counterdiscourses of Petrarchism is in some im-

---

[4] Joel Fineman, *Shakespeare's Perjured Eye: The Invention of Poetic Subjectivity in the Sonnets* (Berkeley: University of California Press, 1986).

[5] Conrad Hilberry, ed., *The Poems of John Collop* (Madison: University of Wisconsin Press, 1962).

portant ways the opposite of his Petrarchan counterpart, much the same can be said of the mistress. In lieu of an unremittingly chaste lady, Craig imports a woman from the territory of the most cynical epigrams, while so-called ugly beauties generally differ from Petrarchan beauties less in their morals than in their physiognomy. Such women may implicitly rebut Petrarchan idealism and thus stage yet again the conflict among contrasting constructions of the female which was being acted in so many different theaters, literal and metaphoric, of their culture. Petrarchan poets and the authors of Petrarchan counterdiscourses struggle for the body of the woman who is at once the mother and the child of their rhetoric.

In another sense, however, that body may have, as it were, a mind if not a room of its own. That is, if the woman is sometimes the object over which Petrarchan discourses and counterdiscourses struggle, elsewhere those counterdiscourses represent her voice in some sense. In certain instances, such as Wyatt's "Whoso List To Hunt," Petrarchan principles are challenged by a female speaker, whereas in other texts that challenge is only implicitly gendered female. But the counterdiscourses cannot be simply and reassuringly classified as protofeminist. For, as the recently cited instances of Craig and the ugly beauty tradition remind us, many Petrarchan counterdiscourses exhibit an overt and intense hostility towards women. In so doing, they draw our attention to comparable antagonisms present in the demands for revenge which are a staple of Petrarchism. But whereas Barnes's counterpart in a typical Petrarchan sonnet merely declares his craving for revenge, at the end of *Parthenophil and Parthenophe* that fantasy is realized in a sexual attack that is itself distanced and excused through the trappings that insistently declare it merely a fantasy.

As Barnes's poem reminds us, whereas the counterdiscourses of Petrarchism manifest disturbingly intense hostility towards women, they also offer techniques for countering that virulence. Indeed, they transfer into safer venues many other kinds of hostility as well, reminding us that displacement is their typical modus operandi. In the ugly beauty tradition, characteristics that might be perceived as associated with all women because of anxieties stemming from gynecological traumas and less material cultural traumas are displaced onto the subject of the poem. Thus these poems, the product of so many kinds of psychic wounds, facilitate love in the age of more literal scar tissue and of other gynecological maladies. And thus their tradition, which both authorizes and delimits misogyny, is attractive in the age of patriarchal choler.

The counterdiscourses of Petrarchism practice many other types of displacement as well. If traits that might be associated with all women are instead attached to the ugly beauty, so too are traits and tendencies that the poet fears in himself; I have seconded the argument that such poems are the product not only of anxieties that women in general and Elizabeth herself will grow old but also that the poet himself is doing so. And, similarly, the practitioners of these counterdiscourses deflect onto other poets characteristics they fear in their own art, a pattern we traced in Sidney and Drayton especially.

These and other strategies, however, are only partially and temporarily successful: the counterdiscourses of Petrarchism typically replicate many of the problems they aim to address, thus offering yet another example of the breakdown of boundaries and of repetition in a literary tradition always marked by it. Often the anti-Petrarchan poets who claim to renounce secular for spiritual love, like Petrarch himself, are not wholly persuasive on that subject. Even the final edition of Drayton's *Idea* includes poems that would not sound out of place in the first edition; even Astrophil's wittily articulated aesthetic principles do not immunize him against the linguistic diseases he diagnoses in others; even Donne's carefully documented status as resident alien does not protect him from being drafted on occasion into the army of Petrarchists.

These replications and reduplications do not support a containment model, now fortunately largely discredited by many new historicists, for some of the challenges the counterdiscourses offer to Petrarchism are indeed telling. Witness, for example, the mockery of stylistic excesses by Sir John Davies. A hit, a very palpable hit. But the repetitions in question do remind us of the tenacity of Petrarchan problematics. When Petrarchism is cut into the hand, it deals a stacked deck; when fort-da is the game, it is played with a trick ball that can never be fully recovered.

The attempt, so often unsuccessful, to distinguish the counterdiscourses of Petrarchism from the discourses is but one example of the diacritical drive that characterizes both of them. Petrarchism is a continuing struggle between difference and sameness, as its signature trope, the oxymoron, would suggest. The distinctions between *then* and *now* which Roland Greene has traced so well are one of many assertions of difference;[6] Petrarchan poets also variously differentiate themselves from other writers, other genres, and other nations. They do so in contrast to and often in reaction against the forms of sameness which characterize the sonnet tradition, notably the repetitiveness of literary imitation and of desire itself. The tension between lyric and narrative within the sonnet is sometimes also realized as a pull between sameness in the sense of entrapped repetition

---

[6] Roland Greene, *Post-Petrarchism: Origins and Innovations of the Western Lyric Sequence* (Princeton: Princeton University Press, 1991), esp. pp. 33–34.

versus movement. Most stanzaic forms play on systems of sameness and difference, but such patterns are especially evident in the sonnet, in part because the relationship among quatrains or between octet and sestet is mirrored in the versions of likeness and unlikeness which characterize the relationship of a single sonnet to the whole sequence. As even this brief summary reminds us, the diacritical markers of Petrarchism include traces of other genres incorporated within the sonnet (witness the references to epic we noted in Chapter 3), poems in other genres juxtaposed with or included within the sonnet sequence (witness the strange bedfellows with whom the *Amoretti* cohabits), allusions to other poets (witness Drayton's poem to Cooke in the 1594 edition of *Idea's Mirrour*), and so on. Above all, the slide between sameness and difference in Petrarchism is gendered. This tradition assigns distinctive roles to the lover and his mistress—the boy wears blue, the girl pink—and then turns one into a mirror version or an echo of the other.

The counterdiscourses of Petrarchism variously respond to these patterns by reestablishing boundaries, notably between their discourse versus putatively lesser forms of love poetry and between male and female, and by reenacting the erasure of such boundaries. My point is not, of course, the tautological one that the authors of those counterdiscourses assert their distinction from Petrarch and many of his imitators but rather that this assertion is but one of many examples of their diacritical impulse. They attempt with varying success to distinguish as well false love from true, English from Other, bad poesy from good, and so on. In so doing they often display anxieties and guilt about their own poetic enterprise. And in so doing they often displace tensions about distinguishing Una from Duessa or the true Florimell from her snowy sister.

Grounded in the assumption that literary drives, like so many other kinds, are often multiply determined, this study has traced a range of etiologies for diacritical desire. If differentiation is central to male subjectivity, as psychoanalysts of many different persuasions have asserted,[7] one needs to inflect that realization with the different sources and manifestations that differentiation may assume in specific cultures. Thus I have argued that the family dynamics of Tudor England, and especially the effects of the mortality crisis of 1557–1559, lie behind the workings of diacritical desire in the society in question. Its appeal should be related as well to that family the nation, and we have traced, in Drayton and elsewhere, its connections

---

[7] See, e.g., the influential statement of this position by Nancy Chodorow in *The Reproduction of Mothering: Psychoanalysis and the Sociology of Gender* (Berkeley: University of California Press, 1978), esp. chap. 6.

to the nationalistic bifurcation of self and Other. Committed to a corrective emphasis on the political and historical spheres, critics today sometimes slight specifically literary issues, and in this case one should emphasize that diacritical desire is often a type of genre criticism practiced in a culture dedicated to that activity. Moreover, in many ways the diacritical desire of anti-Petrarchism serves to respond to the joint criticisms of both love and its poetry by those who claim to be too respectable to indulge in either.[8]

Whatever its sources, diacritical desire not only expresses but also facilitates many agendas of the counterdiscourses of English Petrarchism. It restores agency to the poet, for instance. It permits guilt about other forms of desire, whether they be for Laura or the poetic laurel, to be deflected onto the Other. And, as Donne's "Comparison" among other texts testifies, it is a route for dominating women.

II

Even this brief a summary of issues examined in this study may suggest their relevance to texts outside its scope. A book with as broad a topic as mine must necessarily be selective, but in concluding we can at least glance at some samples of Petrarchan counterdiscourses in genres and modes other than those on which I have focused. *The Faerie Queene, Romeo and Juliet,* and *Paradise Lost* deserve and repay such attention not only because of their significance in their culture and our own literary culture but also because of their representativeness: for all their idiosyncratic characteristics, these three texts provide exemplary instances of some types of diacritical desire. Hence they allow us to summarize patterns traced throughout this study and prepare us to understand the reactions against Petrarchism in additional texts as well.

The impact of Petrarchism and anti-Petrarchism on Spenser's epic has been long acknowledged and often anatomized. Episodes such as the creation of the false Florimell or Busirane's imprisonment of Amoret insistently signal their genealogy through Petrarchan language; in addition, critics have persuasively argued for the influence of that discourse on incidents and characters where its relevance is less overt, such as the vision at Mount Acidale, the behavior of Radigund, and the narratives of the four squires.[9]

---

[8] For useful comments on this issue—and so many others in this book—I am indebted to Anne Lake Prescott.

[9] See, respectively, Barbara L. Estrin, " 'The Longed-for Lands': Petrarch, Spenser, and 'An Ordinary Evening in New Haven,' " *Ariel*, 19 (1988), 6–7; Mark Rose, *Heroic Love: Studies in Sidney and Spenser* (Cambridge: Harvard University Press, 1968), p. 108; and Reed

Yet certain questions have not been fully resolved. Why is Petrarchism, a mode mainly associated with lyric, so pervasive a presence in Spenser's epic poem? And why, given the range of judgments on that discourse presented both within the *Amoretti* and in the dialogue among the texts published with the *Amoretti*, does *The Faerie Queene* offer so negative a view of it? The reinterpretations of love poetry in this study suggest some answers.

The sonnet tradition functions synecdochically in *The Faerie Queene*, as it does in so many of the texts we examined earlier. If, as many readers have recognized, pastoral engages in a contestatory dialogue with epic in Book VI, Petrarchism assumes a comparable role throughout the text: it serves as a countergenre to epic and represents that which impedes and questions epic values.[10] The synecdochic role of Petrarchism is most apparent in Book III, where that discourse plays Dido to Britomart's Aeneas and to the epic as a whole. Britomart is, as many readers have observed, a Petrarchan lover in her laments and an anti-Petrarchan one in her rejection of Petrarchan self-absorption.[11] For the epic to follow its linear track, for the dynasty that will spring from Britomart's womb to be born, she must abandon Petrarchism for some versions of its counterdiscourses: she must eschew the Petrarchan lamentations she delivers by the sea and transform her love into an epic quest for Artegall. As Susanne Lindgren Wofford points out, in delivering them she enacts a struggle between narrative and lyric which parallels the workings of allegory itself.[12] Many readers have commented on Glauce's initial responses to Britomart's lovesickness, but in the context of that battle between narrative and lyric, the nurse's reactions to Britomart's laments by the sea are equally significant:

> Till that old *Glauce* gan with sharpe repriefe,
> Her to restraine, and giue her good reliefe,

Way Dasenbrock, "Escaping the Squires' Double Bind in Books III and IV of *The Faerie Queene*," *SEL*, 26 (1986), 25–45, and the later version of the argument in *Imitating the Italians: Wyatt, Spenser, Synge, Pound, Joyce* (Baltimore: Johns Hopkins University Press, 1991), chap. 3. Also cf. Kenneth Gross's acute suggestions about how both poets demonstrate the limitations of allegory (*Spenserian Poetics: Idolatry, Iconoclasm, and Magic* [Ithaca: Cornell University Press, 1985], pp. 221–224).

[10] Compare A. Leigh DeNeef's observation that genres serve as metaphors throughout the poem ("Ploughing Virgilian Furrows: The Genres of *Faerie Queene* VI," *John Donne Journal*, 1 [1982], 151–166).

[11] On anti-Petrarchan elements in her behavior, see Lauren Silberman, "Singing Unsung Heroines: Androgynous Discourse in Book 3 of *The Faerie Queene*," in *Rewriting the Renaissance: The Discourses of Sexual Difference in Early Modern Europe*, ed. Margaret W. Ferguson, Maureen Quilligan, and Nancy J. Vickers (Chicago: University of Chicago Press, 1986), p. 260.

[12] Susanne Lindgren Wofford, "Britomart's Petrarchan Lament: Allegory and Narrative in *The Faerie Queene*," *CL*, 39 (1987), esp. 53.

> Through hope of those, which *Merlin* had her told
> Should of her name and nation be chiefe,
> And fetch their being from the sacred mould
> Of her immortall wombe, to be in heauen enrold.
>   (III.iv.11)[13]

Glauce in effect impels Britomart from lyric to epic. Here she does not offer a more optimistic view of the world of lyric poetry by asserting, as she did earlier, that this love is a healthy and natural attraction to a deserving man; rather, without even mentioning Artegall, she focuses on the spiritual and nationalistic consequences of the love.

Britomart's responses to love help us to define the Petrarchan values that are played against epic throughout the poem. The world of the sonnet represents not only self-absorbed pity but also, more to our purposes, stasis and repetition. Britomart delivers her lament after alighting from the horse that had been carrying her forward, and she does so to the tune of the repeated surges of the waves. Thus in a sense Petrarchism is the lyric alternative to epic, and the struggle between the two echoes a comparable battle fought and commemorated in the *Amoretti*. But this is only part of the story, for just as satire lives close to the heart of pastoral and the epigram inhabits the body of the sonnet, so the lyric values associated with Britomart's Petrarchism are also inherent to Spenser's epic. The anticlosural impulse manifest in the repetitiveness of the Petrarchan tradition is a version of the pressures that lead Spenser to create marriages that are not consummated and Blatant Beasts that are not securely imprisoned.

Of course, Petrarchism attacks the values of *The Faerie Queene* by representing not only the lyric challenge to epic but also dangerous types of love. Petrarchism is clearly implicated in the episode of Busirane: the color symbolism of Amoret's body in the pageant, among other evidence, signals that the climactic story in this book involves a commentary on Petrarchan love, however one adjudicates its many other interpretive controversies.[14] Amoret is "pend" (III.xi.11) by her captor, a telling word whose literary

---

[13] The Variorum Spenser, ed. Edwin Greenlaw et al., 11 vols. (Baltimore: Johns Hopkins University Press, 1943–1957). I cite this edition throughout this chapter.

[14] For analyses of this controversial episode and of its relationship to Petrarchism, see, e.g., Harry Berger Jr., *Revisionary Play: Studies in the Spenserian Dynamics* (Berkeley: University of California Press, 1988), pp. 114, 172–194; Thomas P. Roche Jr., *The Kindly Flame: A Study of the Third and Fourth Books of Spenser's "Faerie Queene"* (Princeton: Princeton University Press, 1964), esp. pp. 77–88; and Silberman, "Singing Unsung Heroines," pp. 263–267.

connotations many critics have remarked.[15] Similarly, it is no accident that Mirabella inhabits the same canto as Serena, for the Petrarchan victimizer who scorns her lovers is the alter ego of the Petrarchan victim who represents as well the dangers of idolatry in the religion of love.

But the texts analyzed in earlier chapters of this book also direct our attention to less obvious connections in the poem between Petrarchism and dangerous modes of love. If, as I have argued, that discourse is associated in Tudor and Stuart England with problems in differentiation and, in particular, with elisions between male and female roles, it is easier to understand why the witch puts a male spirit in the snowy Florimell.[16] Elsewhere in *The Faerie Queene* the androgyny that confounds Britomart's behavior is resolved, or at least apparently resolved, when she releases her hair. O femina certa. In contrast, the behavior of the witch hints that the literary discourse that she deploys in creating Florimell inscribes a confusion of male and female which cannot be erased that easily.

Similarly, the final poem in Barnes's *Parthenophil and Parthenophe* helps us to explain the emphasis on religion and ritual in the episode of Serena and the cannibals. Serena's captors repeatedly manifest their piety and observe rules about proper behavior at a cannibalistic feast, though not without some reminders from their priest about their faulty table manners. The juxtapositions of the civilized and the barbarous in this incident have been observed by many Spenserians; Jonathan Crewe, for example, reads that paradox in terms of the English presence in Ireland, as well as the development of a culture of consumption.[17] Those explanations and ones rooted in Spenser's attack on Petrarchism are not mutually exclusive. What is most important for our purposes now is that the passage, like Barnes's description of a ceremonious rape, depicts the deployment of ritual to excuse violence against a woman and in so doing raises broad and disturbing questions about the frequency, perhaps even the inescapability, of that maneuver.[18] To what extent, *The Faerie Queene* demands, does Petrarchism use its own equiva-

[15] See esp. Maureen Quilligan, *Milton's Spenser: The Politics of Reading* (Ithaca: Cornell University Press, 1983), p. 198.

[16] Compare Susanne Lindgren Wofford's argument that the false Florimell is associated with social transgression (*The Choice of Achilles: The Ideology of Figure in the Epic* [Stanford: Stanford University Press, 1992], p. 288).

[17] Jonathan Crewe, "Spenser's Saluage Petrarchanism: Pensées Sauvages in *The Faerie Queene,*" *Bucknell Review,* 35 (1992), 89–103. For an alternative explanation, see Donald Cheney, *Spenser's Image of Nature: Wild Man and Shepherd in "The Faerie Queene"* (New Haven: Yale University Press, 1966), pp. 105–106.

[18] Compare my analysis of a similar strategy in Donne's "Epithalamion made at Lincolnes Inne" (*A Happier Eden: The Politics of Marriage in the Stuart Epithalamium* [Ithaca: Cornell University Press, 1990], pp. 162–163).

lents of ritual, notably literary convention, to excuse the violence found in many sequences—in some of Spenser's own descriptions of his tigerish lady, in Shakespeare's attacks on his Dark Lady, and so on? To what extent does art in general proffer such excuses?

One stanza poses these questions in especially pressing form. Throughout the canto, Serena's experiences with the cannibals, like so many other episodes in Petrarchism and anti-Petrarchism, center on eroded boundaries; here the borders between apparently respectful and ritualized behavior on the one hand and brutal savagery on the other are repeatedly violated:

> So round about her they them selues did place
> Vpon the grasse, and diuersely dispose,
> As each thought best to spend the lingring space.
> Some with their eyes the daintest morsels chose;
> Some praise her paps, some praise her lips and nose;
> Some whet their kniues, and strip their elboes bare:
> The Priest him selfe a garland doth compose
> Of finest flowres, and with full busie care
> His bloudy vessels wash, and holy fire prepare.
>
> (VI.viii.39)

Earlier stanzas had emphasized the spirituality of the cannibals ("since by grace of God she there was sent" [VI.viii.38]), but in stanza thirty-nine the juxtaposition of different forms of desire, notably religious aspirations and cannibalistic anticipations, is especially striking. On one level the passage plays the exalted role of the priest against the lower desires of the populace. But that apparent contrast is in turn both replicated and repudiated by the behavior in this passage of that sacerdotal figure and his followers. Making a garland, an act of celebration, is quite different from preparing bloody vessels, but the reader comes to realize that the garland will figure in the ceremony that will, quite literally, draw blood and worse. The priest's dubious aim, after all, is to weave the garlands of repast—and yet in so doing he recalls all the positive characters in *The Faerie Queene* who have festooned their ladies with garlands and the poet's metaphoric version of that activity when he himself "compose[s]" (VI.viii.39) poems of praise. Similarly, the contrast between those who praise Serena and those who whet their knives is striking—and yet Spenser reminds his audience that praise, the activity at the core of Petrarchism, may well be a rhetorical version of whetting one's knife and one's appetite.

Thus far Spenser's attacks on Petrarchism might appear to establish him as a protofeminist. But we have observed throughout this study that while the counterdiscourses of Petrarchism may be gendered female in any number of senses, they may also replicate the problems and tensions of Petrarchism, including its sporadic misogyny. If the anti-Petrarchism in the Serena episode exposes the hostility latent in Petrarchism itself, elsewhere in the poem Spenser's anti-Petrarchism at once exposes and conceals his own gendered antagonisms, a role frequently encountered in such counterdiscourses. In particular, the creation of the false Florimell demonstrates yet again both the fear of women that is often hidden within the responses against Petrarchism and some strategies for deploying that fear. Observe how the description hints that types of behavior associated with the demonic are normative for all women, for true as well as false Florimells: "To stirre and roll them, like a womans eyes" (III.viii.7), and "For he [the devilish spirit in Florimell's body] in counterfeisance did excell, / And all the wyles of wemens wits knew passing well" (III.viii.8). The implicit contrast with the true Florimell ostensibly insists that her snowy sister is not representative of all women; yet like many poems in the ugly beauty tradition, this section of the epic associates with one woman, determinedly presented as the marked case, characteristics its author fears are typical of many others. And, again like those poems, it participates in other forms of deflection as well, attributing to the witch the poet's latent hostility to women. The texts examined earlier in this study also help us to anatomize the sources of the antagonisms hidden beneath the surface of this passage: the false Florimell, like the cannibals, is associated with the breakdown of boundaries, whether they be the divisions of gender (she is inhabited by a male spirit) or the divisions between false and true, beautiful and foul women.

As that breakdown would suggest, during the projected sacrifice of Serena Spenser raises other disturbing questions that extend to his own art. If distinctions between worshipful, disinterested praise and a cannibalism that is self-serving in more senses than one cannot be maintained, might other distinctions be imperiled as well? Can one even separate Petrarchan hyperbole from anti-Petrarchan moderation—or the modes of praise to which this poem is dedicated from the ones in which the cannibals indulge? *The Faerie Queene*, like Petrarchism, is structured around both the erection and the demolition of distinctions. This is one reason allegory, which lends itself to both processes, appeals to Spenser so much, and nowhere are the two more clearly staged than in the relationship between the faults of Petrarchism and their rejection—or apparent rejection—in its counterdiscourses.

We can now better understand why Petrarchism recurs so often in Spenser's epic and why his approach to it is far more negative than, say, the

Amoretti might lead us to expect. That discourse comes to represent several of the states of mind and modes of behavior that most disturb Spenser throughout the poem.[19] As an exemplary instance of the lyric predilection for stasis and repetition, Petrarchism, as much as pastoral, stands for that which threatens epic action. And it represents the threat of violence inherent even, or perhaps especially, in the most civilized discourses about women, including poetry. Petrarchism also testifies to the vulnerability of distinctions of all types, including the ones between Petrarchism and its counterdiscourses and between Petrarchism and its supposed antagonists. Indeed, perhaps the principal reason Spenser attacks Petrarchism so fiercely and repeatedly is that he knows that this Error may simply spawn new heads when one is chopped off, maybe a head bearing Spenser's own face.[20]

Several similar patterns recur in *Romeo and Juliet*, a text almost contemporaneous with the second edition of *The Faerie Queene*. Here too Petrarchism is pervasive: the play opens on a sonnet and later includes other versions of that prosodic structure, oxymora abound, and several of its characters, not just Romeo, borrow Petrarchan language.[21] Indeed, Petrarchism figures in a broader investigation of the relationship between tragedy and lyric discourses of many types, as Shakespeare's incorporation of an aubade and prothalamion would suggest.[22] Many critics assume that behind Shakespeare's allusions to Petrarchism lies a straightforward commentary on that discourse, variously arguing that Romeo's Petrarchan love for Rosaline is contrasted with his more mature devotion to Juliet or that his Petrarchism is played against Mercutio's anti-Petrarchism.[23] Shakes-

---

[19] For a different but compatible overview of Spenser's responses to Petrarchism, see Theresa M. Krier, *Gazing on Secret Sights: Spenser, Classical Imitation, and the Decorums of Vision* (Ithaca: Cornell University Press, 1990), esp. pp. 114–118; this study emphasizes Spenser's concerns about exposure and display.

[20] Compare Joseph F. Loewenstein's reverse version of this argument, his assertion that the 1595 volume criticizes the Petrarchism of the masque of Busirane ("Echo's Ring: Orpheus and Spenser's Career," *ELR*, 16 [1986], 293).

[21] Many readers have observed these characteristics. The best overview of the issue is Jill L. Levenson, "The Definition of Love: Shakespeare's Phrasing in *Romeo and Juliet*," *Shakespeare Studies*, 15 (1982), 21–36; she demonstrates that Shakespeare plays on sonnet conventions throughout the text, often reinvigorating them. Also see Robert O. Evans, *The Osier Cage: Rhetorical Devices in "Romeo and Juliet"* (Lexington: University Press of Kentucky, 1966), chap. 2, on the pervasiveness of the oxymoron; and Brian Gibbons, ed., "Introduction," *Romeo and Juliet* (London: Methuen, 1980), p. 42, on other connections between the play and sonnet sequences. Among the studies discussing the presence of sonnets, complete or fragmentary, are Gideon Rappaport, "Another Sonnet in 'Romeo and Juliet,'" *NQ*, 25 (1978), 124; and Gayle Whittier, "The Sonnet's Body and the Body Sonnetized in *Romeo and Juliet*," *SQ*, 40 (1989), 27–41.

[22] I am indebted to my colleague Susanne Lindgren Wofford for valuable observations about this issue, as well as for many other types of help with this book.

[23] See, e.g., Evans, *Osier Cage*, pp. 24–25. Also cf. David Laird's contention that the lovers

peare's engagement with Petrarchism and its counterdiscourses, however, is more complex and ambivalent than these readings acknowledge.

Romeo and Juliet, even more than most plays, is structured around a series of contrasting perspectives and interpretations. If comedy is played against tragedy,[24] if a private world is played against its public counterpart, if commercial motivations are played against more disinterested ones,[25] so too are different models of love and marriage contrasted with each other. Although Capulet's relationship to his daughter is sometimes read as an instance of patriarchal authoritarianism,[26] earlier in the play he gives evidence as well of respect for her autonomy, announcing to Paris that Juliet's consent is necessary for the marriage: "My will to her consent is but a part" (I.ii.17).[27] The contrast between this declaration and Capulet's indubitably authoritarian pronouncements elsewhere in the text enacts the conflicting constructions of marriage in a culture whose interpretations of that institution were far less hegemonic than many critics have assumed.[28] And, similarly, the drama plays against each other the many different discourses of love. As is the case in the volume containing Spenser's *Amoretti*, "Epithalamion," and Anacreontic poems, the reactions against Petrarchism generate not the dyad one might expect but rather a triad, reminding us again to decline "counterdiscourse" in the plural: the frustrations of unrequited Petrarchan love are contrasted both with a mutual love that issues in marriage and with the cynicism about love expressed by Mercutio and others. Even this pattern is further complicated by other models of love; when Romeo declares that Rosaline will not "ope her lap to saint-seducing gold" (I.i.214), for example, he is closer to the world of the Roman elegies than that of Petrarch, though his use of "saint" juxtaposes the two.

Here, as in *The Faerie Queene* and many of the texts examined earlier, Petrarchism represents a range of issues; in criticizing it, the play comments

---

move from conventional, artificial language towards a new mastery ("The Generation of Style in *Romeo and Juliet*," *JEGP*, 63 [1964], 204–213), and John W. Cole's argument that Romeo is cured of his melancholy and lovesickness by his subsequent love for Juliet ("Romeo and Rosaline," *Neophilologus*, 24 [1939], 285–289).

[24] On this pattern in the play, see Susan Snyder, "*Romeo and Juliet*: Comedy into Tragedy," *EIC*, 20 (1970), 391–402, and the later version in *The Comic Matrix of Shakespeare's Tragedies: "Romeo and Juliet," "Hamlet," "Othello," and "King Lear"* (Princeton: Princeton University Press, 1979), pp. 56–70.

[25] Several readers have noted the sporadic eruption of financial issues in this text; see, e.g., Greg Bentley, "Poetics of Power: Money as Sign and Substance in *Romeo and Juliet*," *Explorations in Renaissance Culture*, 1 (1991), 145–166.

[26] See, e.g., Coppélia Kahn, *Man's Estate: Masculine Identity in Shakespeare* (Berkeley: University of California Press, 1981), p. 95.

[27] I cite G. Blakemore Evans, ed., *The Riverside Shakespeare* (Boston: Houghton Mifflin, 1974).

[28] See my substantiation of this argument in *A Happier Eden*, chap. 1.

on broader habits of language and thought. Thus Petrarchan hyperbole figures in a troubled examination of hyperbolic language of all types. This, like *Arden of Feversham,* is a play where the gods punish those they hate by making their exaggerations come true, with Juliet's playful reference to killing Romeo with "cherishing" (II.ii.183) and Lady Capulet's intemperate wish that Juliet were "married to her grave" (III.v.140) proving tragically proleptic. Rosalie L. Colie discusses "unmetaphoring" in the sense of transforming literary conventions into intrinsic parts of the dramatic action or the characters' psyches;[29] the play, like Donne's poetry and many of the other attacks on Petrarchism examined in this book, also treats hyperbolic assertions in this way. In so doing, it draws our attention to the dangers of getting carried away by language of all types, a peril that also preoccupies Shakespeare in his roughly contemporaneous poem *The Rape of Lucrece.*

Petrarchism also participates in a debate about the relationship of opposites. The feud between two families is, of course, the dramatic embodiment of opposing forces on the level of imagery (night versus day), structure (Mantua versus Verona), and so on. This predilection for pairing is germane to Petrarchism both because the play contrasts that literary practice with its own counterdiscourses, such as Mercutio's mockery of love, and because Petrarchism itself manifests an attraction to opposing dyads, notably realized in the oxymoron. But that figure of speech is not a solution to binary conflicts or a center of values, as some critics have maintained.[30] Rather, in a play that so often draws our attention to the dangers of rhetoric, oxymora are associated primarily with uncontrolled, heightened speech like Juliet's initial response to Tybalt's death.

Petrarchism figures as well in the questioning of repetition that runs throughout the play. In a sense the praxis of *Romeo and Juliet* is a struggle between the compulsion to repeat and the drive to stop doing so.[31] Thus the play thematizes dramatic conventions of recurrence, such as the mirroring of the actions of one class in those of another. Revenge, as I suggested earlier, is a manifestation of reduplication which particularly intrigued and troubled Tudor and Stuart England. An eye for an eye, a

---

[29] Rosalie L. Colie, *Shakespeare's Living Art* (Princeton: Princeton University Press, 1974), p. 145. Also cf. Ann Pasternak Slater's argument that the play repeatedly actualizes Petrarchan language ("Petrarchism Come True in *Romeo and Juliet,*" in Werner Habicht, D. J. Palmer, and Roger Pringle, eds., *Images of Shakespeare: Proceedings of the Third Congress of the International Shakespeare Association, 1986* [Newark and London: University of Delaware Press and Associated University Presses, 1988]).

[30] See, e.g., Lawrence Edward Bowling, "The Thematic Framework of *Romeo and Juliet,*" *PMLA,* 64 (1949), 208–220.

[31] The presence of reduplication in the play is also noted by Harry Levin in "Form and Formality in *Romeo and Juliet,*" *SQ,* 11 (1960), 8.

tooth for a tooth, a Romeo for a Tybalt. The feud, the audience is repeatedly reminded, is grounded in repetition. The Prince's first commentary on it stresses this: "*Three* civil brawls . . . Have *thrice* disturb'd the quiet of our streets" (I.i.89, 91; emphasis added). Ironically, at the tragic conclusion of the drama Romeo and Juliet echo each other's misunderstandings of the situation and repeat the same solution, suicide. Similarly, the text draws attention to the repetitiveness of Romeo's Petrarchan relationship with Rosaline: he uses rhetorical mannerisms involving recurrence, such as his copious lists of the same figures ("Feather of lead, bright smoke, cold fire, sick health" [I.i.180]); he behaves the same way night after night ("Many a morning hath he there been seen" [I.i.131]), and he insists that his love is unchanging ("Farewell, thou canst not teach me to forget" [I.i.237]). Thus Petrarchism, the discourse of repetition, comes to represent the habits of recurrence that lie behind so many of the most misguided actions in the play. If this is a tragedy of patriarchy, as feminist readers have persuasively argued, it is a tragedy of repetition as well and thus in a sense a tragedy propelled by the discourse that legitimates, even revels in, many manifestations of that figure.

One could make a case that *Romeo and Juliet* also celebrates an escape from repetition in that its male lead abandons Petrarchan love for the version of its counterdiscourses that he and Juliet develop. And, as we already observed, certain readers have pursued this argument, pointing to changes in language and to the shift from an unrequited to a mutual love. But *The Faerie Queene* occasionally hints at the difficulty of escaping from Petrarchism, and *Paradise Lost* unambiguously embraces the possibility of doing so, whereas *Romeo and Juliet* occupies an uneasy middle ground on that issue: at some points it holds out the hope of replacing Petrarchism with a better alternative, yet elsewhere it challenges that aspiration.

This pattern, like so many others involving Petrarchism in the play, participates in a broader debate about all potentialities for escape. One way this play reveals its comedic elements is its emphasis on the city;[32] Romeo cannot run away to the woods as do the lovers in *A Midsummer Night's Dream*, and Mercutio cannot retreat to an academy for those who scorn love as does Berowne. Mantua, of course, represents a partial escape, but Romeo is soon called back; it is telling that the climactic escape plan that involves Mantua is compromised in part because plague confines a messenger within a house, thus mirroring the way more central characters are variously confined within a house, a city, or a tomb. Like *Coriolanus*, this

---

[32] Compare Colie, *Shakespeare's Living Art*, p. 137.

play asks whether there is indeed a world elsewhere. The deaths of its title characters suggest that for them all attempts to break loose end in the grave. The same struggle to escape is enacted in the presentation of Petrarchism. In *Romeo and Juliet* Shakespeare engages in the problematics of diacritical desire: he debates whether one can develop an alternative to Petrarchism. Romeo repeatedly announces the differences between his love for Rosaline and his passion for Juliet, and to some extent he is persuasive: one is requited and the other is not, one involves repetitive and frustrated longing, whereas the second culminates in marriage and consummation. Indeed, I suggest that these contrasts help us to understand why, having set up the kind of competitive triangle that structures so many of his dramas (Paris and Romeo both want Juliet), Shakespeare devotes far less attention to the resulting rivalry than his other plays would lead us to expect: erotic competition is displaced onto the tension not only between two families but also between two discourses.

Yet the distinction between Petrarchism and its counterdiscourses blurs at several points in the drama. The love between Romeo and Juliet is surely characterized by the dangerous hyperboles associated with Petrarchism itself, and for all the freshness of the language in the balcony scene, Shakespeare does recycle some images associated with Petrarchism.[33] Juliet is, after all, hardly the first woman to be compared to the sun even if Romeo develops that conceit in a particularly charming manner. It is telling that the Friar, who remains a center of values despite the tragic results of his plots, reacts to Romeo's change of heart as not a rejection but a repetition of folly—telling, too, that he initially sanctions the marriage because of its potentiality for resolving the feud rather than its inherent merits.

> *Fri L.* And art thou chang'd? Pronounce this sentence then:
> Women may fall, when there's no strength in men.
> *Rom.* Thou chidst me oft for loving Rosaline.
> *Fri. L.* For doting, not for loving, pupil mine.
> *Rom.* And badst me bury love.
> *Fri. L.*   Not in a grave,
> To lay one in, another out to have.
> . . . .

[33] Compare James L. Calderwood's contention that Romeo, like Berowne, thinks he has escaped Petrarchism more than he in fact has (*Shakespearean Metadrama: The Argument of the Play in "Titus Andronicus," "Love's Labour's Lost," "Romeo and Juliet," "A Midsummer Night's Dream," and "Richard II"* [Minneapolis: University of Minnesota Press, 1971], p. 89).

But come, young waverer, come go with me,
In one respect, I'll thy assistant be;
For this alliance may so happy prove
To turn your households' rancor to pure love.
(II.iii.79–84, 89–92)

In short, the relationship between Romeo's two loves remains complex and ambiguous. For Shakespeare, like so many other practitioners of the counterdiscourses in question, raises but does not definitively resolve the possibility that new anti-Petrarchism is but old Petrarchism writ large.

Like *Romeo and Juliet*, *Paradise Lost* contrasts marriage with Petrarchan love. Unlike *Romeo and Juliet*, however, Milton's epic draws its battle lines clearly. The alternatives to Petrarchism do not court confusion with it; the valuation of each camp is very clear. Indeed, this poem resembles Spenser's epic in the intensity and clarity of its rejection of Petrarchism. Why, then, is Milton's response to it so negative?

His own work in the sonnet tradition suggests some answers.[34] If his sonnets testify to his attraction to the form developed by Petrarch, his elegies demonstrate his attraction to the erotic sentiments customarily expressed in that verse form. But even in these early poems Milton's responses to Petrarchism are ambivalent. He attaches a recantation to his seventh elegy, thus miming Petrarch's own anti-Petrarchism. And one of his Italian sonnets, "Donna leggiadra," differs strikingly from its analogues in the *Rime sparse* in that the poet distances himself from the emotion of love. Throughout he stresses the way in which the lady affects all men rather than himself in particular, and in so doing his ending both acknowledges and undermines the possibility of escaping her charms: "Grazia sola di sù gli vaglia, innanti / Che'l disio amoroso al cuor s' invecchi" (13–14; "Grace from above alone can avail him to prevent the desire of a lover from becoming fixed immovably in his heart").[35] F. T. Prince's observation that Milton's sonnets resemble "slightly amorous compliments" more than love poetry aptly describes this lyric.[36]

But the ambiguous distancing of this sonnet turns into distrust, disdain, and distaste in *Paradise Lost*: Petrarchism figures in several key episodes of

[34] A. K. Nardo proposes we expand our list of Petrarch's sonnets to include submerged ones in *Paradise Lost*, as well as Milton's shorter poems; certain sections of her argument, however, rest on too loose a definition of that genre ("The Submerged Sonnet as Lyric Moment in Miltonic Epic," *Genre*, 9 [1976], 21–35).

[35] All citations and translations for Milton are from Merritt Y. Hughes, ed., *Complete Poems and Major Prose* (Indianapolis: Odyssey Press, 1957).

[36] F. T. Prince, *The Italian Element in Milton's Verse* (Oxford: Clarendon, 1954), p. 93.

the poem, and, as I suggested, it is typically treated very negatively.[37] Notice first, however, that in the roll call of devils, Thammuz is associated with love lyrics:

> Whose annual wound in *Lebanon* allur'd
> The *Syrian* Damsels to lament his fate
> In amorous ditties all a Summer's day.
> (I.447–449)

The distinguished Miltonist Barbara Kiefer Lewalski observes that the lyric is almost absent from Hell[38]—but one should add that it is closely associated with the fallen angels at several points in the poem.

In a justly renowned passage in Book IV, Milton contrasts the love of Adam and Eve with several forms of love in the fallen world. First he rejects a condemnation of sexuality: "Our Maker bids increase, who bids abstain / But our Destroyer, foe to God and Man" (748–749). The same point is reinforced implicitly elsewhere in Book IV: by using "Rites" both for evening prayer and for sexual intercourse (736, 742) and by associating "mysterious" with the genitals, marriage, and sex (312, 743, 750), Milton establishes the holiness of what the Destroyer attempts to profane.

In the lines in question in Book IV, the poet proceeds to distinguish several reprehensible forms of increase from the proper one enjoyed by Adam and Eve:

>   not in the bought smile
> Of Harlots, loveless, joyless, unindear'd,
> Casual fruition, nor in Court Amours,
> Mixt Dance, or wanton Mask, or Midnight Ball,
> Or Serenate, which the starv'd Lover sings
> To his proud fair, best quitted with disdain.
> (IV. 765–770)

The climactic item in the list again involves song; although this serenade cannot be definitively identified with Petrarchism, the emphasis on unsa-

---

[37] On the presence of Petrarchism in the poem, see esp. an important article by William Kerrigan and Gordon Braden, "Milton's Coy Eve: *Paradise Lost* and Renaissance Love Poetry," *ELH*, 53 (1986), 27–51; their analysis, however, emphasizes the hunt and fame as central characteristics of Petrarchism, whereas I maintain that the primary sources of Milton's interest in Petrarchism lie elsewhere.

[38] Barbara Kiefer Lewalski, *"Paradise Lost" and the Rhetoric of Literary Forms* (Princeton: Princeton University Press, 1985), p. 109.

tisfied love, the reference to a "proud fair" (770), and the Italianate spelling of "Serenate" (769) certainly suggest that discourse.[39] The passage is not merely anti-Petrarchan but also anti-anti-Petrarchan in that those diacritical contrasts encompass an unyielding rejection of one alternative to Petrarchism espoused by many of his predecessors, libertinism.[40] Milton, like so many practitioners of the counterdiscourses studied in this book, is determinedly diacritical: he defines prelapsarian love through contrasts with its postlapsarian alternatives. His repeated use of negatives in a passage immediately preceding those lines—

> nor turn'd I ween
> *Adam* from his fair Spouse, nor *Eve* the Rites
> Mysterious of connubial Love refus'd
> (741–743)

—similarly defines love antithetically, in this instance anticipating the attack on the celibacy advocated by the "Destroyer" (749).

But if the marriage of Adam and Eve is contrasted with Petrarchan as well as other modes of writing and loving, Petrarchism repeatedly rears its ugly and serpentine head in the episodes associated with the Fall. When Satan gazes, frustrated, at Adam and Eve in Book IV, his references to "fierce desire" (509) and "pain of longing" (511) foreshadow the complaints of Petrarchism and his own deployment of that discourse later in the poem. Eve's dream in Book V uses Petrarchan language, as Ilona Bell observes,[41] and one might add that the whole conceit of the dream is in a broader sense Petrarchan: it promises fulfillment of ambitions that cannot and should not be realized in the waking world, much as Petrarchan lovers can achieve erotic satisfaction only in sleep. If Eve is proleptically tempted with the appellation "Goddess" (V.78) in the dream, its language, notably Satan's emphasis on gazing at her beauty, also foreshadows his subsequent

---

[39] For the observation about the spelling of "Serenate" and many other useful suggestions, I thank my colleague David Loewenstein.

[40] The attacks on Petrarchism here are discussed by Lewalski, who also draws attention to a contrast between Milton's celebration of marriage and Petrarch's "Triumph of Love" (*"Paradise Lost" and The Rhetoric of Literary Forms*, p. 194). Also cf. Ilona Bell, "Milton's Dialogue with Petrarch," *Milton Studies*, 28 (1992), esp. 95–96, 108; I am indebted at several points to this study, which emphasizes the contrast between Edenic and Petrarchan love. David S. Berkeley argues persuasively that, given the date of the poem, Milton's attack on applying terminology like "angel" to a woman is targeted against précieuse writing as well as Petrarchism (" 'Précieuse' Gallantry and the Seduction of Eve," *NQ*, 196 [1951], 337–339).

[41] Bell, "Milton's Dialogue with Petrarch," p. 109.

deployment of that discourse. In Book IX, when Milton tells us that the serpent "toward *Eve* / Address'd his way" (495–496), he chooses a verb that links the devil's physical movement towards her with his verbal approach. Satan then proceeds to intone his skilled addresses, which, as many readers have noticed, are laden with the rhetorical maneuvers of Petrarchism:[42] they too deploy hyperbolic compliments and conscript religious language ("a Goddess among Gods" [547]) in the service of a form of seduction.

In *Paradise Lost,* then, Petrarchism represents a whole range of dangers, notably the misuse of rhetoric, idolatry, and the perils of certain types of song. Here, as in *The Faerie Queene,* it bodies forth some of the issues that arouse the most intense and overt anxiety in the poet and his culture. But it represents as well a more covert form of anxiety. Milton's approach to love is intensely diacritical, as we have already observed, and throughout the poem he stresses the necessity for other kinds of precise distinctions too, ones ranging from the light of lamps in contrast to the light of the sky to the gradations of heavenly hierarchies. And he repeatedly associates evil and error with the absence or blurring of distinctions: Adam fails adequately to distinguish love for Eve from love for God, Satan cannot separate subservience from humiliation, the idolatrous do not know the difference between proper and improper objects of worship. Petrarchism itself represents this fateful inability to recognize distinctions, notably the one between real saints and angels and their metaphoric realization in the mistress.

For this and other reasons, the discourse in question is a marker of the changes wrought by the Fall. The prelapsarian world is graced by a love that is contrasted with the values of Petrarchism—and praised by a poet who can, however partially and inadequately, recover a vision of that world precisely by distinguishing modes of love. The postlapsarian world, in contrast, is ushered in by means of Petrarchan rhetoric and characterized by its consequences: frustrated love, misleading language, multiple versions of desire rather than one pure, ideal one, and the erosion of distinctions. In a sense the Fall is a fall into Petrarchism.

As I suggested earlier, in some respects *The Faerie Queene, Romeo and Juliet,* and *Paradise Lost* are typical of reactions against Petrarchism which recur in a number of other texts as well, and so they direct our attention to some specimens of patterns that merit further investigation. Not only

---

[42] See, e.g., Kerrigan and Braden, "Milton's Coy Eve," p. 47; Lewalski, *"Paradise Lost" and the Rhetoric of Literary Forms,* p. 107. Sara Thorne-Thomsen offers related observations about Adam's use of the aubade and the Satanic perversions of that genre in "Adam's Aubade and the Medieval Alba," *South Atlantic Review,* 54 (1989), 13–26.

Romeo and Juliet but also many other plays by Shakespeare and his contemporaries incorporate elements from the sonnet tradition and thus question sonneteering. Jackson G. Barry has argued that the sonnet is well suited to inclusion in drama, involving as it does a lively speaker and a length much like that of the midlength speech in plays.[43] His observations are persuasive but by no means exhaustive, and the characteristics that I have attributed to the counterdiscourses of Petrarchism can help us further to understand the relationship between the sonnet and drama.

One might begin by seeing that interchange as a dialogue between lyric and dramatic modes, with the latter voicing some of the critiques of Petrarchism common in its counterdiscourses. Thus the struggle is one between repetition and movement (inflected with evidence of traces of the repetitive in drama and of the progressive in lyric); in a sense Rosalind guides Orlando into linearity. More specifically, one might trace as well a struggle between the sonnet and comedy. Just as the attitudes—and attitudinizing—of Berowne and his friends resist the pressures of comedic resolution, so the sonnet, the genre most closely associated with their academy, is not simply a-comedic but also anti-comedic, and, similarly, comedy again functions like the counterdiscourses of Petrarchism. The conflict between the two encompasses, of course, a battle between the resolution of marriage and the frustrations of Petrarchan desire and between linearity and circularity or stasis; also involved is a struggle between the uniqueness and isolation for which Petrarchism stands and the pairings of comedy. Eventually not only will Orlando marry Rosalind but also Oliver, Silvius, and even Touchstone will wed as well—each Jack has his Jill. At stake is a contrast between a genre that celebrates the normative and one that claims to be dedicated to the unique (though that pattern is complicated in practice by the conventionality of Petrarchism).

Studying the counterdiscourses of Petrarchism also suggests a new perspective on a subject of interest to many critics: androgyny in drama.[44] Given the centrality of elided genders in Petrarchism, the presence of Petrarchan elements in so many plays, and the oppositional relationship between those elements and drama, I suggest that theatrical cross-dressing responds to the problematics of gender not only in the culture at large but also in the sonnet tradition. Petrarchism is both a source and a target of

---

[43] Jackson G. Barry, "Poem or Speech?: The Sonnet as Dialogue in *Love's Labor's Lost* and *Romeo and Juliet*," *Papers on Language and Literature*, 19 (1983), 13–36.

[44] Among the most important studies of this topic are Phyllis Rackin, "Androgyny, Mimesis, and the Marriage of the Boy Heroine on the English Renaissance Stage," *PMLA*, 102 (1987), 29–41; and Linda Woodbridge, *Women and the English Renaissance: Literature and the Nature of Womankind, 1540–1620* (Urbana: University of Illinois Press, 1984), esp. pt. 2.

the workings of androgyny in the theater. Thus the discourses of love poetry stage the very confusions about gender which impel cross-dressing in the theater, providing an often neglected origin for certain anxieties about sex roles. In one important respect drama responds with an oppositional counterdiscourse, an alternative to the unpredictable shifts in gender which are characteristic of Petrarchism: theater offers the alternative of controlled, delimited androgyny in that it presents cross-dressing as temporary and as theatrical in several senses of that second adjective. In Petrarchism the costume clings to the skin; in many though not all plays, the cross-dressers reassuringly shed their skirts or pantaloons at the end of the masquerade party.

Although I have concentrated on overt reactions against Petrarchism in lyric poetry, many poetic genres as well as dramatic ones enact a covert struggle against that discourse. These relationships, too, would merit further study, perhaps with a focus on how countergenres may serve as counterdiscourses in some of the regards I have traced. Thus Spenser's 1595 volume encourages us to explore the relationship between the sonnet and epithalamium elsewhere as well. Several similarities between the two genres, such as their use of the blazon and of the convention of describing the lady's loose hair, demonstrate their connections. Yet they differ in not simply their modes of love but also their modes of temporality. Petrarchism is typically mired in repetition. The so-called lyric epithalamium, in contrast, is perhaps the most insistently linear of all genres: events, keyed to particular times during the day, culminate in the wedding and its consummation, a pattern mimed by the spatial equivalent of this temporal thrust, the wedding procession.[45] Similarly, Daniel's juxtaposition of *Delia* and "The Complaint of Rosamond" invites us to think further about the relationship between the sonnet and other types of complaint.

The epyllion offers another illuminating example of the relationships between Petrarchism and other literary genres. The parallels between this type of mythological poem and the Petrarchan sonnet create a foil against which the differences stand out more sharply.[46] Though the epyllion tradition includes enough variety to complicate generalizations, by and large

[45] One of the best overviews of this and other characteristics of the genre is Thomas M. Greene, "Spenser and the Epithalamic Convention," *CL*, 9 (1957), 215–228. See also Dubrow, *A Happier Eden*, chaps. 1–3.

[46] Similarities and differences between the two are also trenchantly discussed in Clark Hulse, *Metamorphic Verse: The Elizabethan Minor Epic* (Princeton: Princeton University Press, 1981), esp. chap. 2; and William Keach, *Elizabethan Erotic Narratives: Irony and Pathos in the Ovidian Poetry of Shakespeare, Marlowe, and Their Contemporaries* (New Brunswick, N.J.: Rutgers University Press, 1977), esp. chap. 5. I am indebted to these discussions.

its poems hint at their connections to Petrarchism through their emphasis on unrequited love, their attraction to etiological myths, and their adoption of the blazon and of typically Petrarchan modes of description, such as referring to hair as golden wire.

In other respects, however, this type of narrative firmly positions itself as a Petrarchan counterdiscourse.[47] Some epyllia portray sexually eager women and reluctant or ambivalent men, such as Shakespeare's Venus and Adonis; several others suggest that female diffidence is but a ploy: "she (as some say, all woemen strickly do,) / Faintly deni'd what she was willing too" (Thomas Edwards, *Cephalus and Procris,* 435–436).[48] Thus such poems attack Petrarchan idealization, with the knowing asides of their narrator inviting the reader as well to join a coterie of sophisticates who can see through pretenses of morality and purity. In this and other respects they resemble the amoral, libertine counterdiscourse exemplified by some of Donne's poems. And, as the tone of Edwards's aside demonstrates, whereas the Petrarchan poet revels in his emotions, his counterpart in the epyllion sports an ironic detachment from the follies of love.

These genres, then, invite us to adapt Colie's suggestive terminology and declare that the epyllion is *sal* to the *mel* of the sonnet[49]—as long as we acknowledge that here, as in so many other texts, the relationship between discourse and counterdiscourse is replicated within each of them. Apparently straightforward sonnets contain moments of the type of detachment and cynicism associated with the epyllion, and those mythological poems include visionary reveries that would not be out of place in the sonnet tradition. Just as the authors of Petrarchan counterdiscourses often react against tendencies latent in themselves or manifest in their own earlier poetry, so the genres participating in that counterdiscourse often deflect onto Petrarchism traits within their own makeup. For this reason and others, the connections uniting the Petrarchan sonnet and other literary forms deserve further scrutiny. Indeed, to study the relationship of that discourse to the many genres that may assume the role of counterdiscourse is to trace a knotted family tree of concealed and complex relationships—and thus to understand from some new perspectives the culture in which that tree is rooted.

---

[47] Though they do not analyze the epyllion itself, Kerrigan and Braden observe that seventeenth-century poetry as a whole is often seen as an Ovidian response to Petrarchism ("Milton's Coy Eve," p. 28).

[48] Elizabeth Story Donno, ed., *Elizabethan Minor Epics* (New York and London: Columbia University Press and Routledge and Kegan Paul, 1963).

[49] Colie uses this terminology in discussing the relationship between the sonnet and the epigram (*Shakespeare's Living Art,* pp. 79–134).

III

If examining the counterdiscourses of Petrarchism directs our attention to a range of genres flourishing in Tudor and Stuart England, it also invites renewed analysis of broader literary problems. Witness in particular the gendering of speech and silence. Certainly some of the strongest feminist work of the past two decades has explored the silencing of women, and any future inquiries will build on those foundations.[50] But at this point in the history of feminism, it is both intellectually important and politically advisable variously to nuance and to challenge our earlier assumptions on this subject. Much as students of minority and postcolonial literature have been tracing signs of resistance among suppressed groups,[51] so feminists have questioned certain assumptions about subjectivity and patriarchy that had been cited to deny the very possibility of female agency.[52] Their agenda, like that of this study, is often not to deny repression but to build a model that does full justice to its complexities, including those that open the door to some measure of resistance. Female speech is a case in point. The subaltern can and does speak on occasion, often a limited and truncated language but sometimes an empowered and empowering one.

In particular, the voice of the Petrarchan mistress should not invariably be crammed into the category of disempowered silence. In certain instances, to be sure, it must be described in precisely that way, though with the proviso that the voice of the Petrarchan poet is also muted on occasion. In other cases, mechanically applying the concept of silencing discourages us from discriminating among the many different forms that process may take: muting someone is significantly different from permitting speech but listening selectively or from controlling her by directing her to repeat one's own words, although all three acts might loosely be labeled silencing, and all three are repressive. And in some important instances in the sonnet

[50] See, among a host of other examples, Lynda Boose, "Scolding Brides and Bridling Scolds: Taming the Woman's Unruly Member," *SQ*, 42 (1991), 179–231; Margaret Higonnet, "Speaking Silences: Women's Suicide," in *The Female Body in Western Culture: Contemporary Perspectives*, ed. Susan Rubin Suleiman (Cambridge: Harvard University Press, 1986); and Margaret Homans, *Bearing the Word: Language and Female Experience in Nineteenth-Century Women's Writing* (Chicago: University of Chicago Press, 1986).

[51] See, e.g., the concept of signifying in Henry Louis Gates Jr., *The Signifying Monkey: A Theory of African-American Literary Criticism* (New York: Oxford University Press, 1988); that concept is suggestively similar to some of the descriptions of women's subterranean resistance, a parallel that would reward further scrutiny.

[52] See, e.g., Susan Stanford Friedman, "Post/PostStructuralist Feminist Criticism: The Politics of Recuperation and Negotiation," *NLH*, 22 (1991), 465–490.

tradition, the woman's voice is simply not silenced in any of the literal or metaphoric meanings of that word. Sometimes, indeed, the speech of the sonnet mistress achieves a suasive force that, like the words of Laura, reminds us that Wisdom was gendered female. Many texts, too, draw attention to the sexual power associated with the female voice.

The complexities of speech and silence in English Petrarchism gesture towards the need for further work. In particular, we should rethink the nexus of speech, power, and agency, both in Petrarchan poetry and in other literary and extraliterary arenas. The counterdiscourses of Petrarchism demonstrate that silence may sometimes carry with it a type of power. Being silent, after all, is quite different from being silenced. Conversely, as we have observed throughout this book, speech is not necessarily an unqualified source or sign of power. Witness the ambiguities of telling stories about one's own failures or of writing in a genre condemned by many circles of one's culture. Note, too, the frustrations of the male poet whose words are twisted by an ostensibly subservient and powerless Echo.

Above all, in debating these and other issues, literary critics should challenge the linkage of speech and agency. English Petrarchan mistresses, like Laura, sometimes achieve agency even when they are silent. And English Petrarchan poets, like their principal Italian progenitor, sometimes manifest prolific speech without agency. Pace the term *speech act*, speech need not involve either significant agency or autonomy. Readers of the sonnet tradition have too often deployed that observation about agency in denying the significance of female speech, where it is sometimes but by no means invariably germane, and have too seldom applied it to the speech of the male poet. Indeed, the paradox of speech without agency aptly represents some of the ambiguities in male subjectivity in Tudor and Stuart England— as well as a situation our students confront if the teacher or other members of the class subtly but clearly signal that their opinions are, though tolerated, not respected.

If it is sometimes more precise intellectually to talk about control rather than silence, in future work on these issues it may often be more useful politically to do so as well. Although it is on occasion possible to classify control as a mode of silencing, the former can be a more revealing and precise term. To what extent and in what ways is female speech currently controlled even by those who overtly renounce any attempt to do so? To what extent has an emphasis on not forbidding speech but on controlling it determined how and to what extent it is heard? In an extraordinary moment at a scholarly conference in 1986, a retired professor introduced a panel of women by declaring that its lovely and intelligent members would grace any salon, thus not muting us but framing our papers in a revealing way.[53] Though this anecdote is extreme and hence atypical, the broader issues about contemporary responses to women's speech which it raises are far from unique—and themselves should not be silenced.

Literary and cultural critics also need to extend the current interest in canonicity to which I referred earlier in order to ask some new questions about what is studied and why. In particular, the neglect of Petrarchan counterdiscourses in many circles reminds us that not only this tradition but also lyric poetry in general is currently slighted in favor of drama. Those wishing to accrue symbolic capital in our professional marketplaces are well advised to invest in theatrical stock, for many critics are as dubious about the lyric as sonneteers sometimes profess themselves to be.

The neglect of the lyric is in part simply a consequence of a renewed and generally salutary interest in theater, the many sources of which include the perception that the culture itself was theatrical and the preoccupation with London which is, as I have argued, a central though often overlooked peril of contemporary critical methodologies.[54] The lyric suffers from a kind of double guilt by association in that it was a favored genre first of the middle and upper classes in Tudor and Stuart England and many centuries later of another group currently interpreted as the recipients of undue privilege and unfair advantages, the New Critics. Moreover, lyric is sometimes cast as a mode engaged with the individual rather than the social, the universal rather than the culturally specific, and the timeless rather than the historical; although this book, like many other studies,[55] has demonstrated the inadequacy of such characterizations, their survival contributes to the status of lyric in the current political climate.

But without slighting the exciting results of the emphasis on drama, critics can and should rethink the neglect of lyric and what it suggests about the workings of those academic marketplaces. I have argued for the sig-

[53] Although the emeritus status of this professor helps to explain why he could make his observation without recognizing its inappropriateness, it should not be used to justify generalizations about his age cohort. Most retired professors are more in touch with political realities than this man, whereas certain younger ones hold traditional patriarchal attitudes but are canny enough not to express them. Feminists, themselves subject to prejudice, are in a good position to recognize and reject the widely accepted discrimination against the older members of the profession.

[54] On drama in early modern England and the rationale for the new historicist interest in theater and theatricality, see Stephen Greenblatt, *Shakespearean Negotiations: The Circulation of Social Energy in Renaissance England* (Berkeley: University of California Press, 1988); and Steven Mullaney, *The Place of the Stage: License, Play, and Power in Renaissance England* (Chicago: University of Chicago Press, 1988).

[55] For an analysis of traditional interpretations of the lyric and critical reactions against them, see Patricia Parker, introduction to *Lyric Poetry: Beyond New Criticism*, ed. Chaviva Hošek and Patricia Parker (Ithaca: Cornell University Press, 1985).

nificance of certain problems associated with the lyric which are sometimes overlooked, such as the workings of concatentio and other types of prosodic structure. I have also demonstrated that lyric poetry is well suited, sometimes uniquely suited, to helping us understand many issues that are at the core of early modern studies today. If the theatricality of drama models the workings of power in Tudor and Stuart England, so too does the rhetoric of the sonneteer. If Marlovian drama reveals the development of male subjectivity, Petrarchism and its counterdiscourses demonstrate that type of Renaissance self-fashioning no less clearly.

A renewed attention to lyric poetry could also have the salutary effect of inviting reinterpretations of the relationship between the narrative and lyric modes. As I have shown throughout this book, both Petrarchism and the reactions against it complicate some common assumptions about that issue. In particular, the equation between narrative, male agency, and consummation is problematical for many reasons; students of literature would do well to continue both to question that equation, as a few recent studies in addition to my own have done,[56] and to examine the reasons the scholarly community has been attracted to it. Uncritically applying to sixteenth-century poetry paradigms developed in relation to nineteenth- and twentieth-century novels is risky at best; this is an argument for more contact between scholars studying early modern and modern narrative, a point to which I will return. When we observe how often narrativity in the sonnet tradition is associated with failure, we may wonder whether the frequently cited linkage between narrativity, gender, and achievement tells us more about the masculine and masculinist aspirations of some of the critics propounding it than about the workings of narrative itself. When a line such as Wyatt's "Faynting I folowe" ("Whoso List To Hunt," 7)[57] reminds us that linear movement does not necessarily involve success or even agency, we may speculate about whether contemporary critics are attracted to such movement for reasons we have not yet completely acknowledged.

Hence studying the relationship of narrative and lyric will invite us to think further about another issue that has recurred throughout this book, the temptation of teleology. We have encountered that appeal in many texts, notably in the way the *Rime sparse* itself, sequences like Thomas Watson's *Hecatompathia,* and counterdiscourses such as Barnes's sonnets all strive to move towards some form of culmination, whether it be the wor-

---

[56] For example, see Susan Winnett, "Coming Unstrung: Women, Men, Narrative, and the Principles of Pleasure," *PMLA*, 105 (1990), 505–518.

[57] Kenneth Muir and Patricia Thomson, eds. *Collected Poems of Sir Thomas Wyatt* (Liverpool: Liverpool University Press, 1969).

ship of the Virgin Mary, the rejection of love, or the rape of a woman whose name announces her virginity. Behind that striving, I have suggested, lies the cultural attraction to teleology which attempts to counter types of repetition and stasis which deeply threatened Tudor and Stuart England. This attraction, like several other patterns in Petrarchism and its counterdiscourses, is echoed in the critical practices of many modern students of those movements. For, much as art historians once confidently declared that early Renaissance art anticipates and culminates in the High Renaissance, so literary and cultural critics are prone to impose teleological and other linear patterns on texts and traditions that in fact resist them. Thus some emphasize not the continuing and unresolved fear of the hounds which Petrarch himself stresses when he presents the Actaeon myth in Poem 23 but the tragic denouement of that myth. Others find a clearer plot in Shakespeare's sequence or Spenser's 1595 volume than those texts permit. And still others take the monarch of wit at his word when he declares that Jack Donne is succeeded by Dr. Donne.

Progress is, with due respect to Lyotard, the one master narrative that will not die, and a profound and subterranean attraction to that model, I suggest, impels these misreadings. The liberal paradigm of gradual and steady progress is, of course, different in both its ontological assumptions and its political manifestations from the radical model of ruptural and millenarian change, but in their different ways both impel that attraction to the concept of progress. One might merely assume that critics are attracted to one or the other of the myths depending on their political persuasions, but quite possibly the liberal version, deeply inscribed as it is in our ideologies, exercises an attraction over even critics who would otherwise eschew liberalism, and the optimism implicit in millenarianism might interest those who would otherwise distance themselves from radical paradigms. In any event, for many practitioners of our discipline, not the least appeal of a progress model is professional: it allows academics committed to contemporary methodologies to relegate the criticism of previous generations to the Dark Ages of the university while celebrating their own achievements. Traditional critics, symmetrically, sometimes adduce a model of decline to accomplish similar, and similarly dubious, ends.

IV

These conflicts among critical schools represent but one example, though an important one, of the problems that challenge the academy today. If analyzing reactions against Petrarchism can help us to understand genres like the epyllion and issues like narrativity, so too can it provide a new perspective on some of our most fraught professional practices; in this as in so many other instances, studying literary texts can and should help us to study the academy as text and vice versa. My commentaries on both narrativity and the gendering of speech, for example, direct our attention to a habit that has limited our investigations of those and other subjects: the rigid separation of historical fields despite, or because of, our challenges to the concepts of periodization which distinguish those fields.[58] Though shared theoretical and political agendas sometimes create significant bonds among colleagues who specialize in different historical areas, many institutional practices, such as the emphasis on historical periods at many professional meetings, discourage such contact. Increased interaction among colleagues who share common methodologies but specialize in different historical areas would help us to polish and sharpen our critical tools—and our critical evaluations of those tools.

The two methodologies at the forefront of early modern studies, new historicism and feminism, would especially benefit from such contiguity. For instance, in many institutions new historicists who focus on early modern literature have little contact with those who study American texts, and vice versa. Because the latter group is sometimes more influenced by cultural materialist preoccupations, a dialogue among critics in both fields would encourage them to assess the complex and sometimes tense relationship between new historicist and materialist paradigms. Even more important, early modern studies has witnessed a far more intense clash between feminists and new historicists than has American studies. Analyzing the reasons new historicism has taken different courses in this and other respects would help us to understand the workings of both the academy in general and our critical methodologies in particular.

Such contact among practitioners of the same methodology is even more desirable in the case of feminism. Feminists in the later periods, many of whom have become interested relatively recently in the type of inquiry sometimes termed *gender studies*, could profit from the pioneering work in that field by Coppélia Kahn and Carol Thomas Neely, among others.[59] And feminists specializing in medieval and early modern literature could fruitfully borrow, and in so doing refine, many theoretical concepts from students of later texts; to choose just one example, Margaret Homans's model of "bearing the word" would prove useful in studying the writing

---

[58] For an instance of those challenges, see David Perkins, *Is Literary History Possible?* (Baltimore: Johns Hopkins University Press, 1992), chap. 5.

[59] See esp. Carol Thomas Neely, *Broken Nuptials in Shakespeare's Plays* (New Haven: Yale University Press, 1985); and Kahn, *Man's Estate*.

of many Tudor and Stuart writers, notably Mary Wroth, who indeed bore the word in several relevant senses.[60] Kristeva, who has influenced so many feminist studies of the twentieth century, has not yet had a similar impact on analyses of earlier texts,[61] while the paradigms of object relations theory, which have had so profound and valuable an effect on Shakespeare studies, should be adduced more often by students of nineteenth- and twentieth-century literature. The espousal of gynocritics by many students of nineteenth- and twentieth-century texts has exacerbated this gap between fields, but whatever its causes, the need to bridge it is clear. Only connect. And after that, only intersect and interact.

Those imperatives could also profitably guide the relationship between new historicism and feminism. I have attempted both to advocate and to model some ways of linking the two without subordinating the concerns of either. In studying attitudes towards aging and loss, for example, we can profitably shift back and forth between the wide lens that examines Elizabeth and the fine one that scrutinizes the family unit. Petrarchan politics is local in two interrelated senses: national as well as international conditions impel the movement, and upheavals in the family, especially those generated by the mortality crisis of 1557–1559, as well as conditions in the nation, shape it.

Another gap, as I argued earlier in this chapter, marks and mars the profession today. The contact between practitioners of more traditional and more contemporary modes of criticism—when they have contact at all— is too often characterized by intemperance and intolerance. In lieu of interchange or even productive controversy, ignorant armies clash by night. I am not suggesting that we attempt to ignore the substantive intellectual and ideological distinctions that often divide critics in the embattled camps but rather that we engage with, rather than contemptuously dismiss, the arguments of opposing critics. On the one hand, we will be reminded just how deep some of the disagreements can be. And, on the other hand, we will also recognize that on certain other issues the boundaries between those methodologies are as permeable and unstable as those between Petrarchism and anti-Petrarchism or between gendered roles within those traditions; witness the connections established in this book between formalist genre studies and questions involving power, race, and gender. The current climate of intolerance is particularly destructive when it corrupts

---

[60] Margaret Homans, *Bearing the Word: Language and Female Experience in Nineteenth-Century Women's Writing* (Chicago: University of Chicago Press, 1986).

[61] Naomi J. Miller suggests that students of early modern literature devote more attention to Kristeva and other French feminists ("Changing the Subject: Mary Wroth and Figurations of Gender in Early Modern England," chap. 1, forthcoming).

personnel decisions. In a recent essay Frank E. Haggard observes that "one of the most deplorable situations any department can generate for itself" is "a tenure review process characterized not by patient and thorough discussion of each individual's accomplishments but by impassioned argument about the comparative importance of various fields of work, a situation that can lead to decisions influenced more by competitive programmatic jealousy than by reasoned and humane judgment."[62] Although the type of "impassioned argument" that this quotation rejects can be valuable under certain circumstances, especially if it recognizes and challenges the hierarchical status systems by which fields are still sometimes ranked, the point is unquestionably true if deployed in relation to the prejudices about critical methodologies which may distort personnel votes.

Though I have elsewhere discussed at length the problem of this binary, us-versus-them interpretation of literary and cultural studies,[63] the current professional climate encourages at least a brief rehearsal in relation to the book at hand. Without denying certain important ideological differences among practitioners of different critical methodologies, by both precept and example this study has argued for more interaction among them as well. Though an exclusive devotion to aesthetic issues is inimical to contemporary concerns with history and politics, some attention to formal problems remains useful both in its own right and as an avenue to other investigations. Patricia Parker has persuasively advocated bridging those problems, especially as realized in the study of rhetoric, and more contemporary concerns: "The impasse of a now apparently outworn formalism and a new competing emphasis on politics and history might be breached by questions which fall in between and hence remain unasked by both."[64] It is telling that, as Louis Althusser reminds us, Marx had great respect for Aristotle.[65]

Similarly, in this book I have repeatedly attempted to demonstrate that the often discredited tools of close reading may be deployed without adopting the universalist assumptions or ahistorical practices widely, though not wholly fairly, associated with that method. Analyzing the nuances of language can help us to read both individual texts and whole cultures more acutely. For politics, the deity of our critical generation, is in the details.

In one important respect these and many other professional conflicts

---

[62] Frank E. Haggard, "Hiring in the 1990s," *ADE Bulletin*, 104 (1993), 51.

[63] See esp. Dubrow, *A Happier Eden*, chap. 6.

[64] Patricia Parker, *Literary Fat Ladies: Rhetoric, Gender, Property* (London: Methuen, 1987), p. 96.

[65] Louis Althusser, *Lenin and Philosophy, and Other Essays* (New York: Monthly Review, 1972), p. 166.

could enrich the academy. If, as Gerald Graff has maintained, professors should teach the conflicts,[66] we should study them as well, examining our own professional practices on a range of issues in ways we have thus far neglected. At first that admonition may seem at best unnecessary, at worst ill-informed, for in a sense our universities are already doing precisely what I advocate. The past twenty years have witnessed intense and often fruitful attention to a handful of important problems that bridge those spheres, notably the representation of minorities in the university and our choice of texts to teach and study. But we still need, I maintain, to move in three directions: to direct the scrutiny we have brought to that small group of problems towards others that equally deserve our attention, especially certain issues of pedagogy and collegiality; to bring to bear some questions from our research; and, when feasible, to integrate references to our academic culture with analyses of the other cultures on which we are focusing. In this chapter I attempt to support those goals, especially the last and most controversial of them, both by precept and example.

To put it another way, members of the professoriate tend to compartmentalize our professional lives not only by separating teaching and publication but also by neglecting certain potential connections between our collegial responsibilities and our research. As I have tried to demonstrate, exemplary problems from the classroom and the university as a whole can help us to understand the texts we read, while those texts can in turn can illuminate our professional practices. Such an enterprise must confront challenges and risks: presentism, the assumption that the past merely anticipates the present, remains a peril, and a profession that is perceived in many quarters as arrogantly isolated from the rest of its culture needs to consider the political perils of what might appear mere solipsism. But, despite these dangers, this book aims to show that many issues at the forefront of early modern studies could help us to negotiate many issues at the forefront of academic institutions, and vice versa.

The counterdiscourses of Petrarchism offer a rich arena for those enterprises. The perils of reenactment which haunt both Petrarchism and the reactions against it are also manifest in the academy: tenure and curriculum debates, typically among the most tense and most important decisions we make, are so fraught in no small measure because they too often involve forms of reenactment, of attempting to erase or compensate for what are

---

[66] For the most extensive of his many discussions of this recommendation, see Gerald Graff, *Beyond the Culture Wars: How Teaching the Conflicts Can Revitalize American Education* (New York: Norton, 1992).

perceived as the mistakes of the past. Like other versions of reenactment, too, these debates are often distorted by a covert agenda of retribution; festering resentments about a requirement dropped or a colleague denied or granted tenure in a long distant previous meeting, for example, can compromise current decisions on another requirement or another colleague.

Petrarchism and anti-Petrarchism can also sharpen our awareness of another form of retribution. One strategy of misogyny which survives and even flourishes in the academy today resembles a maneuver of those discourses: targeting one woman for imputed failings as a way of at once denying and asserting the presence of these failings in other or even all women. In particular, how often does an electrifying fear, unspoken and perhaps even unacknowledged, of the increased influence of both women and feminist scholarship in the academy lead to turning a particular feminist colleague into a lightning rod?

Similarly, studying how Petrarchism and its counterdiscourses negotiate the multiple and often conflicting status systems in Tudor and Stuart England can guide us in recognizing and analyzing comparable situations in our own field, and vice versa. Much as the status of any sonneteer varied strikingly from one circle in the culture to the next, so the status of particular scholarly journals varies markedly within the profession. And much as the social position of Sidney varied greatly from one geographical region or one year to another, so professional activities such as writing poetry or chairing important committees will be valued differently in different institutions or even different periods in the same institution's history. Ours is an astronomy of star systems, comets, and black holes—an astronomy whose physics the academic community too seldom tries to understand. Junior colleagues often need guidance in charting this sky and especially in avoiding the debris from falling meteors, and senior faculty members will in turn be better able to advise—and learn from—recently hired professors if we ourselves think more about the workings of status in the profession, perhaps adducing among other analogues the discourses and counterdiscourses of Petrarchism.

Above all, dovetailing our professional practices and our literary investigations could help us to avoid the destructive oversimplifications of alternative critical positions to which I referred earlier. The academy's versions of diacritical desire typically take the form of constructing those binary distinctions between our own work and that of opposing camps. This pursuit, like the forms of diacritical desire traced in this book, is multiply determined, but some of its sources are analogous to those ex-

INDEX

Because of limitations of space, individual texts are indexed only if the book includes a substantial discussion of them.

DATE DUE

DEMCO 38-297